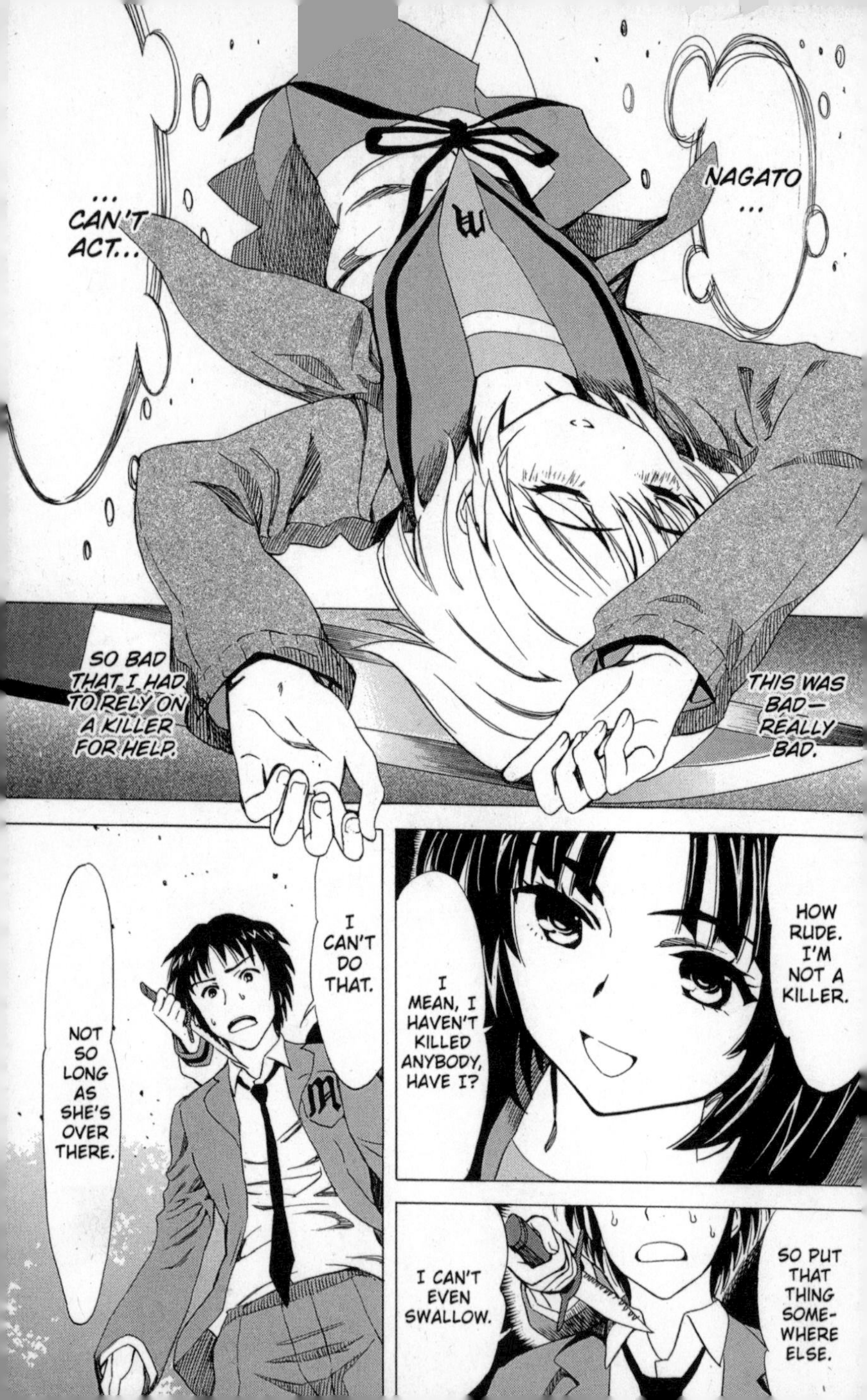

NAGATO ...
... CAN'T ACT...
THIS WAS BAD— REALLY BAD.
SO BAD THAT I HAD TO RELY ON A KILLER FOR HELP.
HOW RUDE. I'M NOT A KILLER.
I MEAN, I HAVEN'T KILLED ANYBODY, HAVE I?
SO PUT THAT THING SOMEWHERE ELSE.
I CAN'T EVEN SWALLOW.
I CAN'T DO THAT.
NOT SO LONG AS SHE'S OVER THERE.

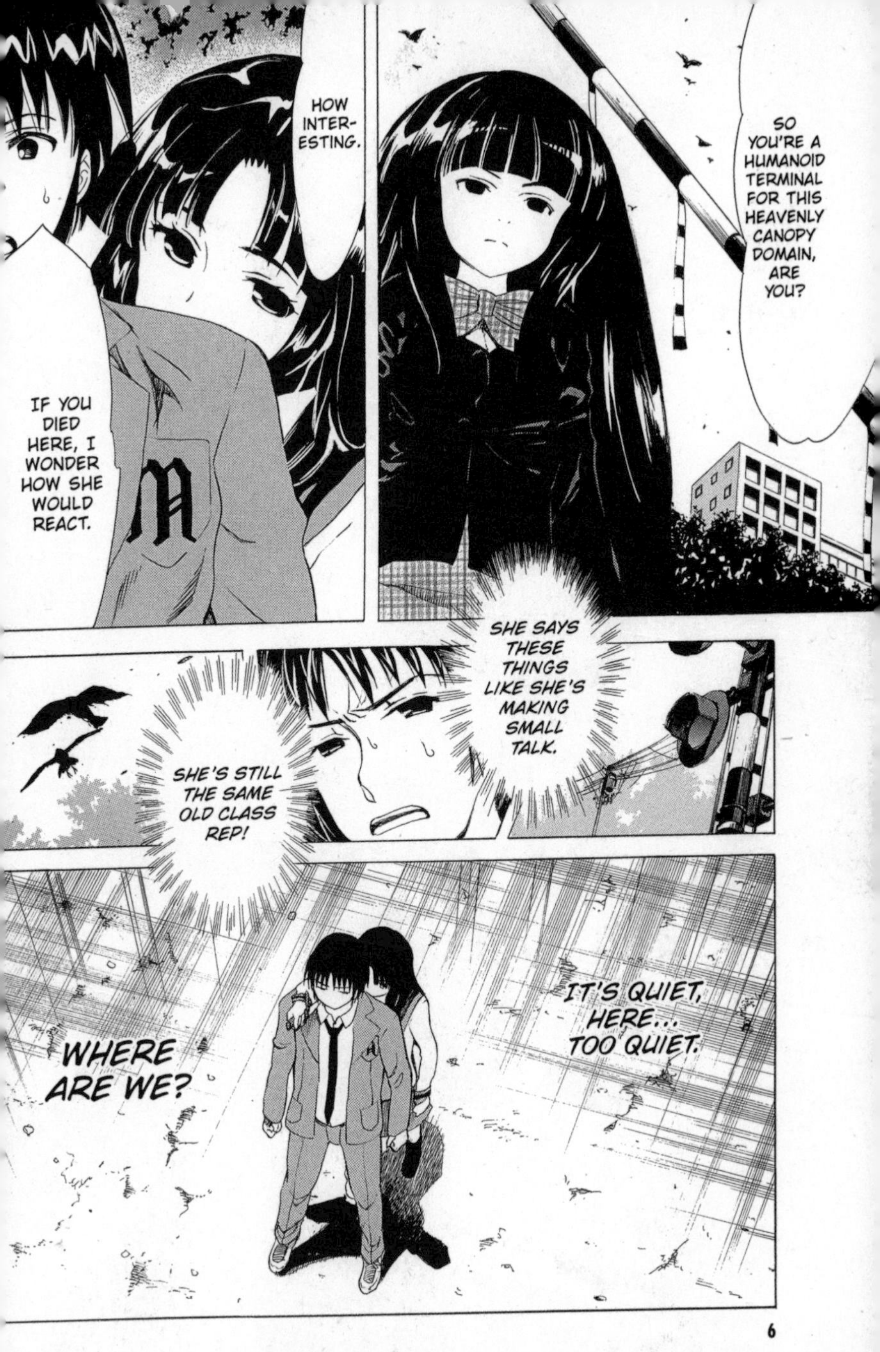
SO YOU'RE A HUMANOID TERMINAL FOR THIS HEAVENLY CANOPY DOMAIN, ARE YOU?
HOW INTER-ESTING.
IF YOU DIED HERE, I WONDER HOW SHE WOULD REACT.
SHE SAYS THESE THINGS LIKE SHE'S MAKING SMALL TALK.
SHE'S STILL THE SAME OLD CLASS REP!
IT'S QUIET, HERE... TOO QUIET.
WHERE ARE WE?

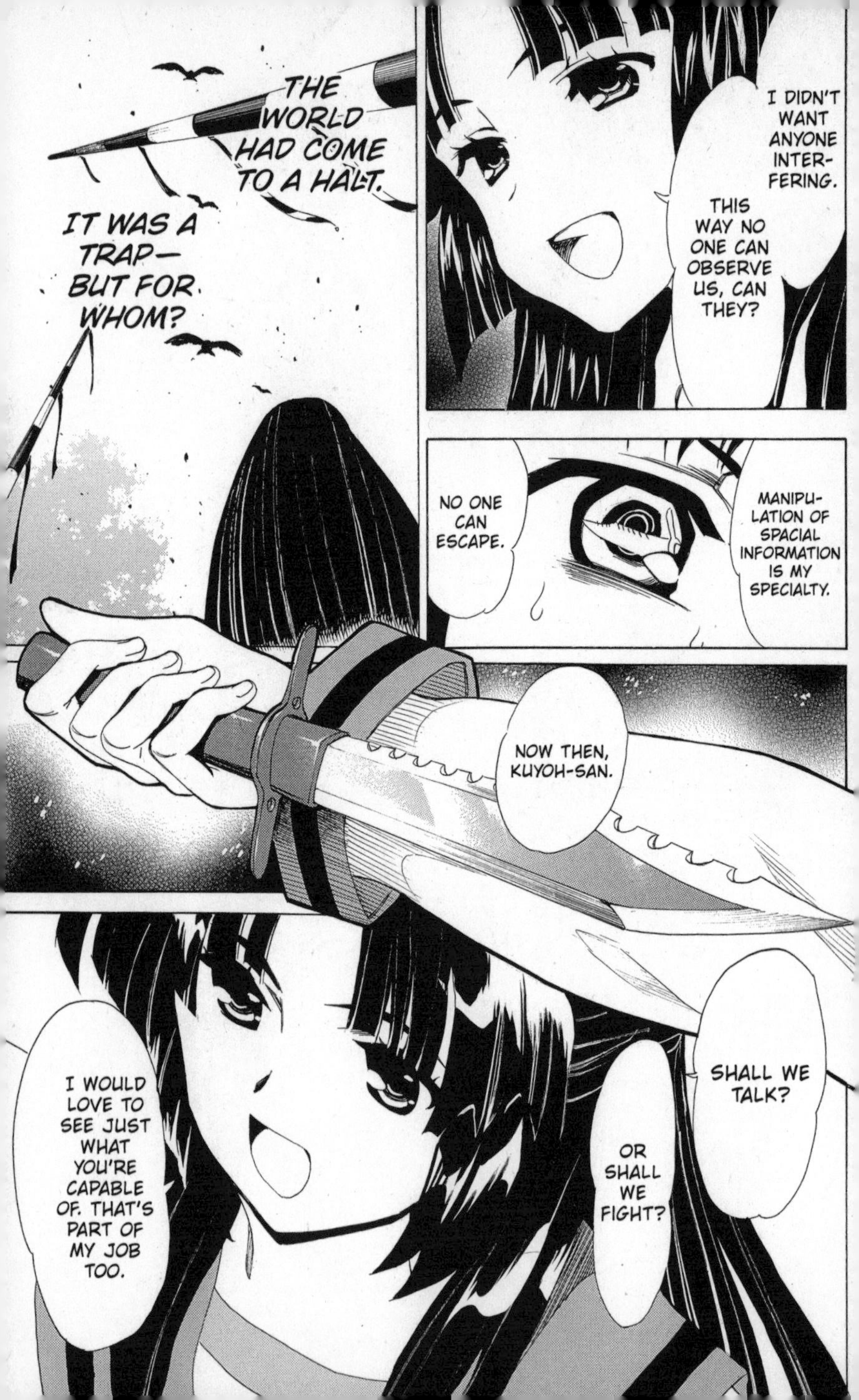
I DIDN'T WANT ANYONE INTERFERING.
THIS WAY NO ONE CAN OBSERVE US, CAN THEY?
MANIPULATION OF SPACIAL INFORMATION IS MY SPECIALTY.
NO ONE CAN ESCAPE.
THE WORLD HAD COME TO A HALT.
IT WAS A TRAP—BUT FOR WHOM?
NOW THEN, KUYOH-SAN.
SHALL WE TALK?
OR SHALL WE FIGHT?
I WOULD LOVE TO SEE JUST WHAT YOU'RE CAPABLE OF. THAT'S PART OF MY JOB TOO.

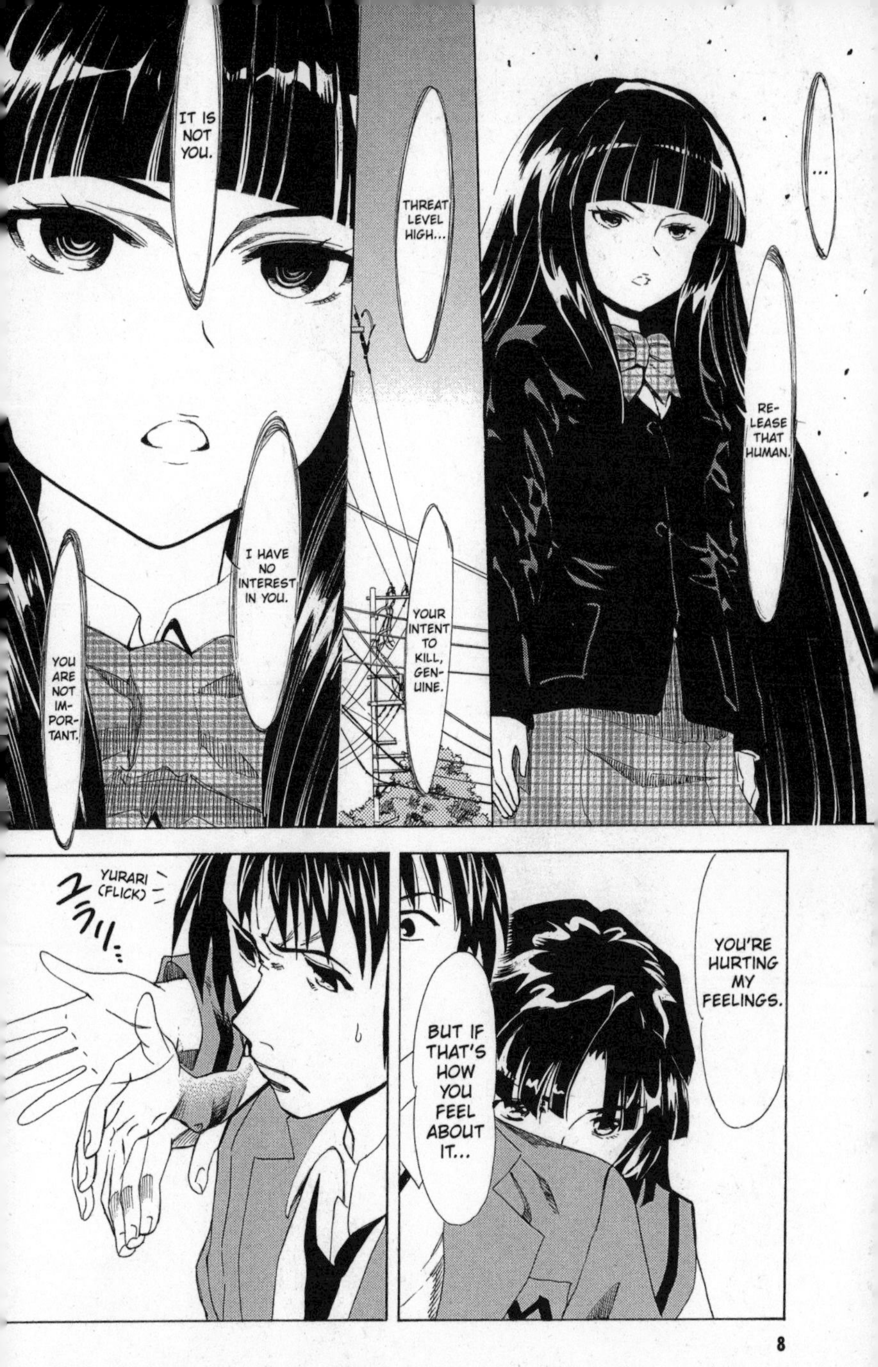
...
RE-LEASE THAT HUMAN.
THREAT LEVEL HIGH...
YOUR INTENT TO KILL, GEN-UINE.
IT IS NOT YOU.
I HAVE NO INTEREST IN YOU.
YOU ARE NOT IM-POR-TANT.
YOU'RE HURTING MY FEELINGS.
BUT IF THAT'S HOW YOU FEEL ABOUT IT...
YURARI (FLICK)

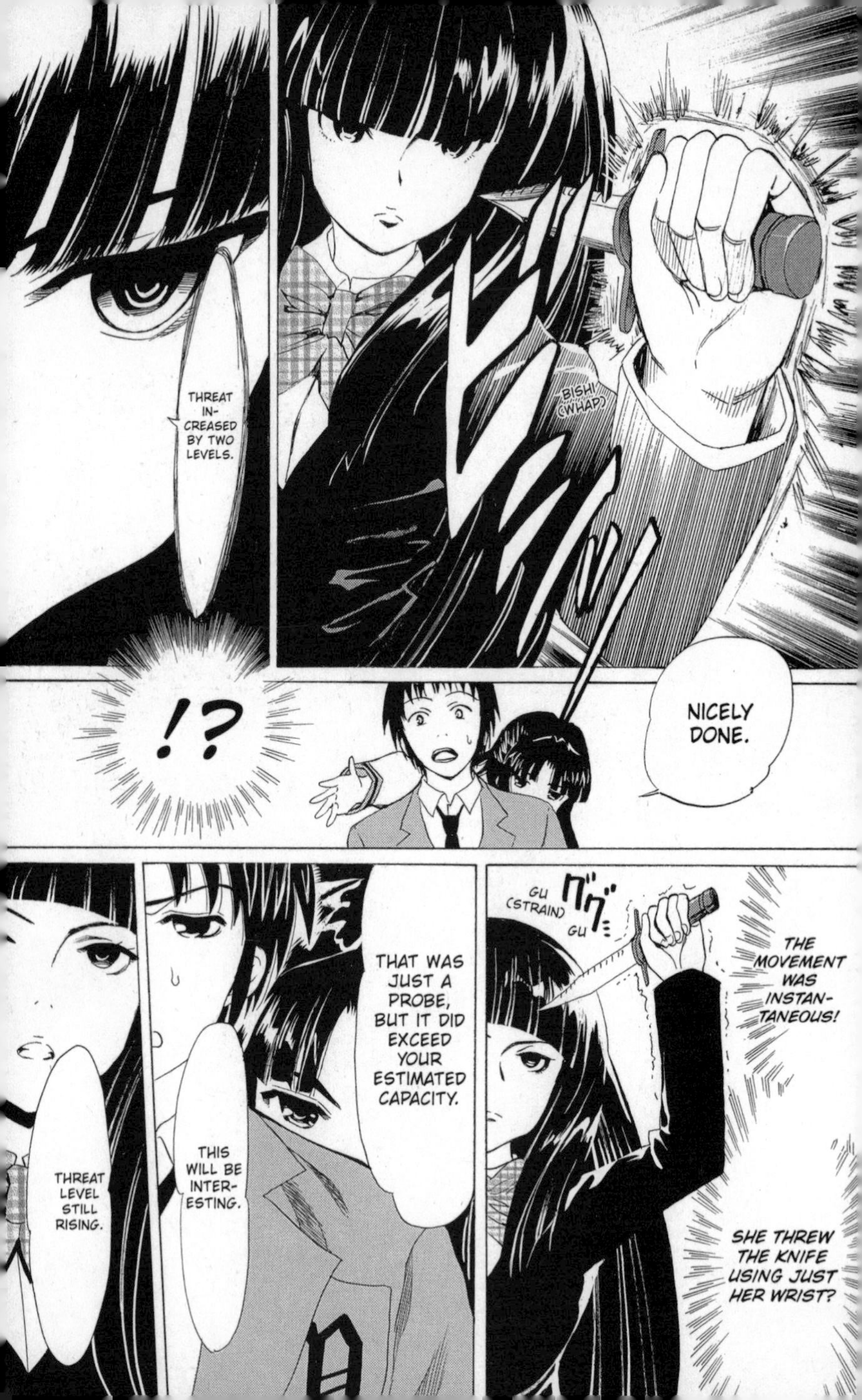
BISHI (WHAP)
THREAT IN-CREASED BY TWO LEVELS.
NICELY DONE.
!?
GU (STRAIN) GU
THE MOVEMENT WAS INSTANTANEOUS!
SHE THREW THE KNIFE USING JUST HER WRIST?
THAT WAS JUST A PROBE, BUT IT DID EXCEED YOUR ESTIMATED CAPACITY.
THIS WILL BE INTERESTING.
THREAT LEVEL STILL RISING.

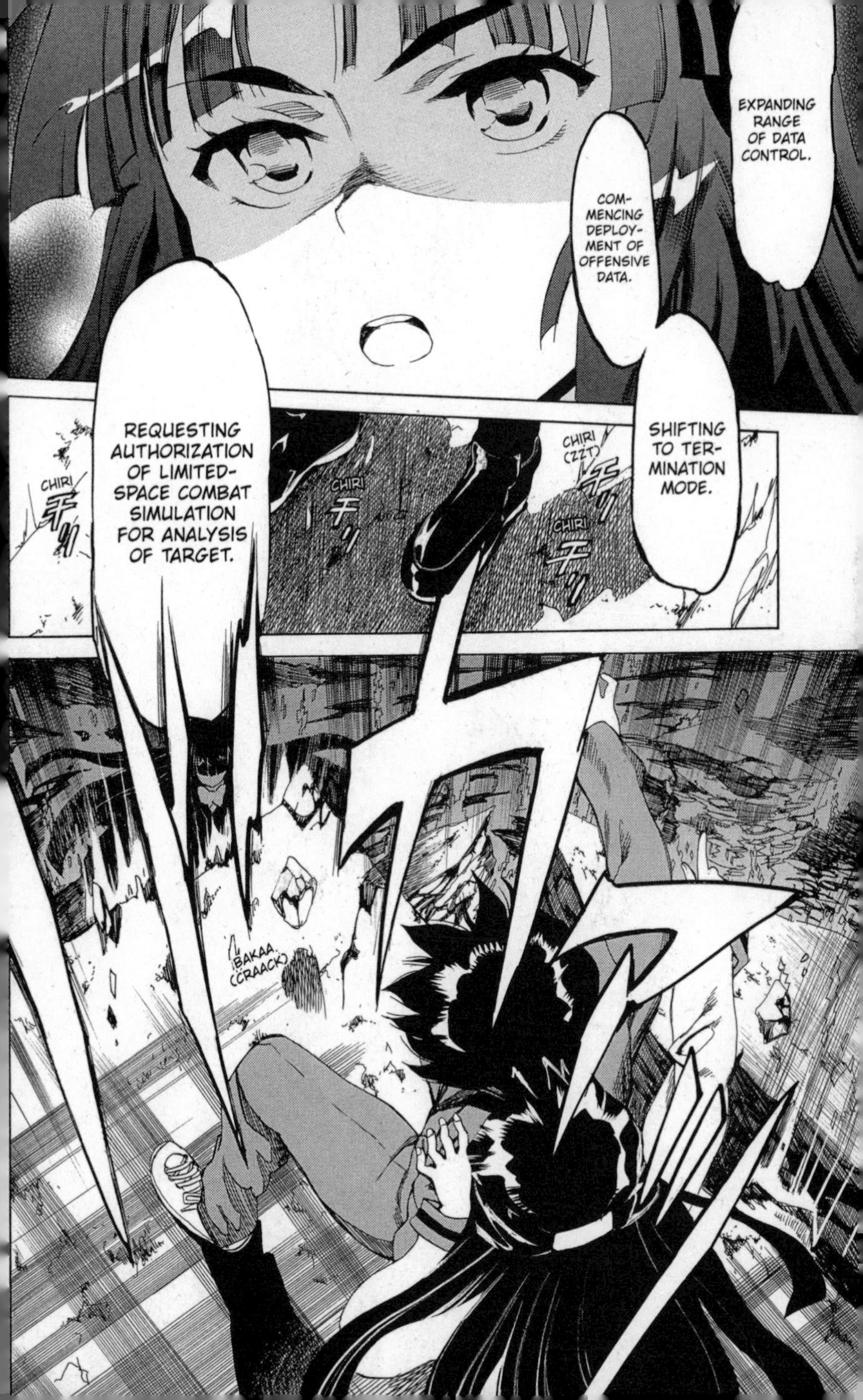

EXPANDING RANGE OF DATA CONTROL.
COM-MENCING DEPLOY-MENT OF OFFENSIVE DATA.
SHIFTING TO TER-MINATION MODE.
CHIRI (ZZT)
CHIRI
CHIRI
REQUESTING AUTHORIZATION OF LIMITED-SPACE COMBAT SIMULATION FOR ANALYSIS OF TARGET.
CHIRI
BAKAA (CRAACK)

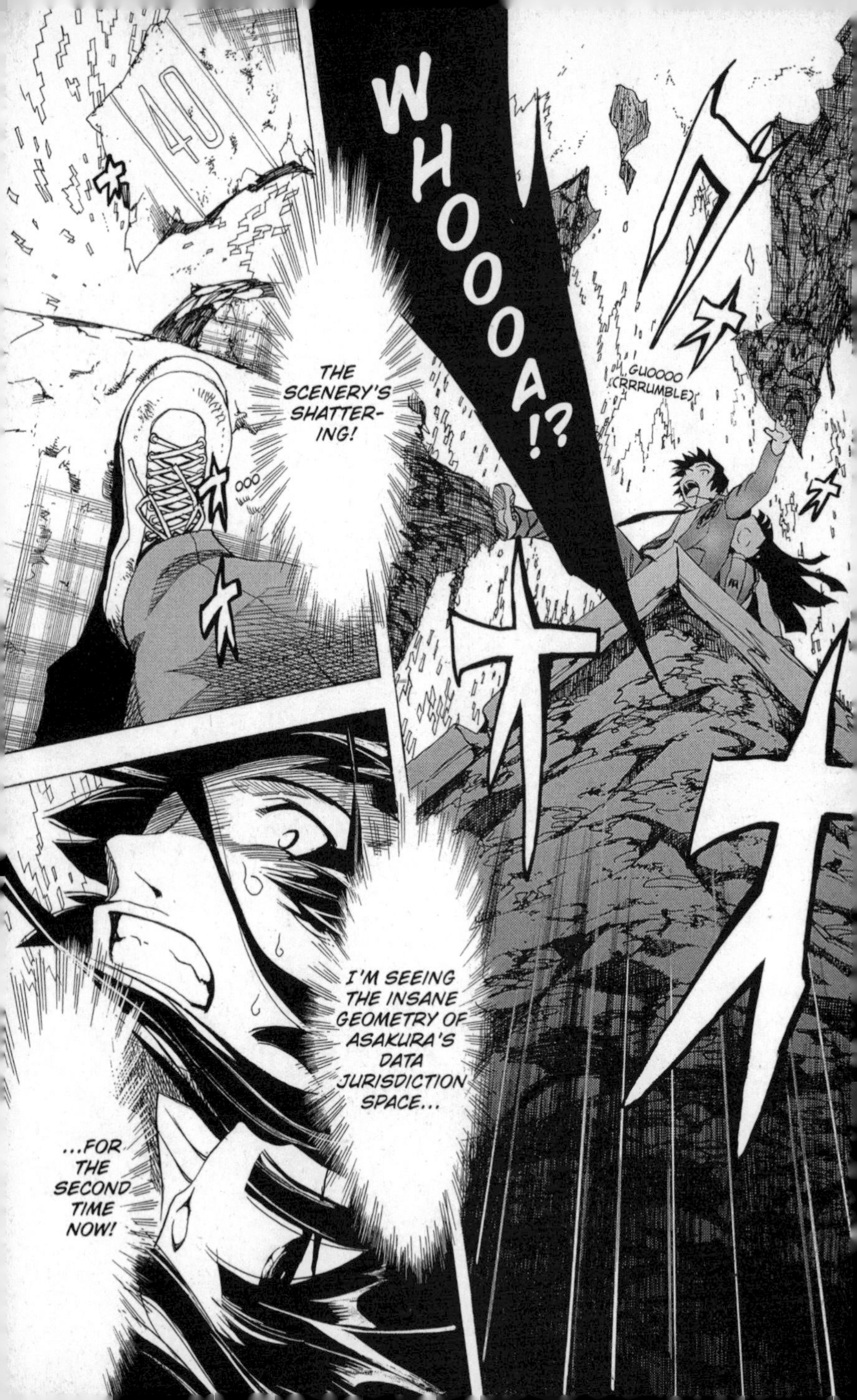
WHOOOA!?
GUOOOO (RRRUMBLE)
THE SCENERY'S SHATTER-ING!
ooo
I'M SEEING THE INSANE GEOMETRY OF ASAKURA'S DATA JURISDICTION SPACE...
...FOR THE SECOND TIME NOW!

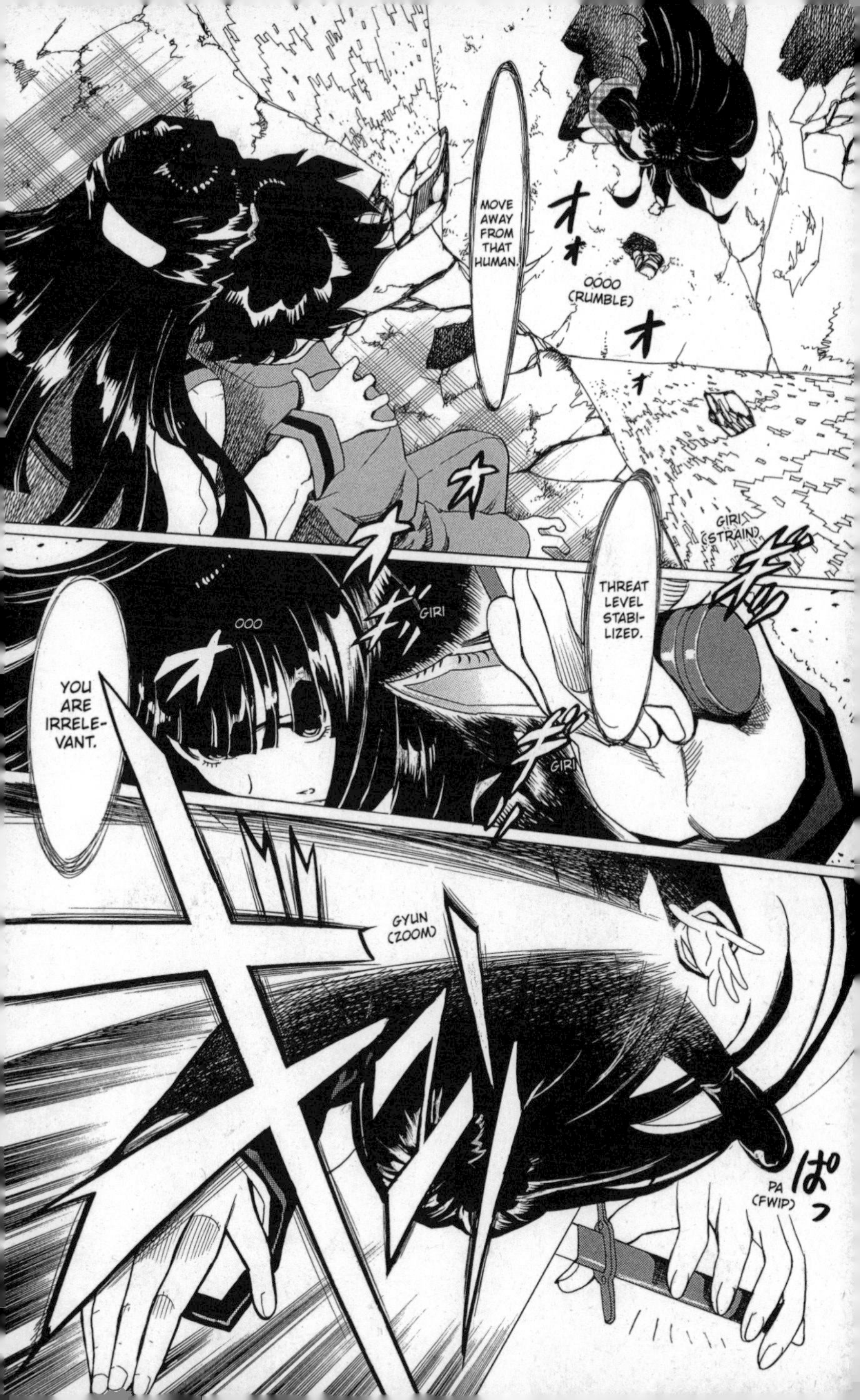
MOVE AWAY FROM THAT HUMAN.
OOOO (RUMBLE)
GIRI (STRAIN)
THREAT LEVEL STABILIZED.
GIRI
OOO
GIRI
YOU ARE IRRELEVANT.
ぱっ
PA (FWIP)
GYUN (ZOOM)

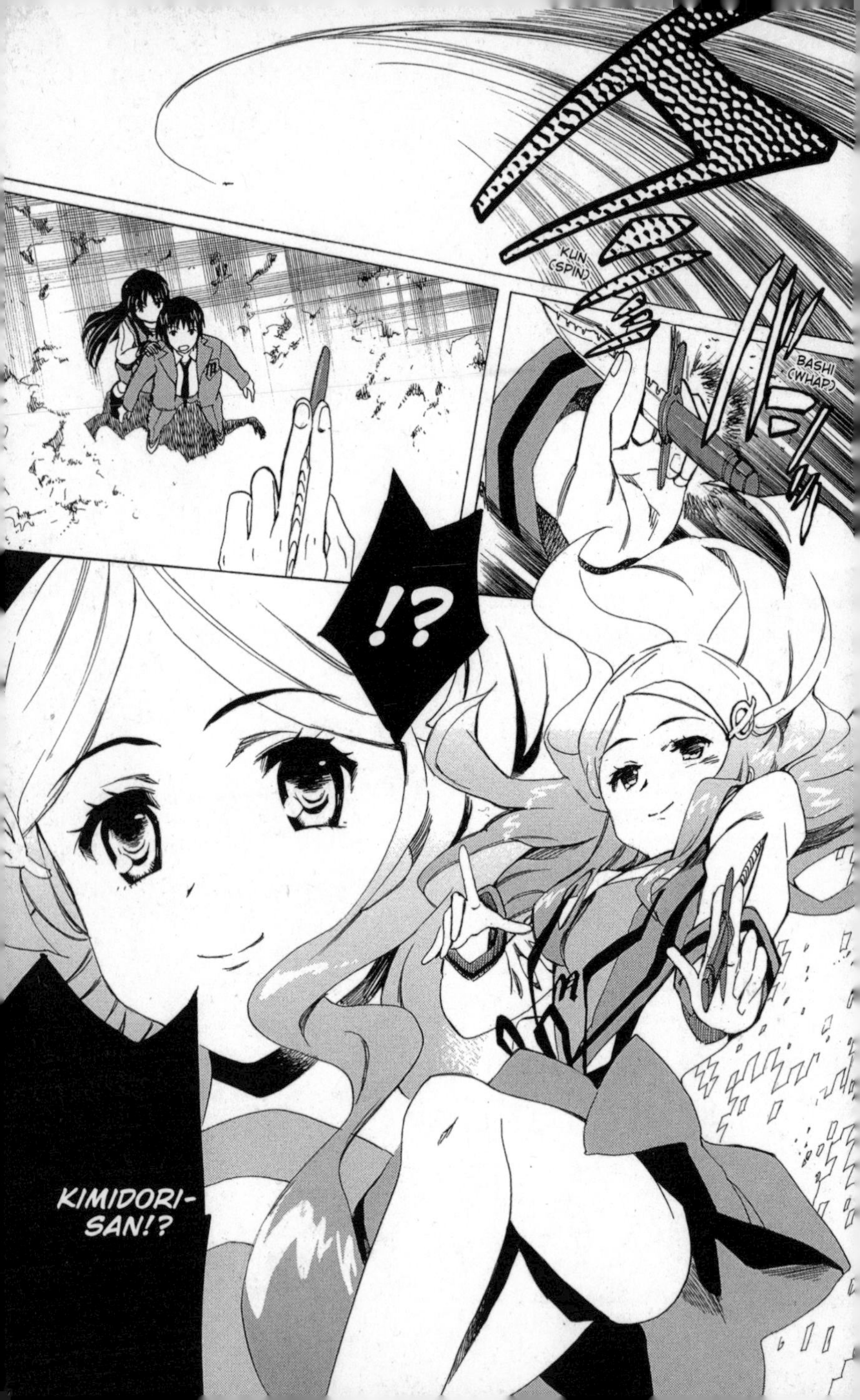
KUN
(SPIN)
BASHI
(WHAP)
!?
KIMIDORI-SAN!?

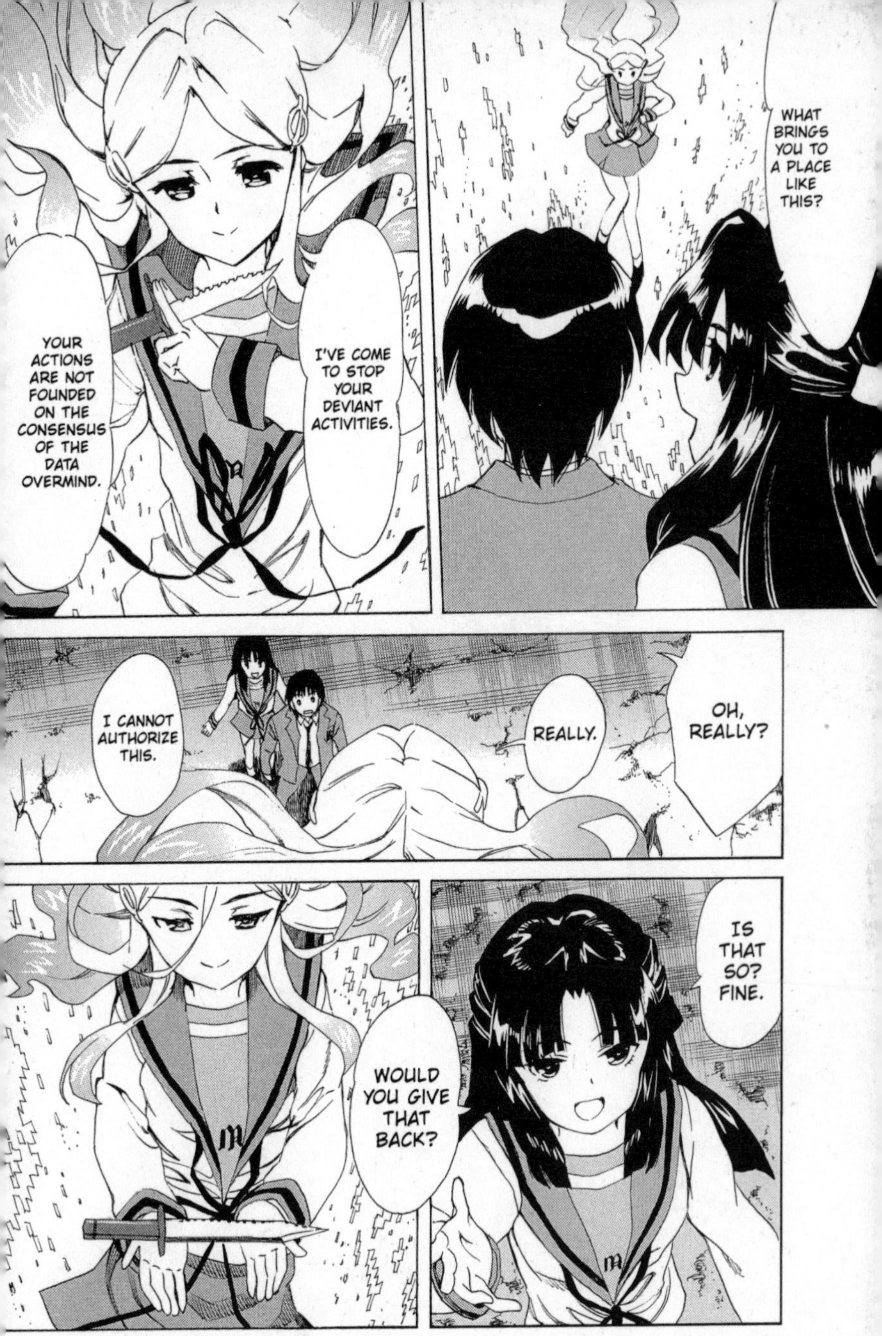
WHAT BRINGS YOU TO A PLACE LIKE THIS?
I'VE COME TO STOP YOUR DEVIANT ACTIVITIES.
YOUR ACTIONS ARE NOT FOUNDED ON THE CONSENSUS OF THE DATA OVERMIND.
OH, REALLY?
REALLY.
I CANNOT AUTHORIZE THIS.
IS THAT SO? FINE.
WOULD YOU GIVE THAT BACK?

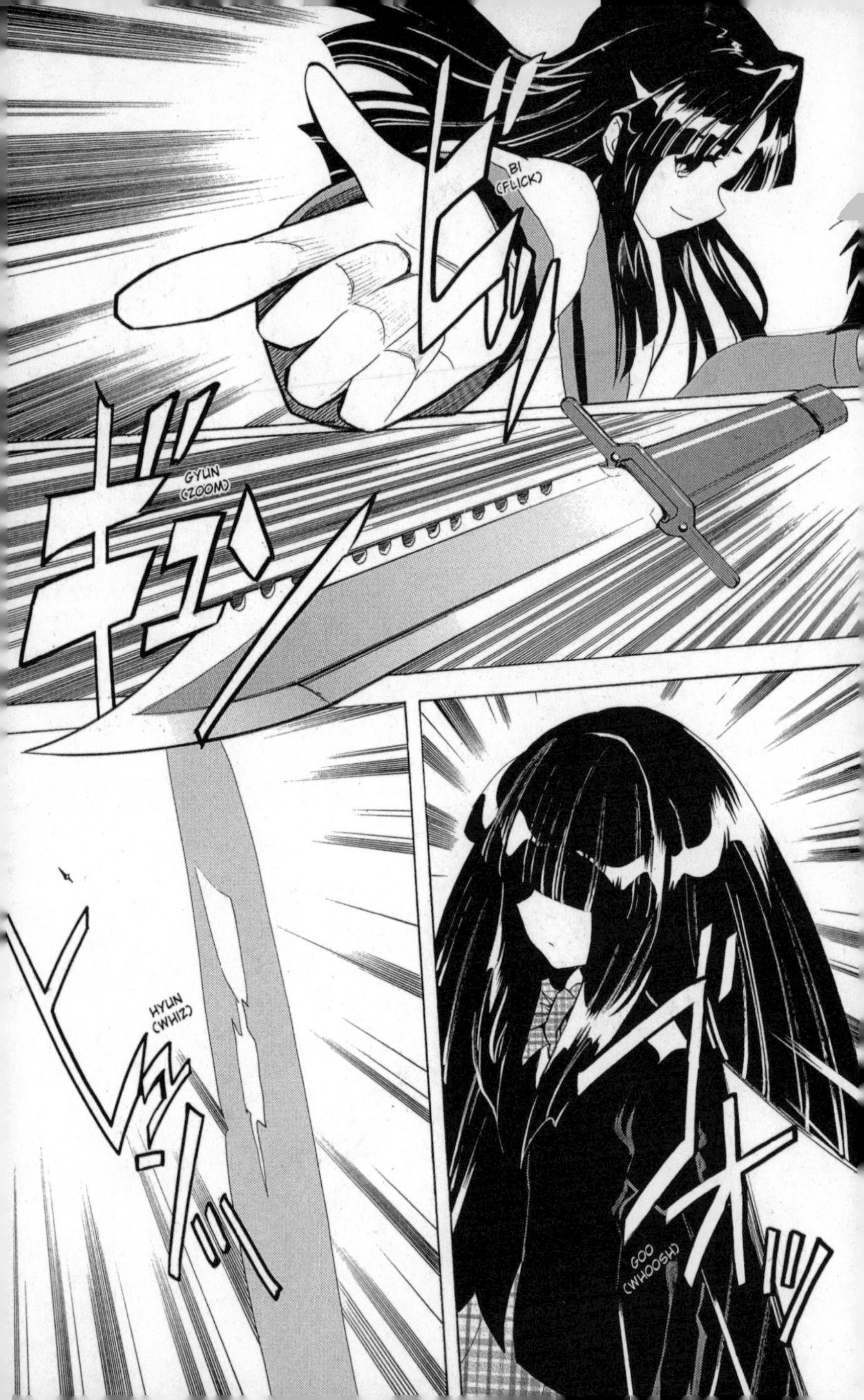
BI
(FLICK)
GYUN
(ZOOM)
GOO
(WHOOSH)
HYUN
(WHIZ)

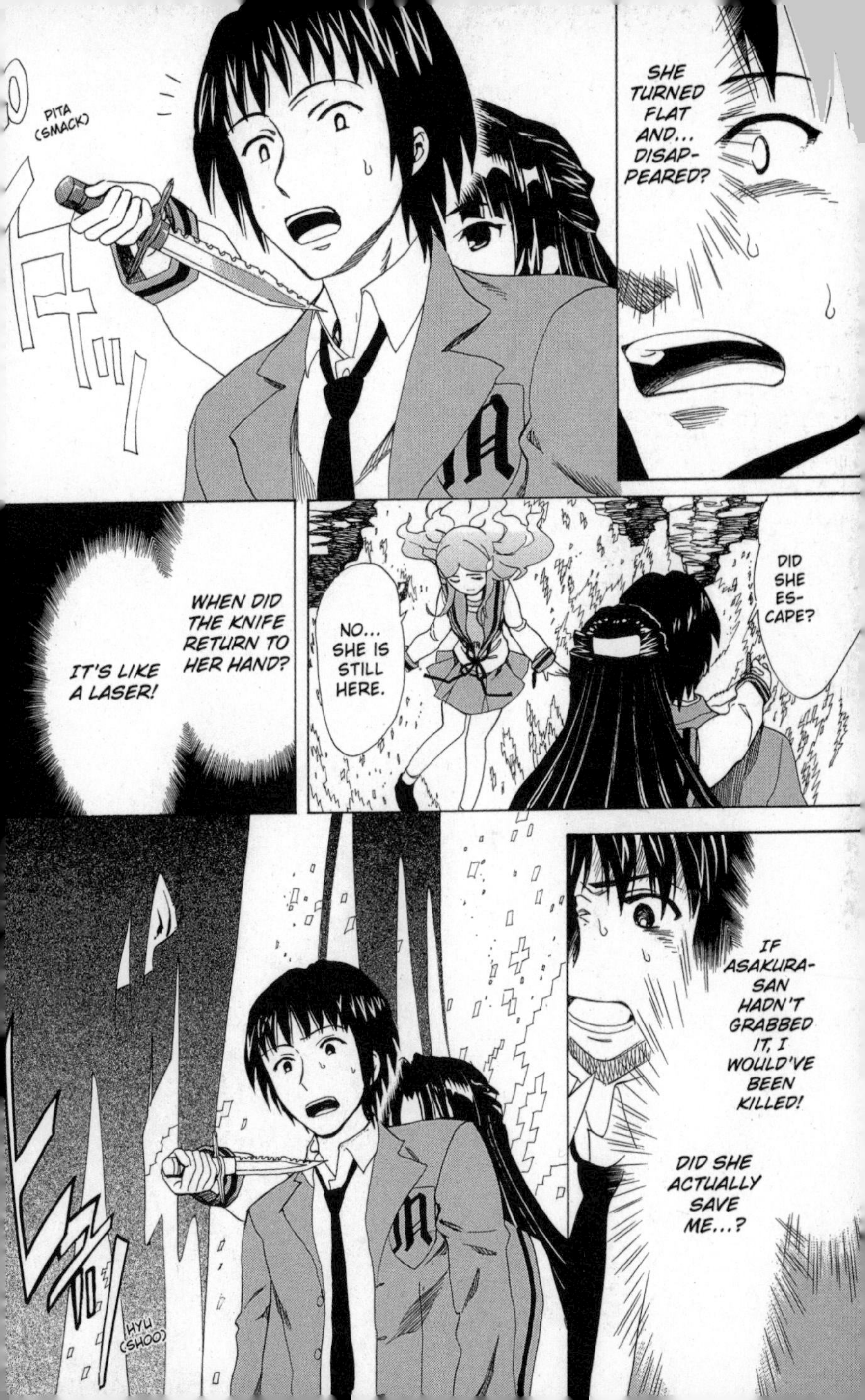
SHE TURNED FLAT AND... DISAPPEARED?
PITA (SMACK)
DID SHE ESCAPE?
NO... SHE IS STILL HERE.
WHEN DID THE KNIFE RETURN TO HER HAND?
IT'S LIKE A LASER!
IF ASAKURA-SAN HADN'T GRABBED IT, I WOULD'VE BEEN KILLED!
DID SHE ACTUALLY SAVE ME...?
HYU (SHOO)

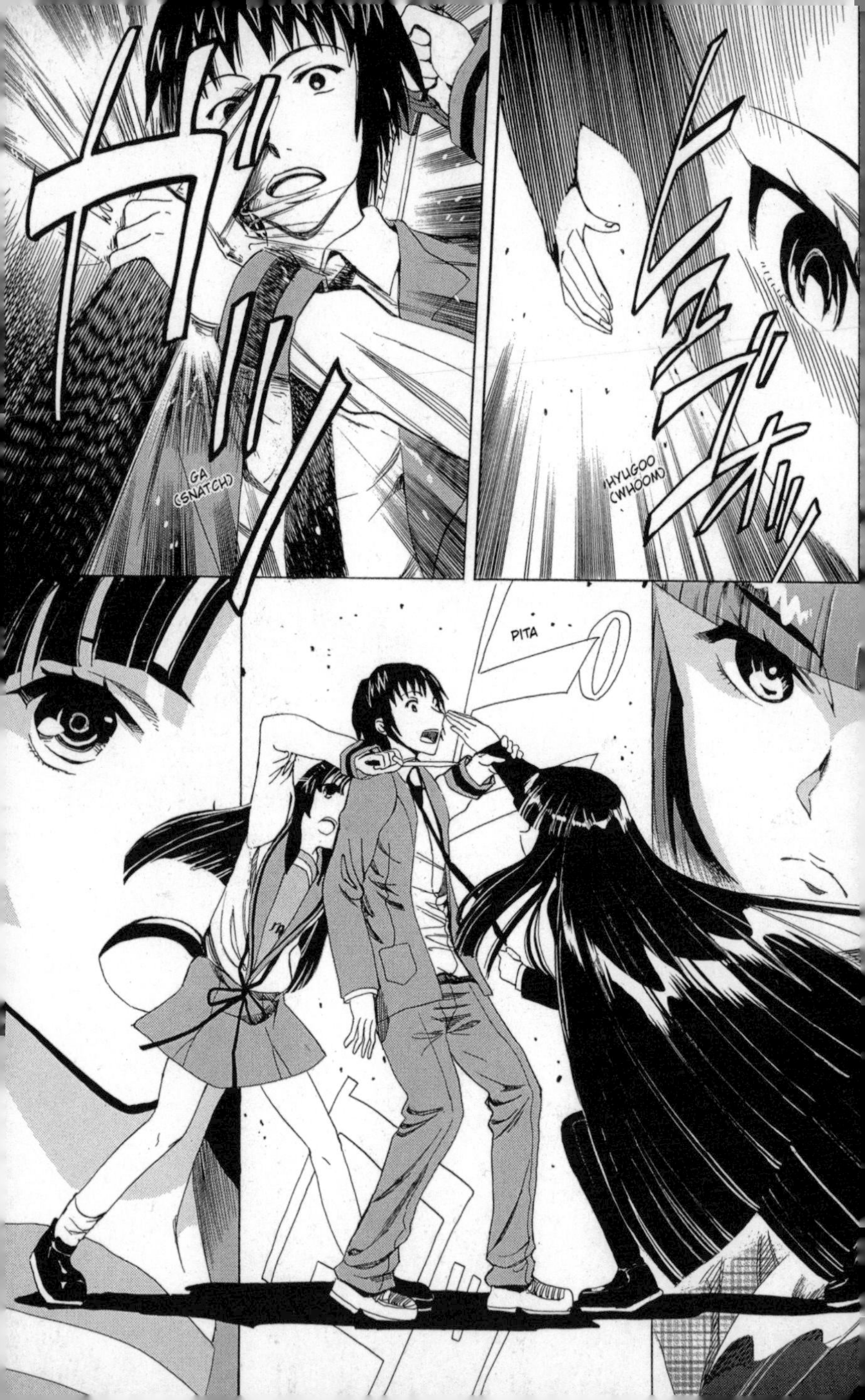
HYUGOO (WHOOM)
GA (SNATCH)
PITA

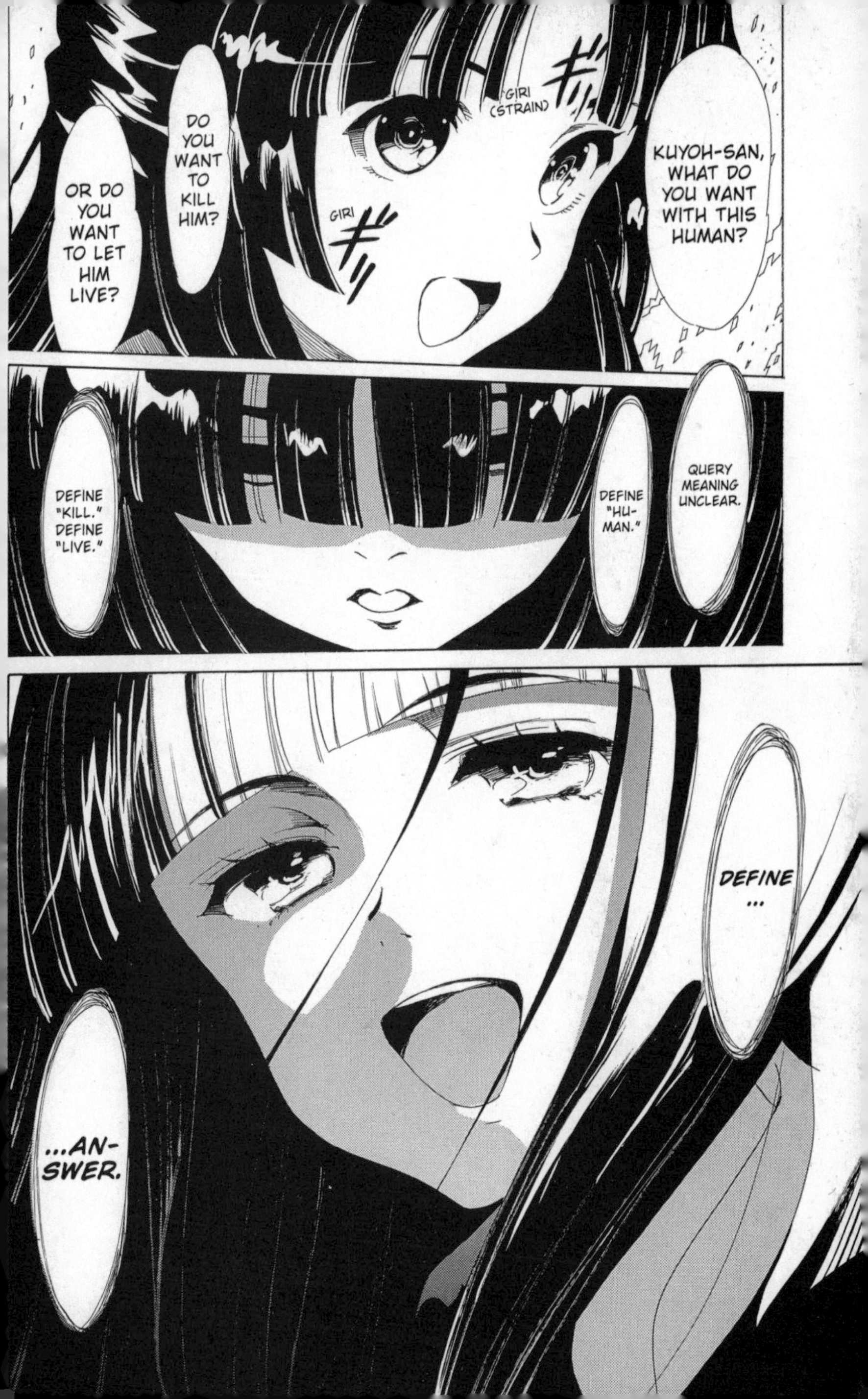

GIRI (STRAIN)
KUYOH-SAN, WHAT DO YOU WANT WITH THIS HUMAN?
GIRI
DO YOU WANT TO KILL HIM?
OR DO YOU WANT TO LET HIM LIVE?
QUERY MEANING UNCLEAR.
DEFINE "HU-MAN."
DEFINE "KILL." DEFINE "LIVE."
DEFINE ...
...AN-SWER.

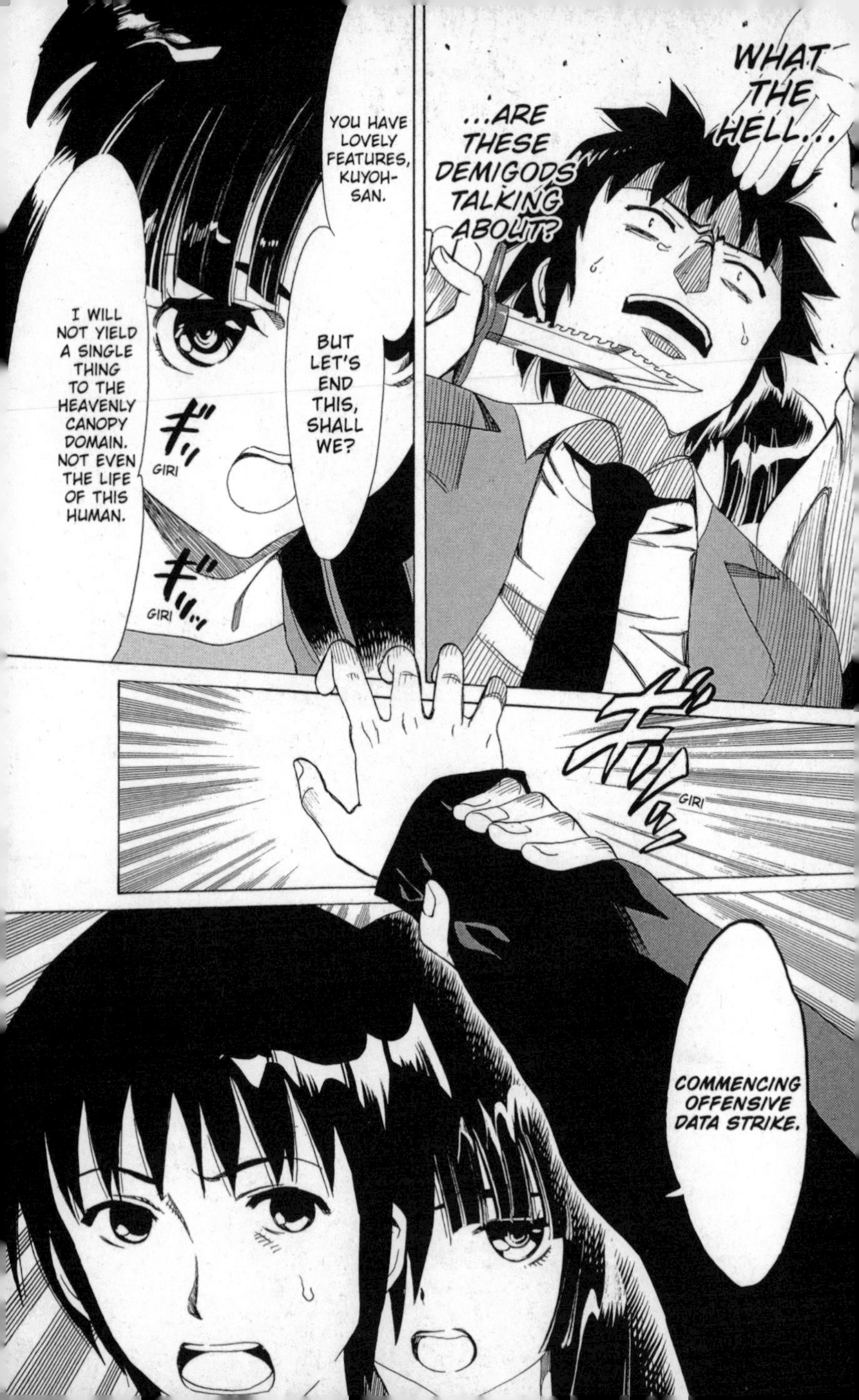
WHAT THE HELL...
...ARE THESE DEMIGODS TALKING ABOUT?
YOU HAVE LOVELY FEATURES, KUYOH-SAN.
BUT LET'S END THIS, SHALL WE?
I WILL NOT YIELD A SINGLE THING TO THE HEAVENLY CANOPY DOMAIN. NOT EVEN THE LIFE OF THIS HUMAN.
ギリ
GIRI
ギリ
GIRI
ギリ
GIRI
COMMENCING OFFENSIVE DATA STRIKE.

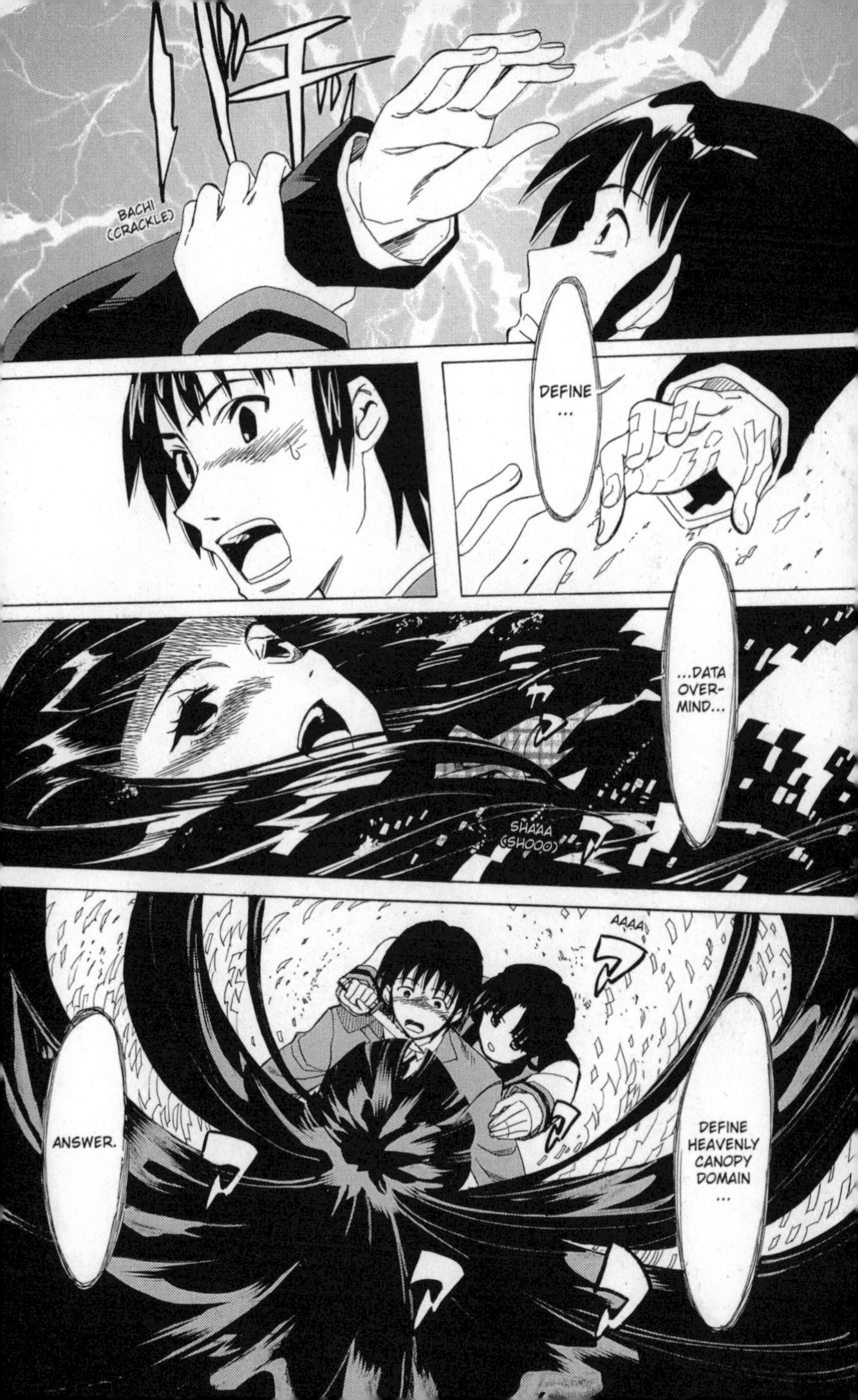
BACHI (CRACKLE)
DEFINE ...
...DATA OVER-MIND...
SHAAA (SHOOO)
DEFINE HEAVENLY CANOPY DOMAIN ...
AAAA
ANSWER.

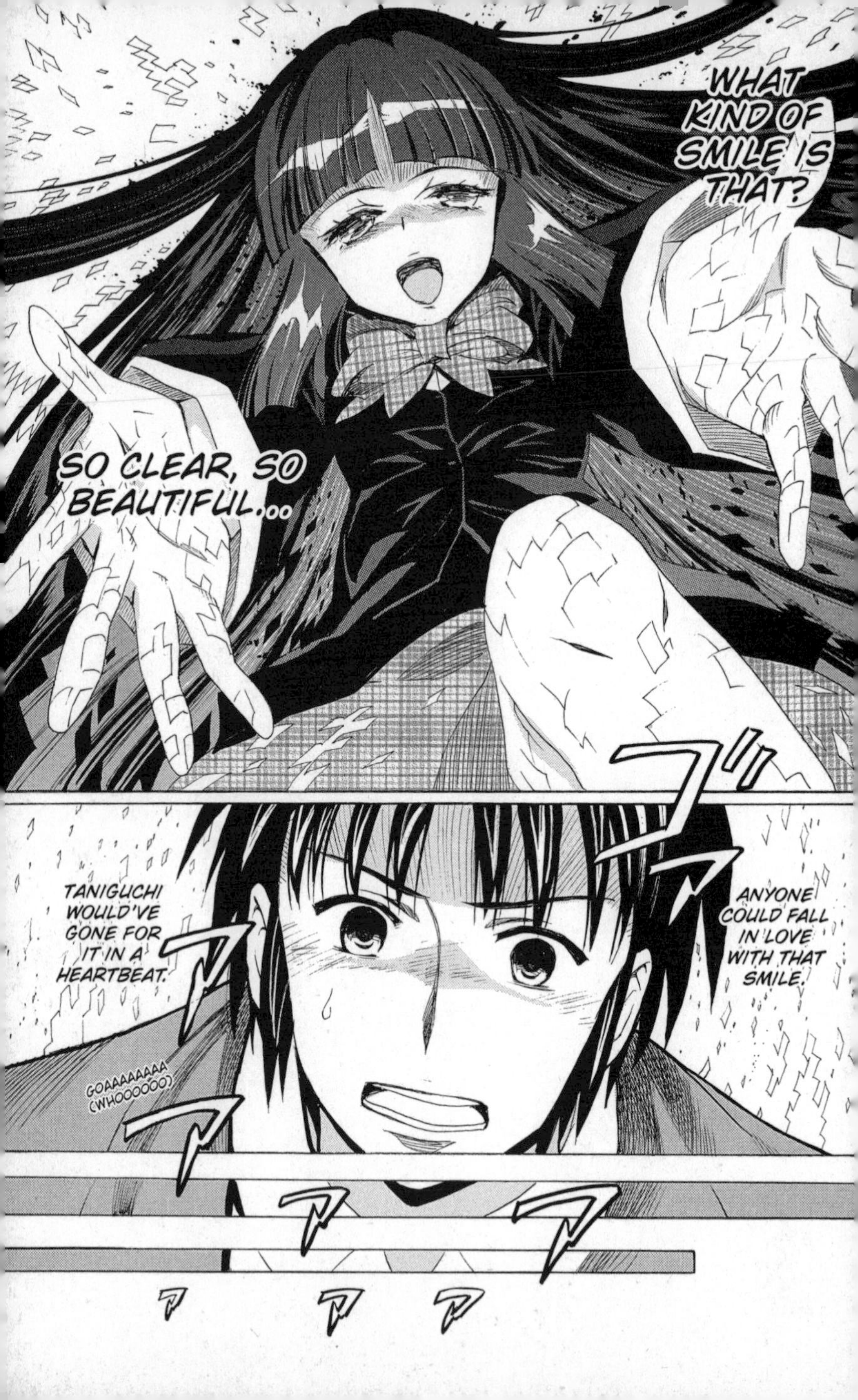
WHAT KIND OF SMILE IS THAT?
SO CLEAR, SO BEAUTIFUL...
ANYONE COULD FALL IN LOVE WITH THAT SMILE.
TANIGUCHI WOULD'VE GONE FOR IT IN A HEARTBEAT.
GOAAAAAAAA (WHOOOOOO)

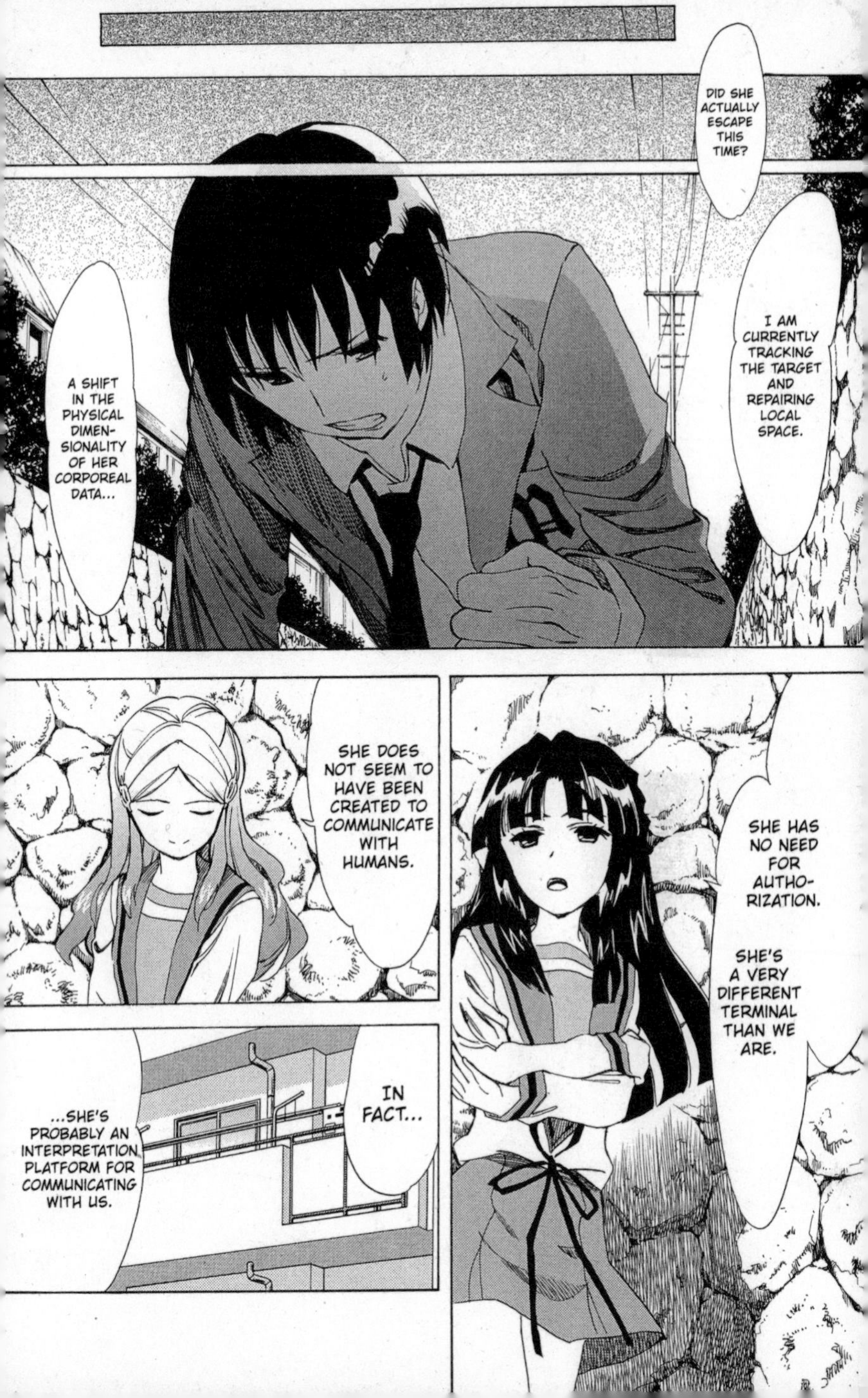
DID SHE ACTUALLY ESCAPE THIS TIME?
I AM CURRENTLY TRACKING THE TARGET AND REPAIRING LOCAL SPACE.
A SHIFT IN THE PHYSICAL DIMEN-SIONALITY OF HER CORPOREAL DATA...
SHE HAS NO NEED FOR AUTHO-RIZATION.
SHE'S A VERY DIFFERENT TERMINAL THAN WE ARE.
SHE DOES NOT SEEM TO HAVE BEEN CREATED TO COMMUNICATE WITH HUMANS.
IN FACT...
...SHE'S PROBABLY AN INTERPRETATION PLATFORM FOR COMMUNICATING WITH US.

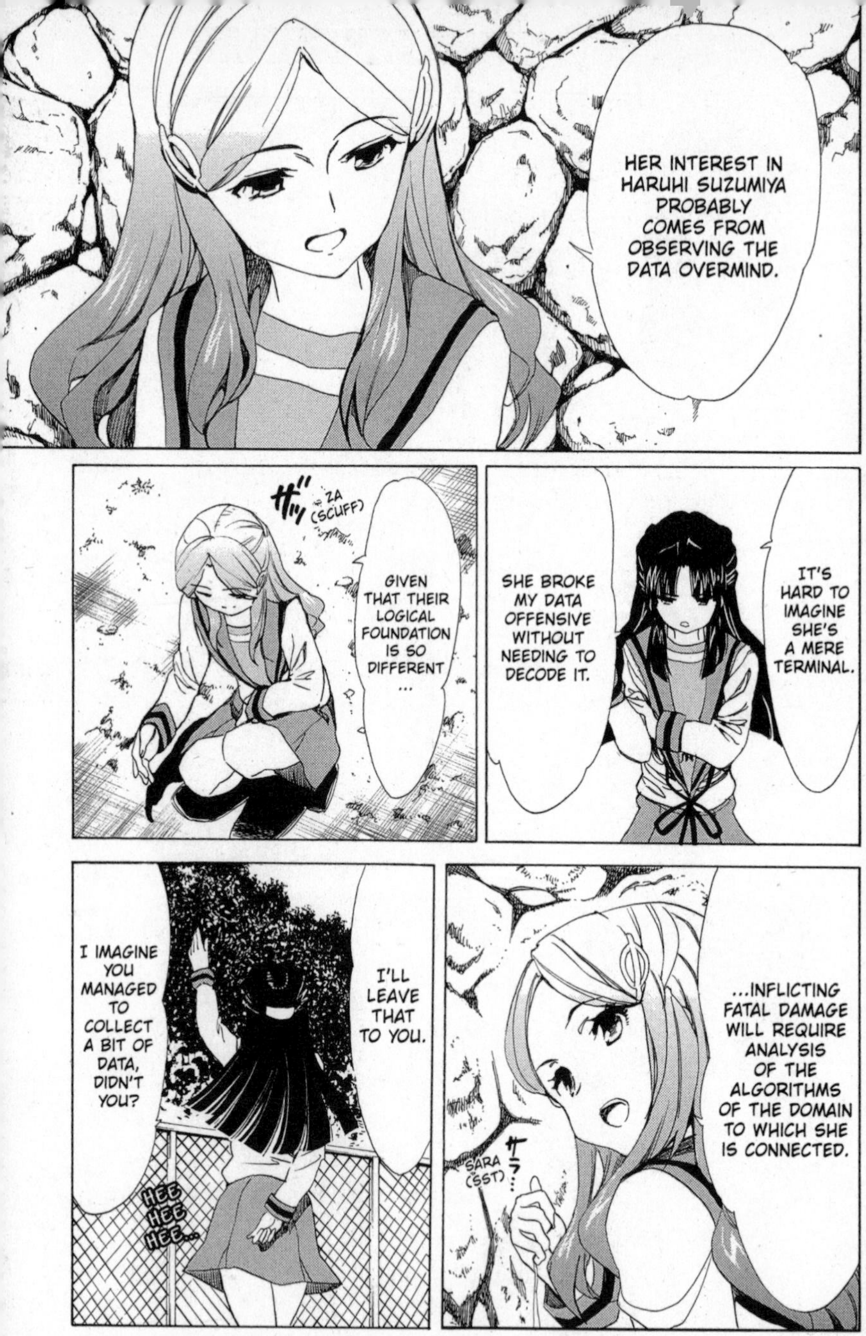
HER INTEREST IN HARUHI SUZUMIYA PROBABLY COMES FROM OBSERVING THE DATA OVERMIND.
IT'S HARD TO IMAGINE SHE'S A MERE TERMINAL.
SHE BROKE MY DATA OFFENSIVE WITHOUT NEEDING TO DECODE IT.
GIVEN THAT THEIR LOGICAL FOUNDATION IS SO DIFFERENT ...
ZA (SCUFF)
...INFLICTING FATAL DAMAGE WILL REQUIRE ANALYSIS OF THE ALGORITHMS OF THE DOMAIN TO WHICH SHE IS CONNECTED.
SARA (SST)
I'LL LEAVE THAT TO YOU.
I IMAGINE YOU MANAGED TO COLLECT A BIT OF DATA, DIDN'T YOU?
HEE HEE HEE...

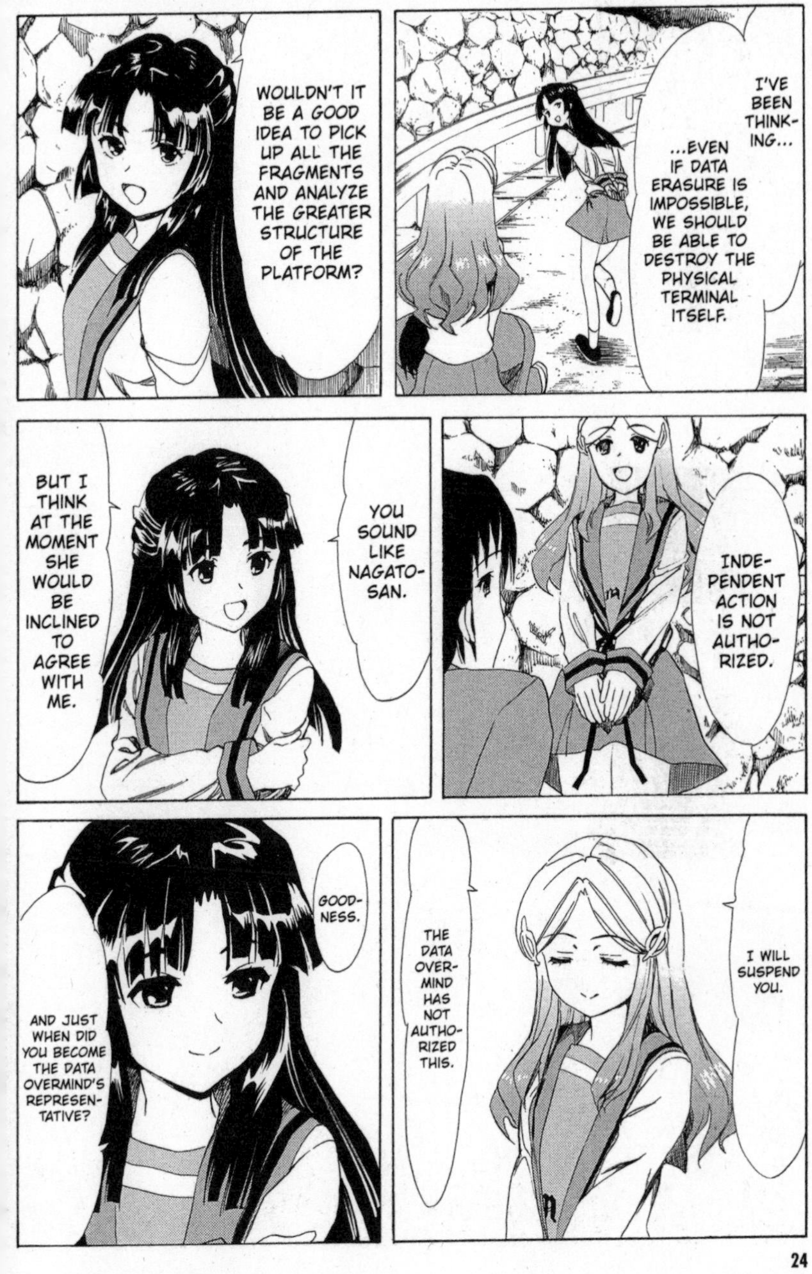
I'VE BEEN THINKING...
...EVEN IF DATA ERASURE IS IMPOSSIBLE, WE SHOULD BE ABLE TO DESTROY THE PHYSICAL TERMINAL ITSELF.
WOULDN'T IT BE A GOOD IDEA TO PICK UP ALL THE FRAGMENTS AND ANALYZE THE GREATER STRUCTURE OF THE PLATFORM?
INDEPENDENT ACTION IS NOT AUTHORIZED.
YOU SOUND LIKE NAGATO-SAN.
BUT I THINK AT THE MOMENT SHE WOULD BE INCLINED TO AGREE WITH ME.
I WILL SUSPEND YOU.
THE DATA OVERMIND HAS NOT AUTHORIZED THIS.
GOODNESS.
AND JUST WHEN DID YOU BECOME THE DATA OVERMIND'S REPRESENTATIVE?

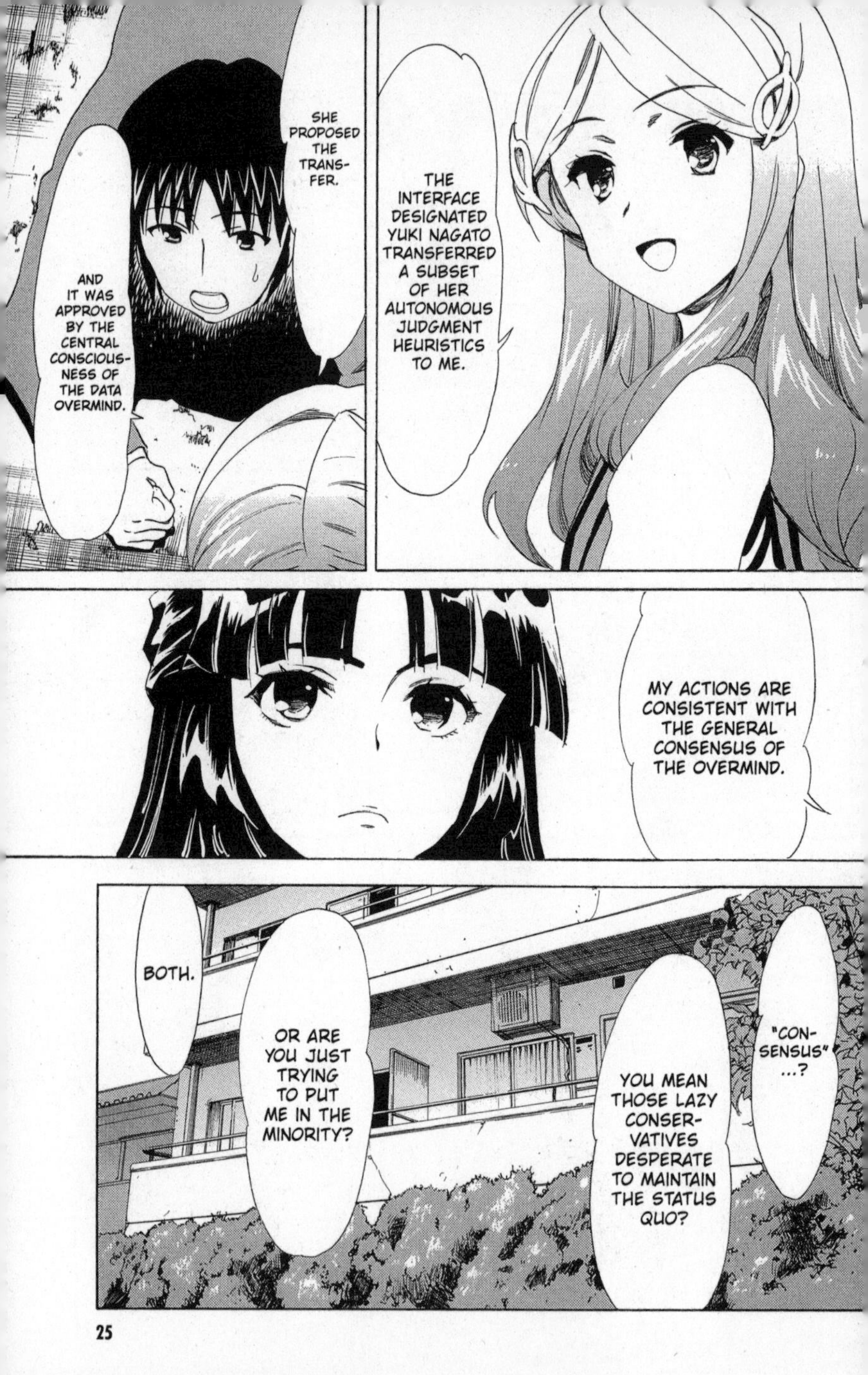
THE INTERFACE DESIGNATED YUKI NAGATO TRANSFERRED A SUBSET OF HER AUTONOMOUS JUDGMENT HEURISTICS TO ME.
SHE PROPOSED THE TRANS-FER.
AND IT WAS APPROVED BY THE CENTRAL CONSCIOUS-NESS OF THE DATA OVERMIND.
MY ACTIONS ARE CONSISTENT WITH THE GENERAL CONSENSUS OF THE OVERMIND.
"CON-SENSUS"...?
YOU MEAN THOSE LAZY CONSER-VATIVES DESPERATE TO MAINTAIN THE STATUS QUO?
OR ARE YOU JUST TRYING TO PUT ME IN THE MINORITY?
BOTH.

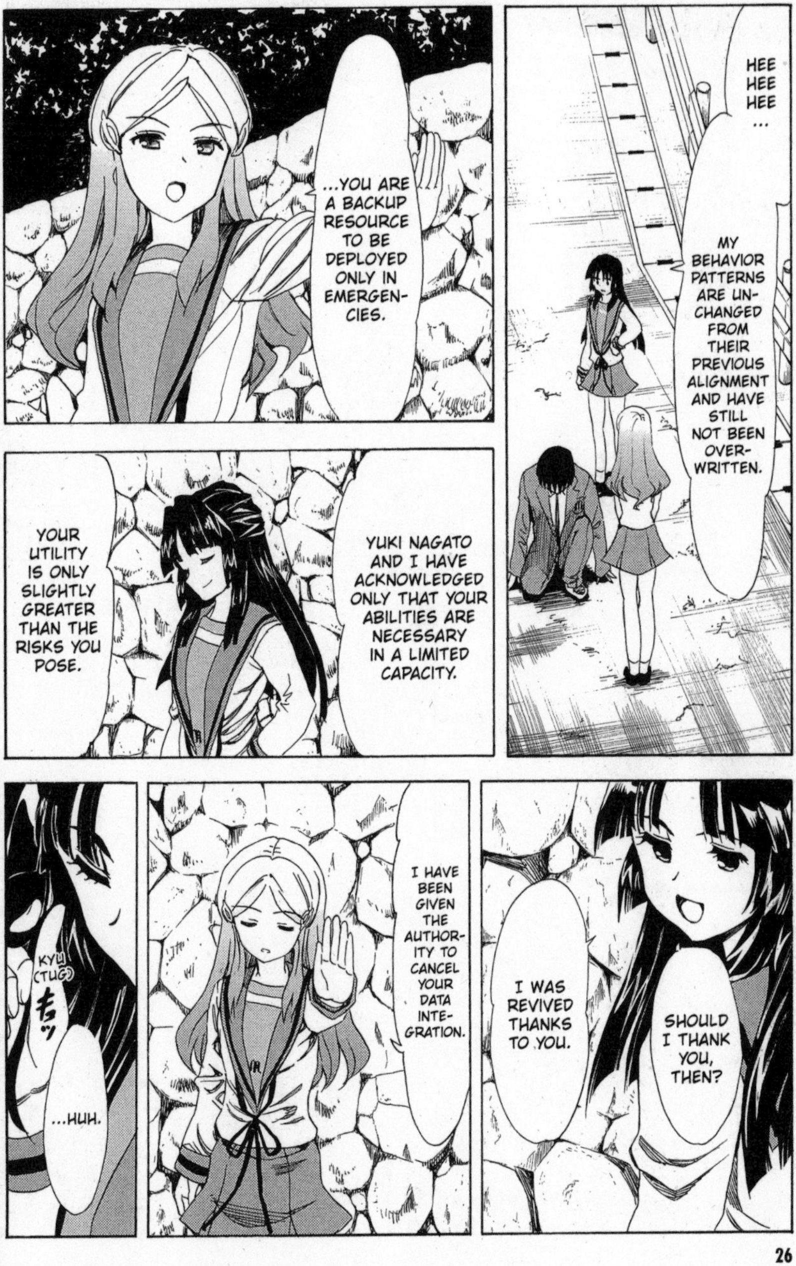
HEE HEE HEE ...
MY BEHAVIOR PATTERNS ARE UN-CHANGED FROM THEIR PREVIOUS ALIGNMENT AND HAVE STILL NOT BEEN OVER-WRITTEN.
...YOU ARE A BACKUP RESOURCE TO BE DEPLOYED ONLY IN EMERGEN-CIES.
YUKI NAGATO AND I HAVE ACKNOWLEDGED ONLY THAT YOUR ABILITIES ARE NECESSARY IN A LIMITED CAPACITY.
YOUR UTILITY IS ONLY SLIGHTLY GREATER THAN THE RISKS YOU POSE.
SHOULD I THANK YOU, THEN?
I WAS REVIVED THANKS TO YOU.
I HAVE BEEN GIVEN THE AUTHOR-ITY TO CANCEL YOUR DATA INTE-GRATION.
KYU (TUG)
キュッ
...HUH.

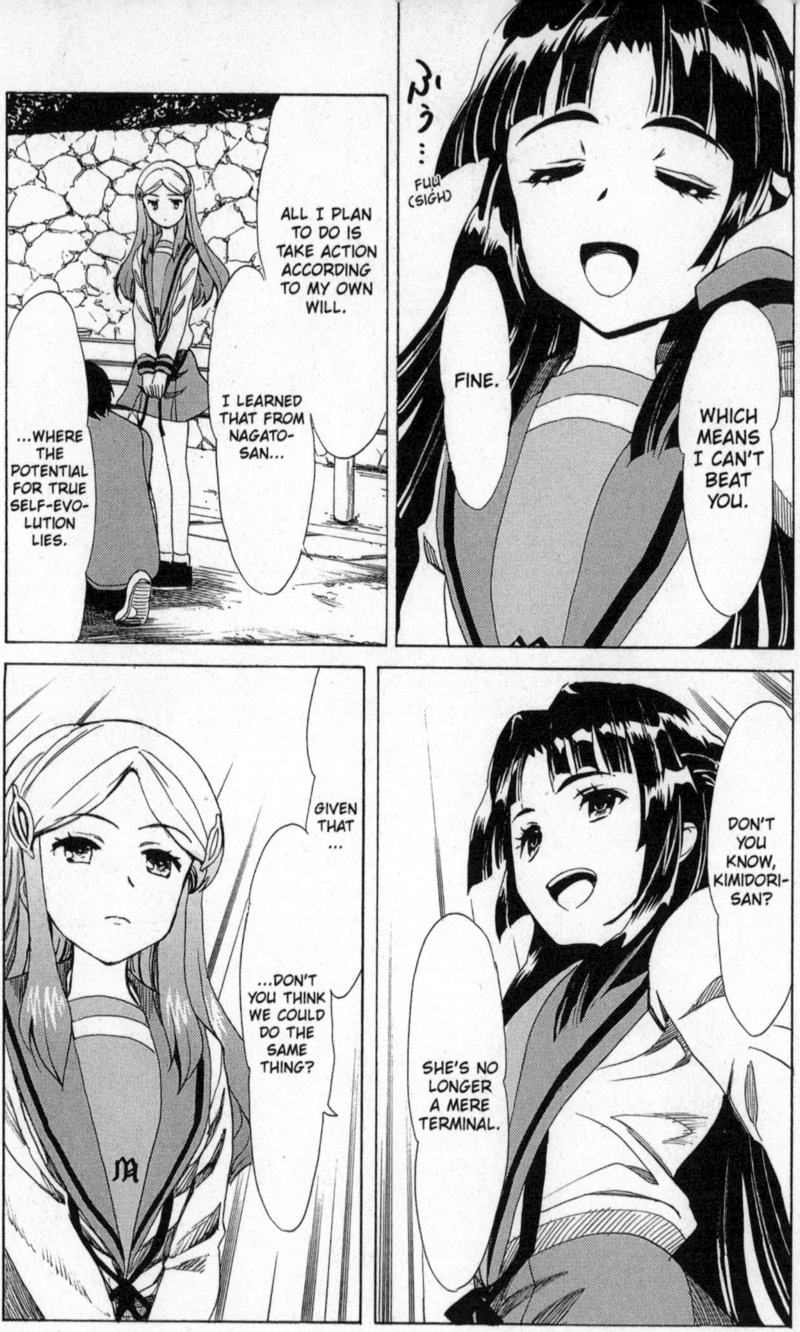
ふう…
FUU (SIGH)
FINE.
WHICH MEANS I CAN'T BEAT YOU.
ALL I PLAN TO DO IS TAKE ACTION ACCORDING TO MY OWN WILL.
I LEARNED THAT FROM NAGATO-SAN...
...WHERE THE POTENTIAL FOR TRUE SELF-EVOLUTION LIES.
DON'T YOU KNOW, KIMIDORI-SAN?
SHE'S NO LONGER A MERE TERMINAL.
GIVEN THAT...
...DON'T YOU THINK WE COULD DO THE SAME THING?

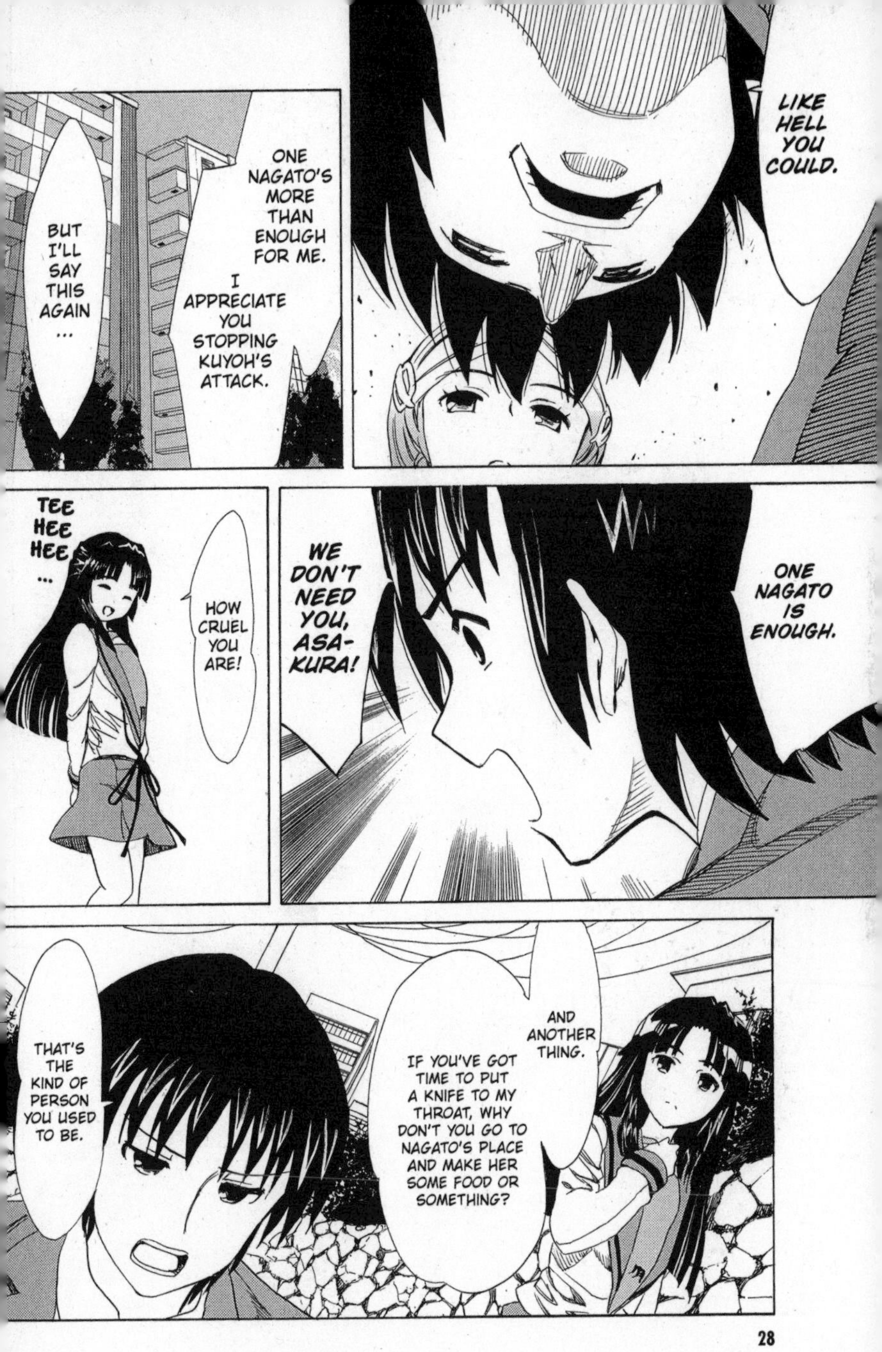
LIKE HELL YOU COULD.
ONE NAGATO'S MORE THAN ENOUGH FOR ME.
I APPRECIATE YOU STOPPING KUYOH'S ATTACK.
BUT I'LL SAY THIS AGAIN ...
ONE NAGATO IS ENOUGH.
WE DON'T NEED YOU, ASA-KURA!
HOW CRUEL YOU ARE!
TEE HEE HEE ...
AND ANOTHER THING.
IF YOU'VE GOT TIME TO PUT A KNIFE TO MY THROAT, WHY DON'T YOU GO TO NAGATO'S PLACE AND MAKE HER SOME FOOD OR SOMETHING?
THAT'S THE KIND OF PERSON YOU USED TO BE.

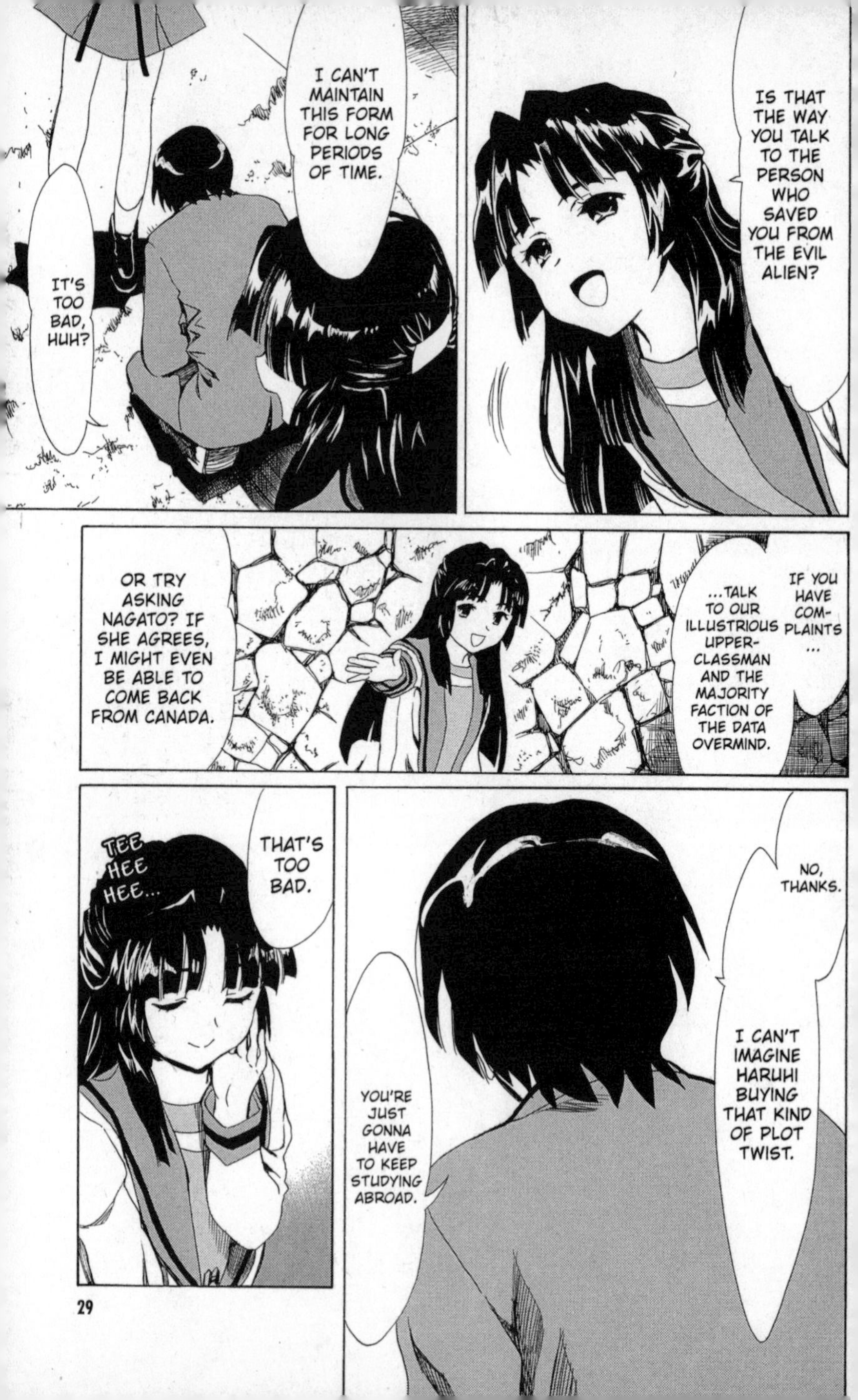
IS THAT THE WAY YOU TALK TO THE PERSON WHO SAVED YOU FROM THE EVIL ALIEN?
I CAN'T MAINTAIN THIS FORM FOR LONG PERIODS OF TIME.
IT'S TOO BAD, HUH?
IF YOU HAVE COM-PLAINTS...
...TALK TO OUR ILLUSTRIOUS UPPER-CLASSMAN AND THE MAJORITY FACTION OF THE DATA OVERMIND.
OR TRY ASKING NAGATO? IF SHE AGREES, I MIGHT EVEN BE ABLE TO COME BACK FROM CANADA.
NO, THANKS.
I CAN'T IMAGINE HARUHI BUYING THAT KIND OF PLOT TWIST.
YOU'RE JUST GONNA HAVE TO KEEP STUDYING ABROAD.
THAT'S TOO BAD.
TEE HEE HEE...

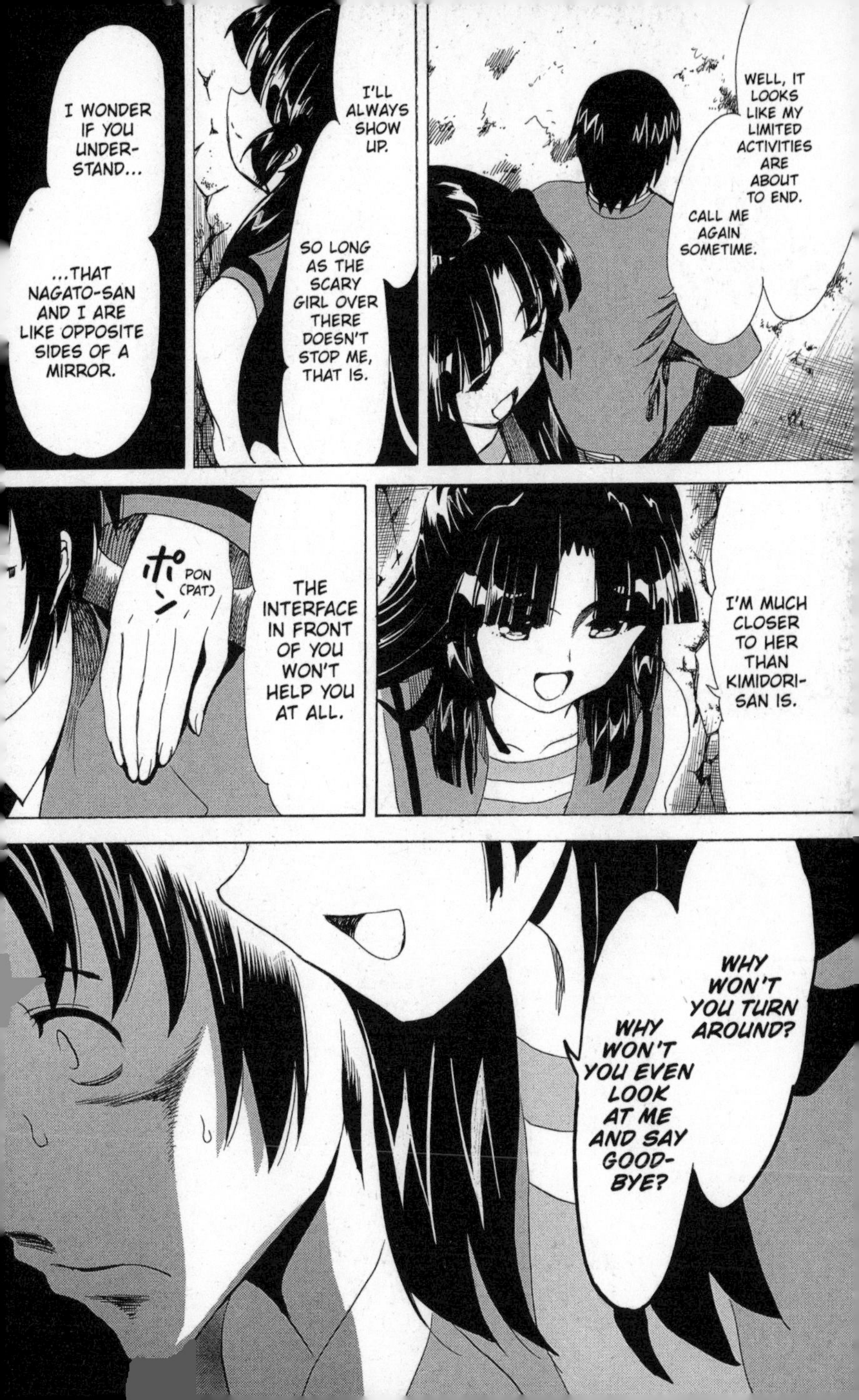
WELL, IT LOOKS LIKE MY LIMITED ACTIVITIES ARE ABOUT TO END.
CALL ME AGAIN SOMETIME.
I'LL ALWAYS SHOW UP.
SO LONG AS THE SCARY GIRL OVER THERE DOESN'T STOP ME, THAT IS.
I WONDER IF YOU UNDER-STAND...
...THAT NAGATO-SAN AND I ARE LIKE OPPOSITE SIDES OF A MIRROR.
I'M MUCH CLOSER TO HER THAN KIMIDORI-SAN IS.
THE INTERFACE IN FRONT OF YOU WON'T HELP YOU AT ALL.
ポン
PON (PAT)
WHY WON'T YOU TURN AROUND?
WHY WON'T YOU EVEN LOOK AT ME AND SAY GOOD-BYE?

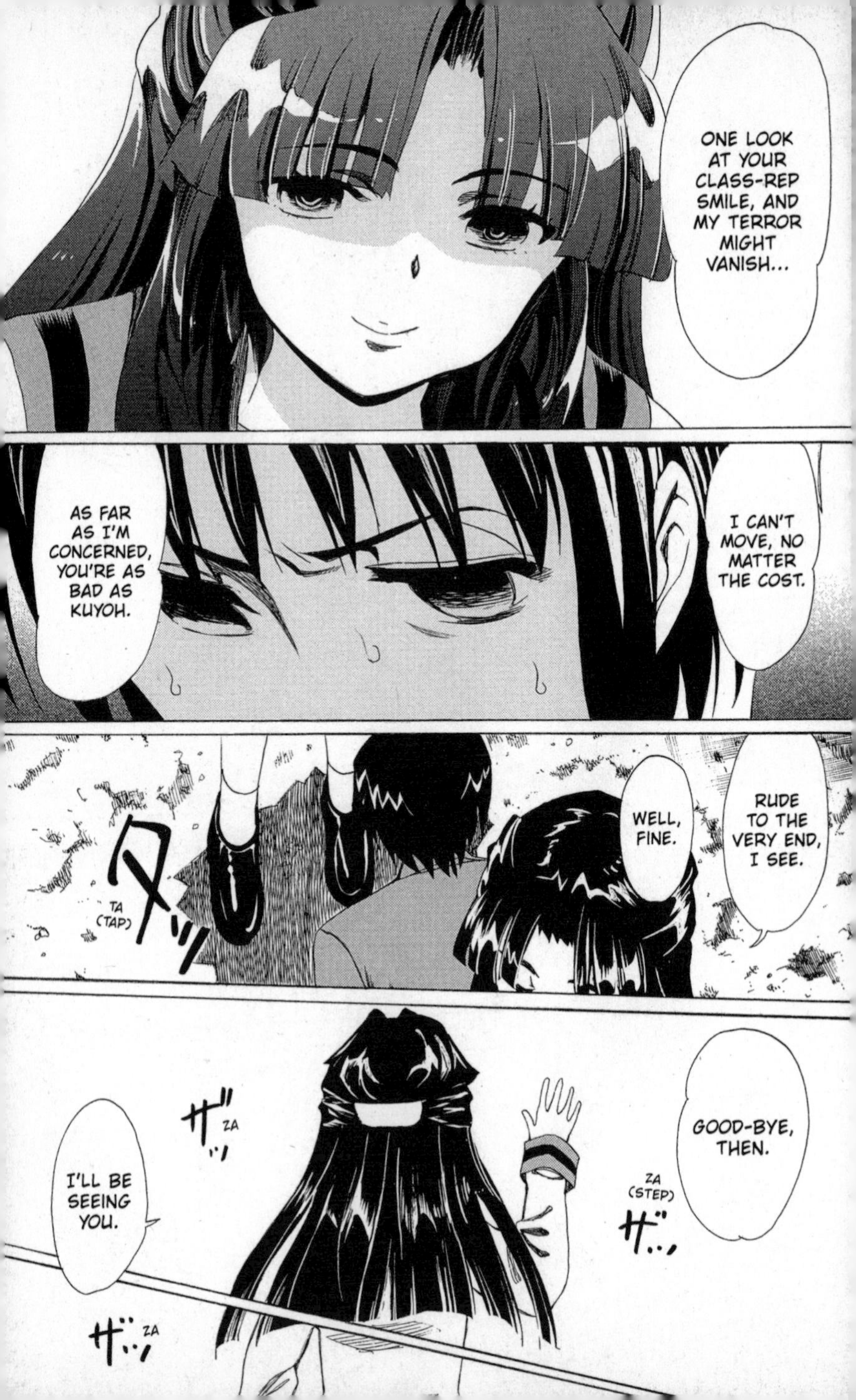
ONE LOOK AT YOUR CLASS-REP SMILE, AND MY TERROR MIGHT VANISH...
I CAN'T MOVE, NO MATTER THE COST.
AS FAR AS I'M CONCERNED, YOU'RE AS BAD AS KUYOH.
RUDE TO THE VERY END, I SEE.
WELL, FINE.
TA (TAP)
GOOD-BYE, THEN.
ZA (STEP)
ZA
I'LL BE SEEING YOU.
ZA

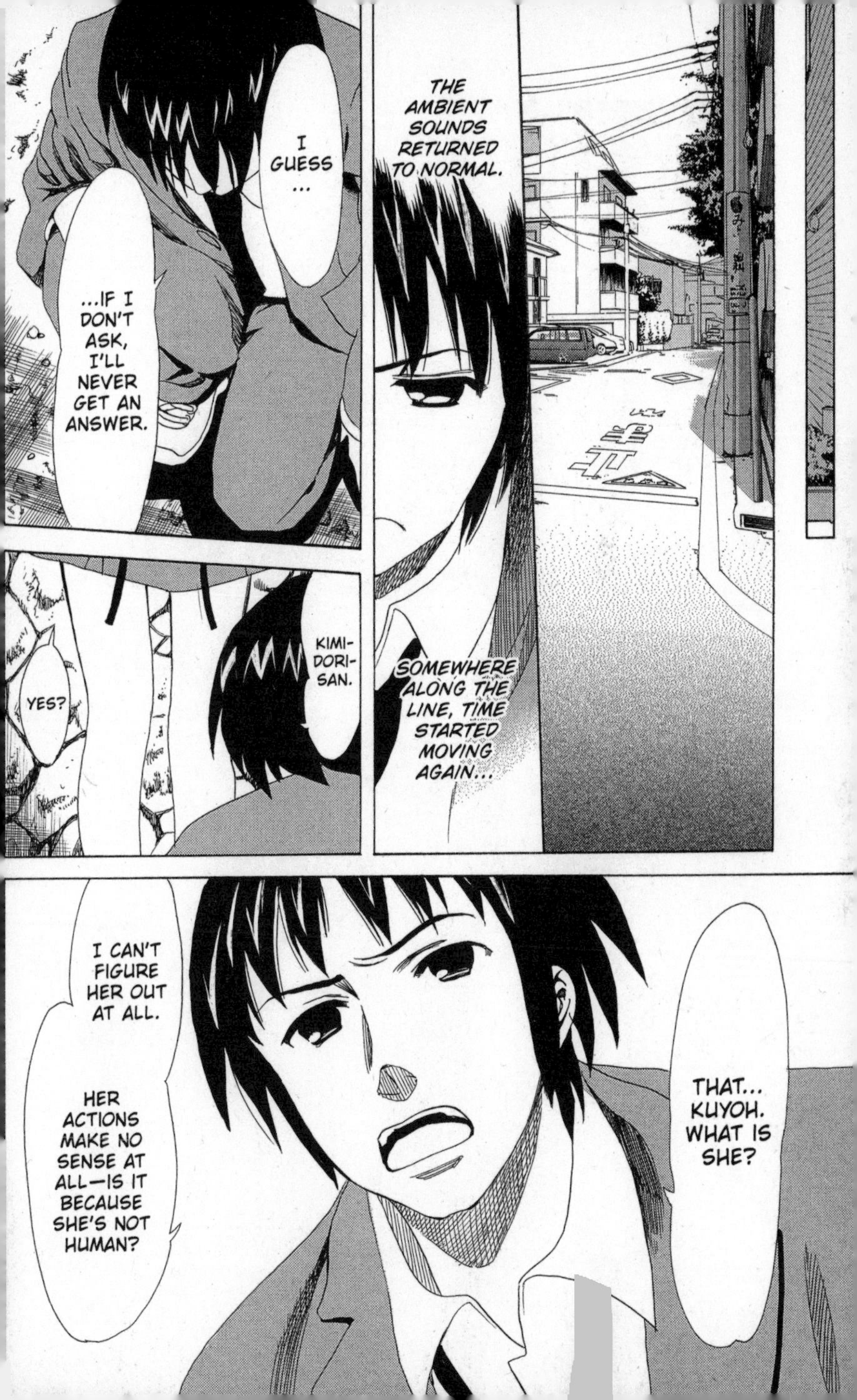
THE AMBIENT SOUNDS RETURNED TO NORMAL.
SOMEWHERE ALONG THE LINE, TIME STARTED MOVING AGAIN...
I GUESS...
...IF I DON'T ASK, I'LL NEVER GET AN ANSWER.
KIMIDORI-SAN.
YES?
THAT... KUYOH. WHAT IS SHE?
I CAN'T FIGURE HER OUT AT ALL.
HER ACTIONS MAKE NO SENSE AT ALL—IS IT BECAUSE SHE'S NOT HUMAN?

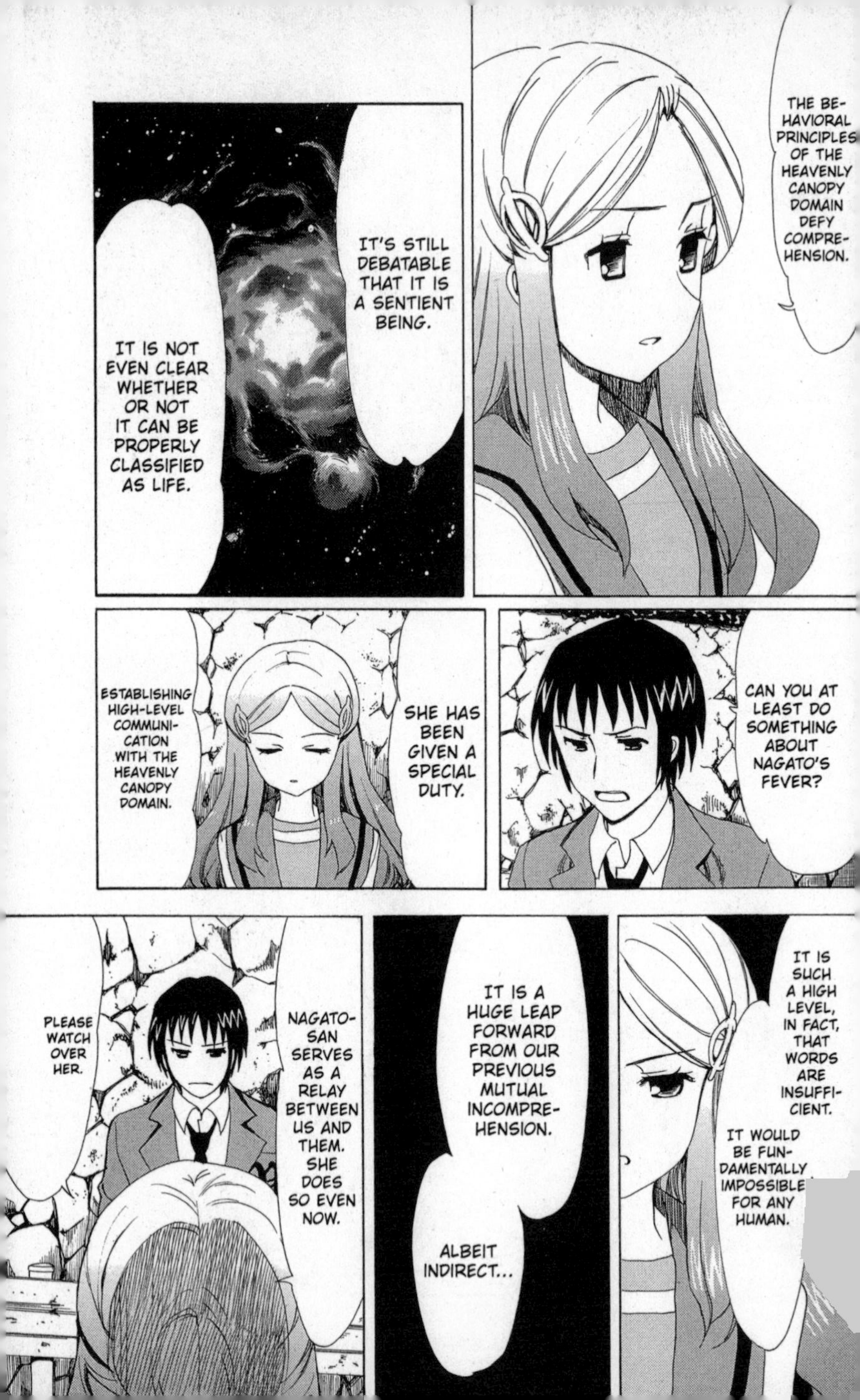
THE BEHAVIORAL PRINCIPLES OF THE HEAVENLY CANOPY DOMAIN DEFY COMPREHENSION.
IT'S STILL DEBATABLE THAT IT IS A SENTIENT BEING.
IT IS NOT EVEN CLEAR WHETHER OR NOT IT CAN BE PROPERLY CLASSIFIED AS LIFE.
CAN YOU AT LEAST DO SOMETHING ABOUT NAGATO'S FEVER?
SHE HAS BEEN GIVEN A SPECIAL DUTY.
ESTABLISHING HIGH-LEVEL COMMUNICATION WITH THE HEAVENLY CANOPY DOMAIN.
IT IS SUCH A HIGH LEVEL, IN FACT, THAT WORDS ARE INSUFFICIENT.
IT WOULD BE FUNDAMENTALLY IMPOSSIBLE FOR ANY HUMAN.
IT IS A HUGE LEAP FORWARD FROM OUR PREVIOUS MUTUAL INCOMPREHENSION.
ALBEIT INDIRECT...
NAGATO-SAN SERVES AS A RELAY BETWEEN US AND THEM. SHE DOES SO EVEN NOW.
PLEASE WATCH OVER HER.

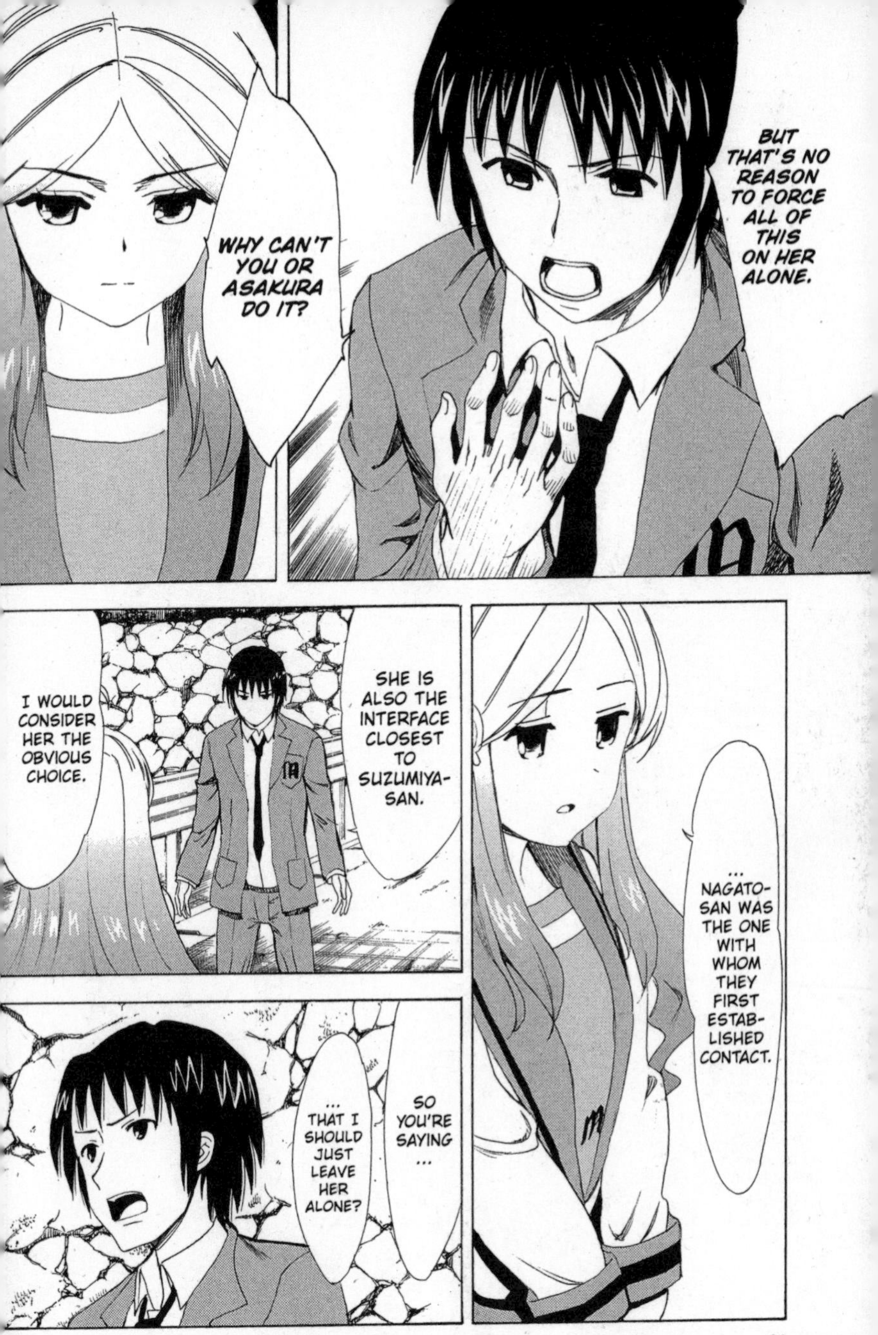
BUT THAT'S NO REASON TO FORCE ALL OF THIS ON HER ALONE.
WHY CAN'T YOU OR ASAKURA DO IT?
... NAGATO-SAN WAS THE ONE WITH WHOM THEY FIRST ESTAB-LISHED CONTACT.
SHE IS ALSO THE INTERFACE CLOSEST TO SUZUMIYA-SAN.
I WOULD CONSIDER HER THE OBVIOUS CHOICE.
SO YOU'RE SAYING ...
... THAT I SHOULD JUST LEAVE HER ALONE?

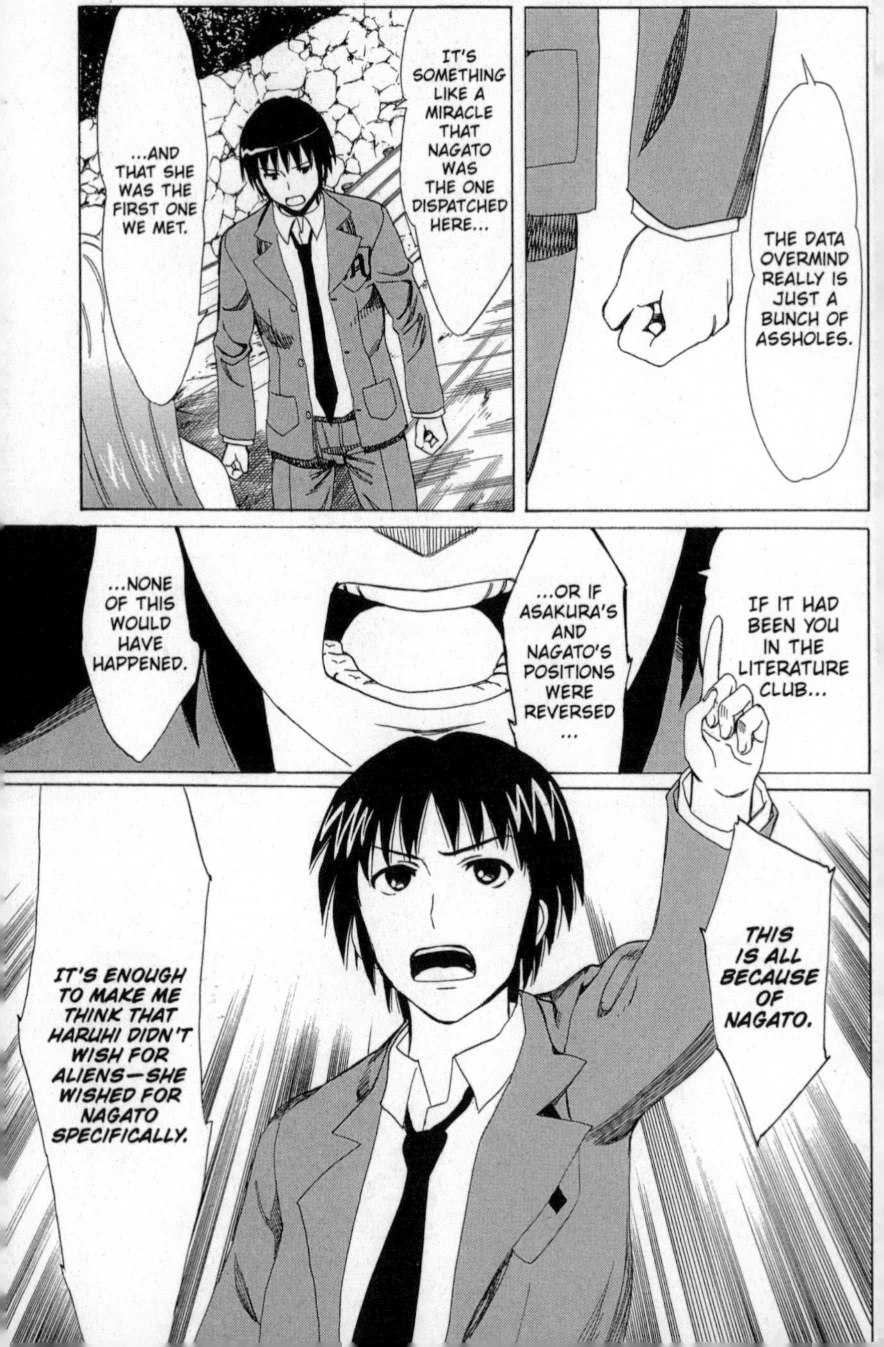
THE DATA OVERMIND REALLY IS JUST A BUNCH OF ASSHOLES.
IT'S SOMETHING LIKE A MIRACLE THAT NAGATO WAS THE ONE DISPATCHED HERE...
...AND THAT SHE WAS THE FIRST ONE WE MET.
IF IT HAD BEEN YOU IN THE LITERATURE CLUB...
...OR IF ASAKURA'S AND NAGATO'S POSITIONS WERE REVERSED...
...NONE OF THIS WOULD HAVE HAPPENED.
THIS IS ALL BECAUSE OF NAGATO.
IT'S ENOUGH TO MAKE ME THINK THAT HARUHI DIDN'T WISH FOR ALIENS—SHE WISHED FOR NAGATO SPECIFICALLY.

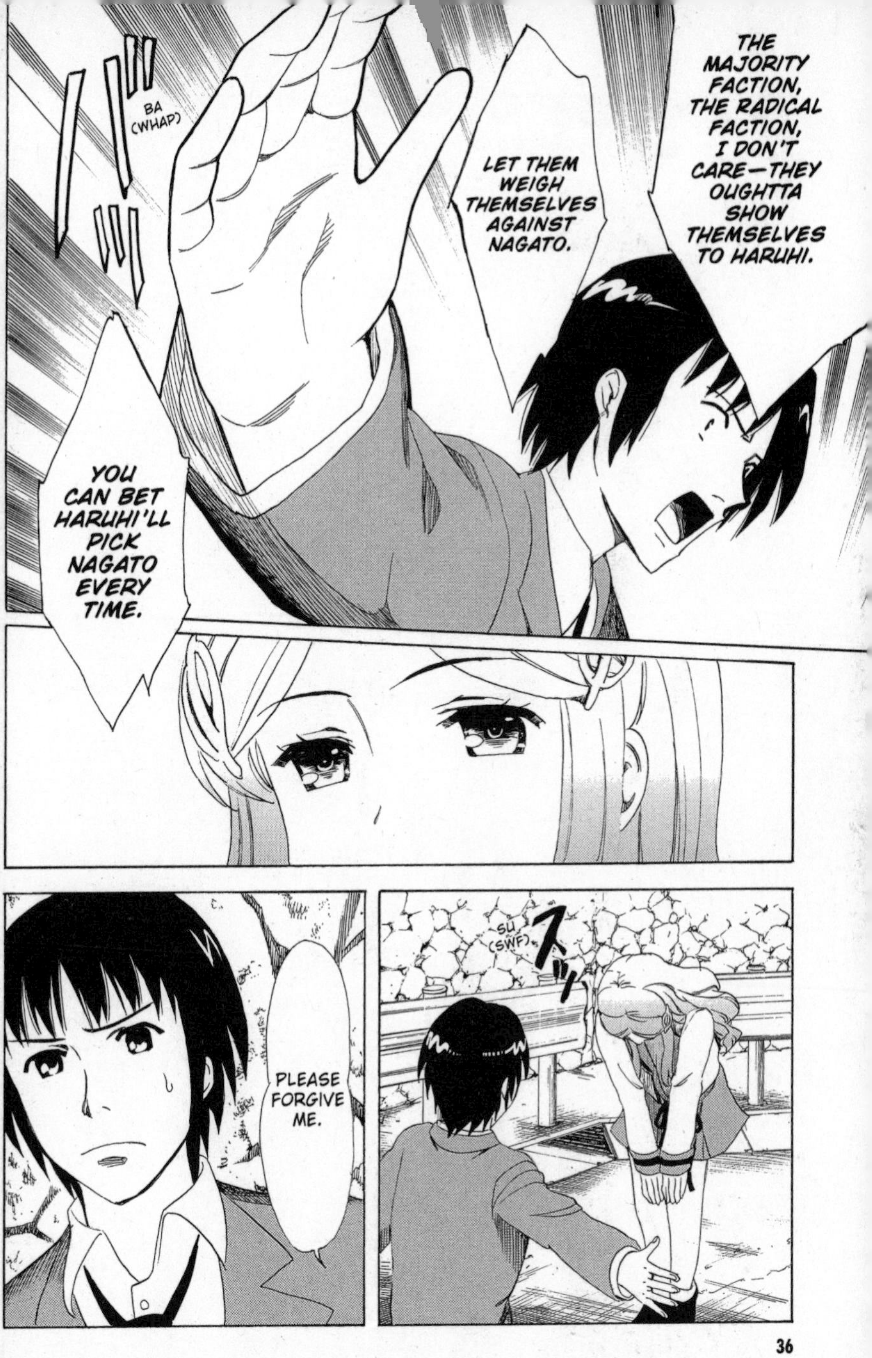
THE MAJORITY FACTION, THE RADICAL FACTION, I DON'T CARE—THEY OUGHTTA SHOW THEMSELVES TO HARUHI.
LET THEM WEIGH THEMSELVES AGAINST NAGATO.
BA (WHAP)
YOU CAN BET HARUHI'LL PICK NAGATO EVERY TIME.
SU (SWF)
PLEASE FORGIVE ME.

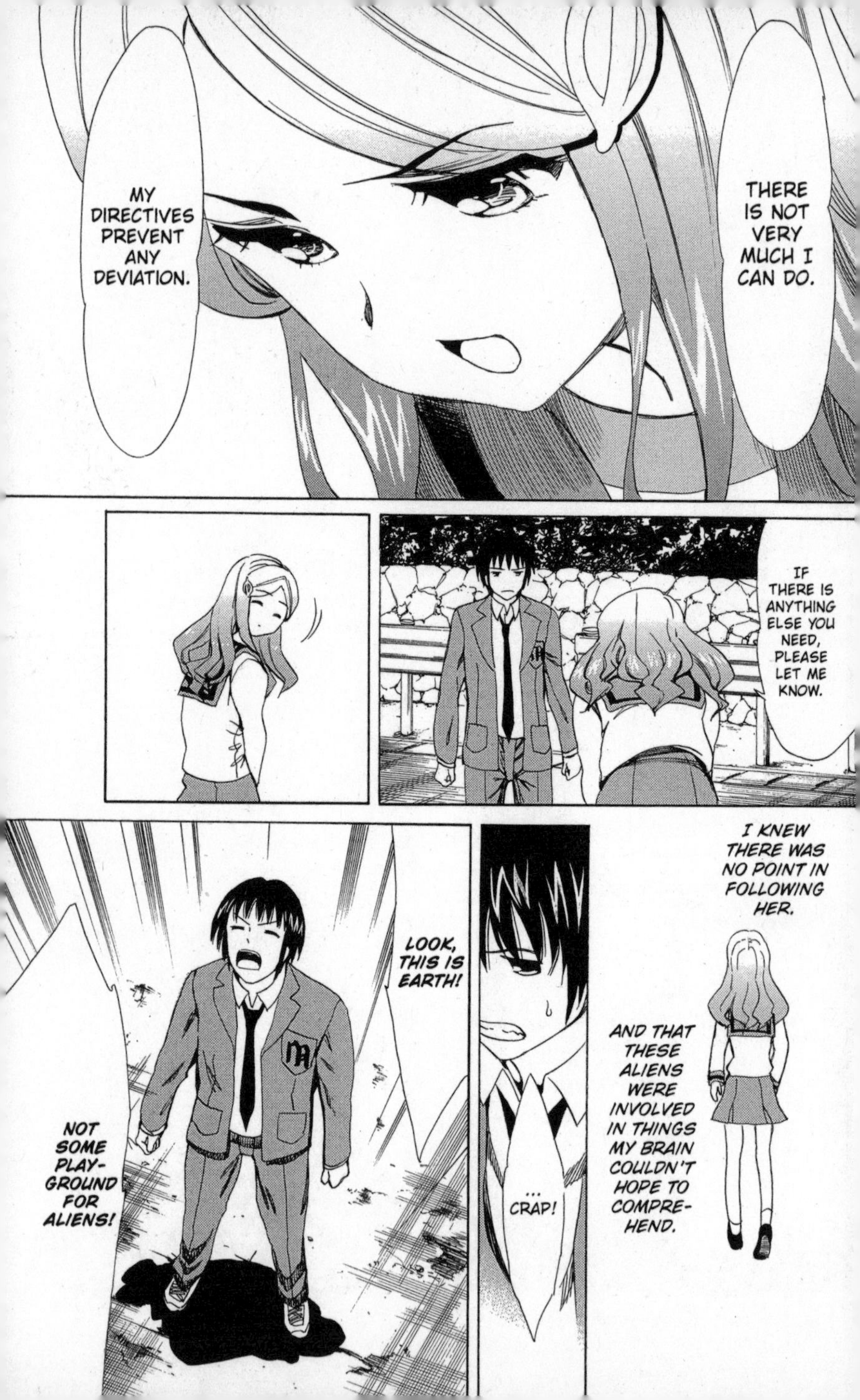
THERE IS NOT VERY MUCH I CAN DO.
MY DIRECTIVES PREVENT ANY DEVIATION.
IF THERE IS ANYTHING ELSE YOU NEED, PLEASE LET ME KNOW.
I KNEW THERE WAS NO POINT IN FOLLOWING HER.
AND THAT THESE ALIENS WERE INVOLVED IN THINGS MY BRAIN COULDN'T HOPE TO COMPRE-HEND.
...CRAP!
LOOK, THIS IS EARTH!
NOT SOME PLAY-GROUND FOR ALIENS!

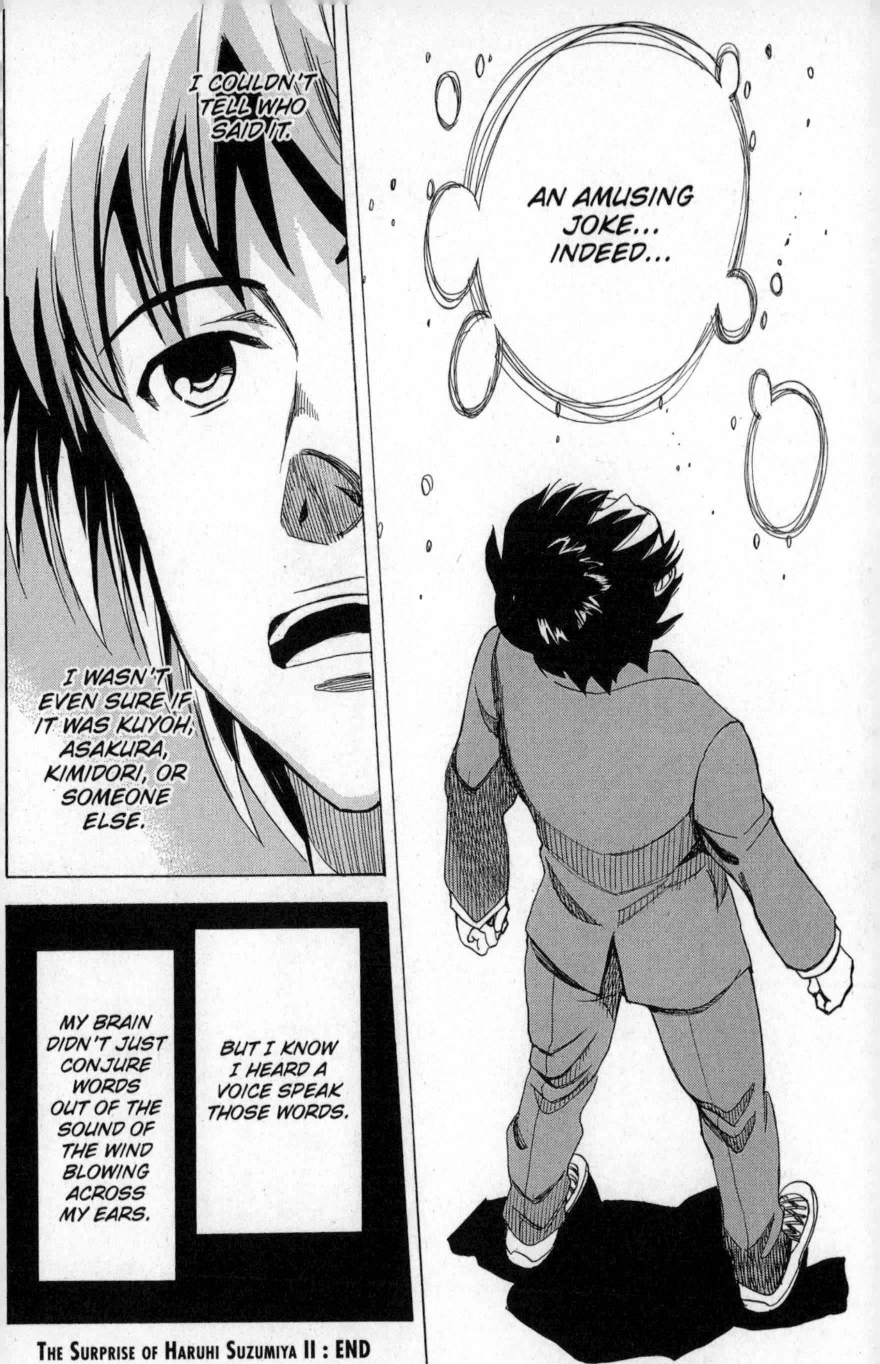
AN AMUSING JOKE... INDEED...
I COULDN'T TELL WHO SAID IT.
I WASN'T EVEN SURE IF IT WAS KUYOH, ASAKURA, KIMIDORI, OR SOMEONE ELSE.
BUT I KNOW I HEARD A VOICE SPEAK THOSE WORDS.
MY BRAIN DIDN'T JUST CONJURE WORDS OUT OF THE SOUND OF THE WIND BLOWING ACROSS MY EARS.

THE SURPRISE OF HARUHI SUZUMIYA II : END

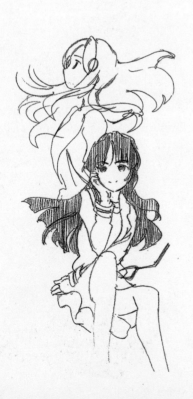

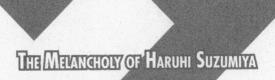

THE MELANCHOLY OF HARUHI SUZUMIYA

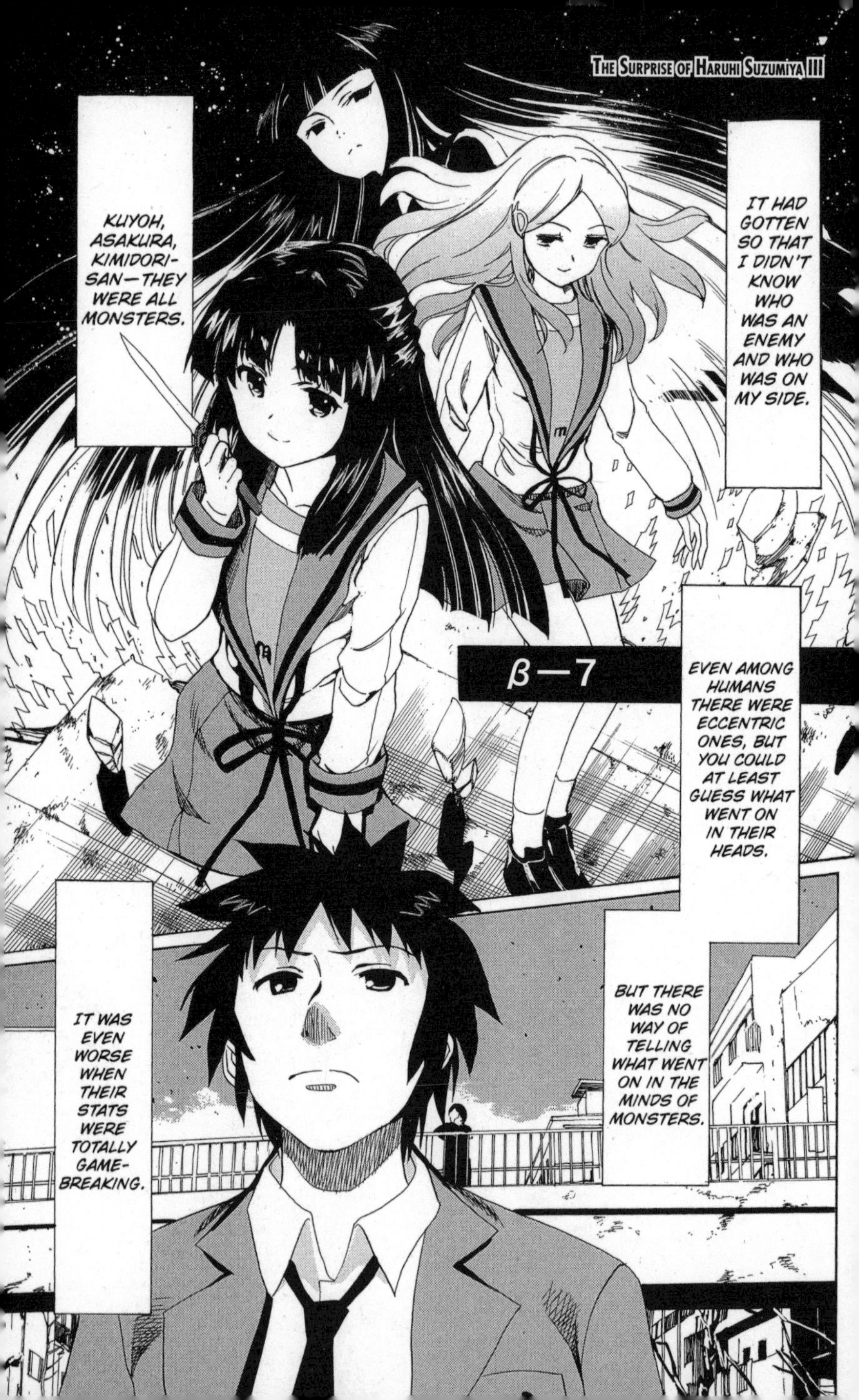
IT HAD GOTTEN SO THAT I DIDN'T KNOW WHO WAS AN ENEMY AND WHO WAS ON MY SIDE.
KUYOH, ASAKURA, KIMIDORI-SAN—THEY WERE ALL MONSTERS.
β—7
EVEN AMONG HUMANS THERE WERE ECCENTRIC ONES, BUT YOU COULD AT LEAST GUESS WHAT WENT ON IN THEIR HEADS.
BUT THERE WAS NO WAY OF TELLING WHAT WENT ON IN THE MINDS OF MONSTERS.
IT WAS EVEN WORSE WHEN THEIR STATS WERE TOTALLY GAME-BREAKING.

◎ THE SURPRISE OF HARUHI SUZUMIYA III

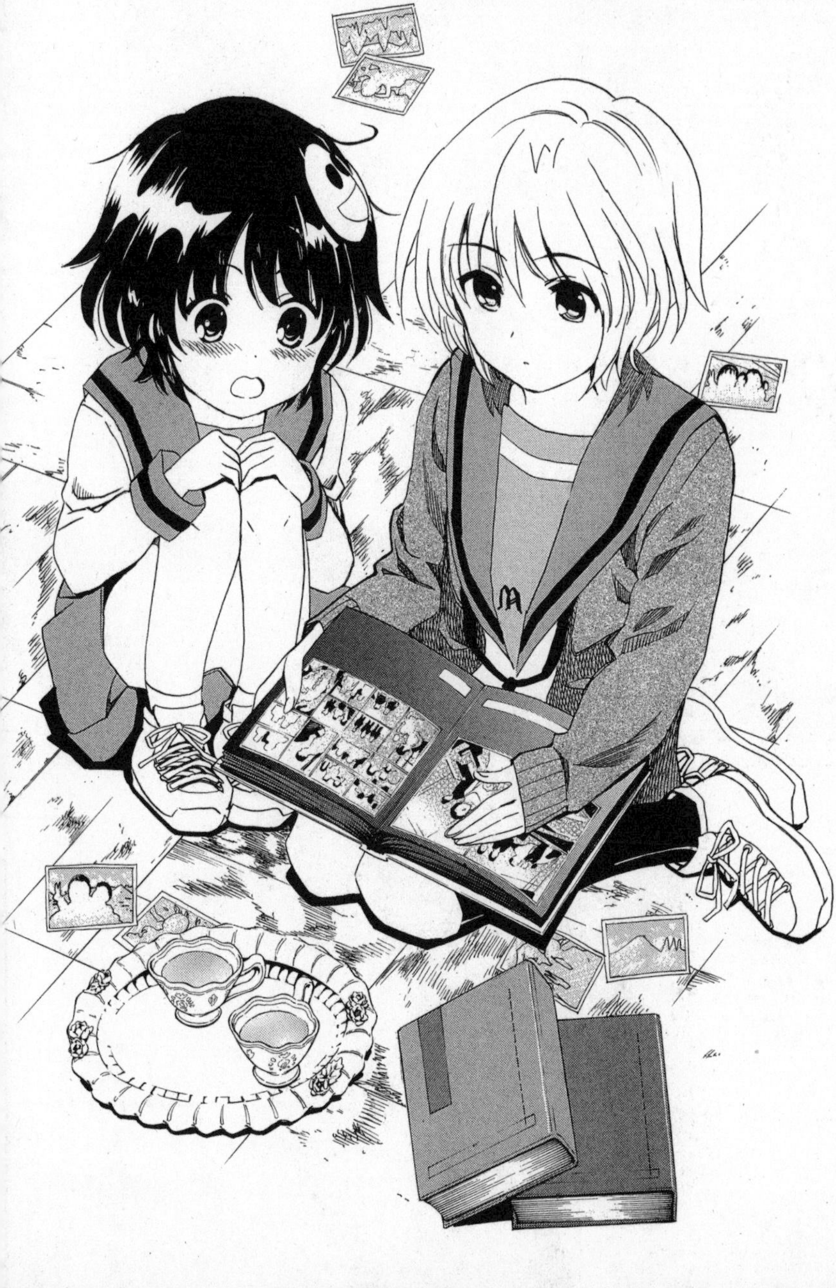

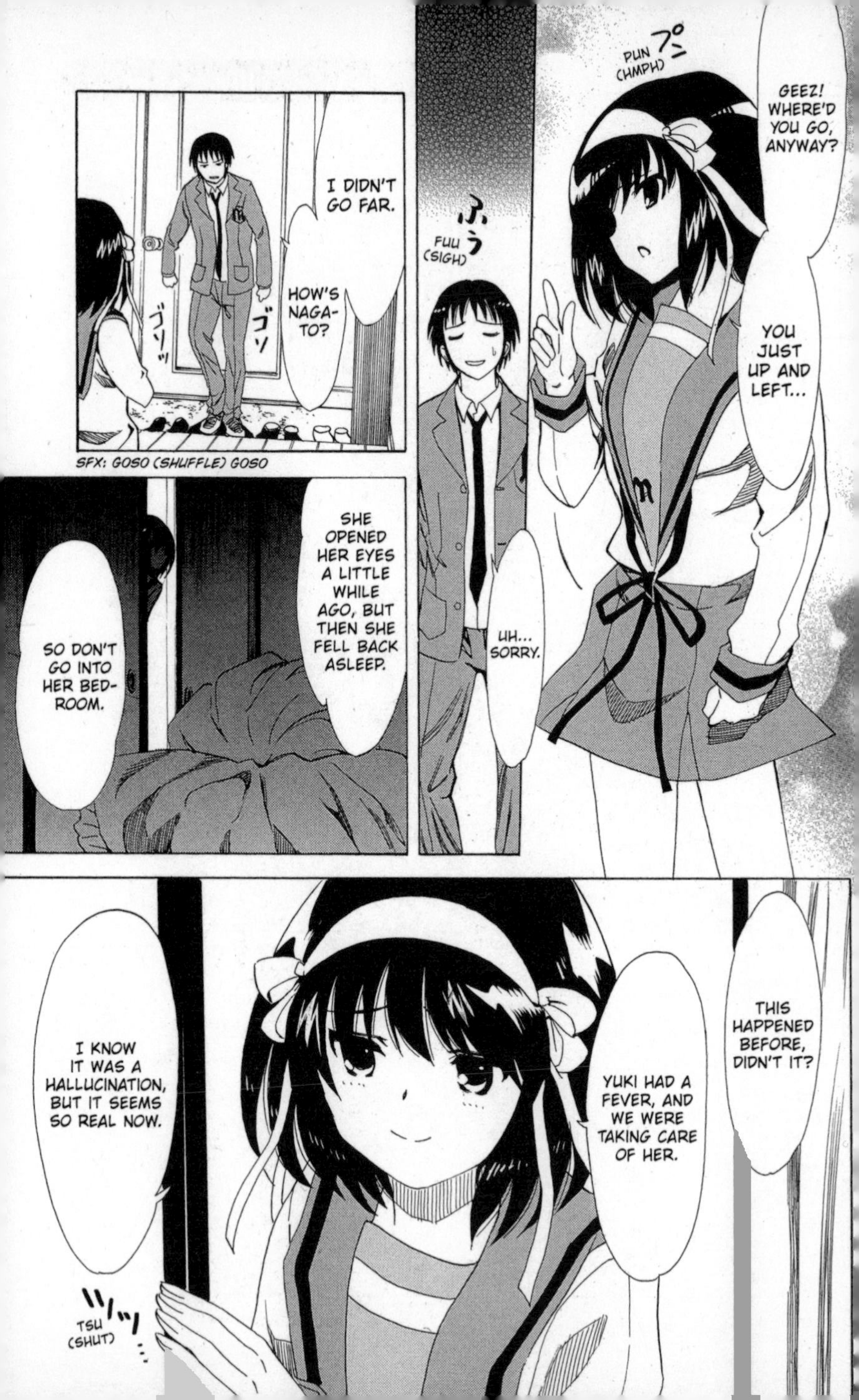
プン
PUN (HMPH)
GEEZ! WHERE'D YOU GO, ANYWAY?
YOU JUST UP AND LEFT...
ふう
FUU (SIGH)
UH... SORRY.
I DIDN'T GO FAR.
HOW'S NAGATO?
ゴソッ
ゴソ
SFX: GOSO (SHUFFLE) GOSO
SHE OPENED HER EYES A LITTLE WHILE AGO, BUT THEN SHE FELL BACK ASLEEP.
SO DON'T GO INTO HER BEDROOM.
THIS HAPPENED BEFORE, DIDN'T IT?
YUKI HAD A FEVER, AND WE WERE TAKING CARE OF HER.
I KNOW IT WAS A HALLUCINATION, BUT IT SEEMS SO REAL NOW.
TSU (SHUT)

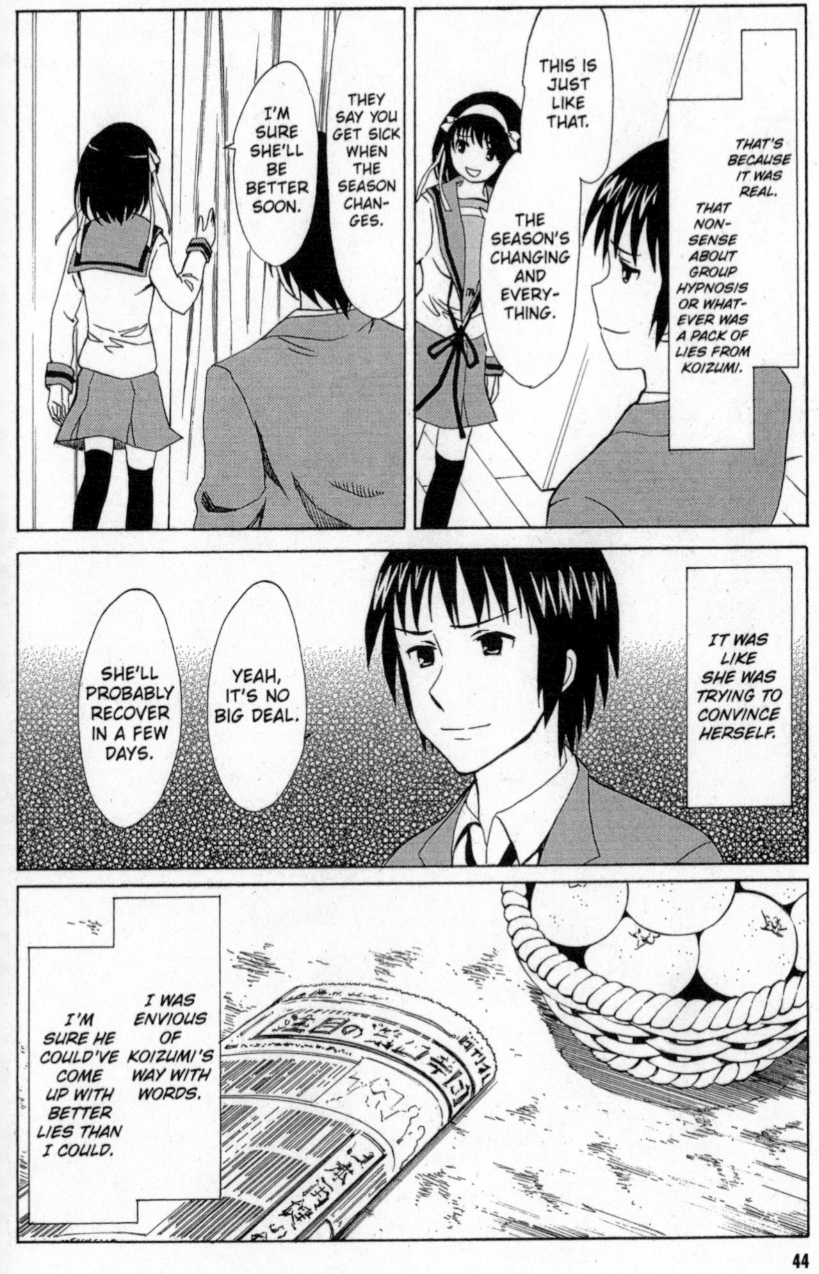
THIS IS JUST LIKE THAT.
THE SEASON'S CHANGING AND EVERY-THING.
THAT'S BECAUSE IT WAS REAL.
THAT NON-SENSE ABOUT GROUP HYPNOSIS OR WHAT-EVER WAS A PACK OF LIES FROM KOIZUMI.
THEY SAY YOU GET SICK WHEN THE SEASON CHAN-GES.
I'M SURE SHE'LL BE BETTER SOON.
IT WAS LIKE SHE WAS TRYING TO CONVINCE HERSELF.
YEAH, IT'S NO BIG DEAL.
SHE'LL PROBABLY RECOVER IN A FEW DAYS.
I WAS ENVIOUS OF KOIZUMI'S WAY WITH WORDS.
I'M SURE HE COULD'VE COME UP WITH BETTER LIES THAN I COULD.

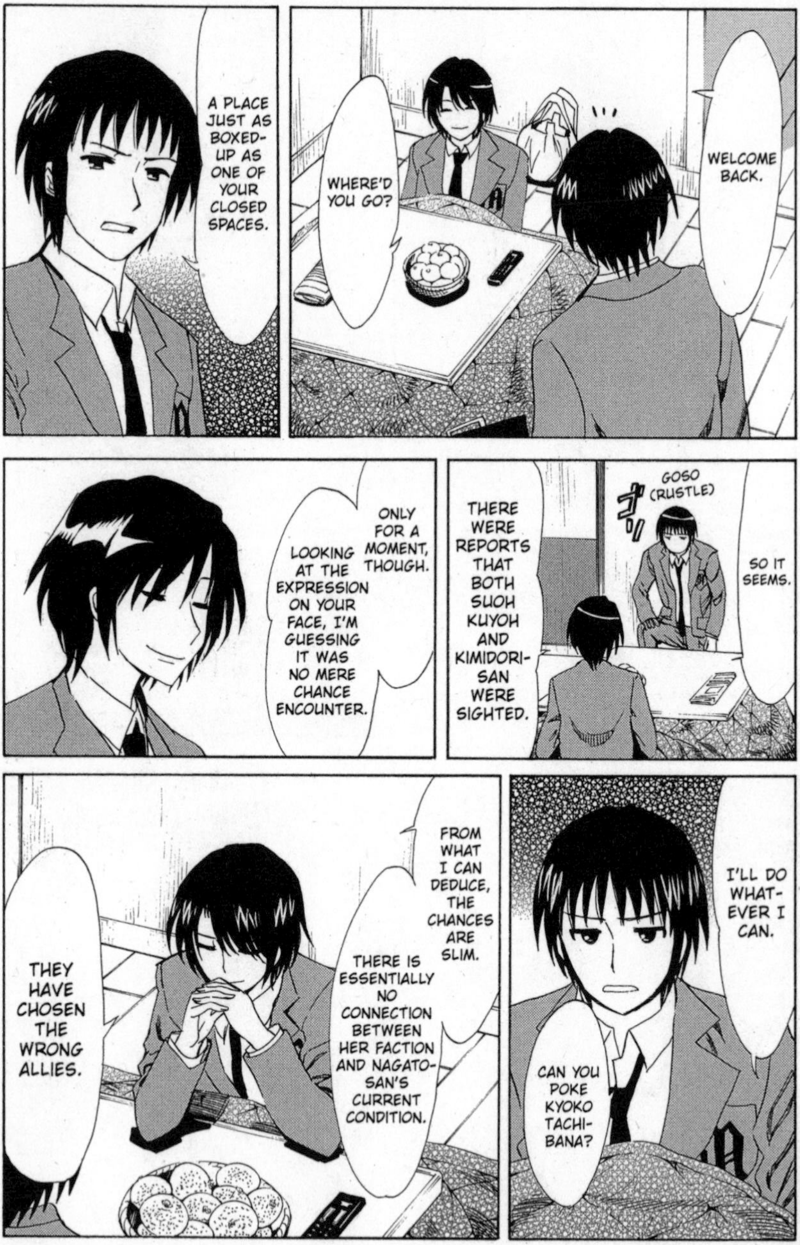
WELCOME BACK.
WHERE'D YOU GO?
A PLACE JUST AS BOXED-UP AS ONE OF YOUR CLOSED SPACES.
SO IT SEEMS.
GOSO (RUSTLE)
THERE WERE REPORTS THAT BOTH SUOH KUYOH AND KIMIDORI-SAN WERE SIGHTED.
ONLY FOR A MOMENT, THOUGH.
LOOKING AT THE EXPRESSION ON YOUR FACE, I'M GUESSING IT WAS NO MERE CHANCE ENCOUNTER.
I'LL DO WHATEVER I CAN.
CAN YOU POKE KYOKO TACHIBANA?
FROM WHAT I CAN DEDUCE, THE CHANCES ARE SLIM.
THERE IS ESSENTIALLY NO CONNECTION BETWEEN HER FACTION AND NAGATO-SAN'S CURRENT CONDITION.
THEY HAVE CHOSEN THE WRONG ALLIES.

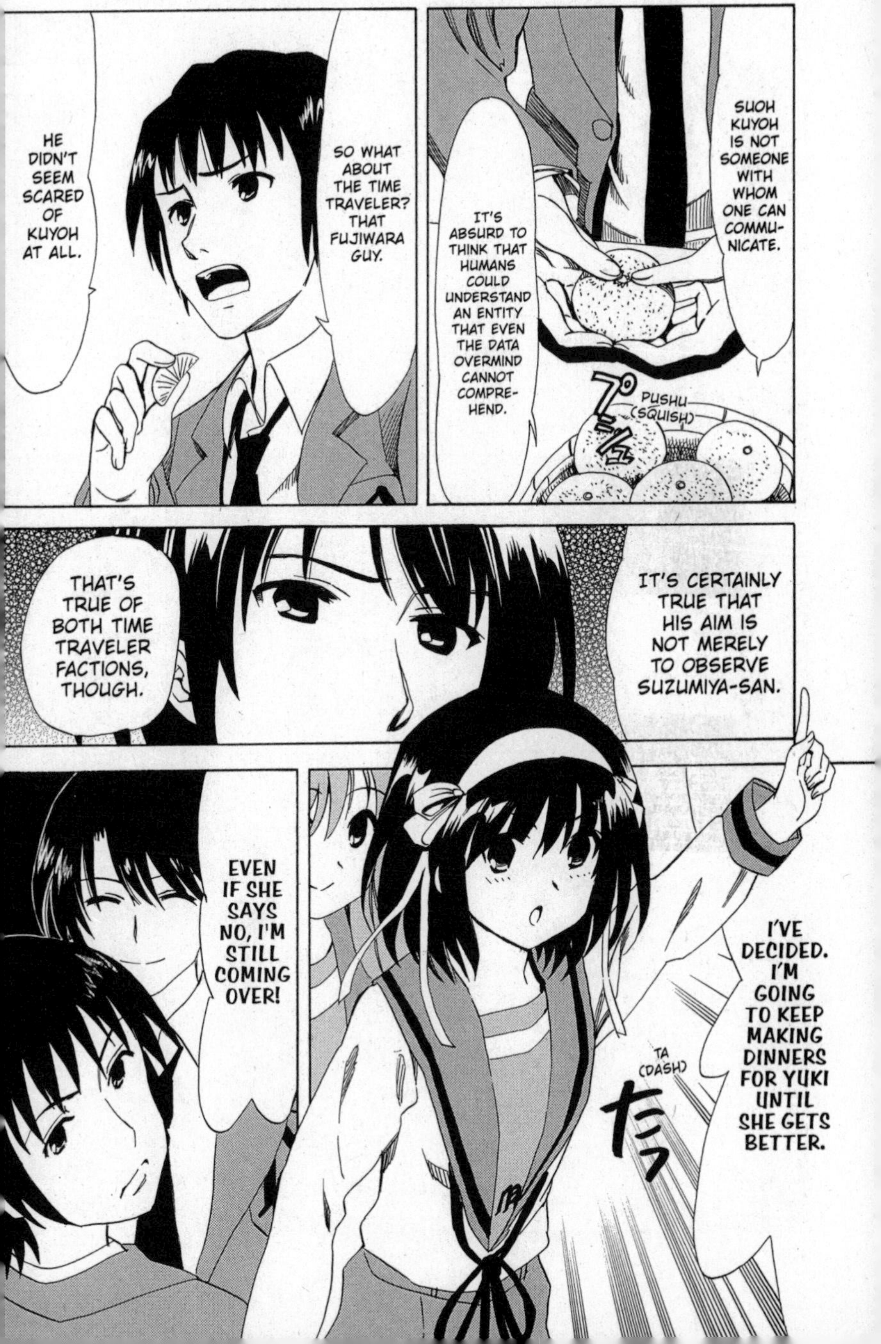
SUOH KUYOH IS NOT SOMEONE WITH WHOM ONE CAN COMMUNICATE.
IT'S ABSURD TO THINK THAT HUMANS COULD UNDERSTAND AN ENTITY THAT EVEN THE DATA OVERMIND CANNOT COMPREHEND.
PUSHU (SQUISH)
SO WHAT ABOUT THE TIME TRAVELER? THAT FUJIWARA GUY.
HE DIDN'T SEEM SCARED OF KUYOH AT ALL.
IT'S CERTAINLY TRUE THAT HIS AIM IS NOT MERELY TO OBSERVE SUZUMIYA-SAN.
THAT'S TRUE OF BOTH TIME TRAVELER FACTIONS, THOUGH.
I'VE DECIDED. I'M GOING TO KEEP MAKING DINNERS FOR YUKI UNTIL SHE GETS BETTER.
TA (DASH)
EVEN IF SHE SAYS NO, I'M STILL COMING OVER!

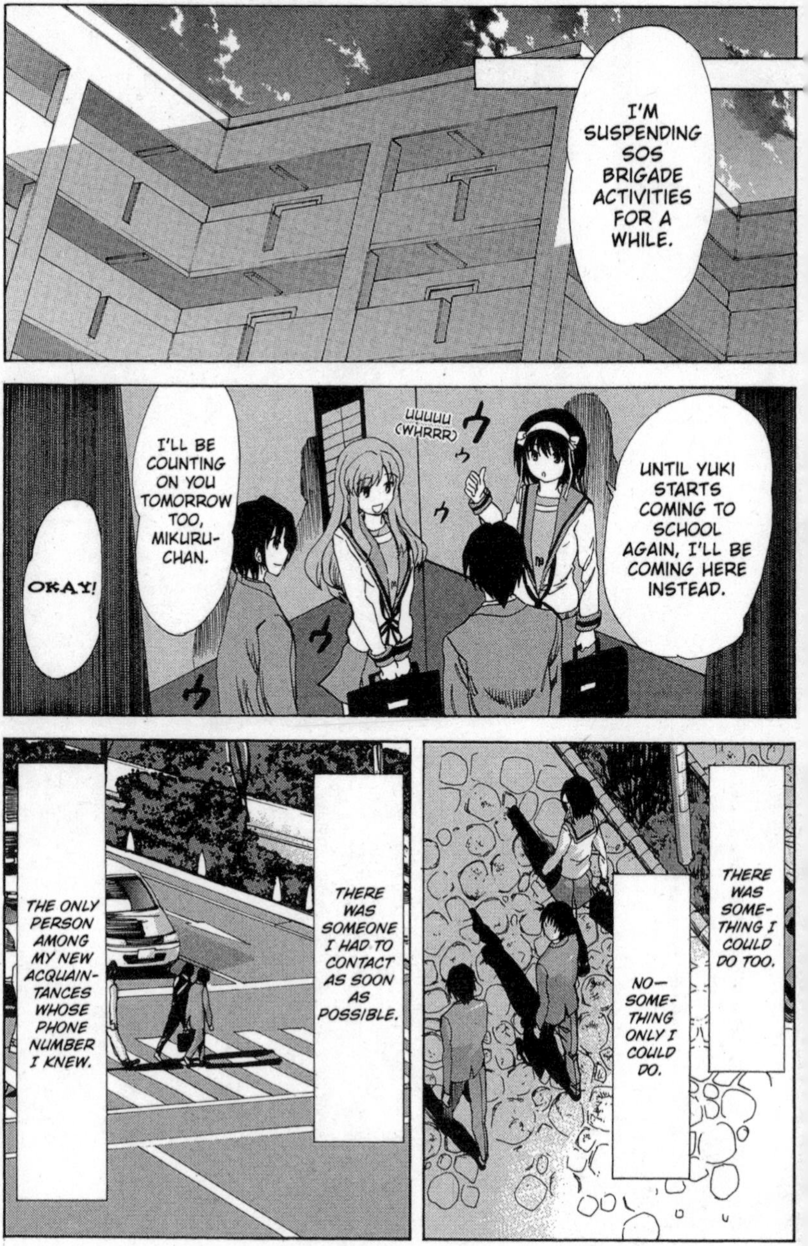
I'M SUSPENDING SOS BRIGADE ACTIVITIES FOR A WHILE.
UNTIL YUKI STARTS COMING TO SCHOOL AGAIN, I'LL BE COMING HERE INSTEAD.
UUUUUU (WHRRR)
I'LL BE COUNTING ON YOU TOMORROW TOO, MIKURU-CHAN.
OKAY!
THERE WAS SOME-THING I COULD DO TOO.
NO— SOME-THING ONLY I COULD DO.
THERE WAS SOMEONE I HAD TO CONTACT AS SOON AS POSSIBLE.
THE ONLY PERSON AMONG MY NEW ACQUAIN-TANCES WHOSE PHONE NUMBER I KNEW.

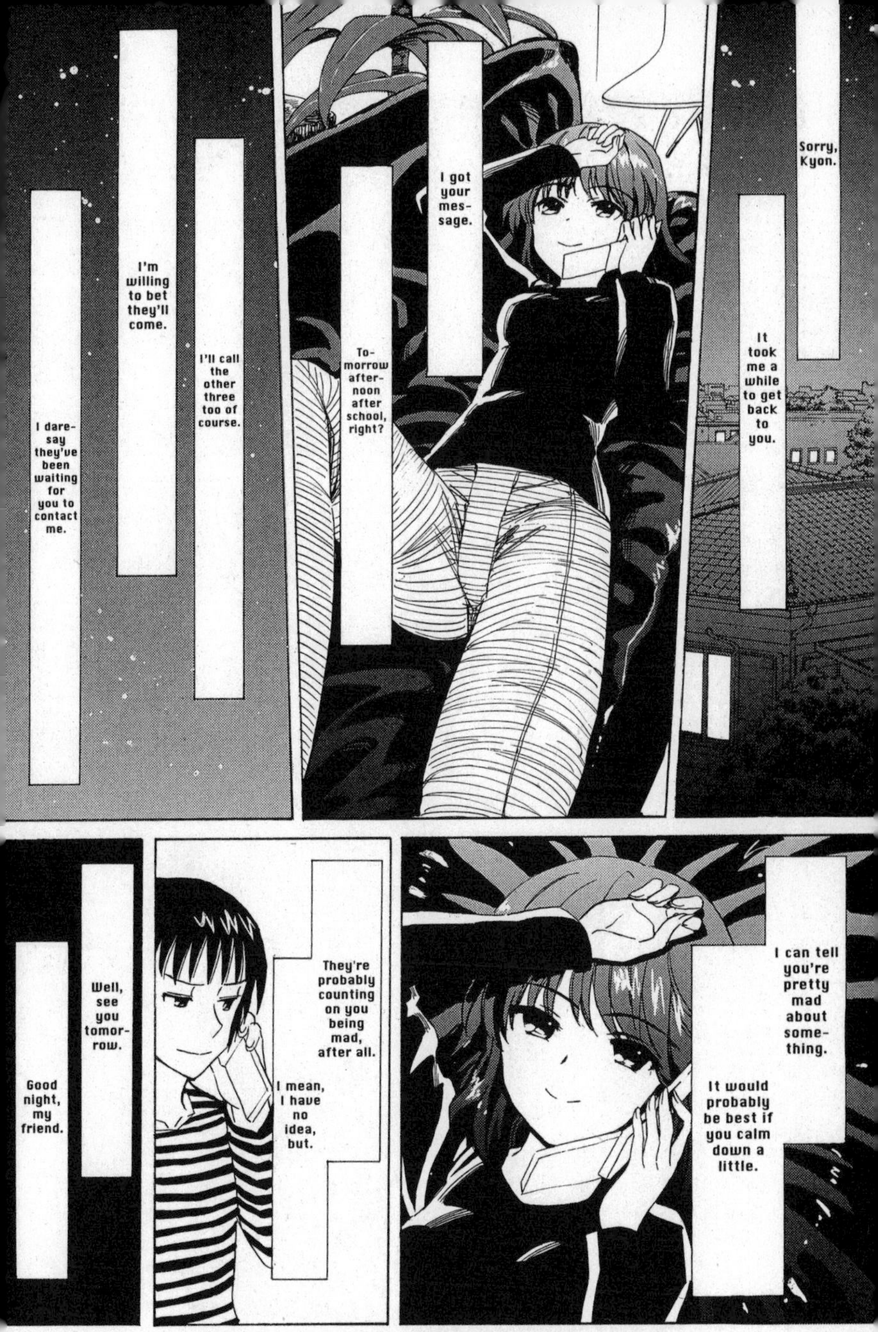
Sorry, Kyon.
It took me a while to get back to you.
I got your message.
Tomorrow afternoon after school, right?
I'll call the other three too of course.
I'm willing to bet they'll come.
I daresay they've been waiting for you to contact me.
I can tell you're pretty mad about something.
It would probably be best if you calm down a little.
They're probably counting on you being mad, after all.
I mean, I have no idea, but.
Well, see you tomorrow.
Good night, my friend.

α—8

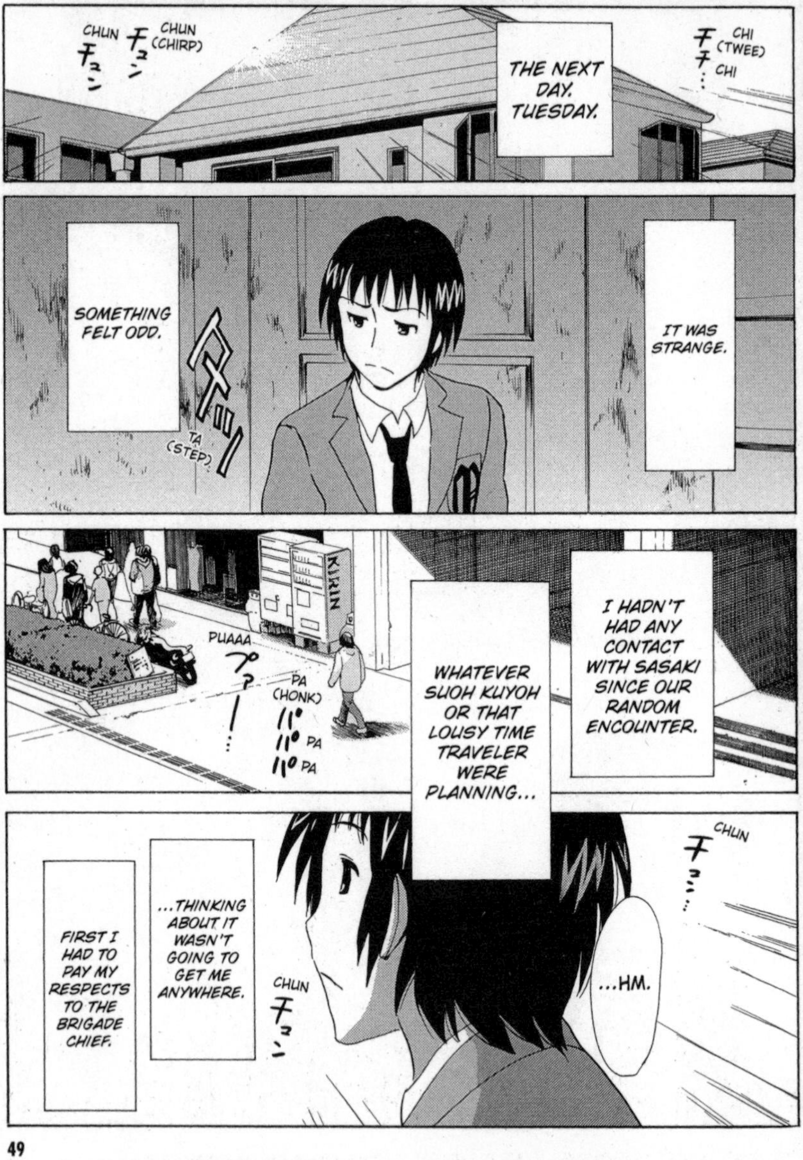
CHI (TWEE) CHI...
THE NEXT DAY. TUESDAY.
CHUN (CHIRP)
CHUN
IT WAS STRANGE.
TA (STEP)
SOMETHING FELT ODD.
I HADN'T HAD ANY CONTACT WITH SASAKI SINCE OUR RANDOM ENCOUNTER.
WHATEVER SUOH KUYOH OR THAT LOUSY TIME TRAVELER WERE PLANNING...
PA (HONK) PA PA
PUAAA
KIRIN
CHUN
...HM.
CHUN
...THINKING ABOUT IT WASN'T GOING TO GET ME ANYWHERE.
FIRST I HAD TO PAY MY RESPECTS TO THE BRIGADE CHIEF.

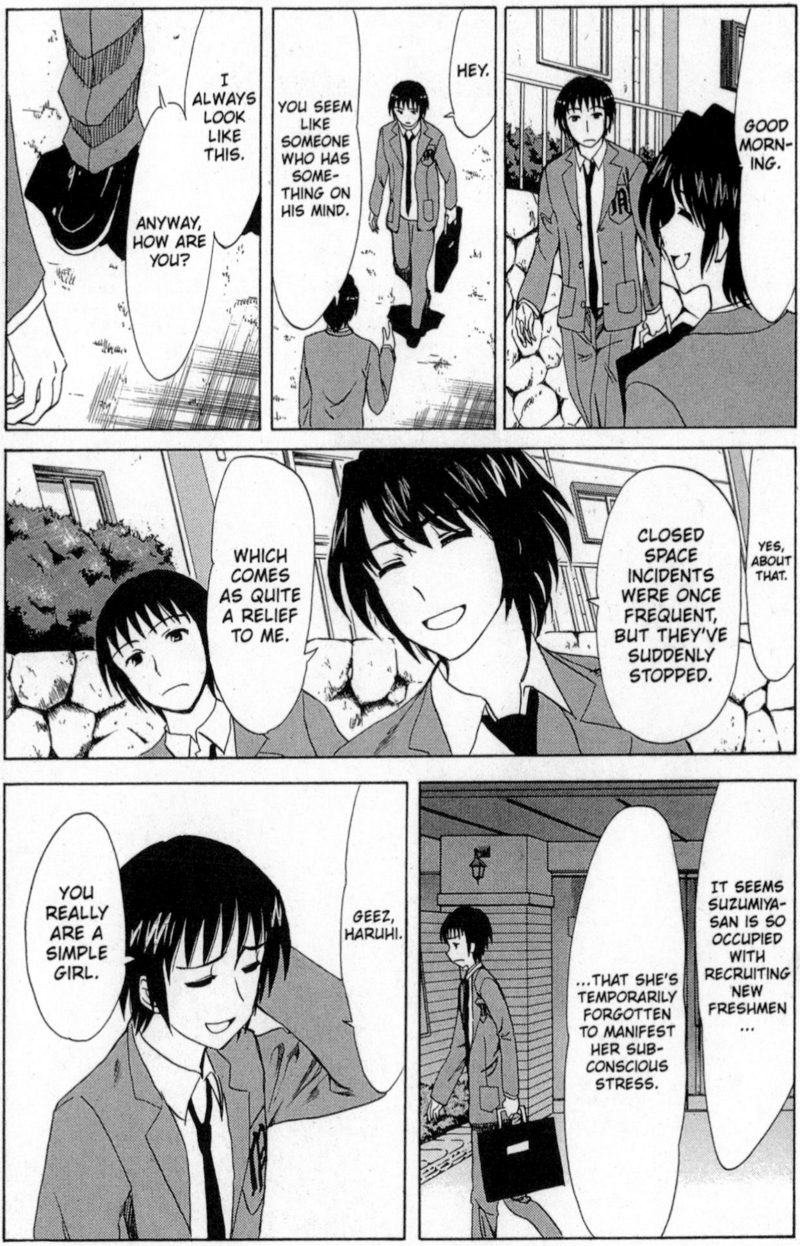
GOOD MORN-ING.
HEY.
YOU SEEM LIKE SOMEONE WHO HAS SOME-THING ON HIS MIND.
I ALWAYS LOOK LIKE THIS.
ANYWAY, HOW ARE YOU?
YES, ABOUT THAT.
CLOSED SPACE INCIDENTS WERE ONCE FREQUENT, BUT THEY'VE SUDDENLY STOPPED.
WHICH COMES AS QUITE A RELIEF TO ME.
IT SEEMS SUZUMIYA-SAN IS SO OCCUPIED WITH RECRUITING NEW FRESHMEN ...
...THAT SHE'S TEMPORARILY FORGOTTEN TO MANIFEST HER SUB-CONSCIOUS STRESS.
GEEZ, HARUHI.
YOU REALLY ARE A SIMPLE GIRL.

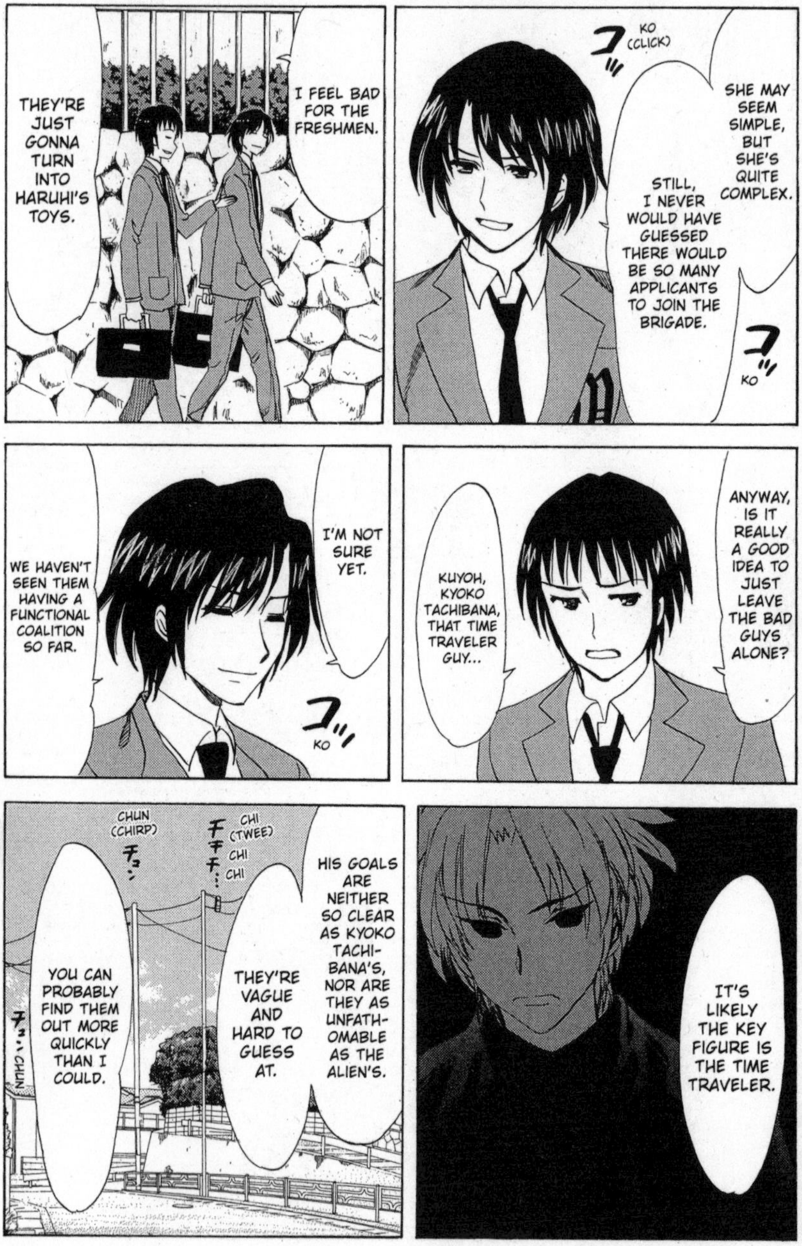
KO (CLICK)
SHE MAY SEEM SIMPLE, BUT SHE'S QUITE COMPLEX.
STILL, I NEVER WOULD HAVE GUESSED THERE WOULD BE SO MANY APPLICANTS TO JOIN THE BRIGADE.
KO
I FEEL BAD FOR THE FRESHMEN.
THEY'RE JUST GONNA TURN INTO HARUHI'S TOYS.
ANYWAY, IS IT REALLY A GOOD IDEA TO JUST LEAVE THE BAD GUYS ALONE?
KUYOH, KYOKO TACHIBANA, THAT TIME TRAVELER GUY...
I'M NOT SURE YET.
WE HAVEN'T SEEN THEM HAVING A FUNCTIONAL COALITION SO FAR.
KO
IT'S LIKELY THE KEY FIGURE IS THE TIME TRAVELER.
HIS GOALS ARE NEITHER SO CLEAR AS KYOKO TACHI-BANA'S, NOR ARE THEY AS UNFATH-OMABLE AS THE ALIEN'S.
CHI (TWEE) CHI CHI
CHUN (CHIRP)
THEY'RE VAGUE AND HARD TO GUESS AT.
YOU CAN PROBABLY FIND THEM OUT MORE QUICKLY THAN I COULD.
CHUN

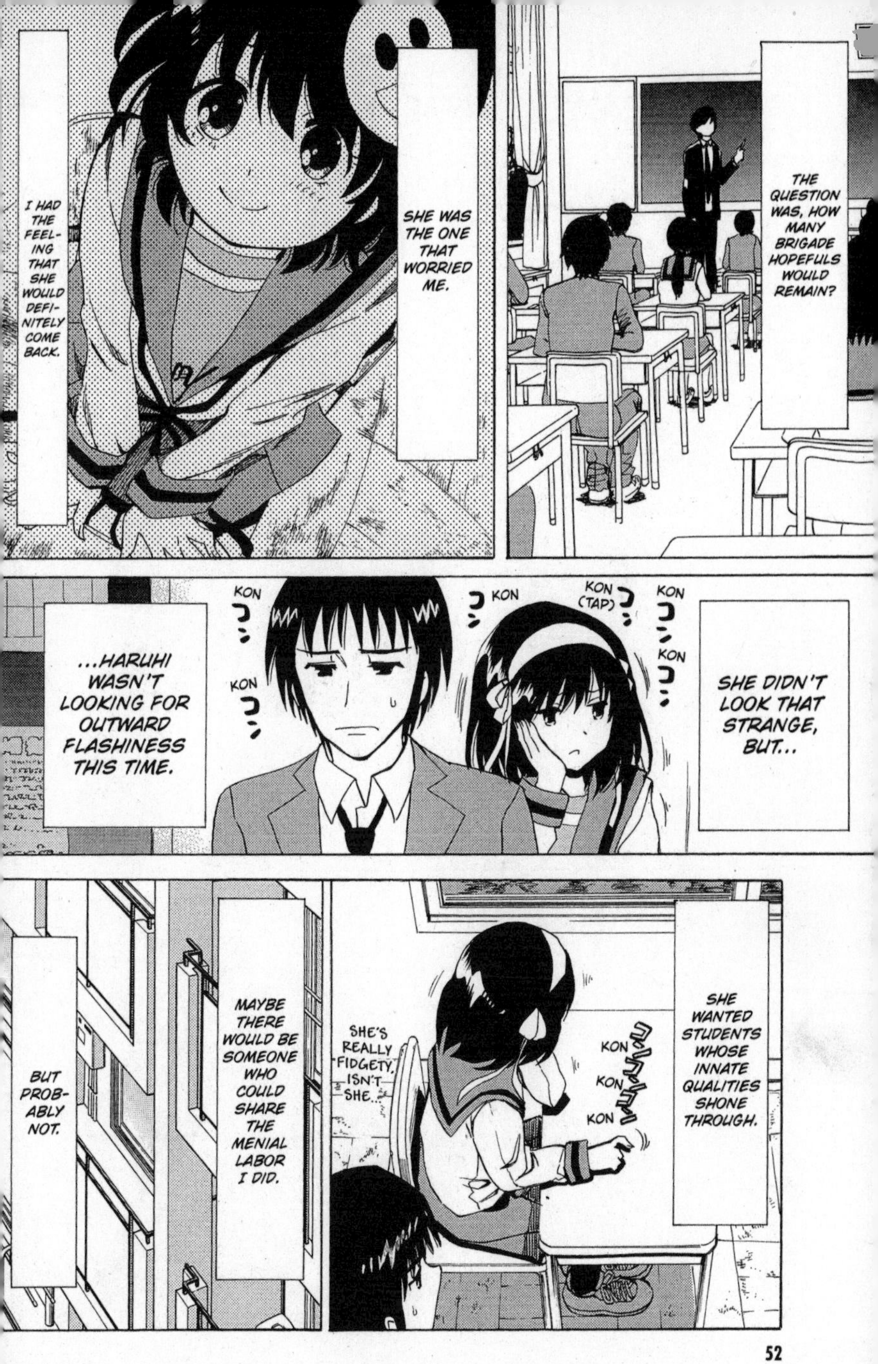
THE QUESTION WAS, HOW MANY BRIGADE HOPEFULS WOULD REMAIN?
SHE WAS THE ONE THAT WORRIED ME.
I HAD THE FEELING THAT SHE WOULD DEFINITELY COME BACK.
SHE DIDN'T LOOK THAT STRANGE, BUT...
KON
KON
KON (TAP)
KON
KON
KON
...HARUHI WASN'T LOOKING FOR OUTWARD FLASHINESS THIS TIME.
SHE WANTED STUDENTS WHOSE INNATE QUALITIES SHONE THROUGH.
KON
KON
KON
SHE'S REALLY FIDGETY, ISN'T SHE...
MAYBE THERE WOULD BE SOMEONE WHO COULD SHARE THE MENIAL LABOR I DID.
BUT PROBABLY NOT.

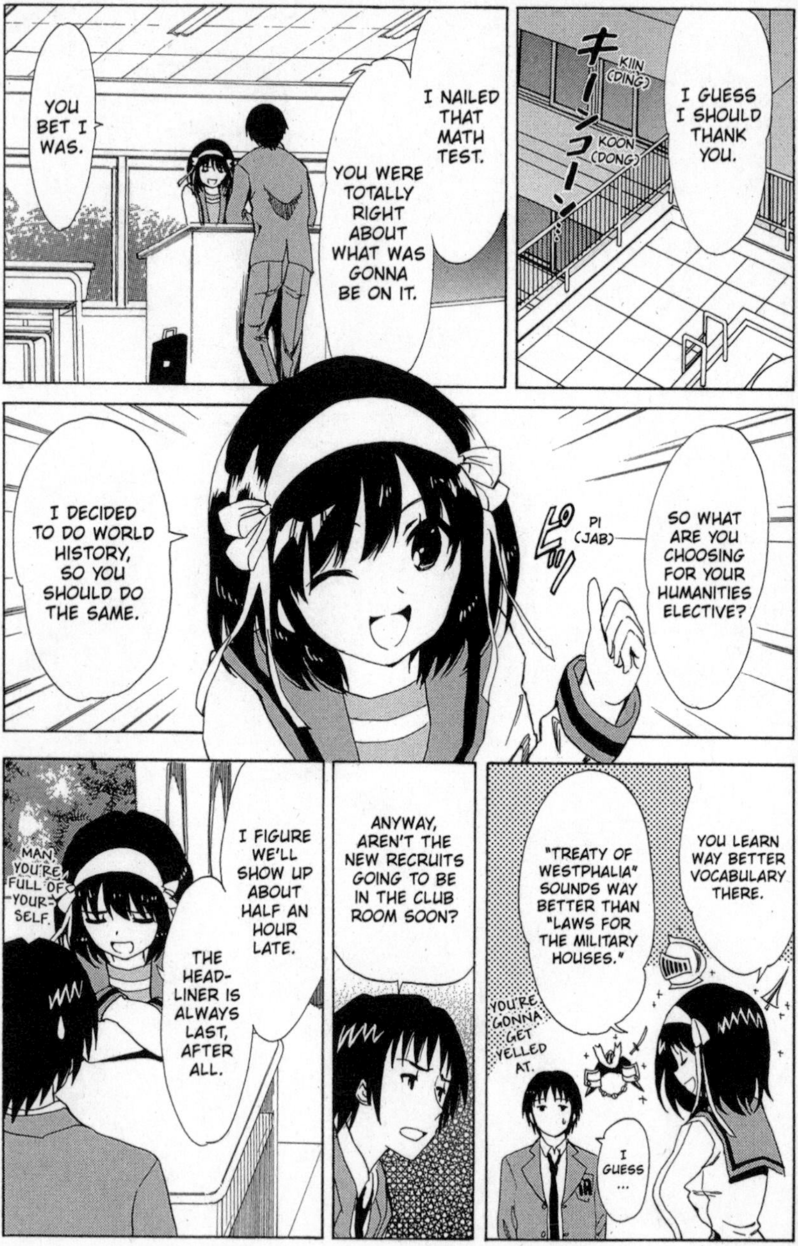
KIIN (DING)
KOON (DONG)
I GUESS I SHOULD THANK YOU.
I NAILED THAT MATH TEST.
YOU WERE TOTALLY RIGHT ABOUT WHAT WAS GONNA BE ON IT.
YOU BET I WAS.
PI (JAB)
SO WHAT ARE YOU CHOOSING FOR YOUR HUMANITIES ELECTIVE?
I DECIDED TO DO WORLD HISTORY, SO YOU SHOULD DO THE SAME.
YOU LEARN WAY BETTER VOCABULARY THERE.
"TREATY OF WESTPHALIA" SOUNDS WAY BETTER THAN "LAWS FOR THE MILITARY HOUSES."
YOU'RE GONNA GET YELLED AT.
I GUESS ...
ANYWAY, AREN'T THE NEW RECRUITS GOING TO BE IN THE CLUB ROOM SOON?
I FIGURE WE'LL SHOW UP ABOUT HALF AN HOUR LATE.
THE HEAD-LINER IS ALWAYS LAST, AFTER ALL.
MAN YOU'RE FULL OF YOUR-SELF.

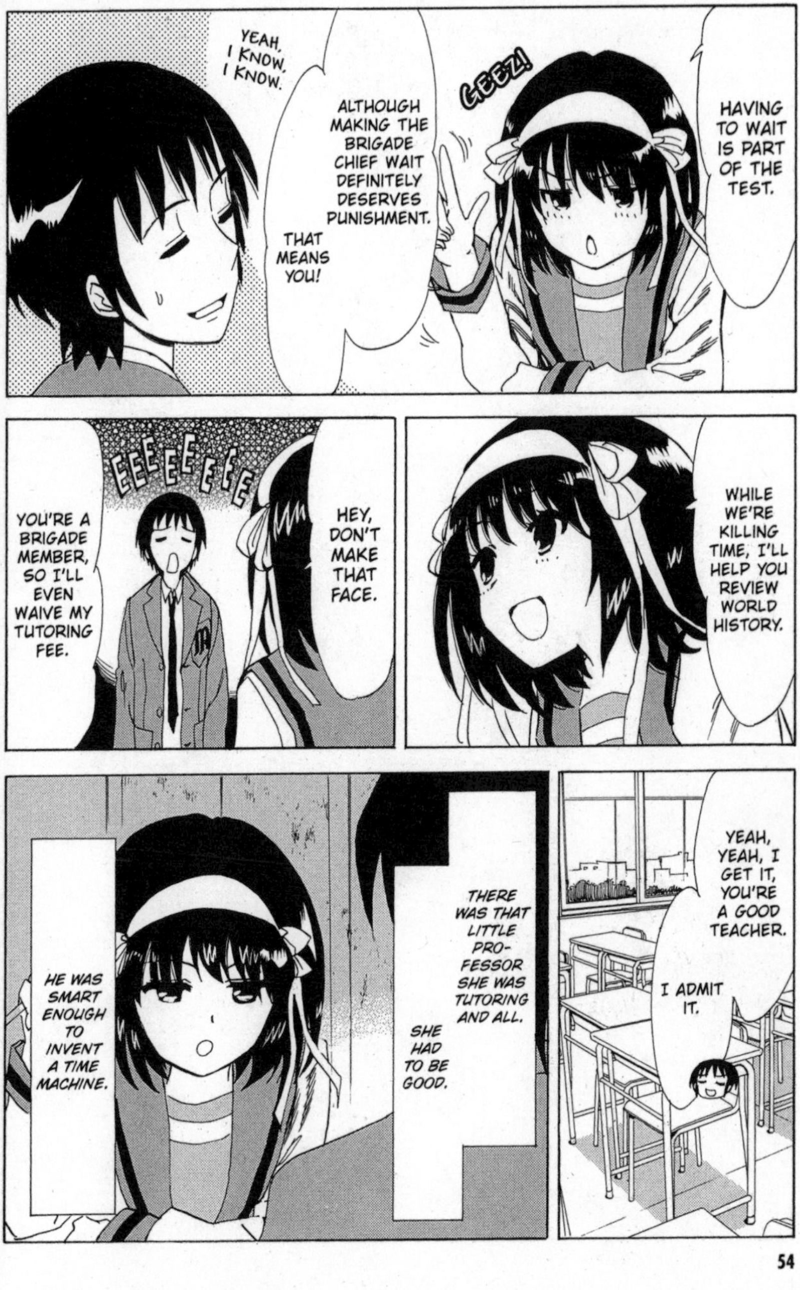
HAVING TO WAIT IS PART OF THE TEST.
GEEZ!
ALTHOUGH MAKING THE BRIGADE CHIEF WAIT DEFINITELY DESERVES PUNISHMENT.
THAT MEANS YOU!
YEAH, I KNOW, I KNOW.
WHILE WE'RE KILLING TIME, I'LL HELP YOU REVIEW WORLD HISTORY.
HEY, DON'T MAKE THAT FACE.
EEEEEEEE
YOU'RE A BRIGADE MEMBER, SO I'LL EVEN WAIVE MY TUTORING FEE.
YEAH, YEAH, I GET IT, YOU'RE A GOOD TEACHER.
I ADMIT IT.
THERE WAS THAT LITTLE PRO-FESSOR SHE WAS TUTORING AND ALL.
SHE HAD TO BE GOOD.
HE WAS SMART ENOUGH TO INVENT A TIME MACHINE.

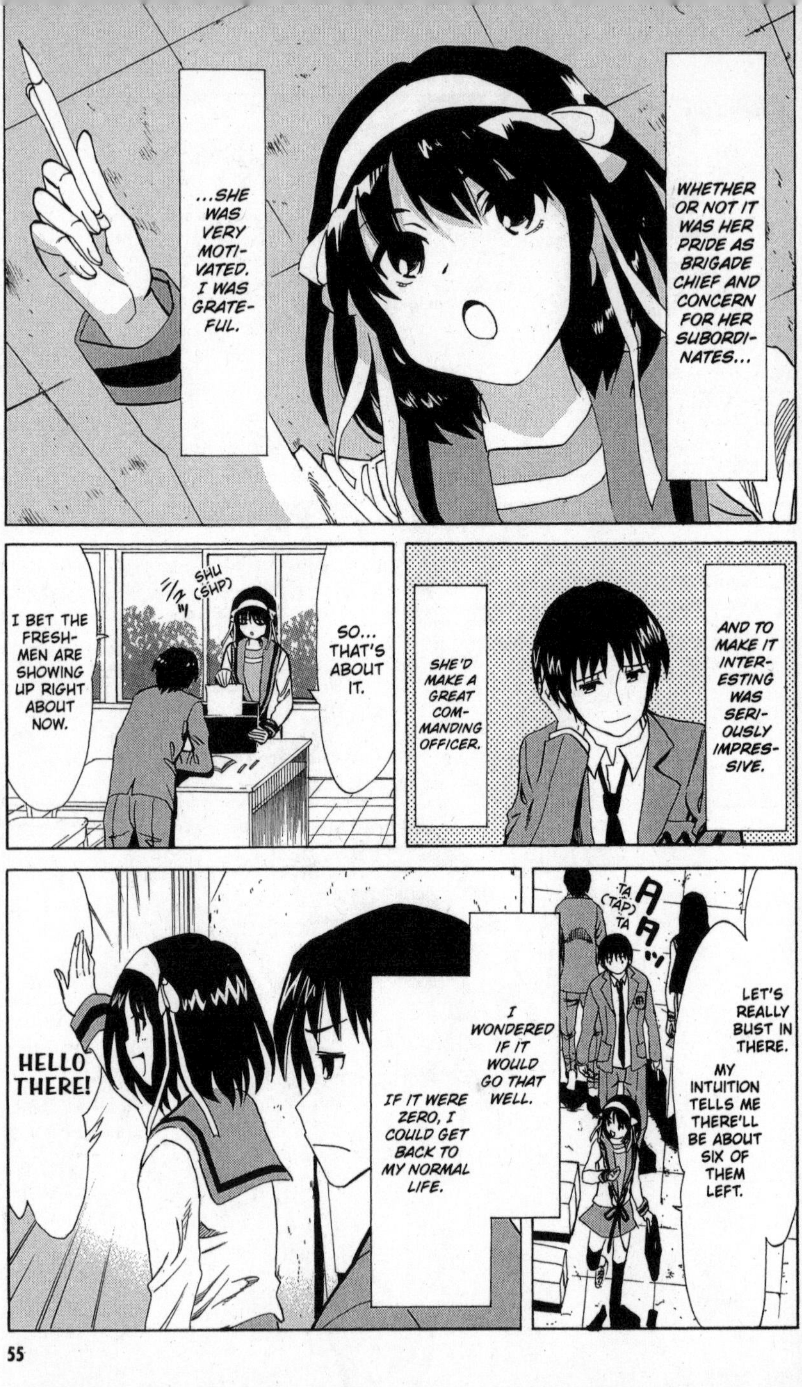
WHETHER OR NOT IT WAS HER PRIDE AS BRIGADE CHIEF AND CONCERN FOR HER SUBORDINATES...
...SHE WAS VERY MOTIVATED. I WAS GRATEFUL.
AND TO MAKE IT INTERESTING WAS SERIOUSLY IMPRESSIVE.
SHE'D MAKE A GREAT COMMANDING OFFICER.
SO... THAT'S ABOUT IT.
SHU (SHP)
I BET THE FRESHMEN ARE SHOWING UP RIGHT ABOUT NOW.
TA (TAP) TA
LET'S REALLY BUST IN THERE.
MY INTUITION TELLS ME THERE'LL BE ABOUT SIX OF THEM LEFT.
I WONDERED IF IT WOULD GO THAT WELL.
IF IT WERE ZERO, I COULD GET BACK TO MY NORMAL LIFE.
HELLO THERE!

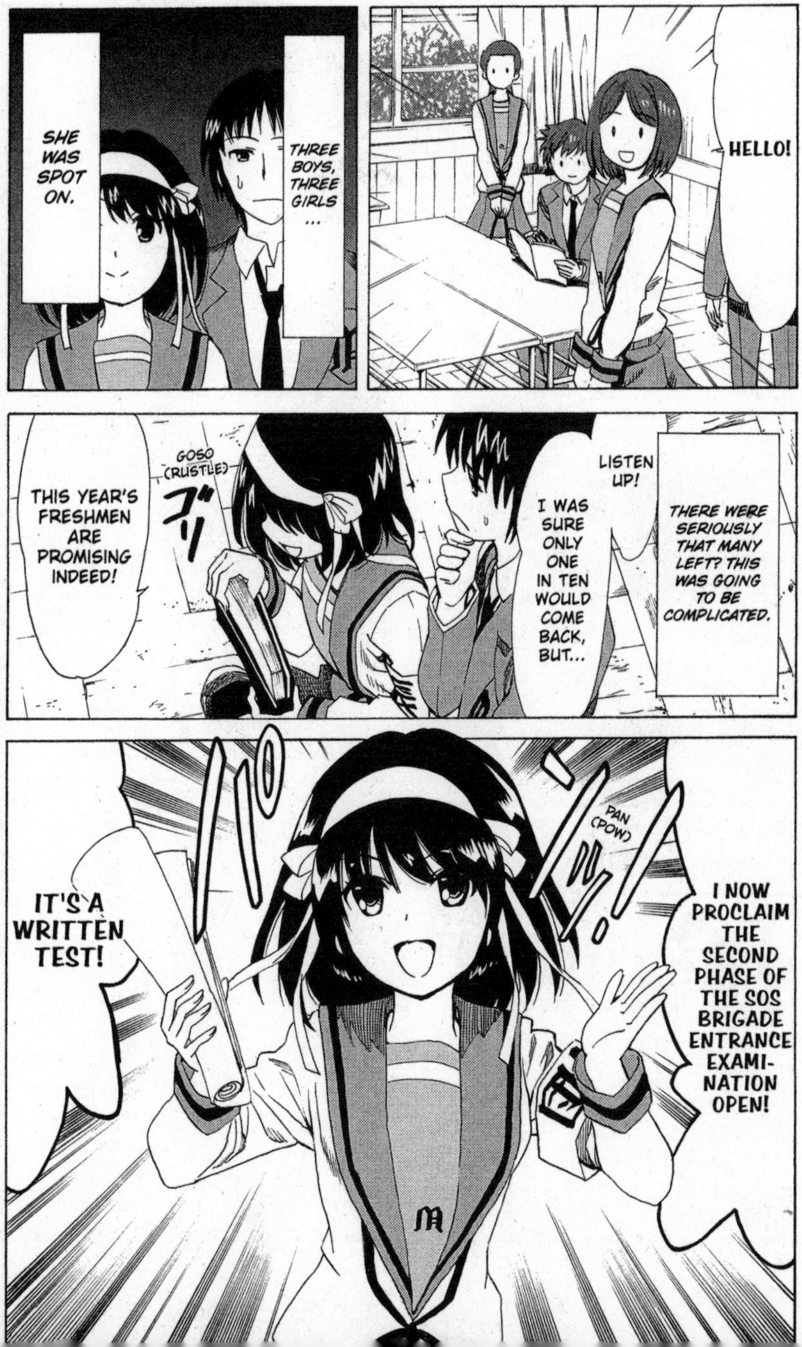
HELLO!
THREE BOYS, THREE GIRLS...
SHE WAS SPOT ON.
THERE WERE SERIOUSLY THAT MANY LEFT? THIS WAS GOING TO BE COMPLICATED.
LISTEN UP!
I WAS SURE ONLY ONE IN TEN WOULD COME BACK, BUT...
GOSO (RUSTLE)
THIS YEAR'S FRESHMEN ARE PROMISING INDEED!
I NOW PROCLAIM THE SECOND PHASE OF THE SOS BRIGADE ENTRANCE EXAMINATION OPEN!
PAN (POW)
IT'S A WRITTEN TEST!

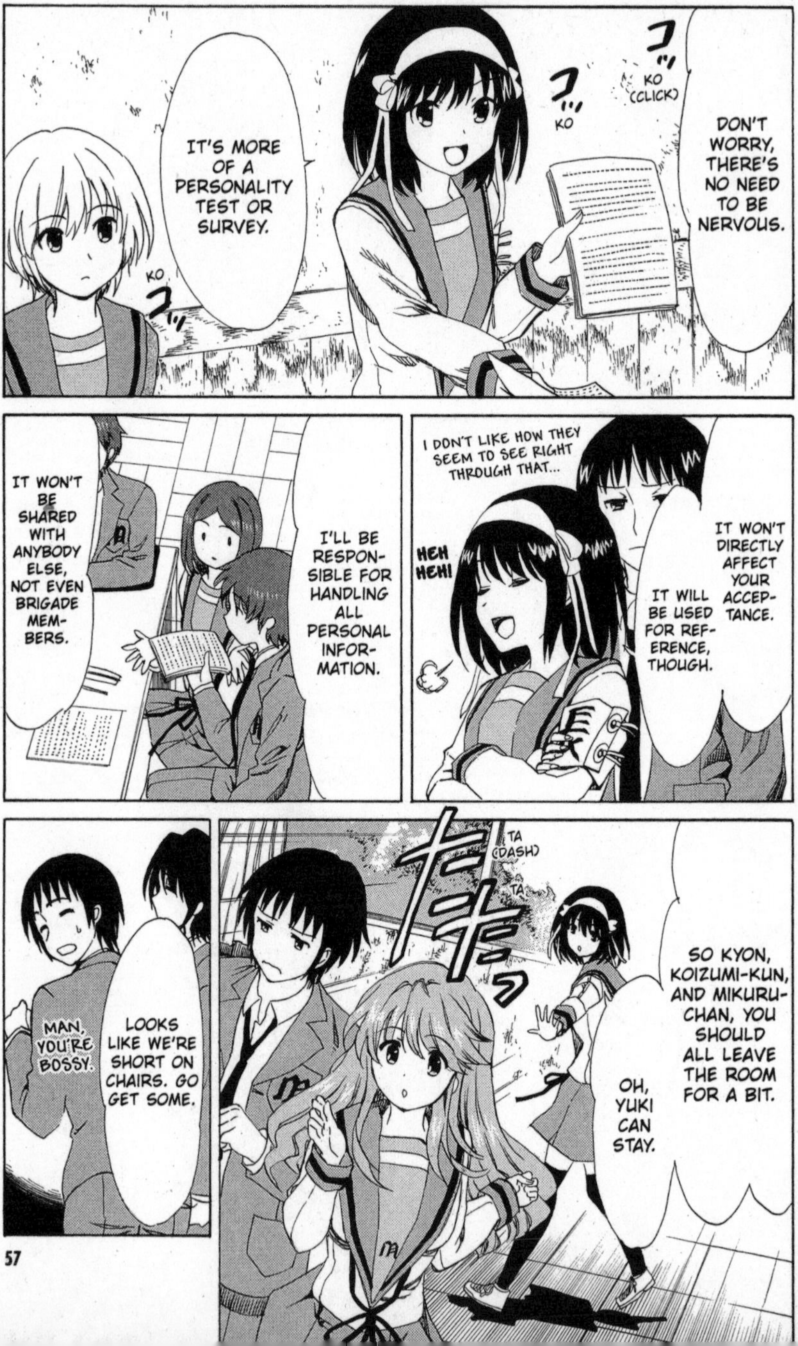
DON'T WORRY, THERE'S NO NEED TO BE NERVOUS.
KO (CLICK)
KO
IT'S MORE OF A PERSONALITY TEST OR SURVEY.
KO
IT WON'T DIRECTLY AFFECT YOUR ACCEPTANCE.
IT WILL BE USED FOR REFERENCE, THOUGH.
HEH HEH!
I DON'T LIKE HOW THEY SEEM TO SEE RIGHT THROUGH THAT...
I'LL BE RESPONSIBLE FOR HANDLING ALL PERSONAL INFORMATION.
IT WON'T BE SHARED WITH ANYBODY ELSE, NOT EVEN BRIGADE MEMBERS.
SO KYON, KOIZUMI-KUN, AND MIKURU-CHAN, YOU SHOULD ALL LEAVE THE ROOM FOR A BIT.
OH, YUKI CAN STAY.
TA (DASH)
TA
LOOKS LIKE WE'RE SHORT ON CHAIRS. GO GET SOME.
MAN, YOU'RE BOSSY.

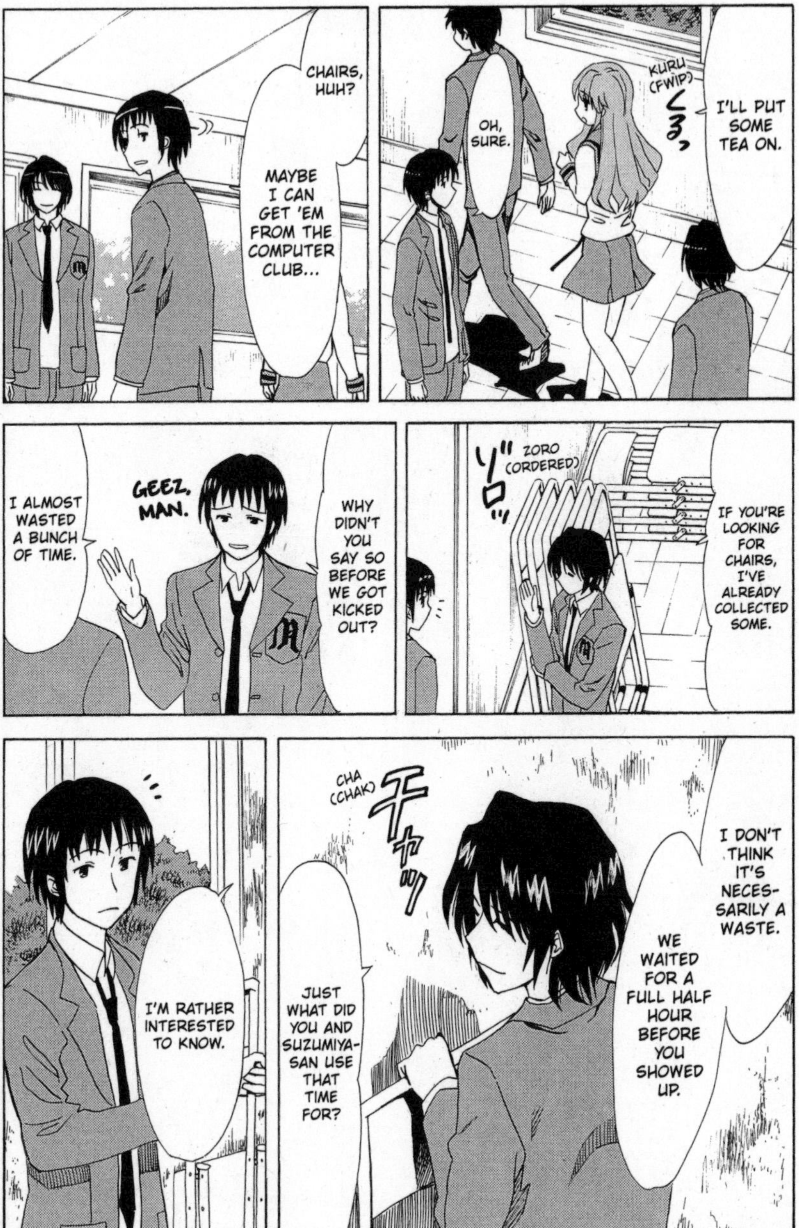
KURU (FWIP)
くるっ
I'LL PUT SOME TEA ON.
OH, SURE.
CHAIRS, HUH?
MAYBE I CAN GET 'EM FROM THE COMPUTER CLUB...
ゾロッ
ZORO (ORDERED)
IF YOU'RE LOOKING FOR CHAIRS, I'VE ALREADY COLLECTED SOME.
WHY DIDN'T YOU SAY SO BEFORE WE GOT KICKED OUT?
GEEZ, MAN.
I ALMOST WASTED A BUNCH OF TIME.
I DON'T THINK IT'S NECES-SARILY A WASTE.
WE WAITED FOR A FULL HALF HOUR BEFORE YOU SHOWED UP.
CHA (CHAK)
チャッ
JUST WHAT DID YOU AND SUZUMIYA-SAN USE THAT TIME FOR?
I'M RATHER INTERESTED TO KNOW.

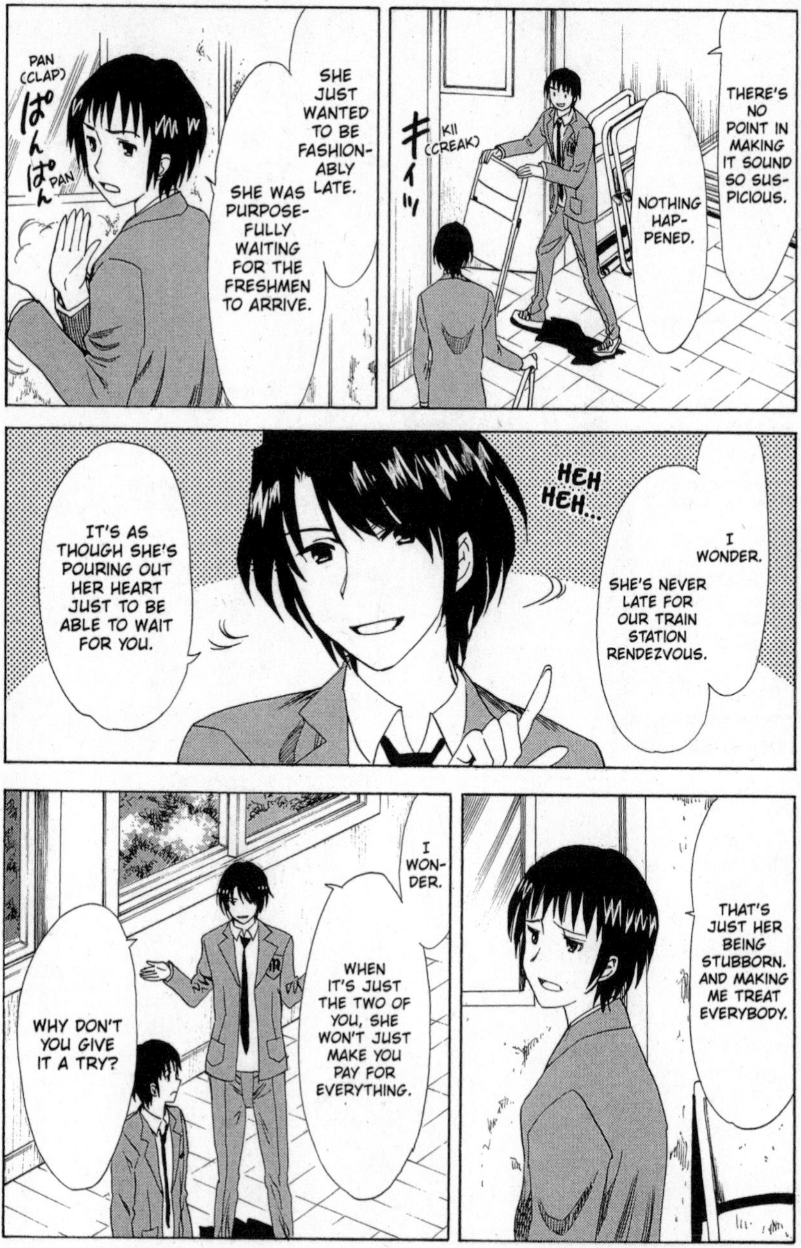
THERE'S NO POINT IN MAKING IT SOUND SO SUSPICIOUS.
NOTHING HAP-PENED.
キイッ
KII (CREAK)
SHE JUST WANTED TO BE FASHION-ABLY LATE.
SHE WAS PURPOSE-FULLY WAITING FOR THE FRESHMEN TO ARRIVE.
ぱんぱん
PAN (CLAP) PAN
I WONDER.
SHE'S NEVER LATE FOR OUR TRAIN STATION RENDEZVOUS.
HEH HEH...
IT'S AS THOUGH SHE'S POURING OUT HER HEART JUST TO BE ABLE TO WAIT FOR YOU.
THAT'S JUST HER BEING STUBBORN. AND MAKING ME TREAT EVERYBODY.
I WON-DER.
WHEN IT'S JUST THE TWO OF YOU, SHE WON'T JUST MAKE YOU PAY FOR EVERYTHING.
WHY DON'T YOU GIVE IT A TRY?

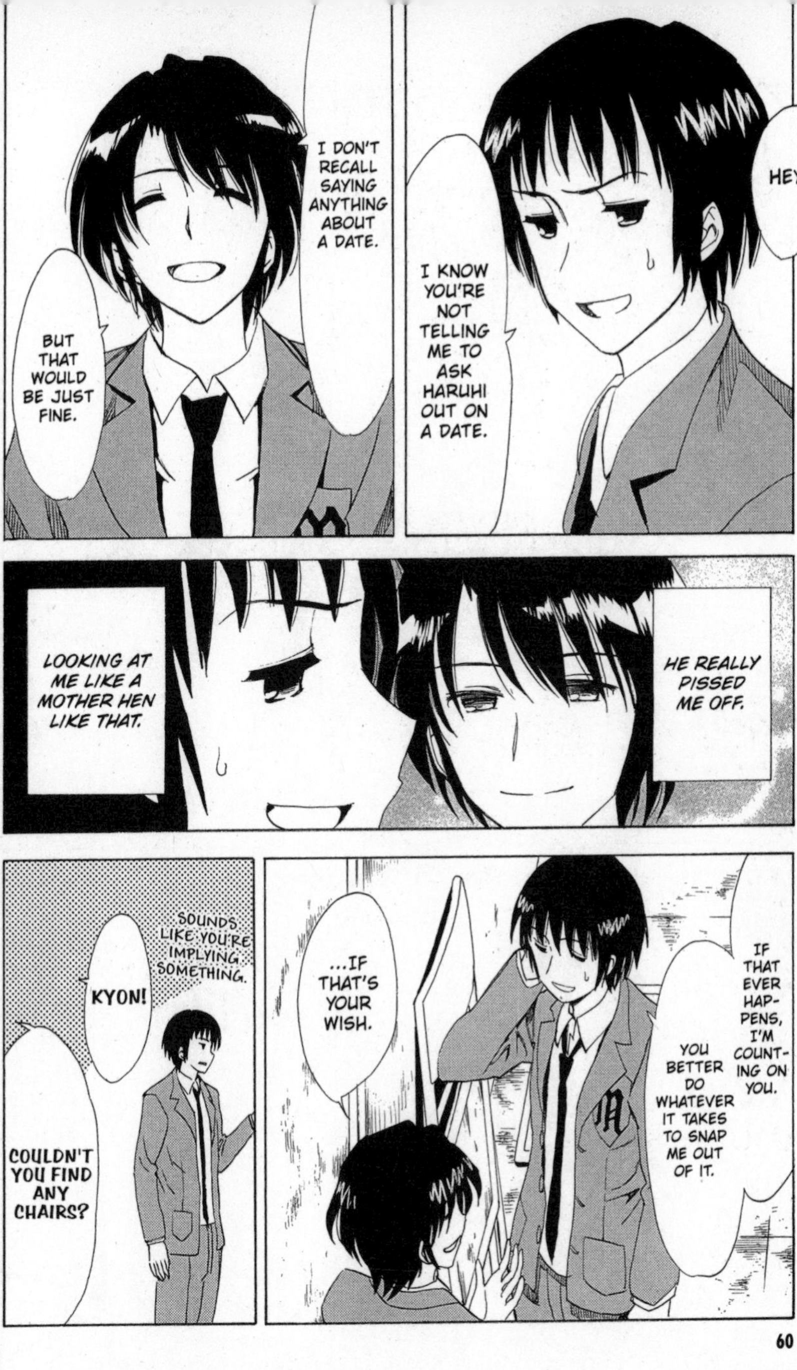
HEY.
I KNOW YOU'RE NOT TELLING ME TO ASK HARUHI OUT ON A DATE.
I DON'T RECALL SAYING ANYTHING ABOUT A DATE.
BUT THAT WOULD BE JUST FINE.
HE REALLY PISSED ME OFF.
LOOKING AT ME LIKE A MOTHER HEN LIKE THAT.
IF THAT EVER HAP-PENS, I'M COUNT-ING ON YOU.
YOU BETTER DO WHATEVER IT TAKES TO SNAP ME OUT OF IT.
...IF THAT'S YOUR WISH.
SOUNDS LIKE YOU'RE IMPLYING SOMETHING.
KYON!
COULDN'T YOU FIND ANY CHAIRS?

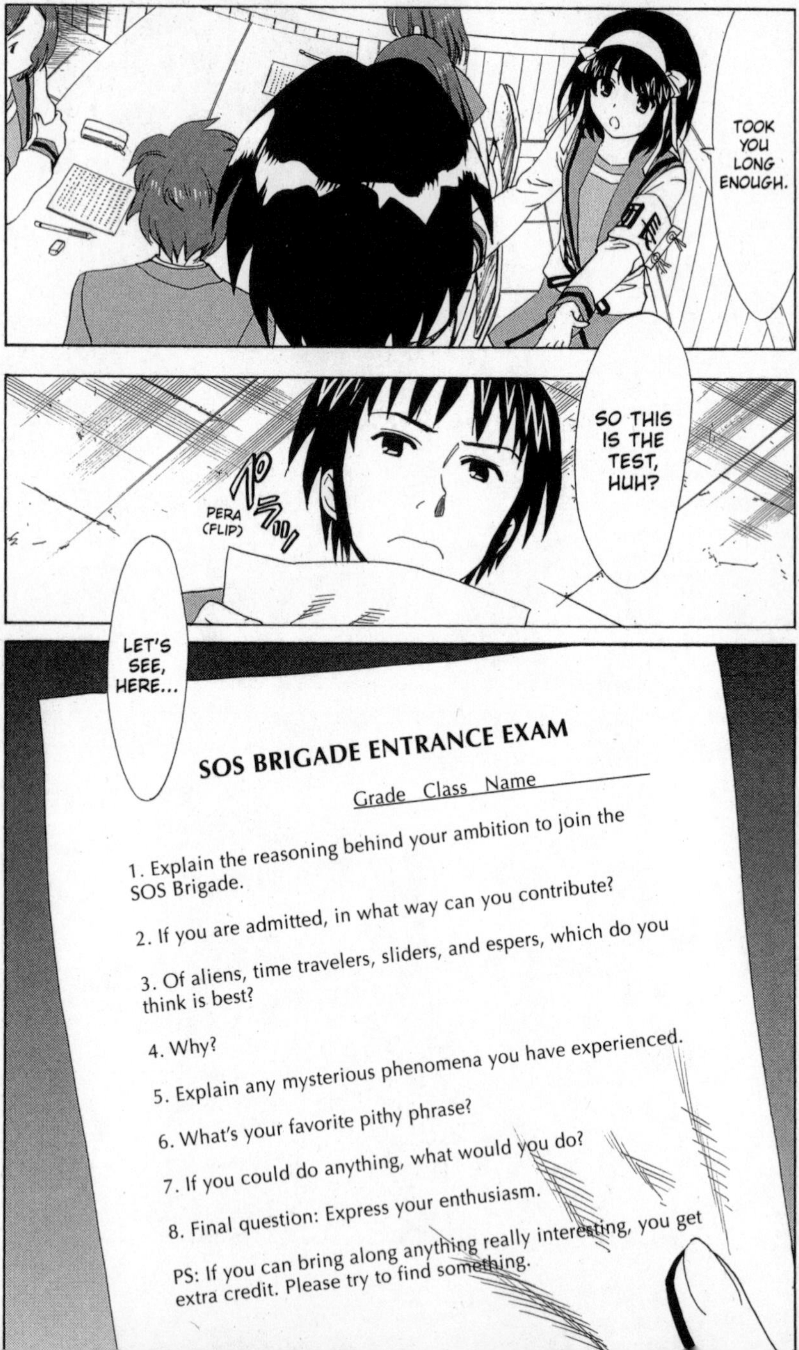
TOOK YOU LONG ENOUGH.
SO THIS IS THE TEST, HUH?
PERA (FLIP)
LET'S SEE, HERE...
SOS BRIGADE ENTRANCE EXAM
Grade Class Name
1. Explain the reasoning behind your ambition to join the SOS Brigade.
2. If you are admitted, in what way can you contribute?
3. Of aliens, time travelers, sliders, and espers, which do you think is best?
4. Why?
5. Explain any mysterious phenomena you have experienced.
6. What's your favorite pithy phrase?
7. If you could do anything, what would you do?
8. Final question: Express your enthusiasm.
PS: If you can bring along anything really interesting, you get extra credit. Please try to find something.

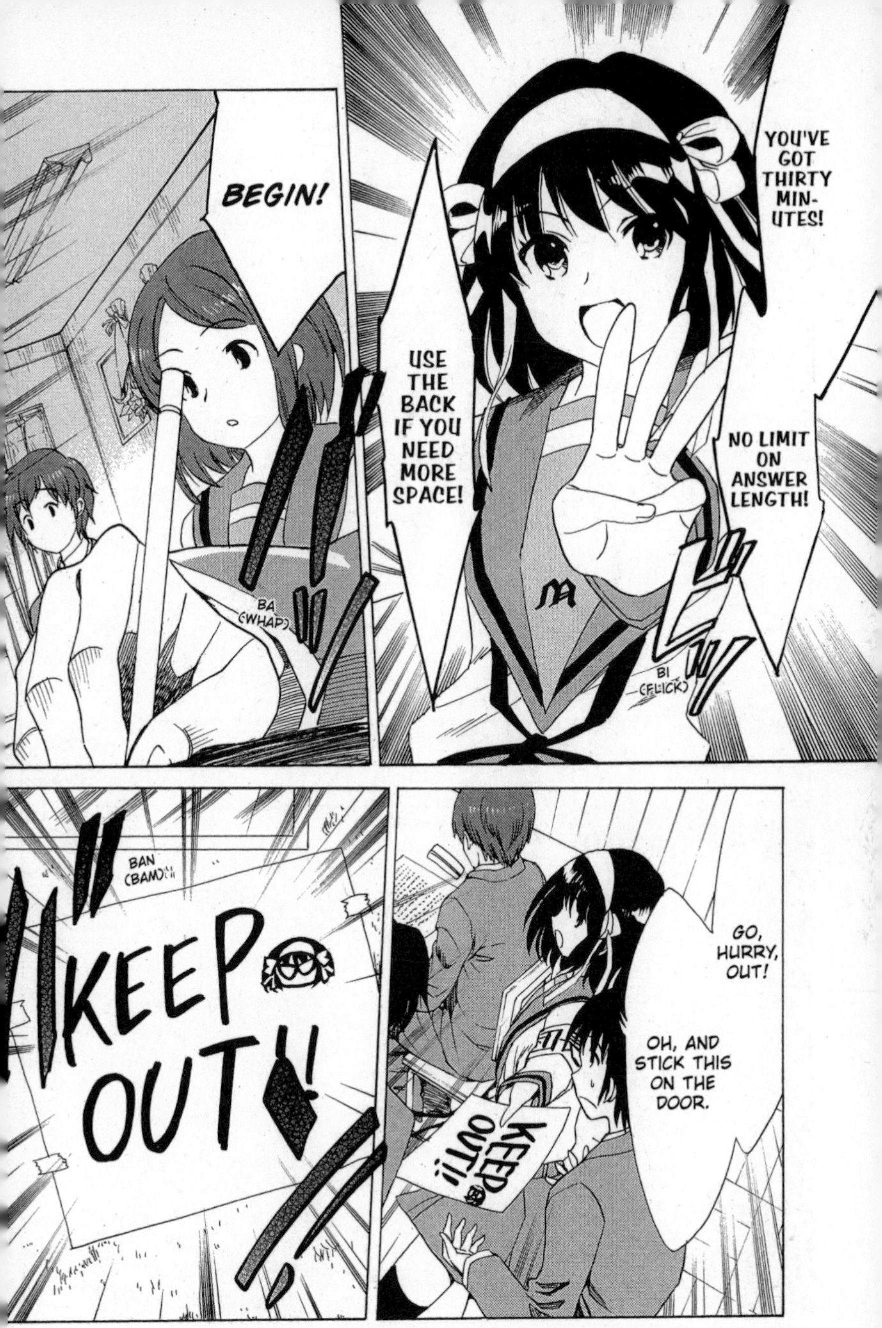
YOU'VE GOT THIRTY MIN-UTES!
NO LIMIT ON ANSWER LENGTH!
USE THE BACK IF YOU NEED MORE SPACE!
BI (FLICK)
BEGIN!
BA (WHAP)
GO, HURRY, OUT!
OH, AND STICK THIS ON THE DOOR.
KEEP OUT!!
BAN (BAM)
KEEP OUT!

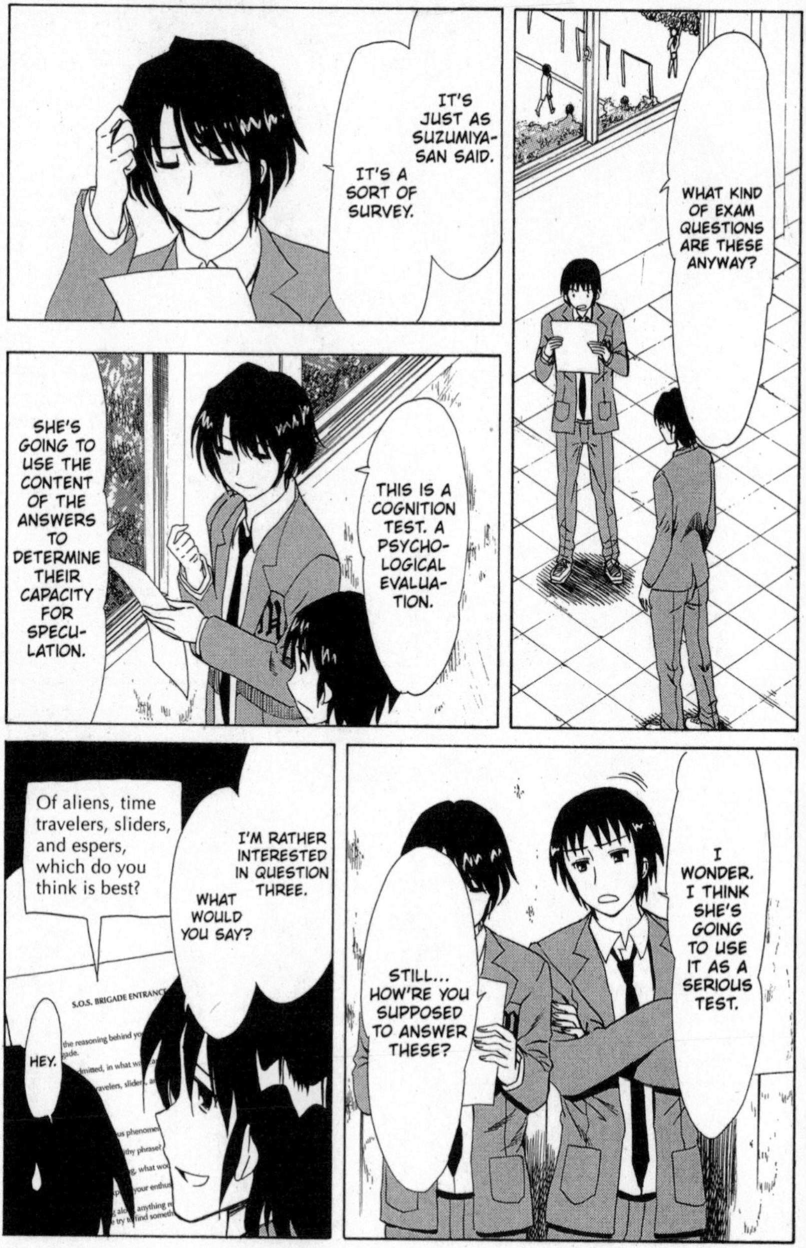
WHAT KIND OF EXAM QUESTIONS ARE THESE ANYWAY?
IT'S JUST AS SUZUMIYA-SAN SAID.
IT'S A SORT OF SURVEY.
THIS IS A COGNITION TEST. A PSYCHOLOGICAL EVALUATION.
SHE'S GOING TO USE THE CONTENT OF THE ANSWERS TO DETERMINE THEIR CAPACITY FOR SPECULATION.
I WONDER. I THINK SHE'S GOING TO USE IT AS A SERIOUS TEST.
STILL... HOW'RE YOU SUPPOSED TO ANSWER THESE?
I'M RATHER INTERESTED IN QUESTION THREE.
WHAT WOULD YOU SAY?
Of aliens, time travelers, sliders, and espers, which do you think is best?
HEY.

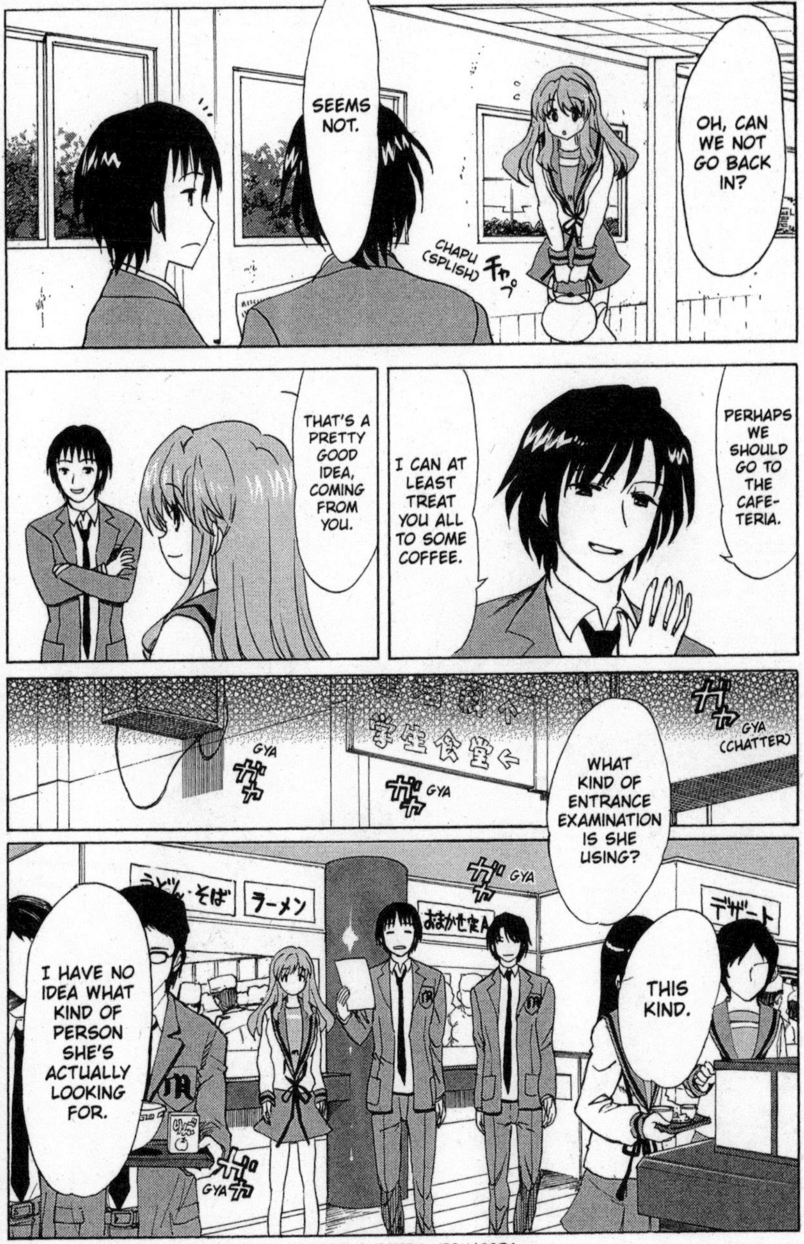
OH, CAN WE NOT GO BACK IN?
CHAPU (SPLISH)
SEEMS NOT.
PERHAPS WE SHOULD GO TO THE CAFETERIA.
I CAN AT LEAST TREAT YOU ALL TO SOME COFFEE.
THAT'S A PRETTY GOOD IDEA, COMING FROM YOU.
GYA (CHATTER)
WHAT KIND OF ENTRANCE EXAMINATION IS SHE USING?
GYA
GYA
GYA
THIS KIND.
I HAVE NO IDEA WHAT KIND OF PERSON SHE'S ACTUALLY LOOKING FOR.
GYA

SIGNS: STUDENT CAFETERIA, DESSERT, SET MEAL A, RAMEN, UDON/SOBA

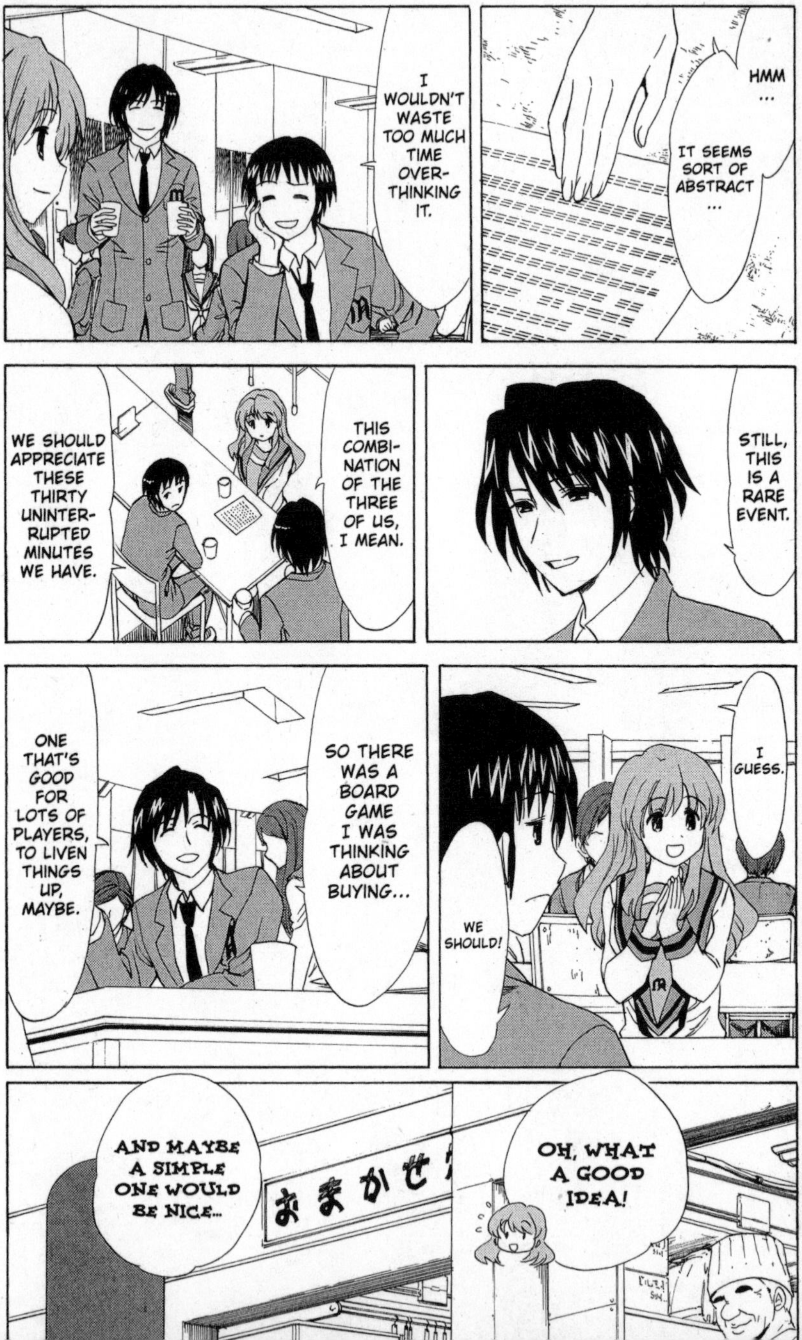
HMM ...
IT SEEMS SORT OF ABSTRACT ...
I WOULDN'T WASTE TOO MUCH TIME OVER-THINKING IT.
STILL, THIS IS A RARE EVENT.
THIS COMBINATION OF THE THREE OF US, I MEAN.
WE SHOULD APPRECIATE THESE THIRTY UNINTERRUPTED MINUTES WE HAVE.
I GUESS.
WE SHOULD!
SO THERE WAS A BOARD GAME I WAS THINKING ABOUT BUYING...
ONE THAT'S GOOD FOR LOTS OF PLAYERS, TO LIVEN THINGS UP, MAYBE.
OH, WHAT A GOOD IDEA!
AND MAYBE A SIMPLE ONE WOULD BE NICE...
おまかせ

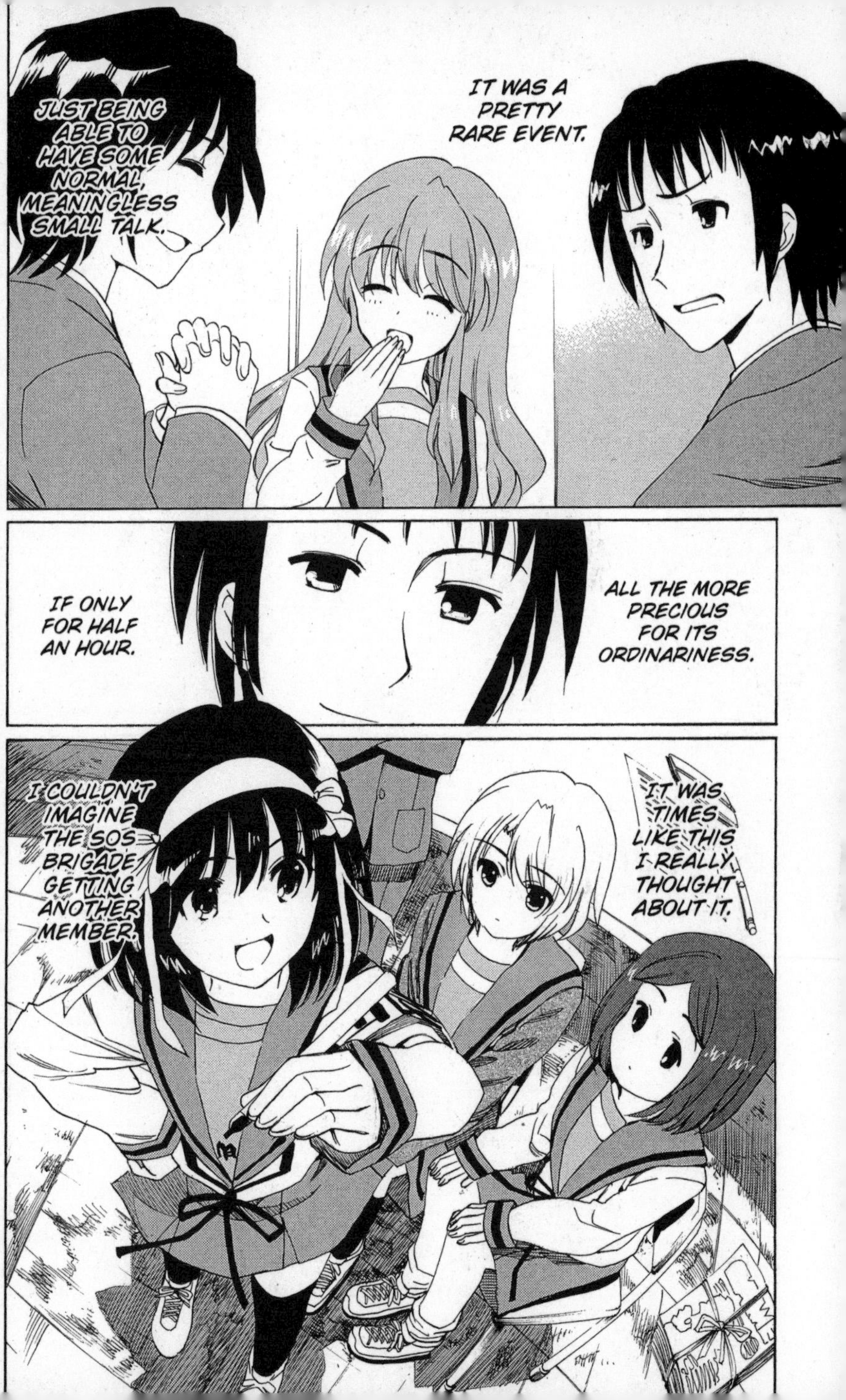
IT WAS A PRETTY RARE EVENT.
JUST BEING ABLE TO HAVE SOME NORMAL, MEANINGLESS SMALL TALK.
ALL THE MORE PRECIOUS FOR ITS ORDINARINESS.
IF ONLY FOR HALF AN HOUR.
IT WAS TIMES LIKE THIS I REALLY THOUGHT ABOUT IT.
I COULDN'T IMAGINE THE SOS BRIGADE GETTING ANOTHER MEMBER.

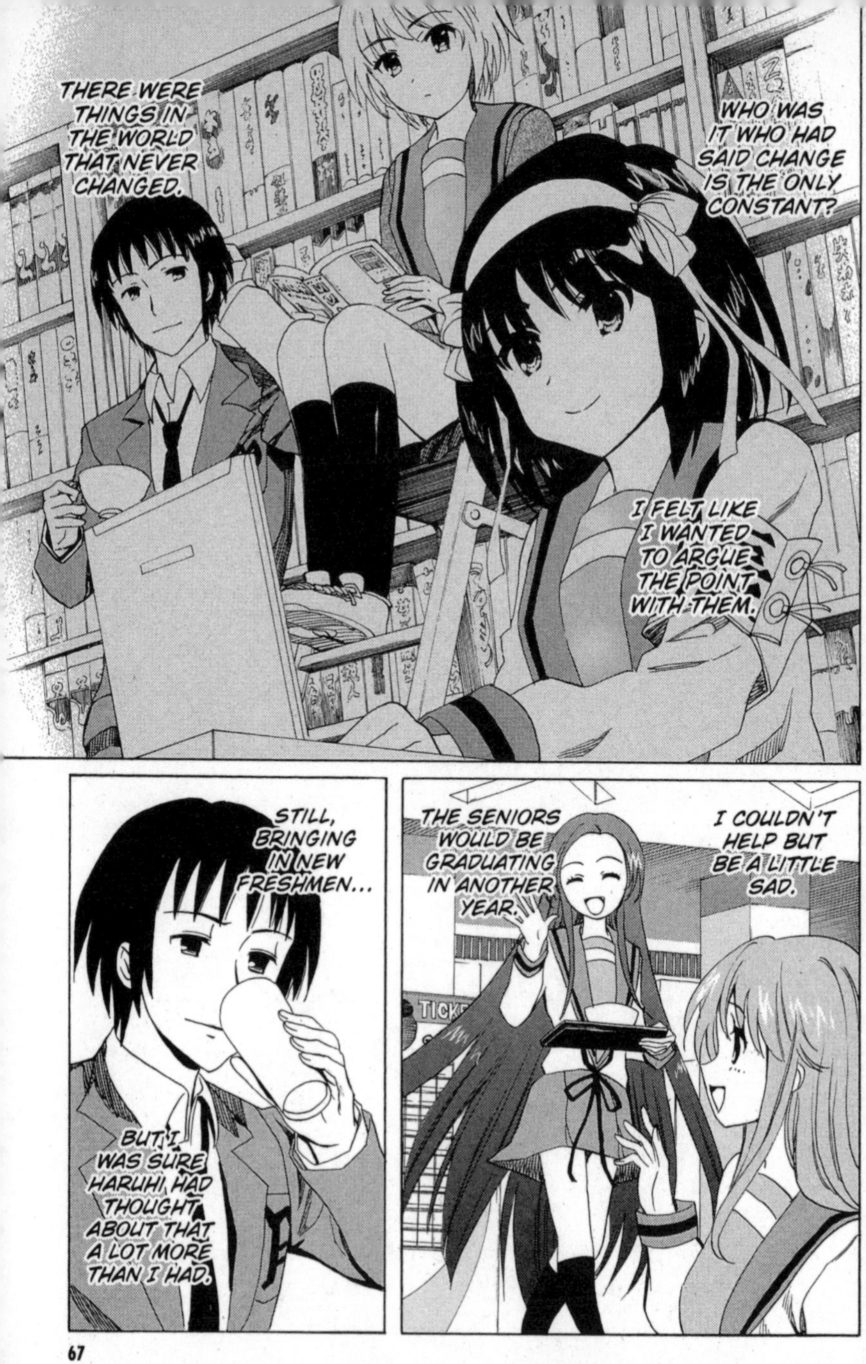
WHO WAS IT WHO HAD SAID CHANGE IS THE ONLY CONSTANT?
THERE WERE THINGS IN THE WORLD THAT NEVER CHANGED.
I FELT LIKE I WANTED TO ARGUE THE POINT WITH THEM.
THE SENIORS WOULD BE GRADUATING IN ANOTHER YEAR.
I COULDN'T HELP BUT BE A LITTLE SAD.
STILL, BRINGING IN NEW FRESHMEN...
BUT I WAS SURE HARUHI HAD THOUGHT ABOUT THAT A LOT MORE THAN I HAD.

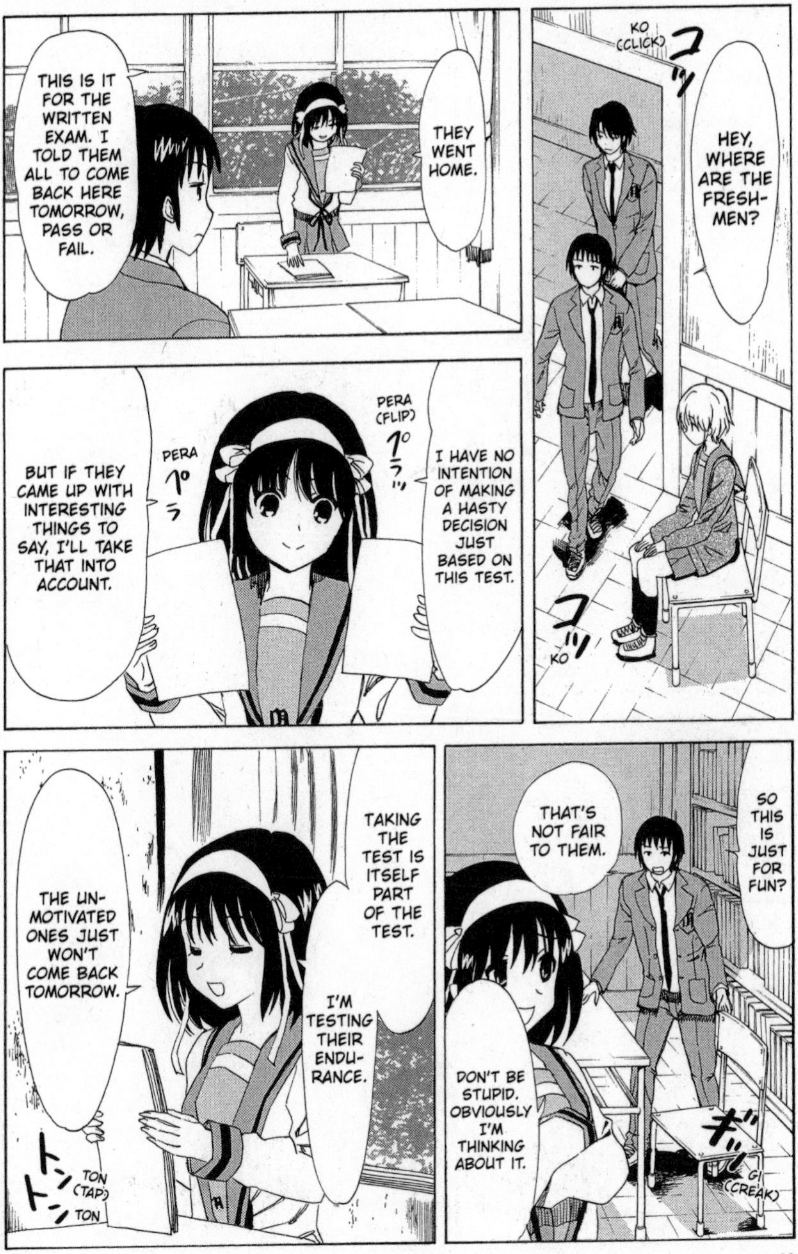
KO (CLICK)
HEY, WHERE ARE THE FRESH-MEN?
KO
THEY WENT HOME.
THIS IS IT FOR THE WRITTEN EXAM. I TOLD THEM ALL TO COME BACK HERE TOMORROW, PASS OR FAIL.
PERA (FLIP)
I HAVE NO INTENTION OF MAKING A HASTY DECISION JUST BASED ON THIS TEST.
PERA
BUT IF THEY CAME UP WITH INTERESTING THINGS TO SAY, I'LL TAKE THAT INTO ACCOUNT.
SO THIS IS JUST FOR FUN?
THAT'S NOT FAIR TO THEM.
DON'T BE STUPID. OBVIOUSLY I'M THINKING ABOUT IT.
GI (CREAK)
TAKING THE TEST IS ITSELF PART OF THE TEST.
I'M TESTING THEIR ENDU-RANCE.
THE UN-MOTIVATED ONES JUST WON'T COME BACK TOMORROW.
TON (TAP)
TON

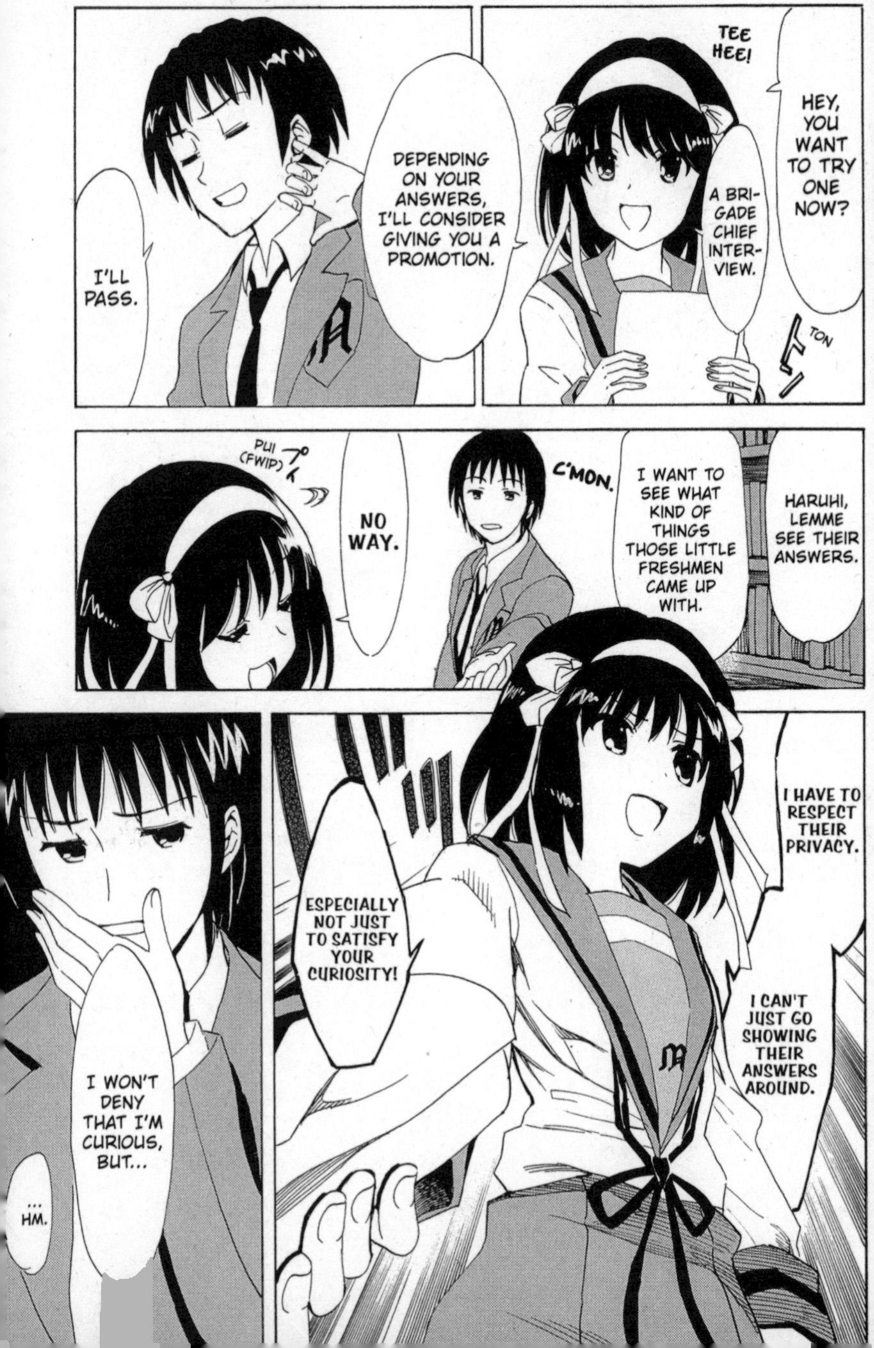
HEY, YOU WANT TO TRY ONE NOW?
TEE HEE!
A BRI-GADE CHIEF INTER-VIEW.
TON
DEPENDING ON YOUR ANSWERS, I'LL CONSIDER GIVING YOU A PROMOTION.
I'LL PASS.
HARUHI, LEMME SEE THEIR ANSWERS.
I WANT TO SEE WHAT KIND OF THINGS THOSE LITTLE FRESHMEN CAME UP WITH.
C'MON.
NO WAY.
PUI (FWIP)
I HAVE TO RESPECT THEIR PRIVACY.
I CAN'T JUST GO SHOWING THEIR ANSWERS AROUND.
ESPECIALLY NOT JUST TO SATISFY YOUR CURIOSITY!
I WON'T DENY THAT I'M CURIOUS, BUT...
...HM.

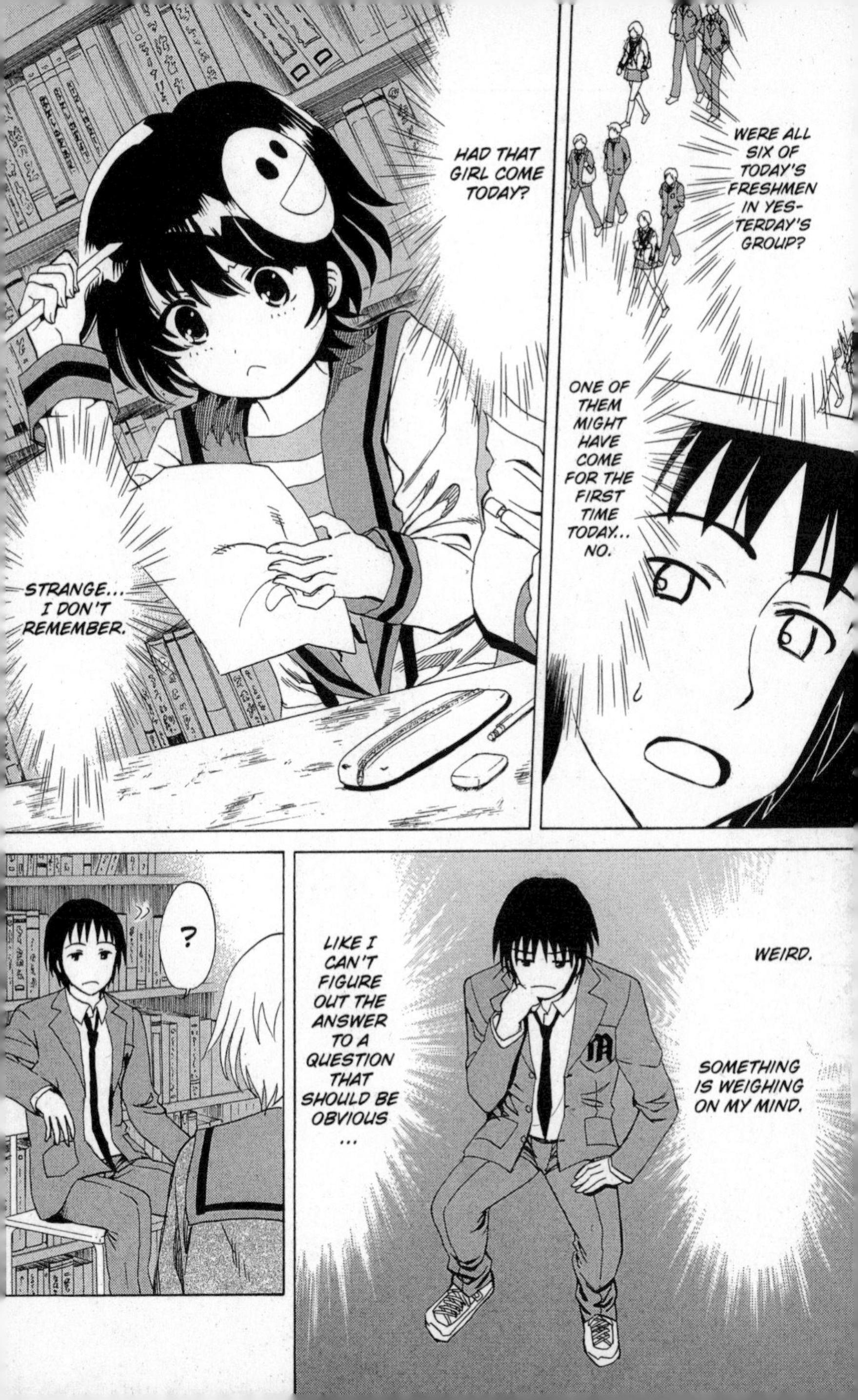
WERE ALL SIX OF TODAY'S FRESHMEN IN YES-TERDAY'S GROUP?
ONE OF THEM MIGHT HAVE COME FOR THE FIRST TIME TODAY... NO.
HAD THAT GIRL COME TODAY?
STRANGE... I DON'T REMEMBER.
WEIRD.
SOMETHING IS WEIGHING ON MY MIND.
LIKE I CAN'T FIGURE OUT THE ANSWER TO A QUESTION THAT SHOULD BE OBVIOUS ...
?

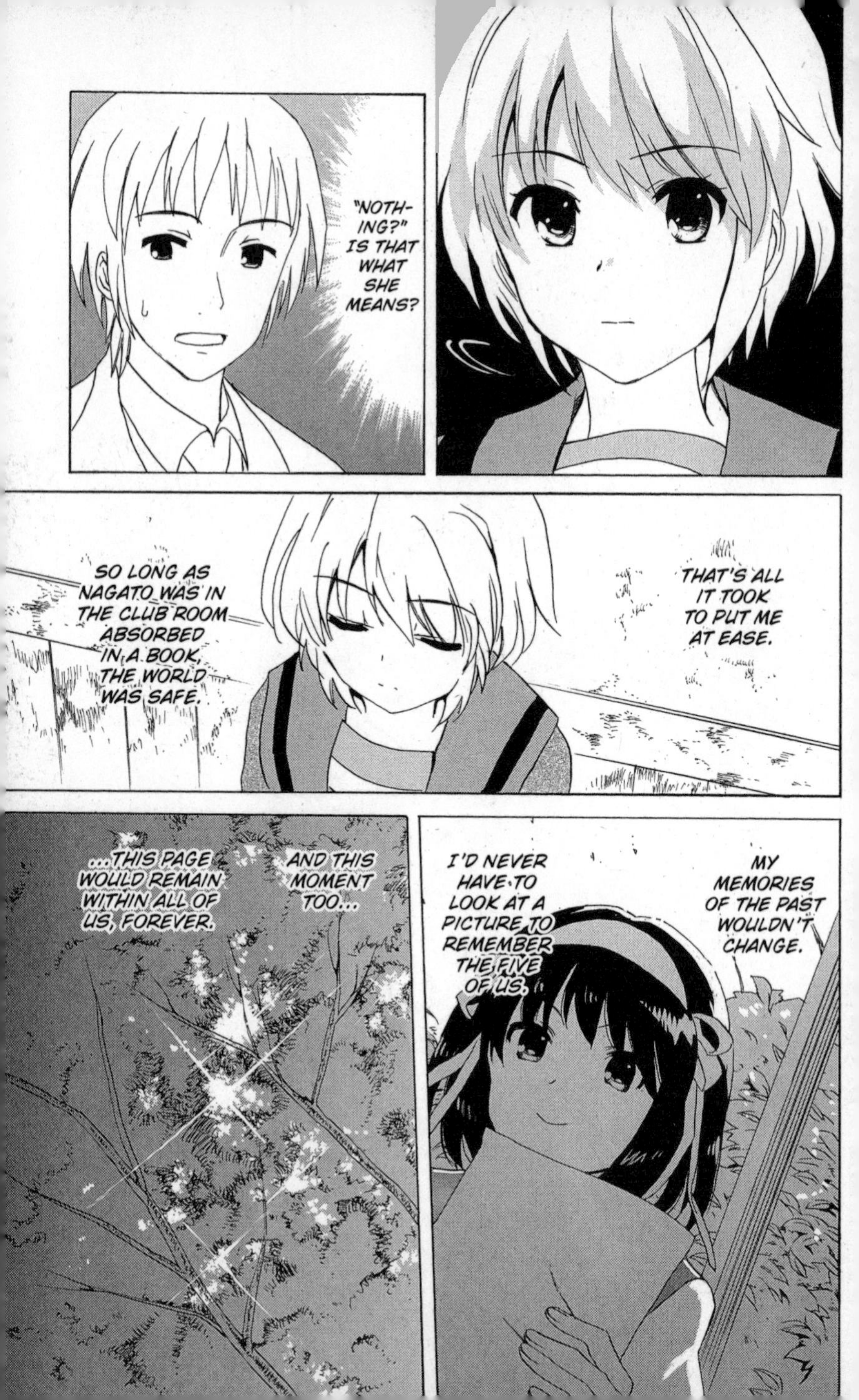
"NOTHING?" IS THAT WHAT SHE MEANS?
THAT'S ALL IT TOOK TO PUT ME AT EASE.
SO LONG AS NAGATO WAS IN THE CLUB ROOM ABSORBED IN A BOOK, THE WORLD WAS SAFE.
MY MEMORIES OF THE PAST WOULDN'T CHANGE.
I'D NEVER HAVE TO LOOK AT A PICTURE TO REMEMBER THE FIVE OF US.
AND THIS MOMENT TOO...
...THIS PAGE WOULD REMAIN WITHIN ALL OF US, FOREVER.

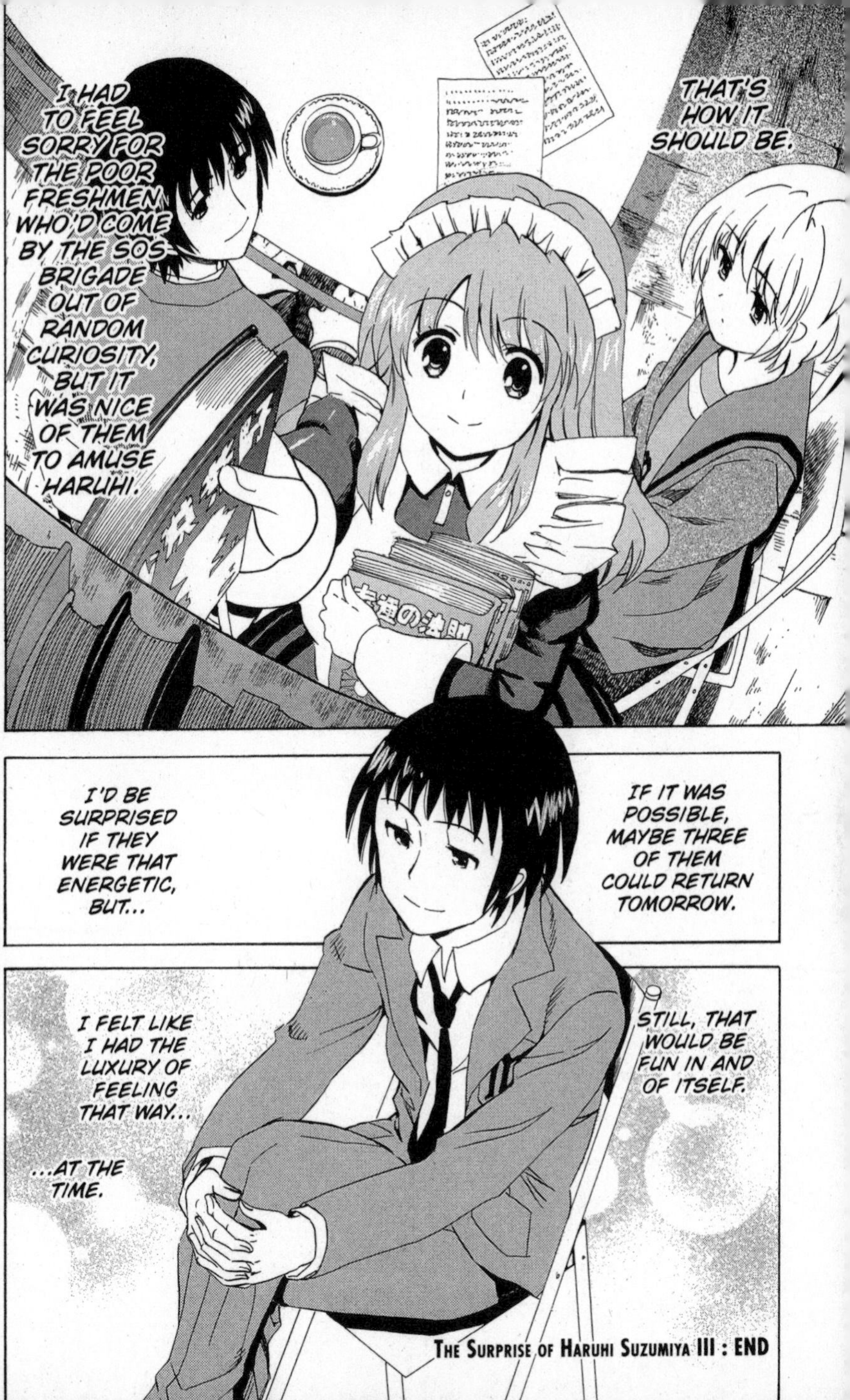
THAT'S HOW IT SHOULD BE.
I HAD TO FEEL SORRY FOR THE POOR FRESHMEN WHO'D COME BY THE SOS BRIGADE OUT OF RANDOM CURIOSITY, BUT IT WAS NICE OF THEM TO AMUSE HARUHI.
IF IT WAS POSSIBLE, MAYBE THREE OF THEM COULD RETURN TOMORROW.
I'D BE SURPRISED IF THEY WERE THAT ENERGETIC, BUT...
STILL, THAT WOULD BE FUN IN AND OF ITSELF.
I FELT LIKE I HAD THE LUXURY OF FEELING THAT WAY...
...AT THE TIME.
THE SURPRISE OF HARUHI SUZUMIYA III : END

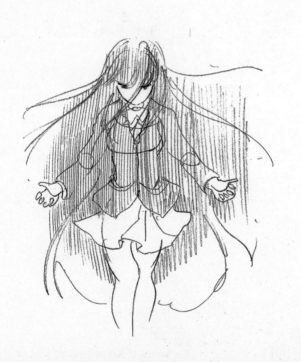

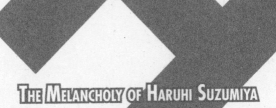

THE MELANCHOLY OF HARUHI SUZUMIYA

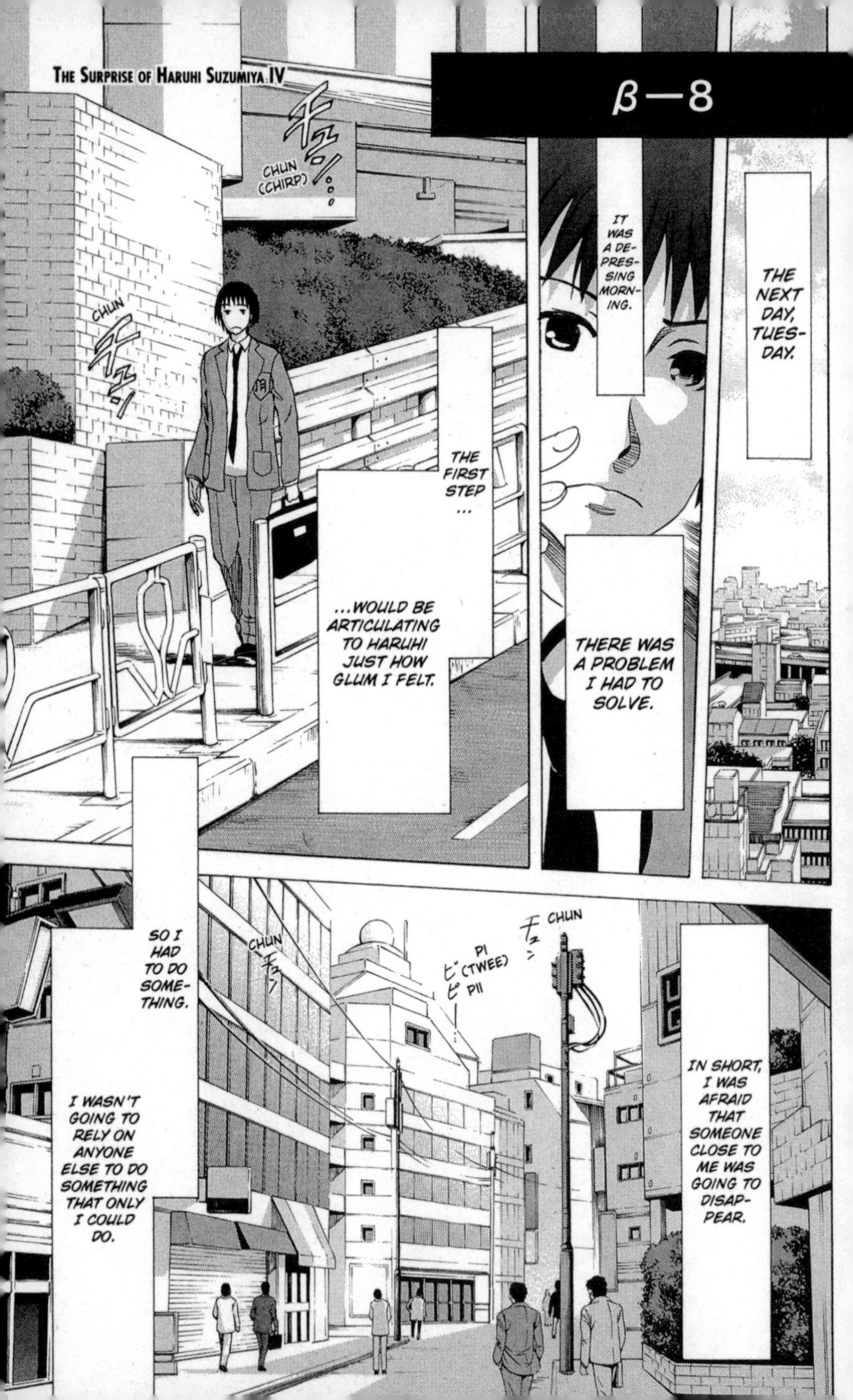
β—8
THE NEXT DAY, TUESDAY.
IT WAS A DEPRESSING MORNING.
THERE WAS A PROBLEM I HAD TO SOLVE.
CHUN (CHIRP)
CHUN
THE FIRST STEP...
...WOULD BE ARTICULATING TO HARUHI JUST HOW GLUM I FELT.
IN SHORT, I WAS AFRAID THAT SOMEONE CLOSE TO ME WAS GOING TO DISAPPEAR.
CHUN
PI (TWEE) PII
CHUN
SO I HAD TO DO SOMETHING.
I WASN'T GOING TO RELY ON ANYONE ELSE TO DO SOMETHING THAT ONLY I COULD DO.

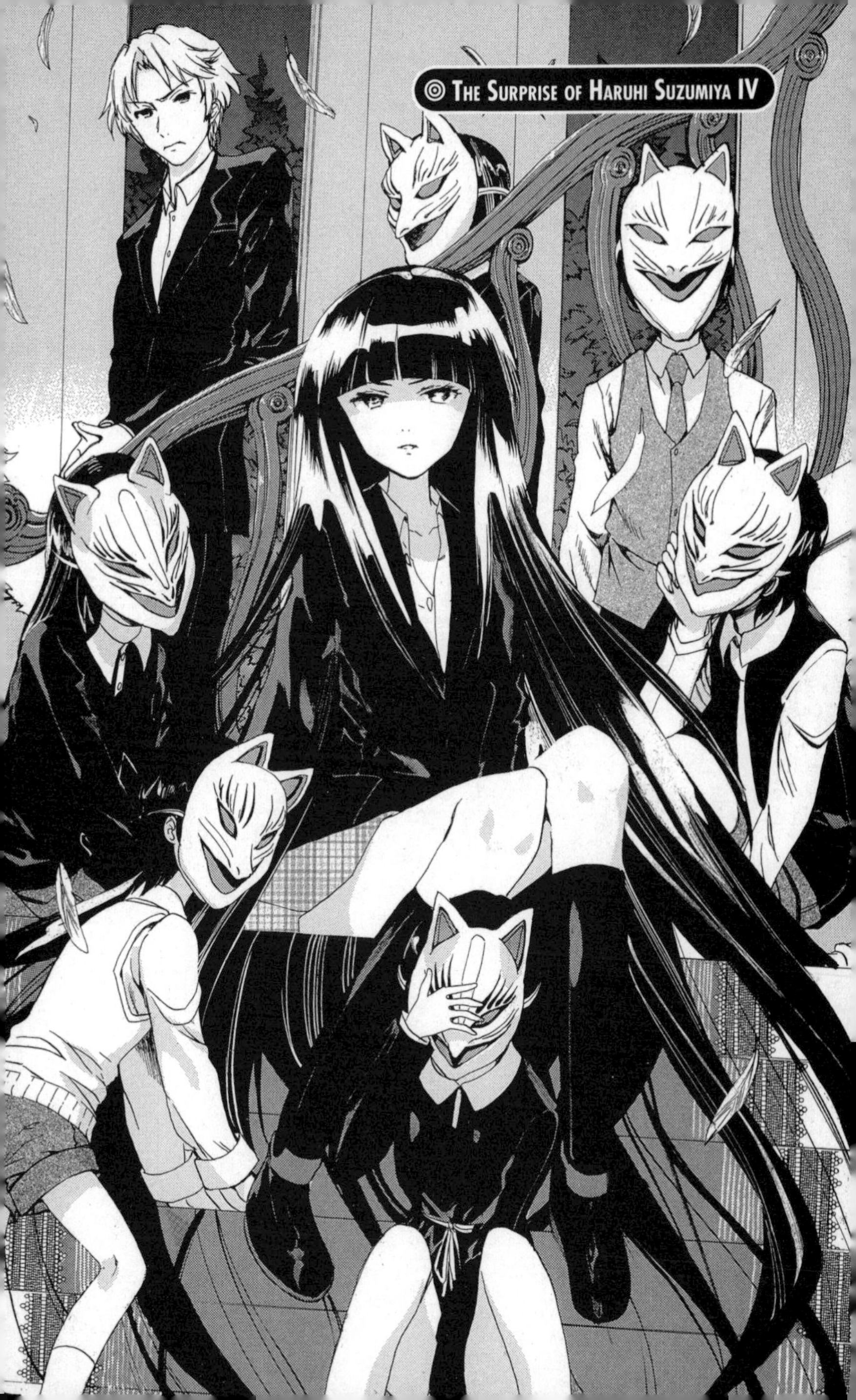
◎ The Surprise of Haruhi Suzumiya IV

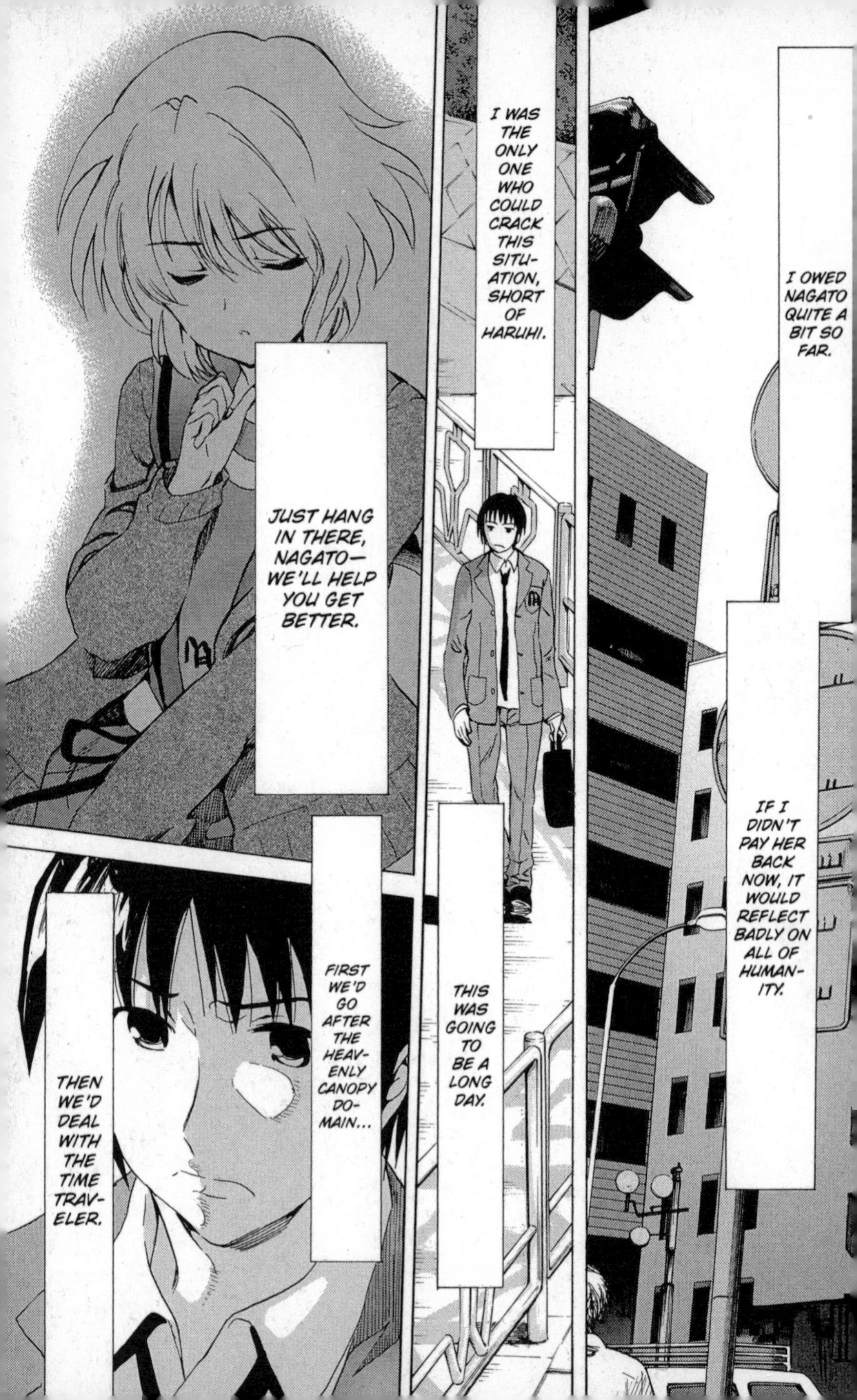
I OWED NAGATO QUITE A BIT SO FAR.
IF I DIDN'T PAY HER BACK NOW, IT WOULD REFLECT BADLY ON ALL OF HUMAN-ITY.
I WAS THE ONLY ONE WHO COULD CRACK THIS SITU-ATION, SHORT OF HARUHI.
JUST HANG IN THERE, NAGATO—WE'LL HELP YOU GET BETTER.
FIRST WE'D GO AFTER THE HEAV-ENLY CANOPY DO-MAIN...
THEN WE'D DEAL WITH THE TIME TRAV-ELER.
THIS WAS GOING TO BE A LONG DAY.

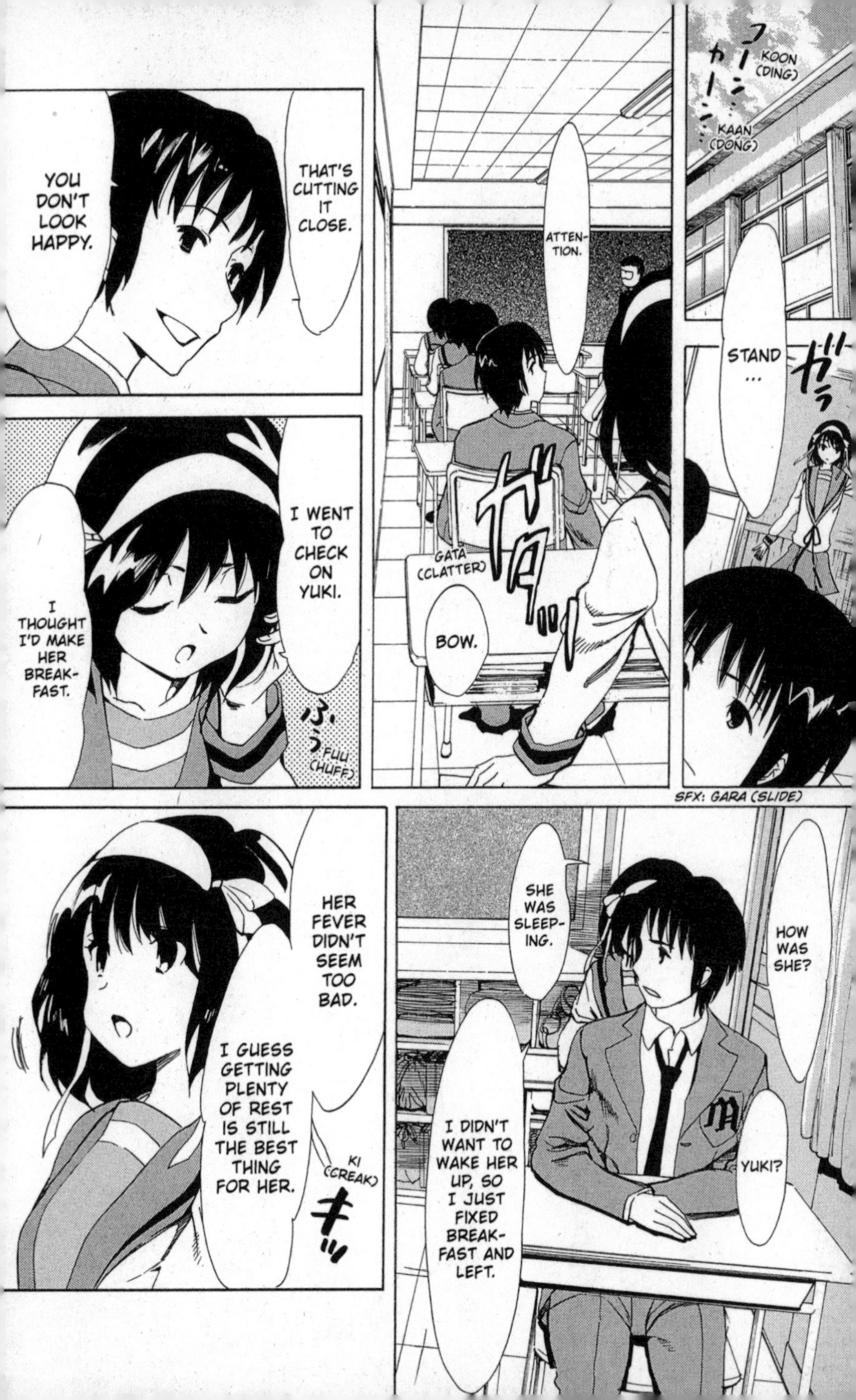

KOON (DING)
KAAN (DONG)
STAND...
SFX: GARA (SLIDE)
ATTEN-TION.
GATA (CLATTER)
BOW.
THAT'S CUTTING IT CLOSE.
YOU DON'T LOOK HAPPY.
I WENT TO CHECK ON YUKI.
I THOUGHT I'D MAKE HER BREAK-FAST.
FUU (HUFF)
HOW WAS SHE?
YUKI?
SHE WAS SLEEP-ING.
I DIDN'T WANT TO WAKE HER UP, SO I JUST FIXED BREAK-FAST AND LEFT.
HER FEVER DIDN'T SEEM TOO BAD.
I GUESS GETTING PLENTY OF REST IS STILL THE BEST THING FOR HER.
KI (CREAK)

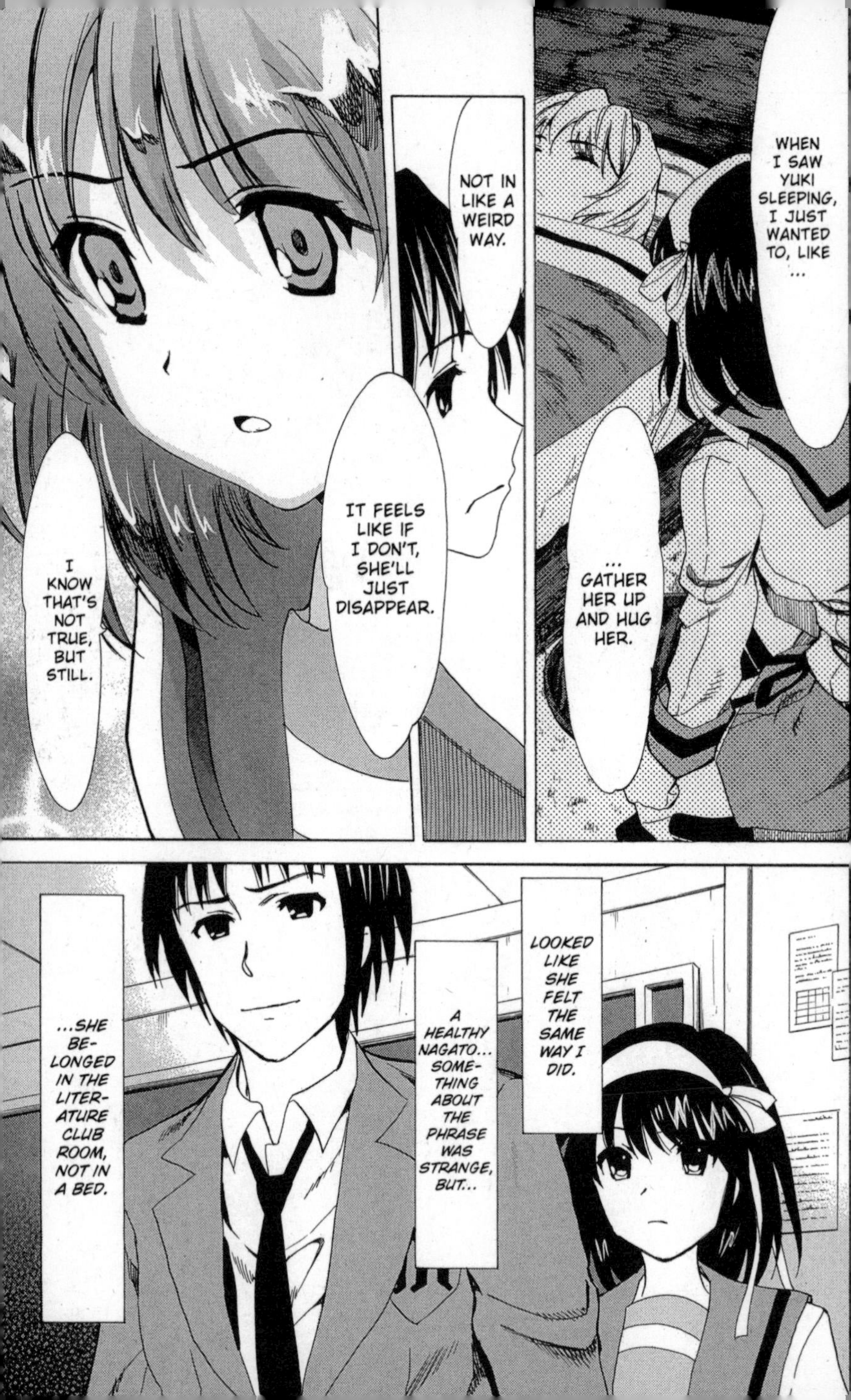
WHEN I SAW YUKI SLEEPING, I JUST WANTED TO, LIKE ...
... GATHER HER UP AND HUG HER.
NOT IN LIKE A WEIRD WAY.
IT FEELS LIKE IF I DON'T, SHE'LL JUST DISAPPEAR.
I KNOW THAT'S NOT TRUE, BUT STILL.
LOOKED LIKE SHE FELT THE SAME WAY I DID.
A HEALTHY NAGATO... SOMETHING ABOUT THE PHRASE WAS STRANGE, BUT...
...SHE BE-LONGED IN THE LITER-ATURE CLUB ROOM, NOT IN A BED.

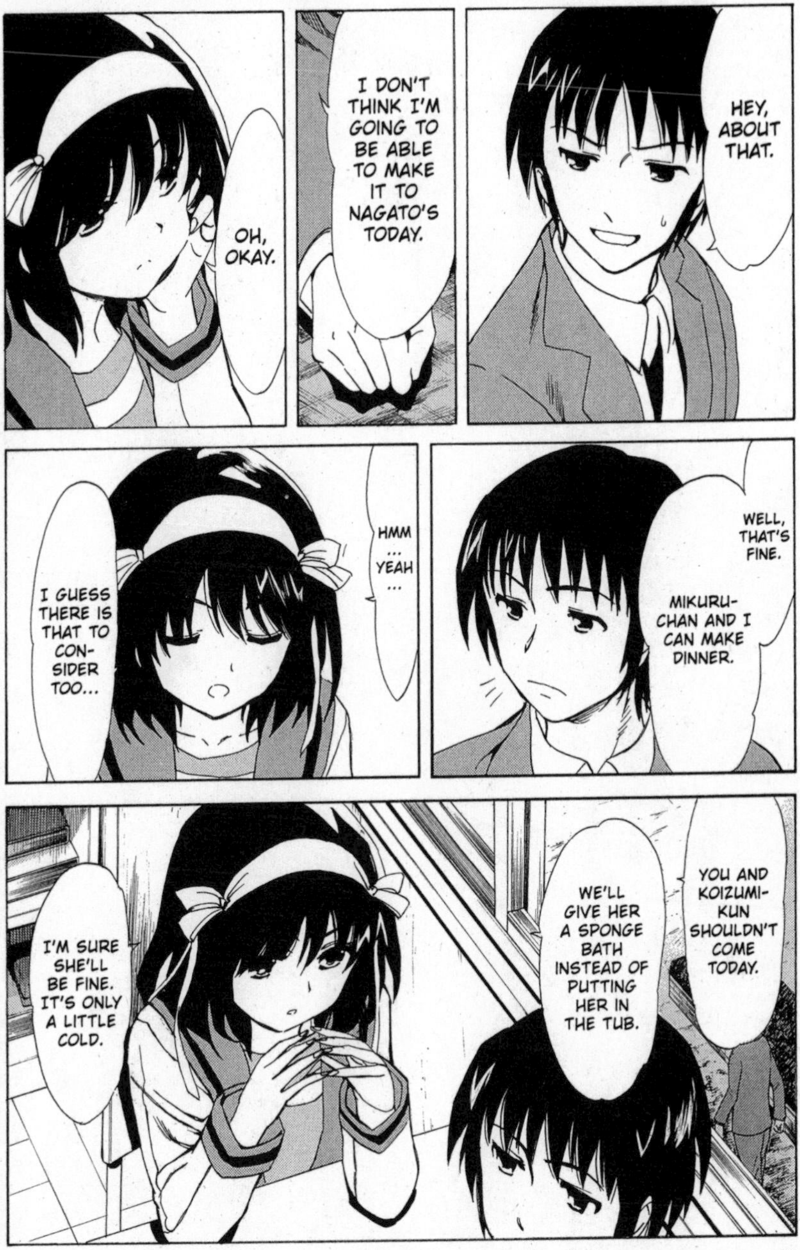
HEY, ABOUT THAT.
I DON'T THINK I'M GOING TO BE ABLE TO MAKE IT TO NAGATO'S TODAY.
OH, OKAY.
WELL, THAT'S FINE.
MIKURU-CHAN AND I CAN MAKE DINNER.
HMM ... YEAH ...
I GUESS THERE IS THAT TO CONSIDER TOO...
YOU AND KOIZUMI-KUN SHOULDN'T COME TODAY.
WE'LL GIVE HER A SPONGE BATH INSTEAD OF PUTTING HER IN THE TUB.
I'M SURE SHE'LL BE FINE. IT'S ONLY A LITTLE COLD.

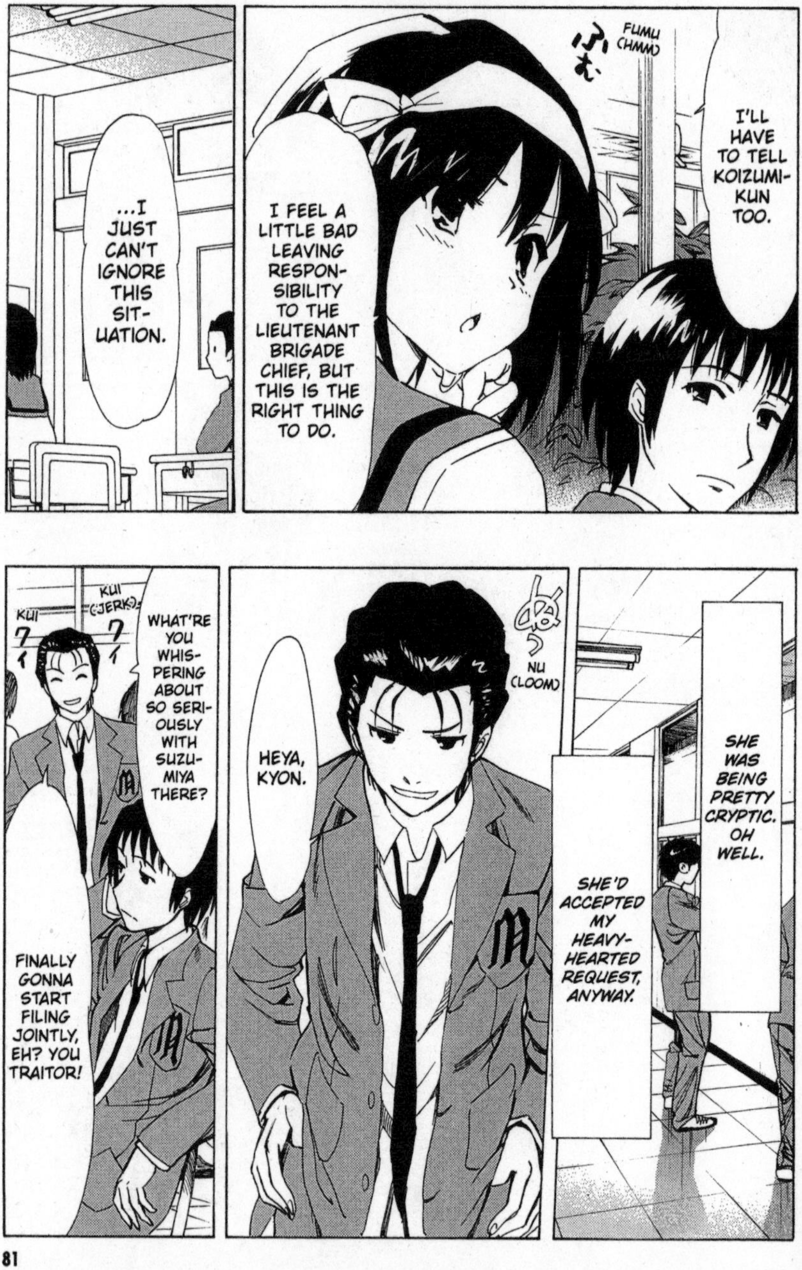
I'LL HAVE TO TELL KOIZUMI-KUN TOO.
ふむ FUMU (HMM)
I FEEL A LITTLE BAD LEAVING RESPONSIBILITY TO THE LIEUTENANT BRIGADE CHIEF, BUT THIS IS THE RIGHT THING TO DO.
...I JUST CAN'T IGNORE THIS SITUATION.
SHE WAS BEING PRETTY CRYPTIC. OH WELL.
SHE'D ACCEPTED MY HEAVY-HEARTED REQUEST, ANYWAY.
ぬっ NU (LOOM)
HEYA, KYON.
クイ KUI (JERK)
クイ KUI
WHAT'RE YOU WHISPERING ABOUT SO SERIOUSLY WITH SUZUMIYA THERE?
FINALLY GONNA START FILING JOINTLY, EH? YOU TRAITOR!

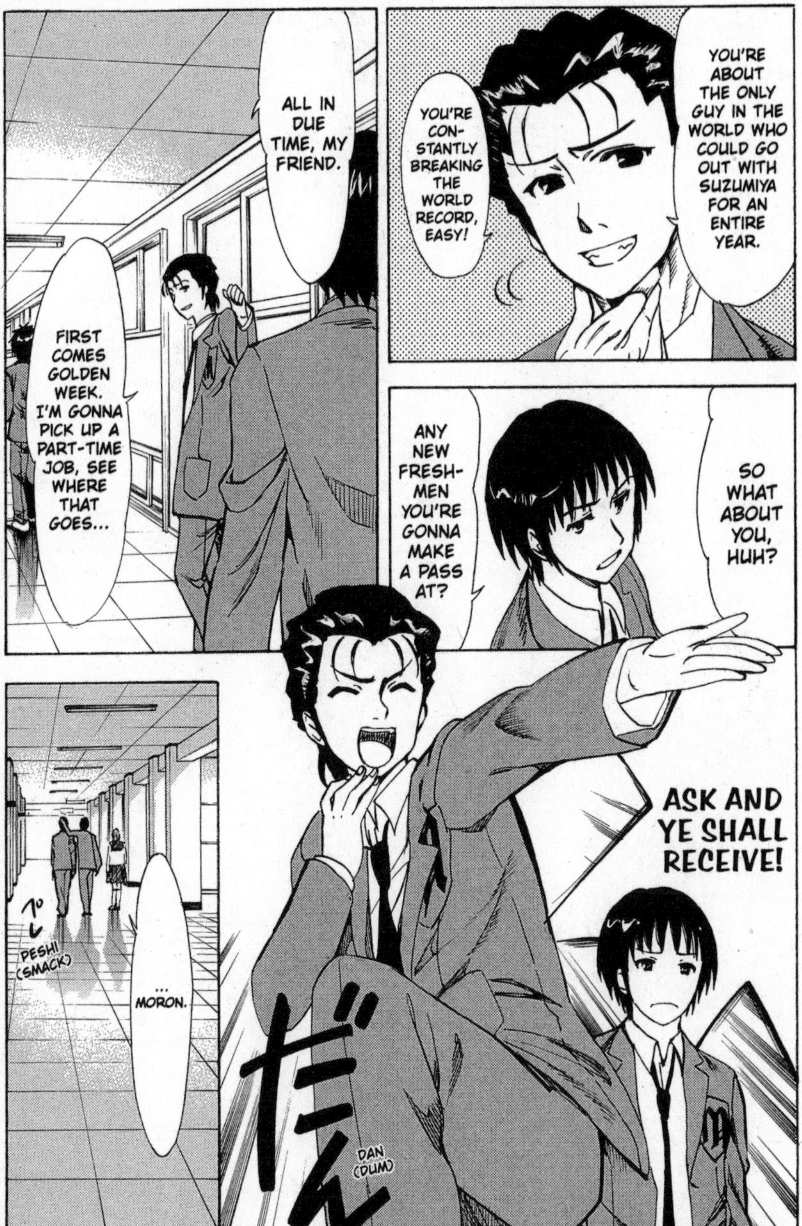
YOU'RE ABOUT THE ONLY GUY IN THE WORLD WHO COULD GO OUT WITH SUZUMIYA FOR AN ENTIRE YEAR.
YOU'RE CON-STANTLY BREAKING THE WORLD RECORD, EASY!
SO WHAT ABOUT YOU, HUH?
ANY NEW FRESH-MEN YOU'RE GONNA MAKE A PASS AT?
ALL IN DUE TIME, MY FRIEND.
FIRST COMES GOLDEN WEEK. I'M GONNA PICK UP A PART-TIME JOB, SEE WHERE THAT GOES...
ASK AND YE SHALL RECEIVE!
だん
DAN (DUM)
... MORON.
PESHI (SMACK)

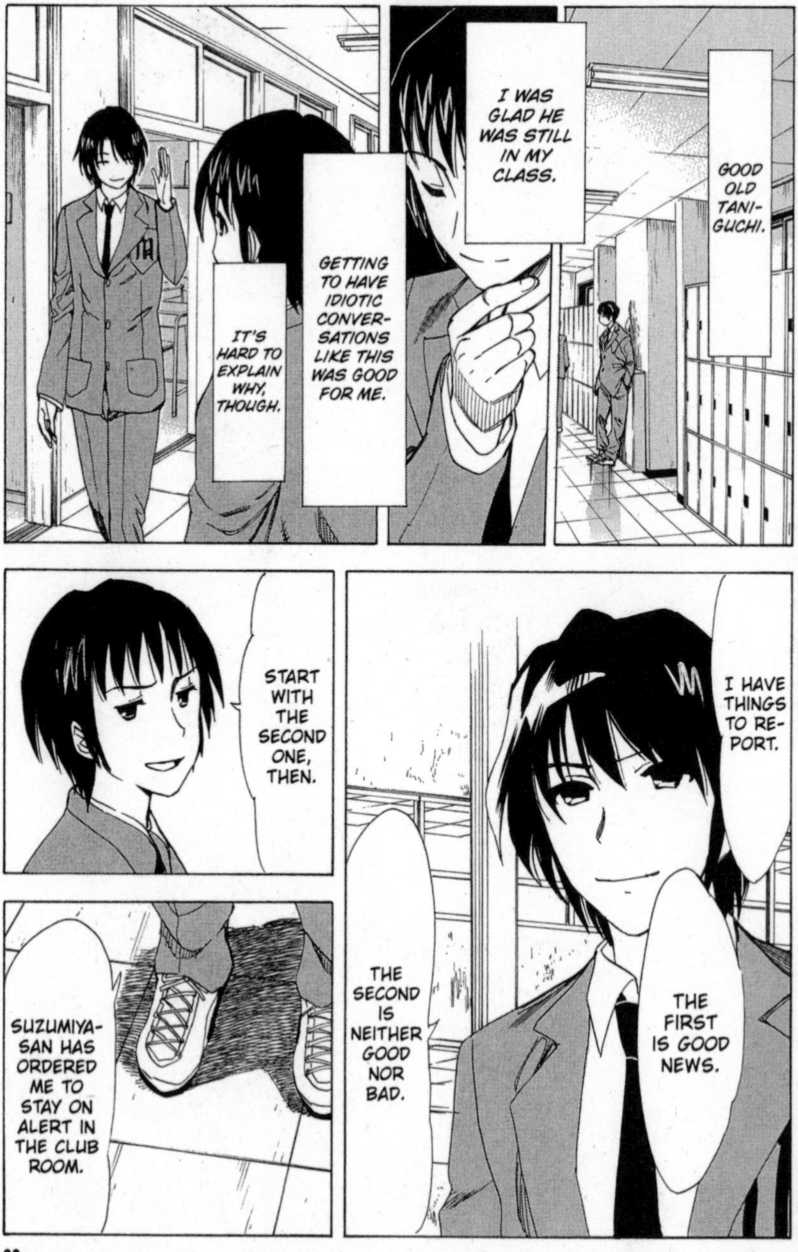
GOOD OLD TANI-GUCHI.
I WAS GLAD HE WAS STILL IN MY CLASS.
GETTING TO HAVE IDIOTIC CONVER-SATIONS LIKE THIS WAS GOOD FOR ME.
IT'S HARD TO EXPLAIN WHY, THOUGH.
I HAVE THINGS TO RE-PORT.
THE FIRST IS GOOD NEWS.
THE SECOND IS NEITHER GOOD NOR BAD.
START WITH THE SECOND ONE, THEN.
SUZUMIYA-SAN HAS ORDERED ME TO STAY ON ALERT IN THE CLUB ROOM.

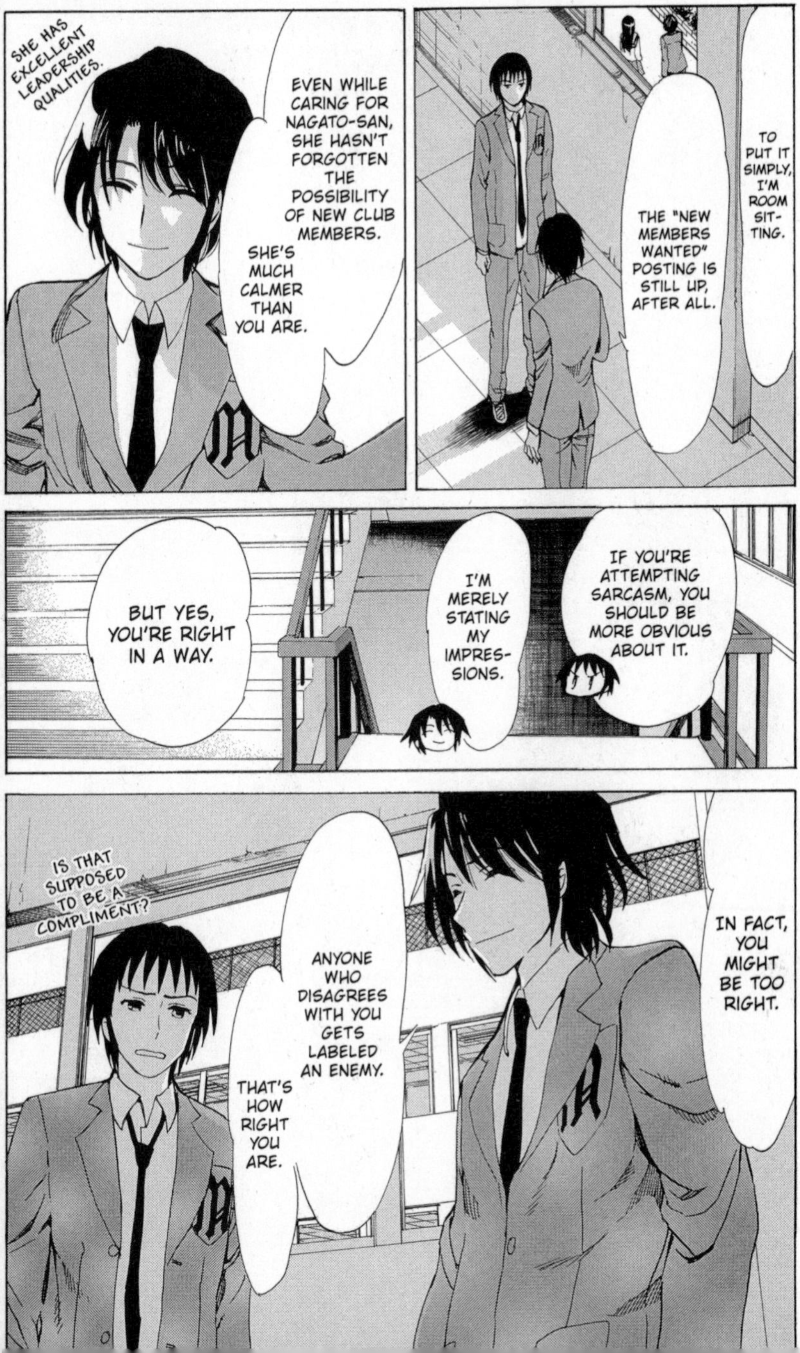
TO PUT IT SIMPLY, I'M ROOM SITTING.
THE "NEW MEMBERS WANTED" POSTING IS STILL UP, AFTER ALL.
EVEN WHILE CARING FOR NAGATO-SAN, SHE HASN'T FORGOTTEN THE POSSIBILITY OF NEW CLUB MEMBERS.
SHE HAS EXCELLENT LEADERSHIP QUALITIES.
SHE'S MUCH CALMER THAN YOU ARE.
IF YOU'RE ATTEMPTING SARCASM, YOU SHOULD BE MORE OBVIOUS ABOUT IT.
I'M MERELY STATING MY IMPRESSIONS.
BUT YES, YOU'RE RIGHT IN A WAY.
IN FACT, YOU MIGHT BE TOO RIGHT.
ANYONE WHO DISAGREES WITH YOU GETS LABELED AN ENEMY.
THAT'S HOW RIGHT YOU ARE.
IS THAT SUPPOSED TO BE A COMPLIMENT?

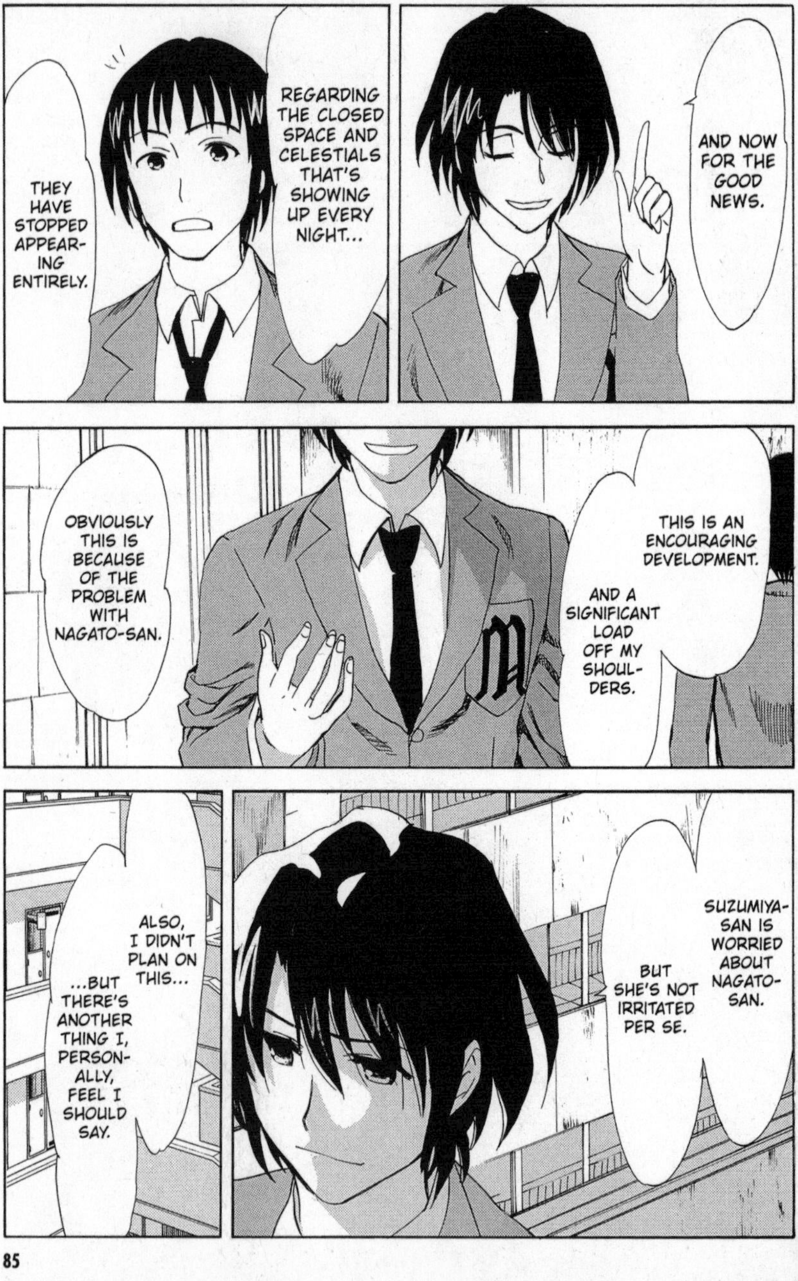
AND NOW FOR THE GOOD NEWS.
REGARDING THE CLOSED SPACE AND CELESTIALS THAT'S SHOWING UP EVERY NIGHT...
THEY HAVE STOPPED APPEARING ENTIRELY.
THIS IS AN ENCOURAGING DEVELOPMENT.
AND A SIGNIFICANT LOAD OFF MY SHOULDERS.
OBVIOUSLY THIS IS BECAUSE OF THE PROBLEM WITH NAGATO-SAN.
SUZUMIYA-SAN IS WORRIED ABOUT NAGATO-SAN.
BUT SHE'S NOT IRRITATED PER SE.
ALSO, I DIDN'T PLAN ON THIS...
...BUT THERE'S ANOTHER THING I, PERSONALLY, FEEL I SHOULD SAY.

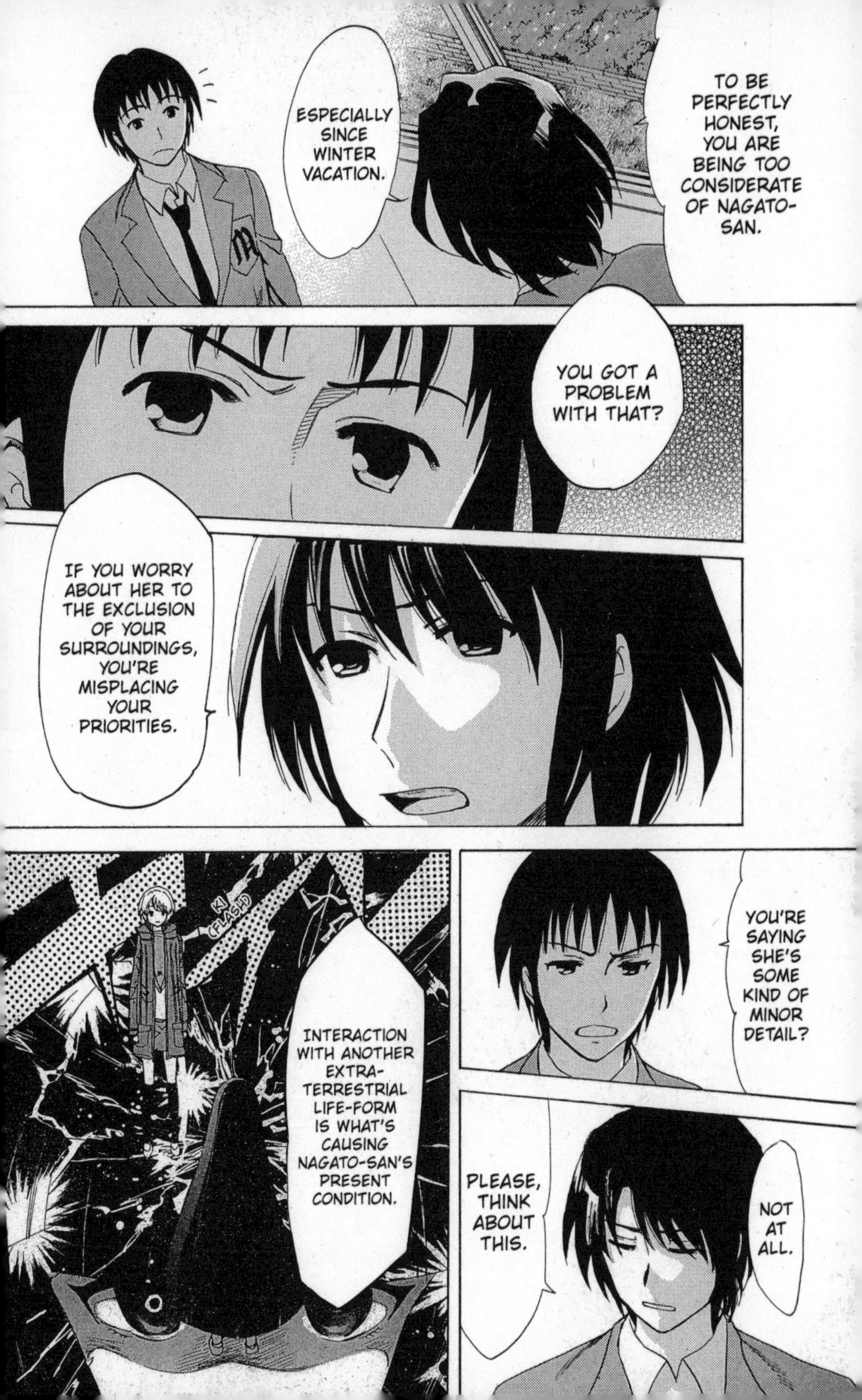
TO BE PERFECTLY HONEST, YOU ARE BEING TOO CONSIDERATE OF NAGATO-SAN.
ESPECIALLY SINCE WINTER VACATION.
YOU GOT A PROBLEM WITH THAT?
IF YOU WORRY ABOUT HER TO THE EXCLUSION OF YOUR SURROUNDINGS, YOU'RE MISPLACING YOUR PRIORITIES.
YOU'RE SAYING SHE'S SOME KIND OF MINOR DETAIL?
NOT AT ALL.
PLEASE, THINK ABOUT THIS.
KI (FLASH)
INTERACTION WITH ANOTHER EXTRA-TERRESTRIAL LIFE-FORM IS WHAT'S CAUSING NAGATO-SAN'S PRESENT CONDITION.

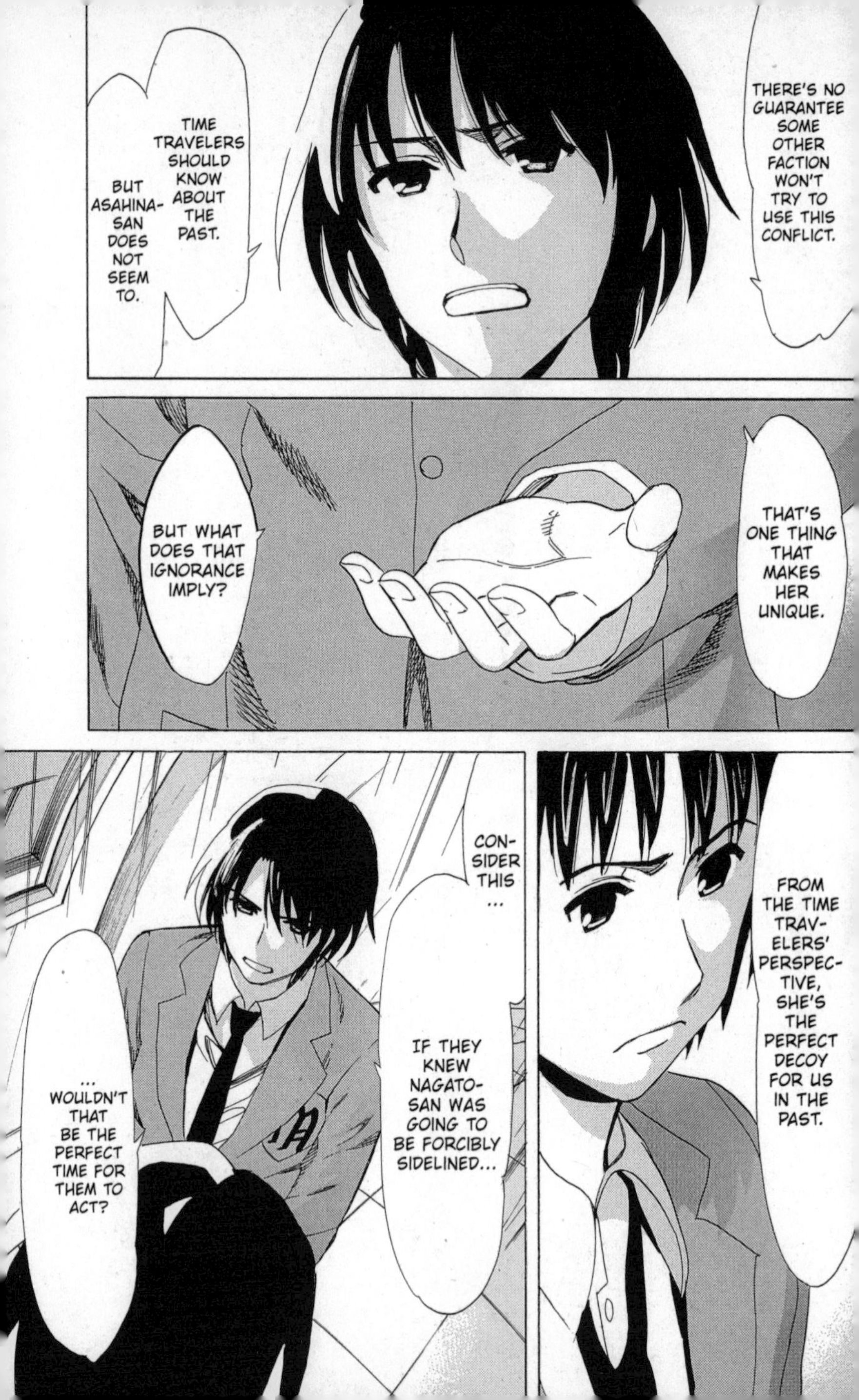
THERE'S NO GUARANTEE SOME OTHER FACTION WON'T TRY TO USE THIS CONFLICT.
TIME TRAVELERS SHOULD KNOW ABOUT THE PAST.
BUT ASAHINA-SAN DOES NOT SEEM TO.
THAT'S ONE THING THAT MAKES HER UNIQUE.
BUT WHAT DOES THAT IGNORANCE IMPLY?
FROM THE TIME TRAVELERS' PERSPECTIVE, SHE'S THE PERFECT DECOY FOR US IN THE PAST.
CONSIDER THIS...
IF THEY KNEW NAGATO-SAN WAS GOING TO BE FORCIBLY SIDELINED...
...WOULDN'T THAT BE THE PERFECT TIME FOR THEM TO ACT?

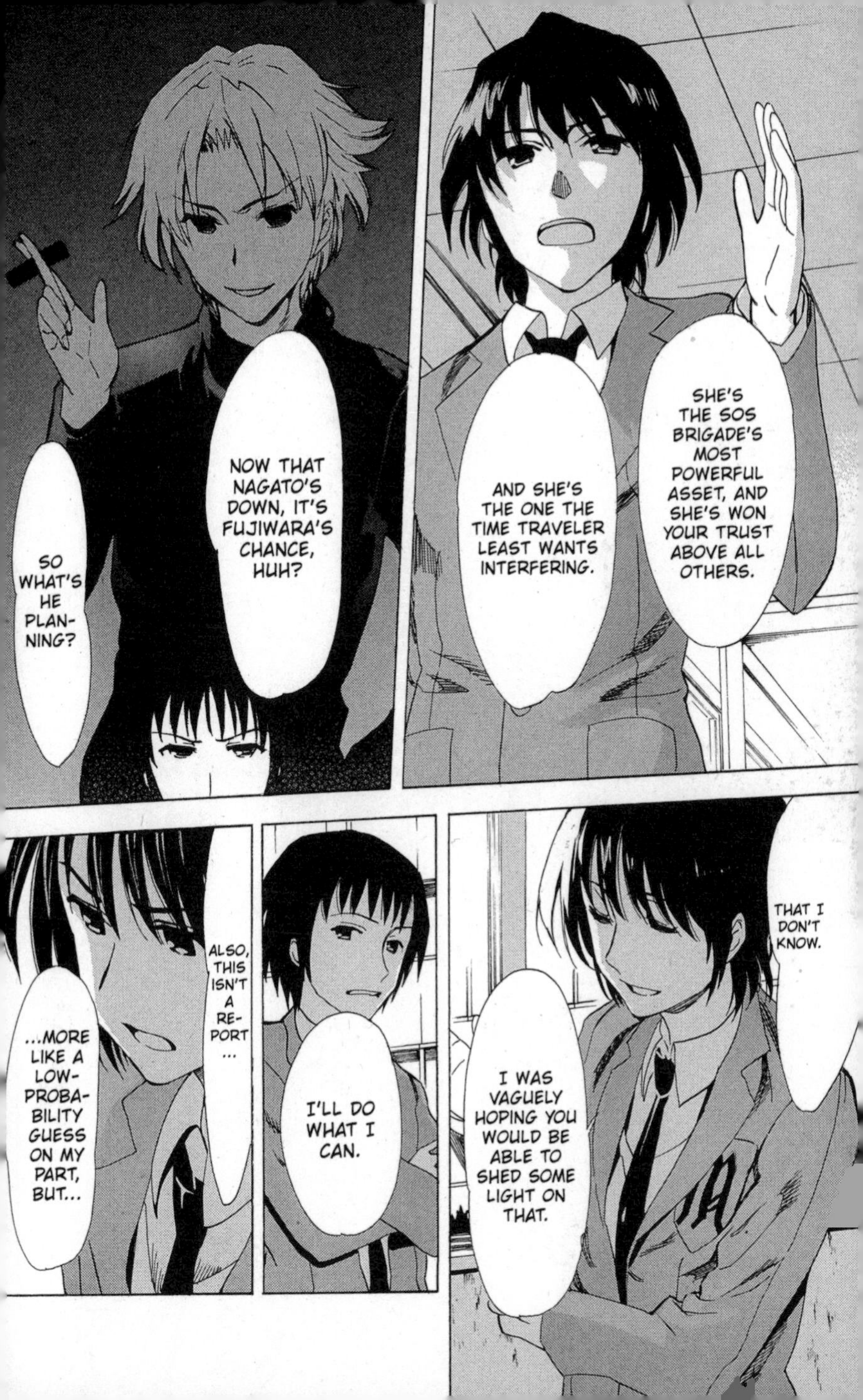
SHE'S THE SOS BRIGADE'S MOST POWERFUL ASSET, AND SHE'S WON YOUR TRUST ABOVE ALL OTHERS.
AND SHE'S THE ONE THE TIME TRAVELER LEAST WANTS INTERFERING.
NOW THAT NAGATO'S DOWN, IT'S FUJIWARA'S CHANCE, HUH?
SO WHAT'S HE PLANNING?
THAT I DON'T KNOW.
I WAS VAGUELY HOPING YOU WOULD BE ABLE TO SHED SOME LIGHT ON THAT.
I'LL DO WHAT I CAN.
ALSO, THIS ISN'T A REPORT...
...MORE LIKE A LOW-PROBABILITY GUESS ON MY PART, BUT...

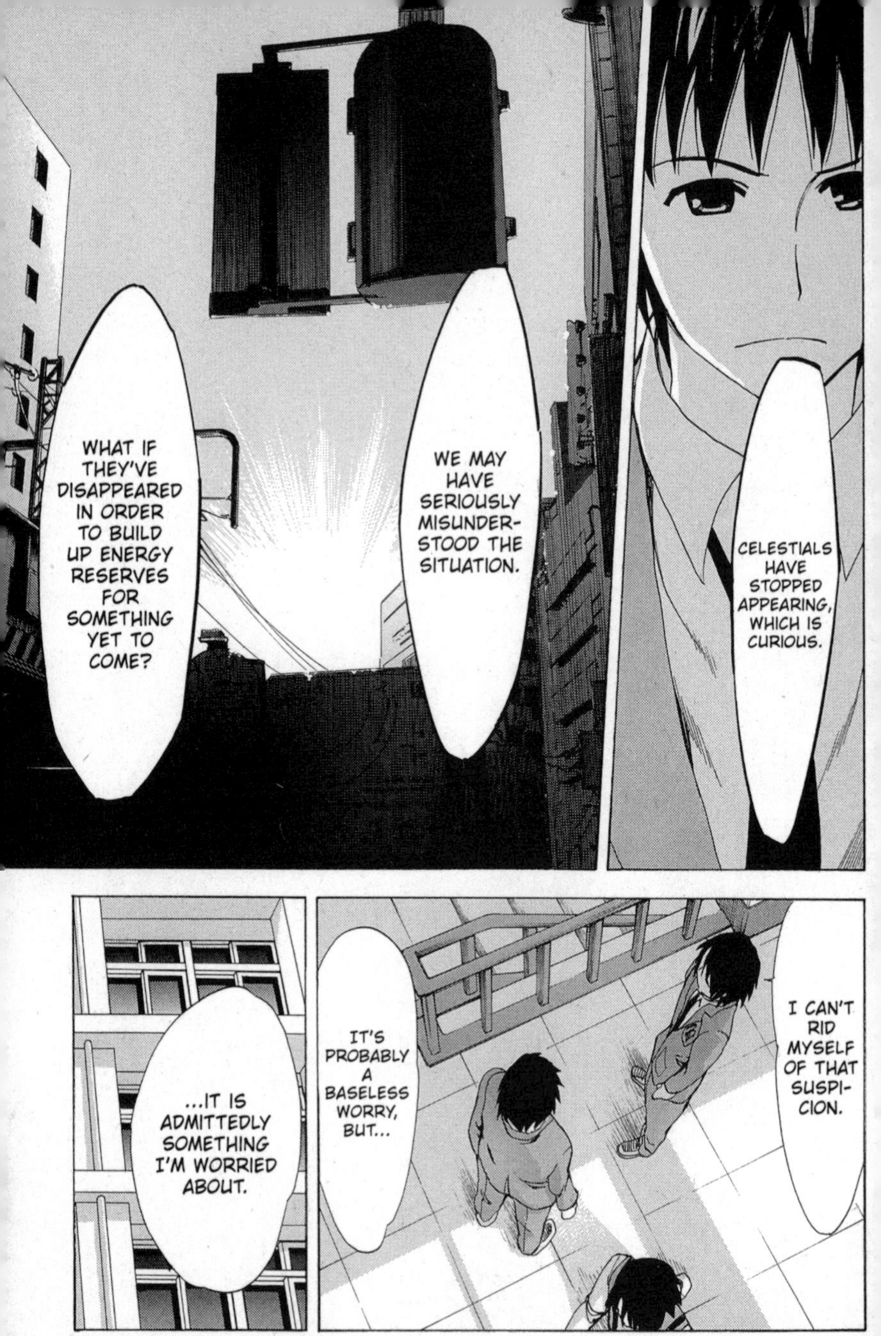
CELESTIALS HAVE STOPPED APPEARING, WHICH IS CURIOUS.
WE MAY HAVE SERIOUSLY MISUNDER-STOOD THE SITUATION.
WHAT IF THEY'VE DISAPPEARED IN ORDER TO BUILD UP ENERGY RESERVES FOR SOMETHING YET TO COME?
I CAN'T RID MYSELF OF THAT SUSPI-CION.
IT'S PROBABLY A BASELESS WORRY, BUT...
...IT IS ADMITTEDLY SOMETHING I'M WORRIED ABOUT.

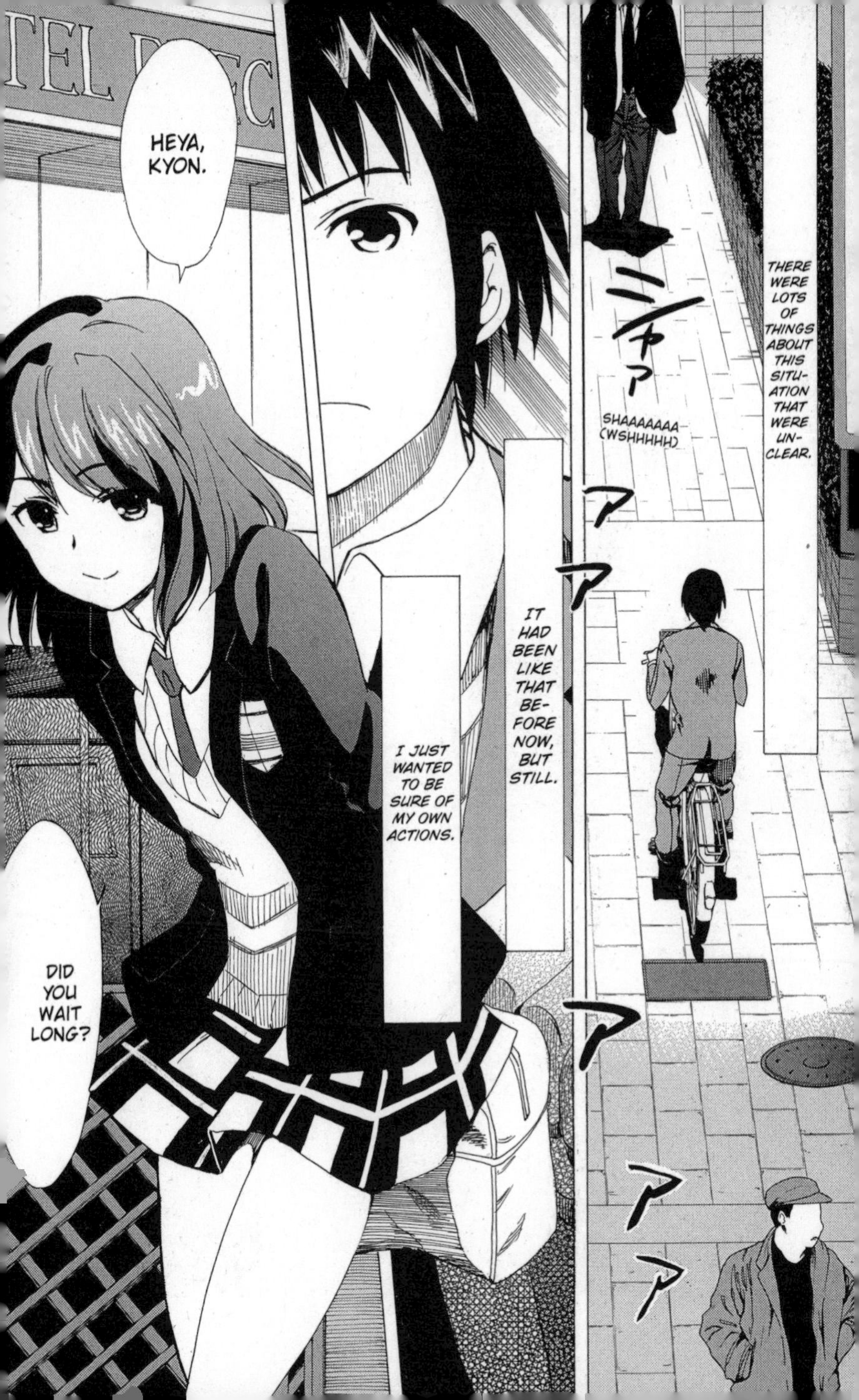
THERE WERE LOTS OF THINGS ABOUT THIS SITU-ATION THAT WERE UN-CLEAR.
SHAAAAAAA (WSHHHHH)
IT HAD BEEN LIKE THAT BE-FORE NOW, BUT STILL.
I JUST WANTED TO BE SURE OF MY OWN ACTIONS.
HEYA, KYON.
DID YOU WAIT LONG?

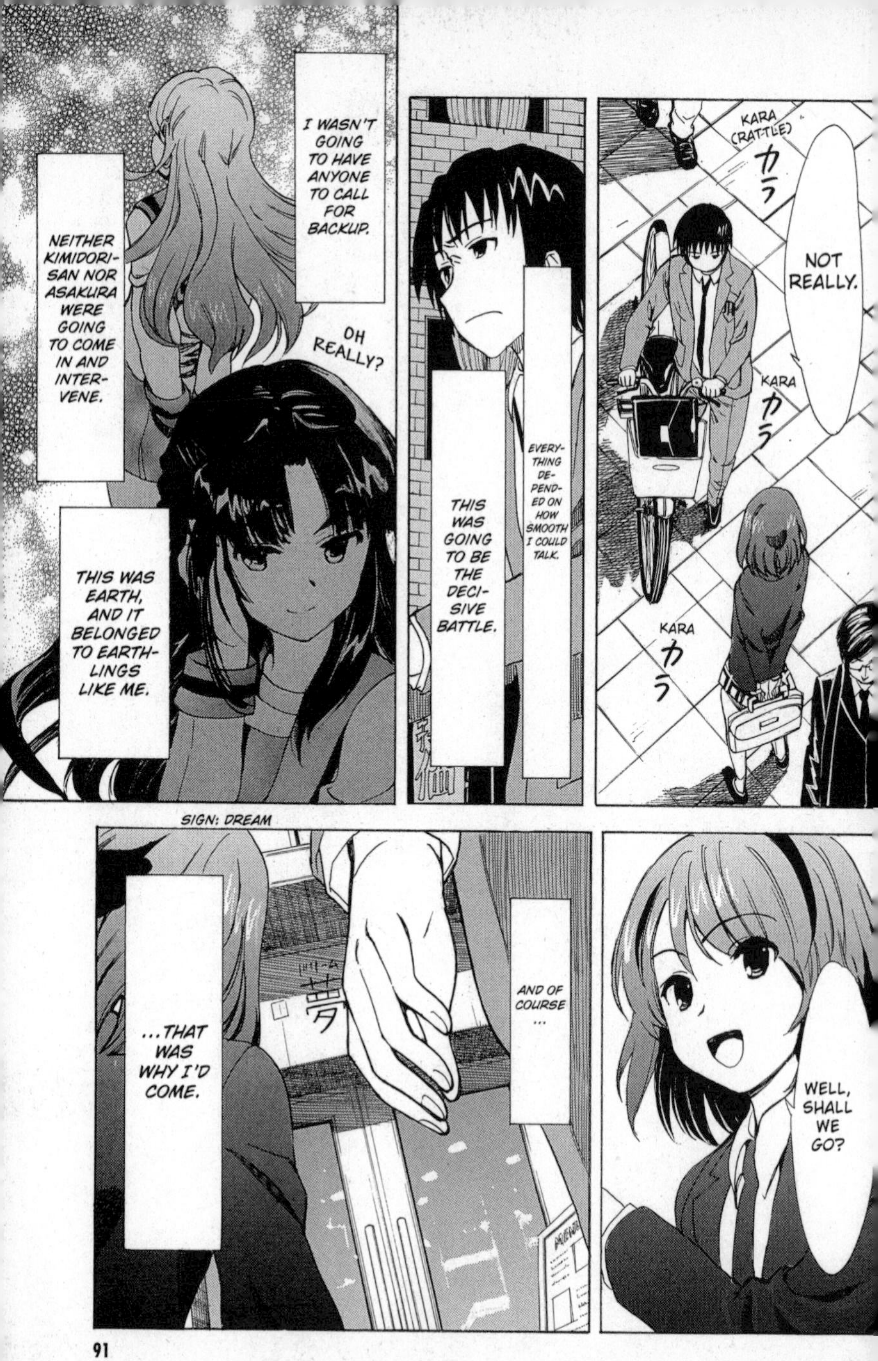
KARA (RATTLE)
カラ
NOT REALLY.
KARA
カラ
KARA
カラ
EVERYTHING DEPENDED ON HOW SMOOTH I COULD TALK.
THIS WAS GOING TO BE THE DECISIVE BATTLE.
I WASN'T GOING TO HAVE ANYONE TO CALL FOR BACKUP.
OH REALLY?
NEITHER KIMIDORI-SAN NOR ASAKURA WERE GOING TO COME IN AND INTERVENE.
THIS WAS EARTH, AND IT BELONGED TO EARTHLINGS LIKE ME.
WELL, SHALL WE GO?
AND OF COURSE...
...THAT WAS WHY I'D COME.
SIGN: DREAM
夢

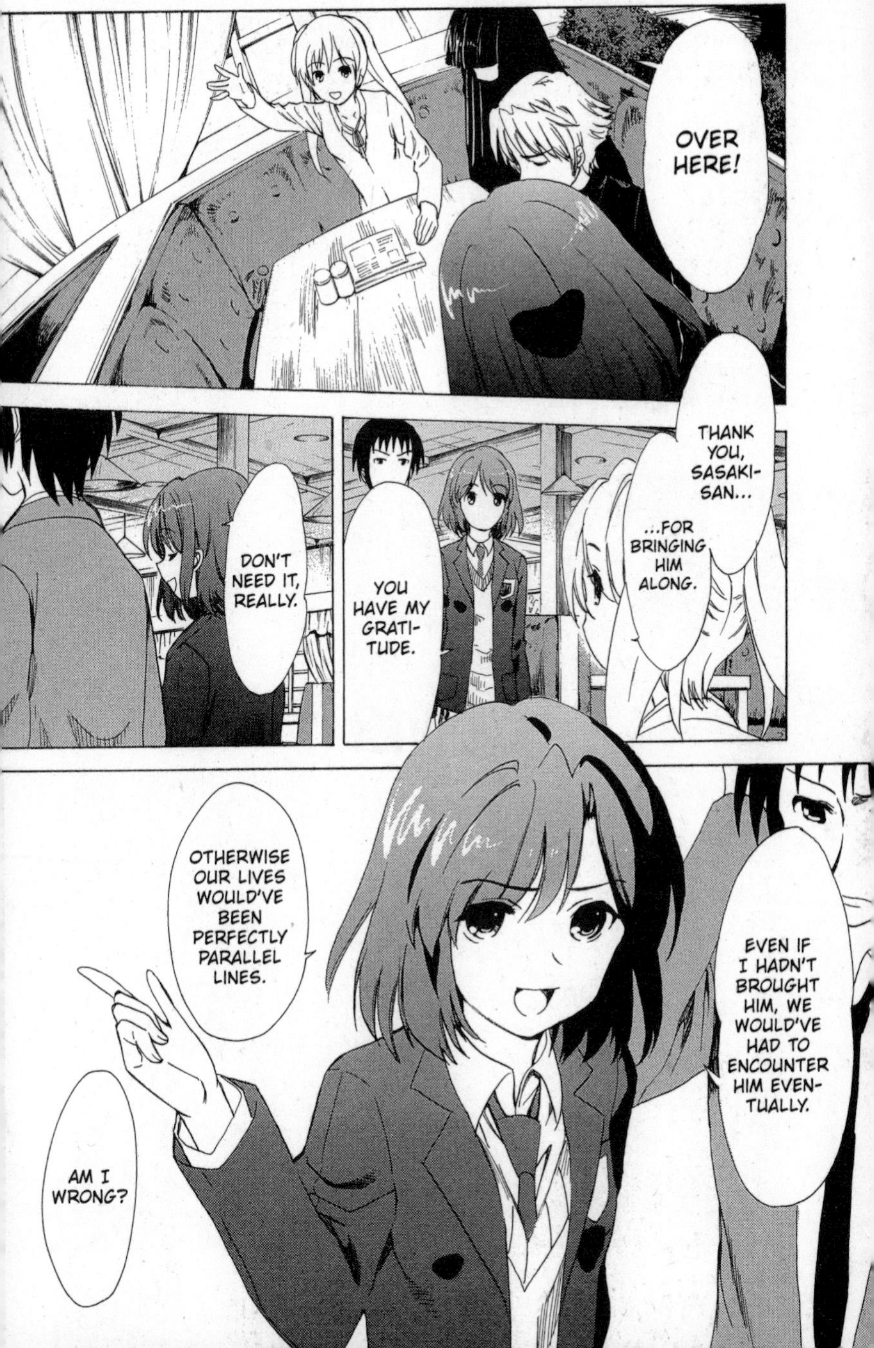
OVER HERE!
THANK YOU, SASAKI-SAN...
...FOR BRINGING HIM ALONG.
YOU HAVE MY GRATITUDE.
DON'T NEED IT, REALLY.
EVEN IF I HADN'T BROUGHT HIM, WE WOULD'VE HAD TO ENCOUNTER HIM EVENTUALLY.
OTHERWISE OUR LIVES WOULD'VE BEEN PERFECTLY PARALLEL LINES.
AM I WRONG?

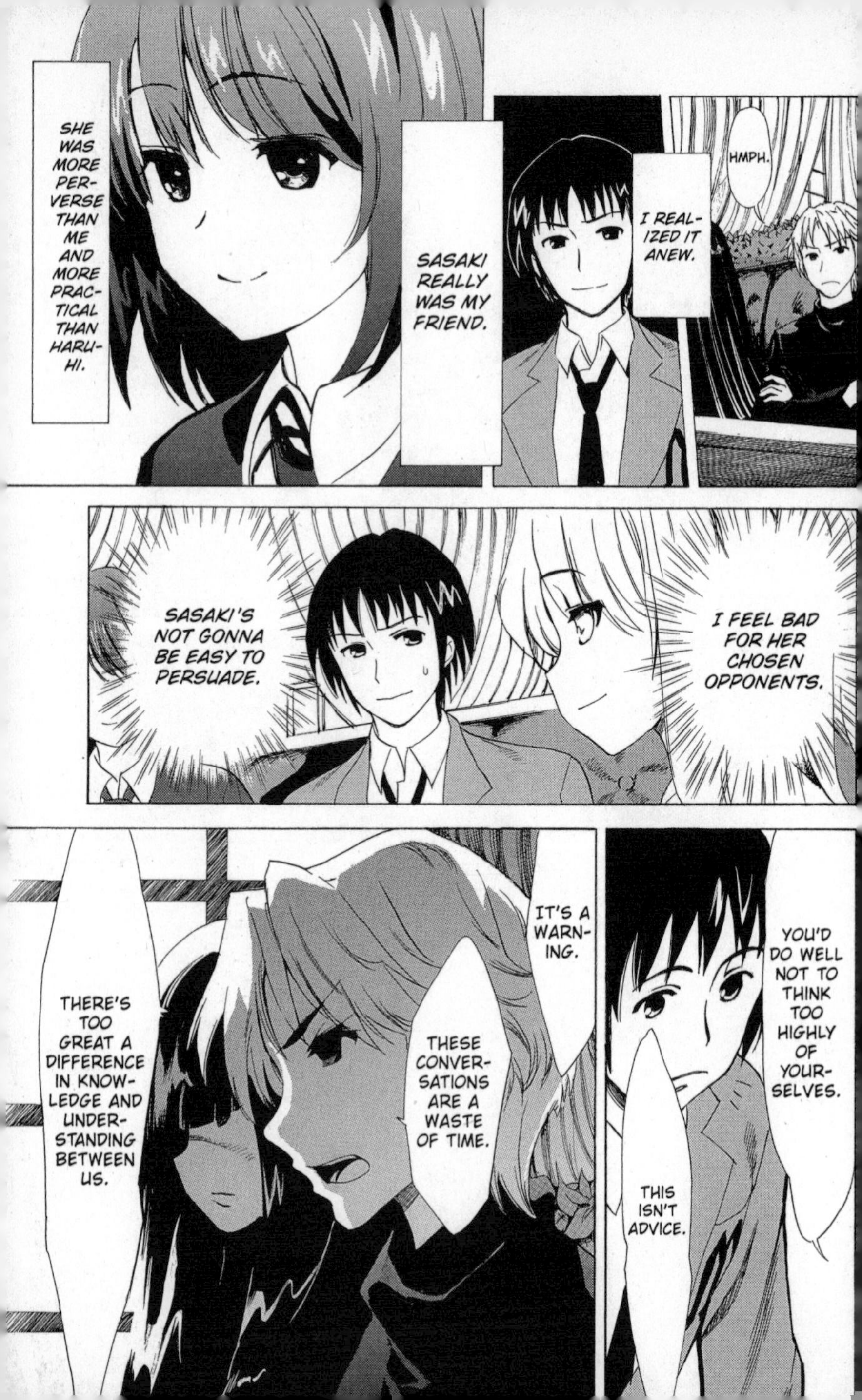
HMPH.
I REALIZED IT ANEW.
SASAKI REALLY WAS MY FRIEND.
SHE WAS MORE PERVERSE THAN ME AND MORE PRACTICAL THAN HARUHI.
I FEEL BAD FOR HER CHOSEN OPPONENTS.
SASAKI'S NOT GONNA BE EASY TO PERSUADE.
YOU'D DO WELL NOT TO THINK TOO HIGHLY OF YOURSELVES.
THIS ISN'T ADVICE.
IT'S A WARNING.
THESE CONVERSATIONS ARE A WASTE OF TIME.
THERE'S TOO GREAT A DIFFERENCE IN KNOWLEDGE AND UNDERSTANDING BETWEEN US.

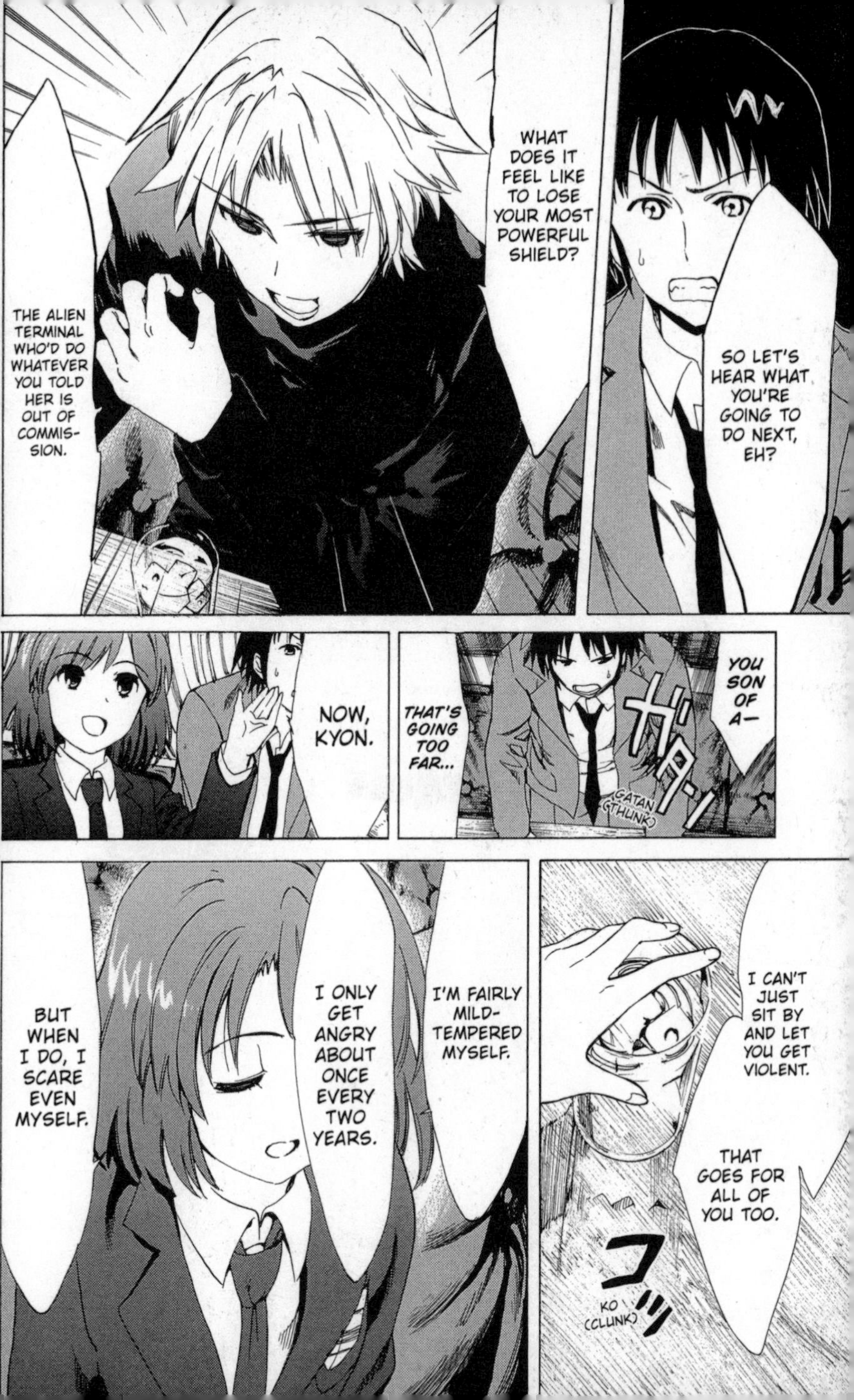

SO LET'S HEAR WHAT YOU'RE GOING TO DO NEXT, EH?
WHAT DOES IT FEEL LIKE TO LOSE YOUR MOST POWERFUL SHIELD?
THE ALIEN TERMINAL WHO'D DO WHATEVER YOU TOLD HER IS OUT OF COMMISSION.
YOU SON OF A—
GATAN (THUNK)
THAT'S GOING TOO FAR...
NOW, KYON.
I CAN'T JUST SIT BY AND LET YOU GET VIOLENT.
THAT GOES FOR ALL OF YOU TOO.
KO (CLUNK)
I'M FAIRLY MILD-TEMPERED MYSELF.
I ONLY GET ANGRY ABOUT ONCE EVERY TWO YEARS.
BUT WHEN I DO, I SCARE EVEN MYSELF.

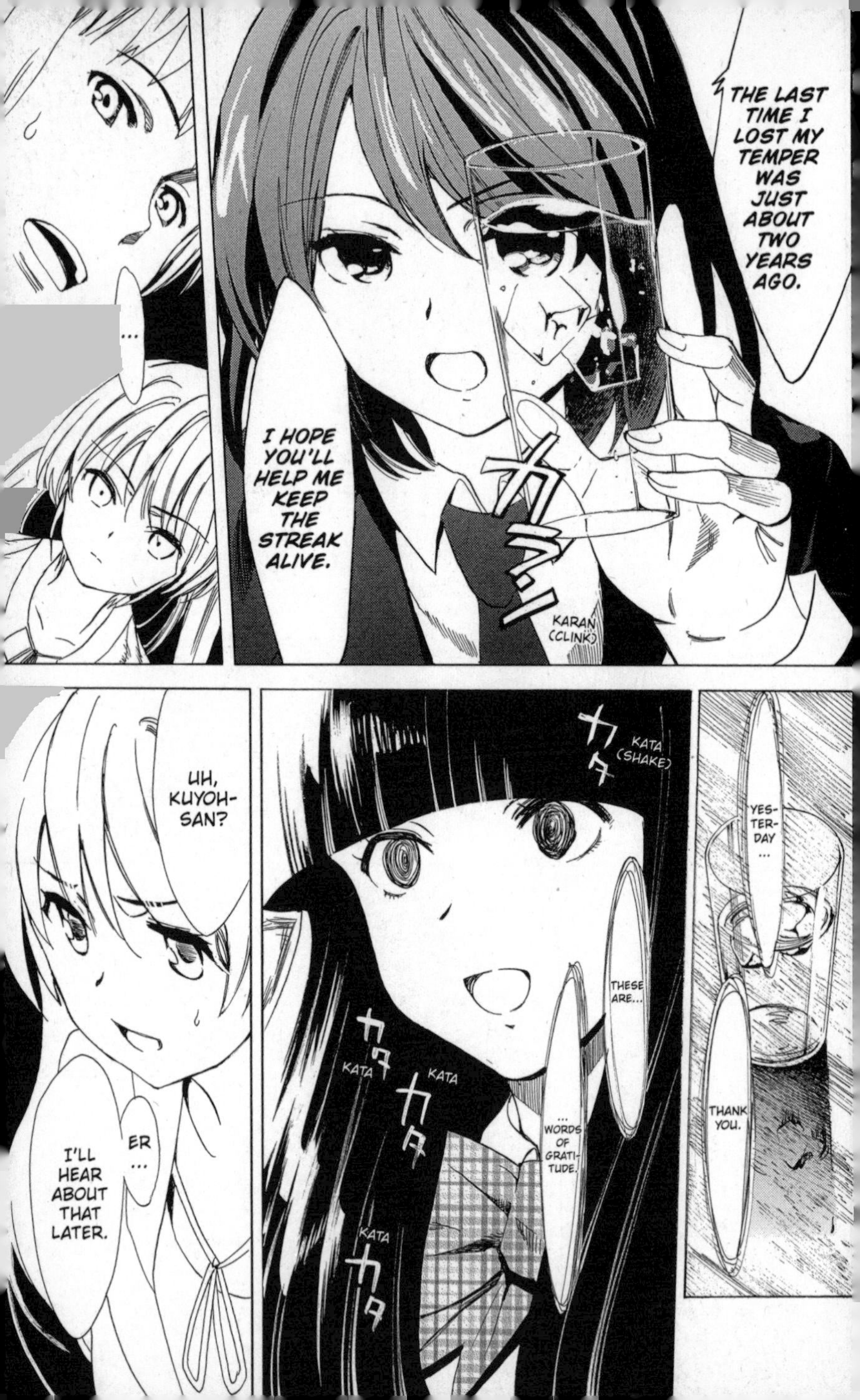
THE LAST TIME I LOST MY TEMPER WAS JUST ABOUT TWO YEARS AGO.
I HOPE YOU'LL HELP ME KEEP THE STREAK ALIVE.
KARAN (CLINK)
...
YES-TER-DAY...
THANK YOU.
KATA (SHAKE)
THESE ARE...
...WORDS OF GRATI-TUDE.
KATA
KATA
KATA
UH, KUYOH-SAN?
ER...
I'LL HEAR ABOUT THAT LATER.

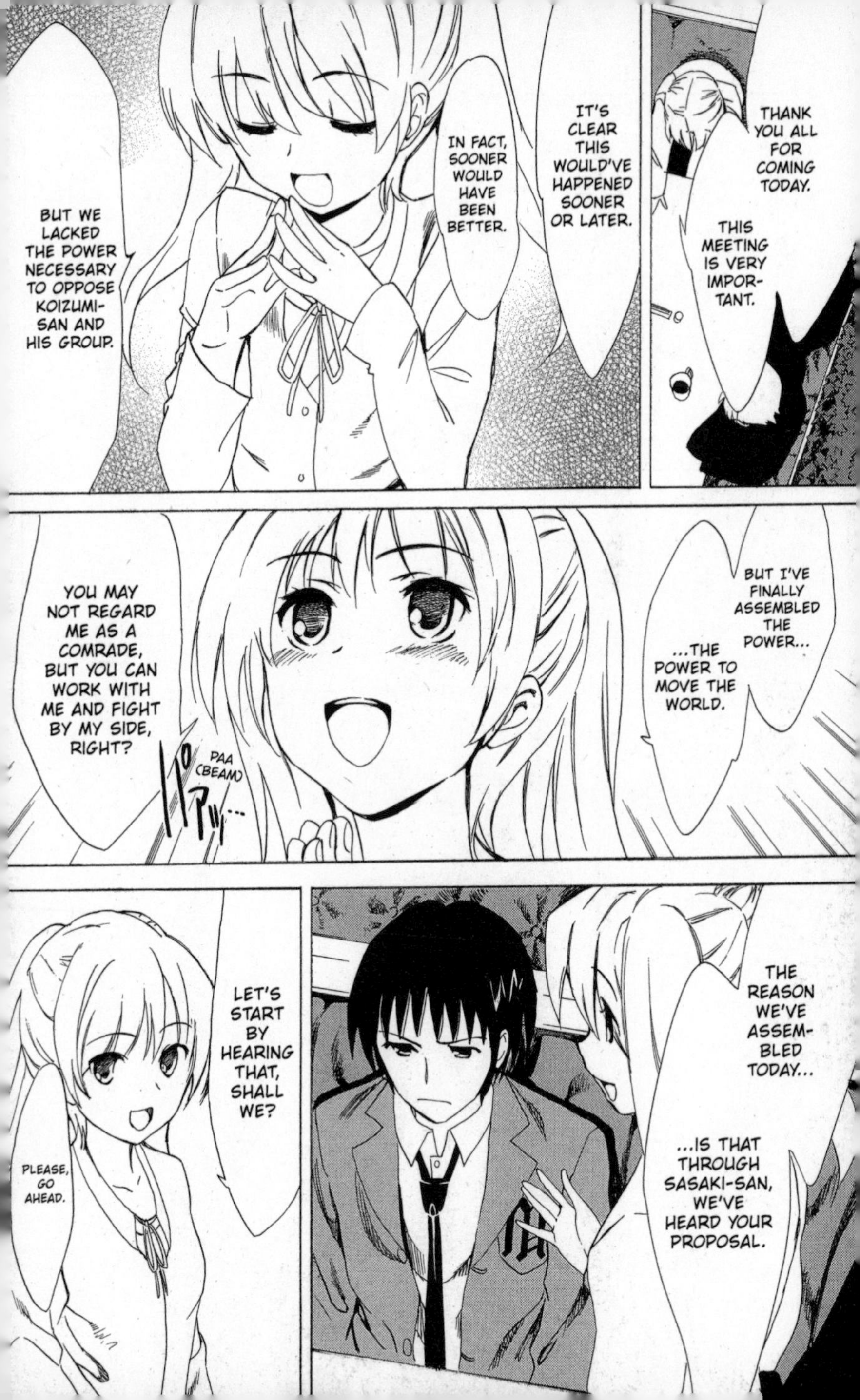
THANK YOU ALL FOR COMING TODAY.
THIS MEETING IS VERY IMPOR-TANT.
IT'S CLEAR THIS WOULD'VE HAPPENED SOONER OR LATER.
IN FACT, SOONER WOULD HAVE BEEN BETTER.
BUT WE LACKED THE POWER NECESSARY TO OPPOSE KOIZUMI-SAN AND HIS GROUP.
BUT I'VE FINALLY ASSEMBLED THE POWER...
...THE POWER TO MOVE THE WORLD.
PAA (BEAM)
YOU MAY NOT REGARD ME AS A COMRADE, BUT YOU CAN WORK WITH ME AND FIGHT BY MY SIDE, RIGHT?
THE REASON WE'VE ASSEM-BLED TODAY...
...IS THAT THROUGH SASAKI-SAN, WE'VE HEARD YOUR PROPOSAL.
LET'S START BY HEARING THAT, SHALL WE?
PLEASE, GO AHEAD.

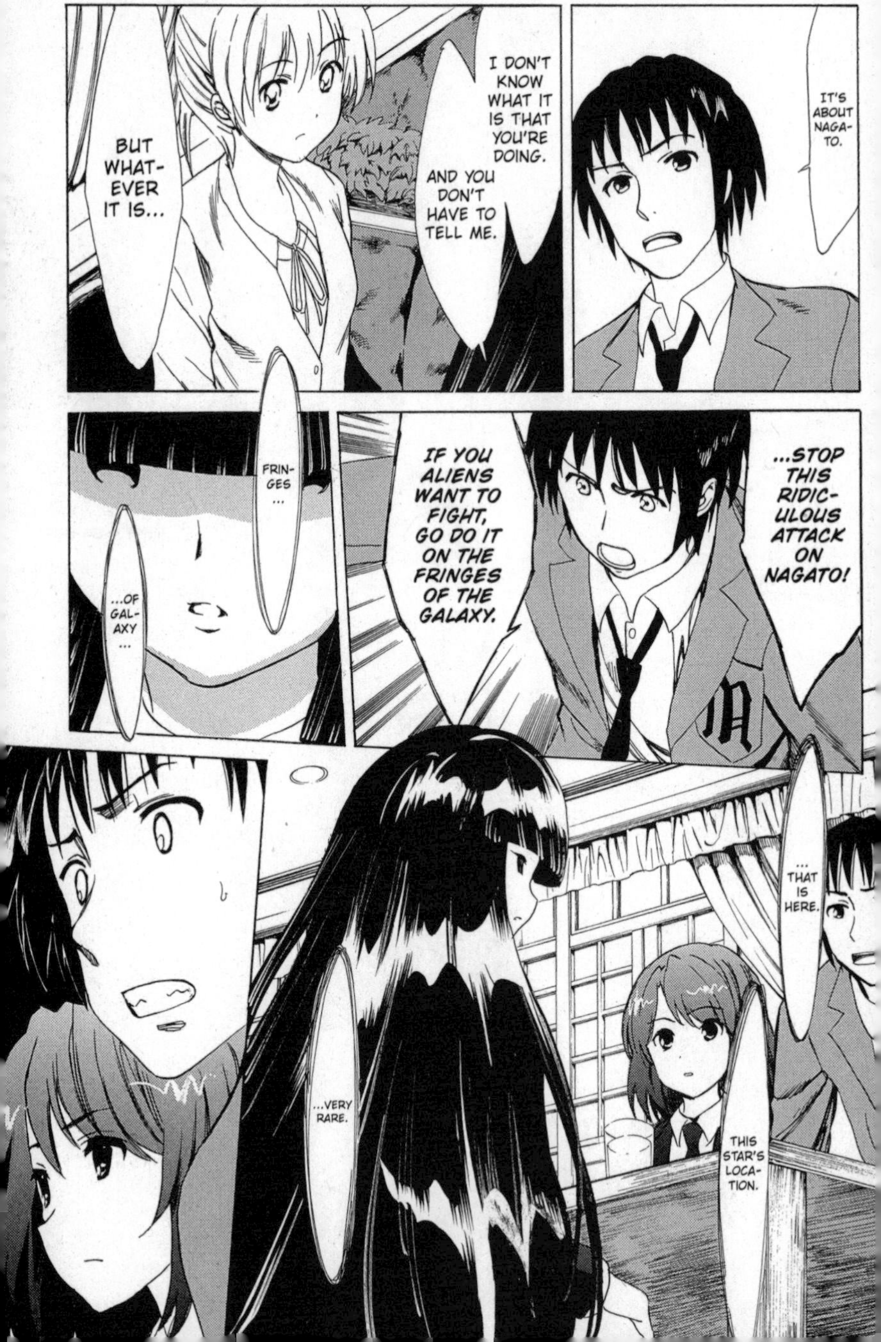
IT'S ABOUT NAGATO.
I DON'T KNOW WHAT IT IS THAT YOU'RE DOING.
AND YOU DON'T HAVE TO TELL ME.
BUT WHATEVER IT IS...
...STOP THIS RIDICULOUS ATTACK ON NAGATO!
IF YOU ALIENS WANT TO FIGHT, GO DO IT ON THE FRINGES OF THE GALAXY.
FRINGES...
...OF GALAXY...
...THAT IS HERE.
THIS STAR'S LOCATION.
...VERY RARE.

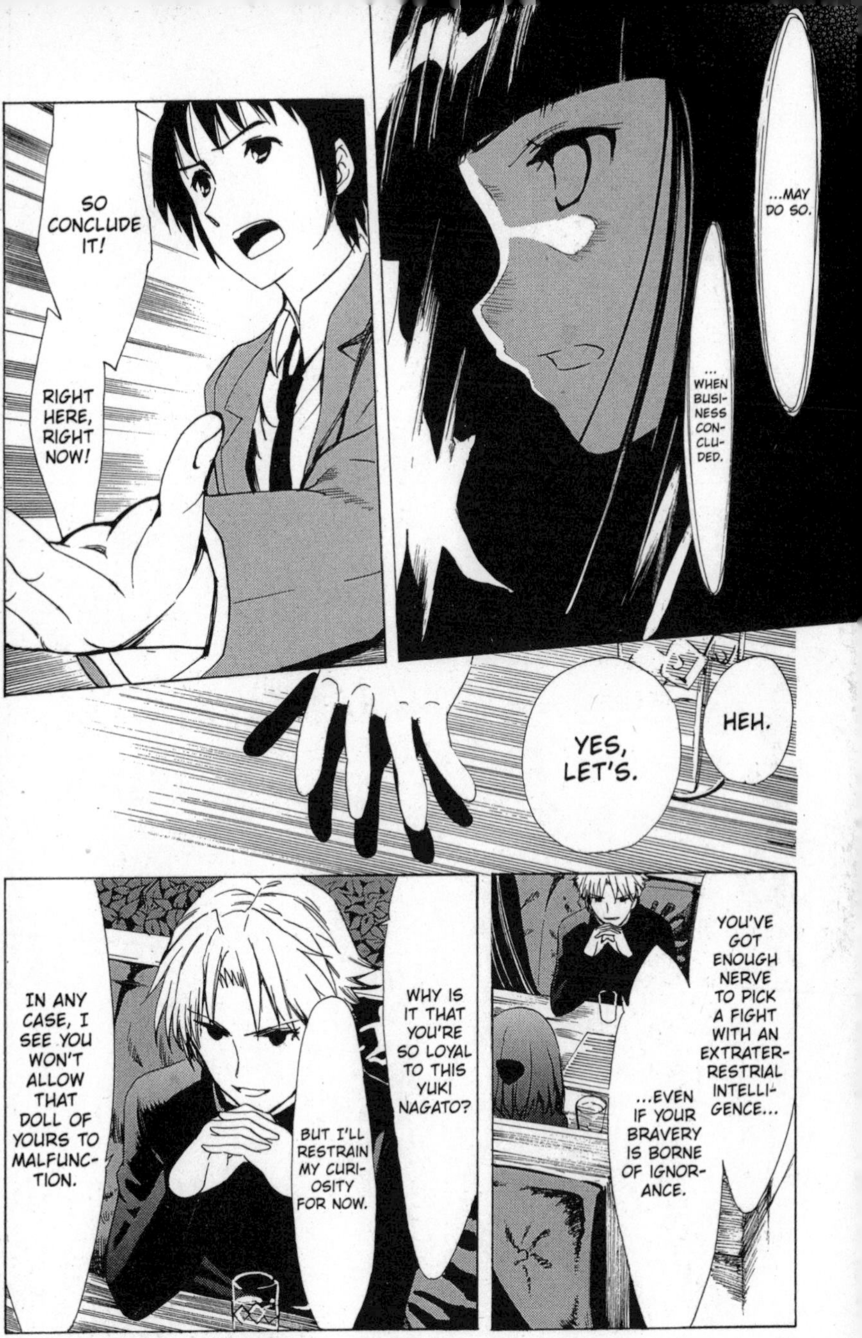
...MAY DO SO.
...WHEN BUSINESS CONCLUDED.
SO CONCLUDE IT!
RIGHT HERE, RIGHT NOW!
HEH.
YES, LET'S.
YOU'VE GOT ENOUGH NERVE TO PICK A FIGHT WITH AN EXTRATERRESTRIAL INTELLIGENCE...
...EVEN IF YOUR BRAVERY IS BORNE OF IGNORANCE.
WHY IS IT THAT YOU'RE SO LOYAL TO THIS YUKI NAGATO?
BUT I'LL RESTRAIN MY CURIOSITY FOR NOW.
IN ANY CASE, I SEE YOU WON'T ALLOW THAT DOLL OF YOURS TO MALFUNCTION.

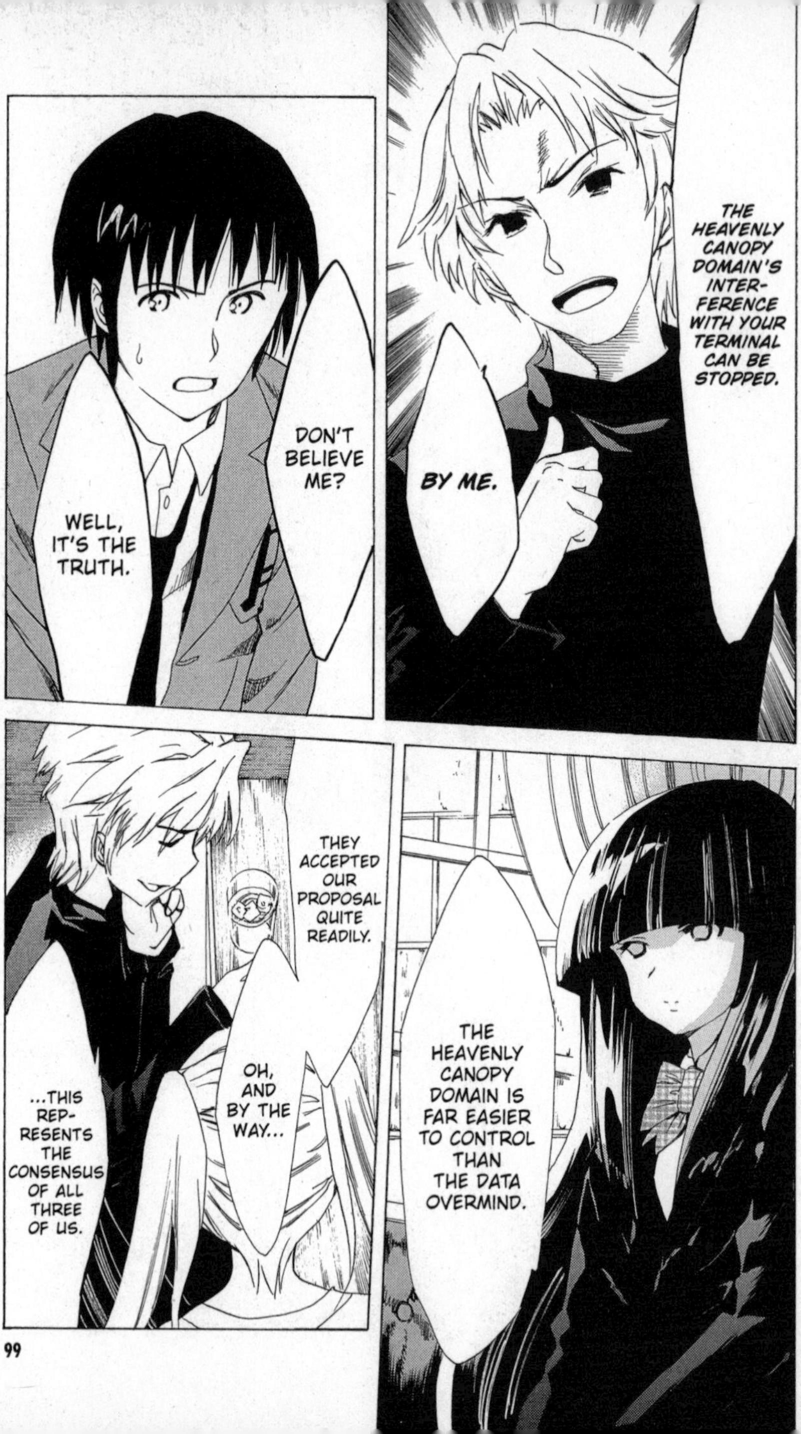
THE HEAVENLY CANOPY DOMAIN'S INTERFERENCE WITH YOUR TERMINAL CAN BE STOPPED.
BY ME.
DON'T BELIEVE ME?
WELL, IT'S THE TRUTH.
THE HEAVENLY CANOPY DOMAIN IS FAR EASIER TO CONTROL THAN THE DATA OVERMIND.
THEY ACCEPTED OUR PROPOSAL QUITE READILY.
OH, AND BY THE WAY...
...THIS REPRESENTS THE CONSENSUS OF ALL THREE OF US.

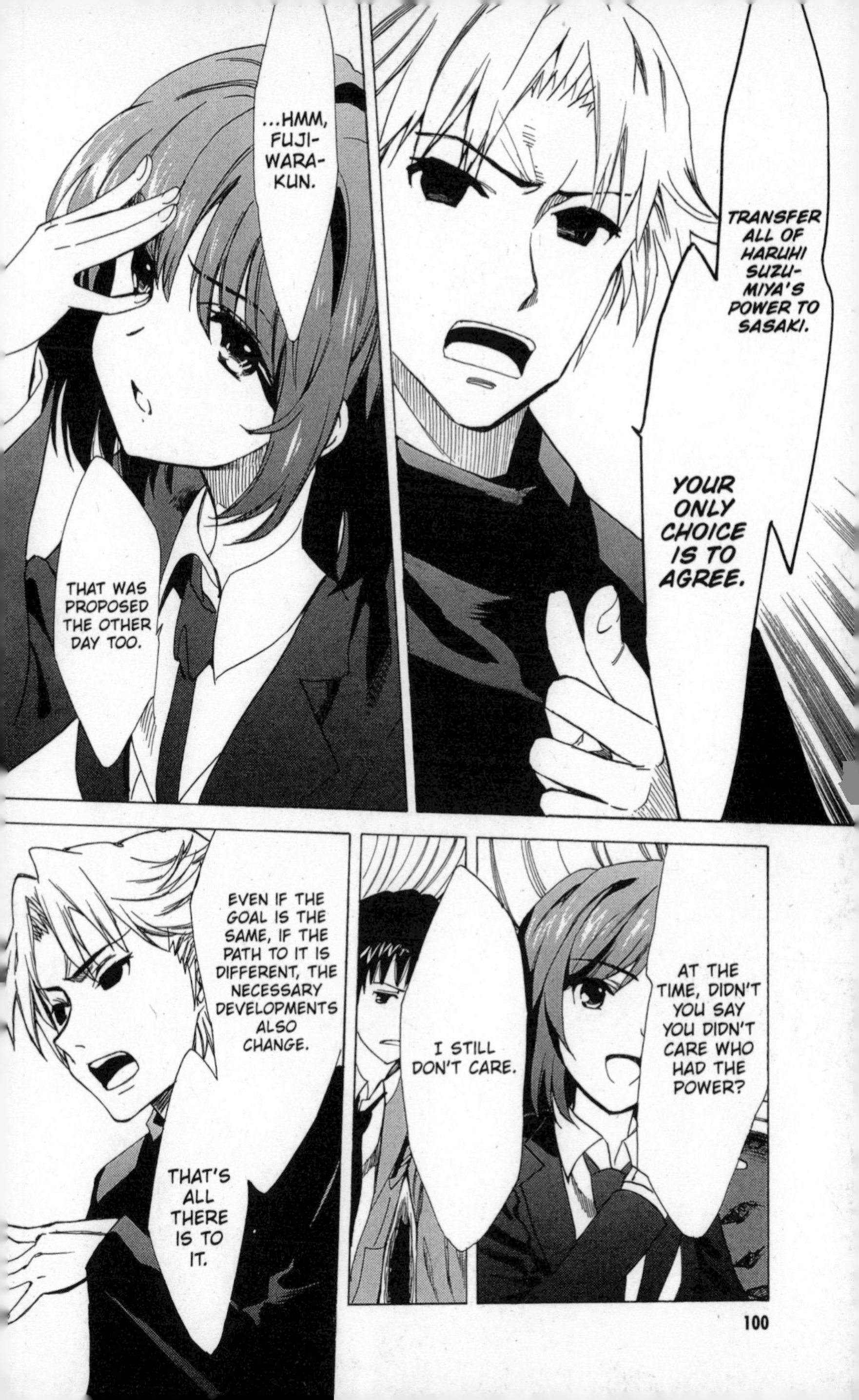
TRANSFER ALL OF HARUHI SUZUMIYA'S POWER TO SASAKI.
YOUR ONLY CHOICE IS TO AGREE.
...HMM, FUJIWARA-KUN.
THAT WAS PROPOSED THE OTHER DAY TOO.
AT THE TIME, DIDN'T YOU SAY YOU DIDN'T CARE WHO HAD THE POWER?
I STILL DON'T CARE.
EVEN IF THE GOAL IS THE SAME, IF THE PATH TO IT IS DIFFERENT, THE NECESSARY DEVELOPMENTS ALSO CHANGE.
THAT'S ALL THERE IS TO IT.

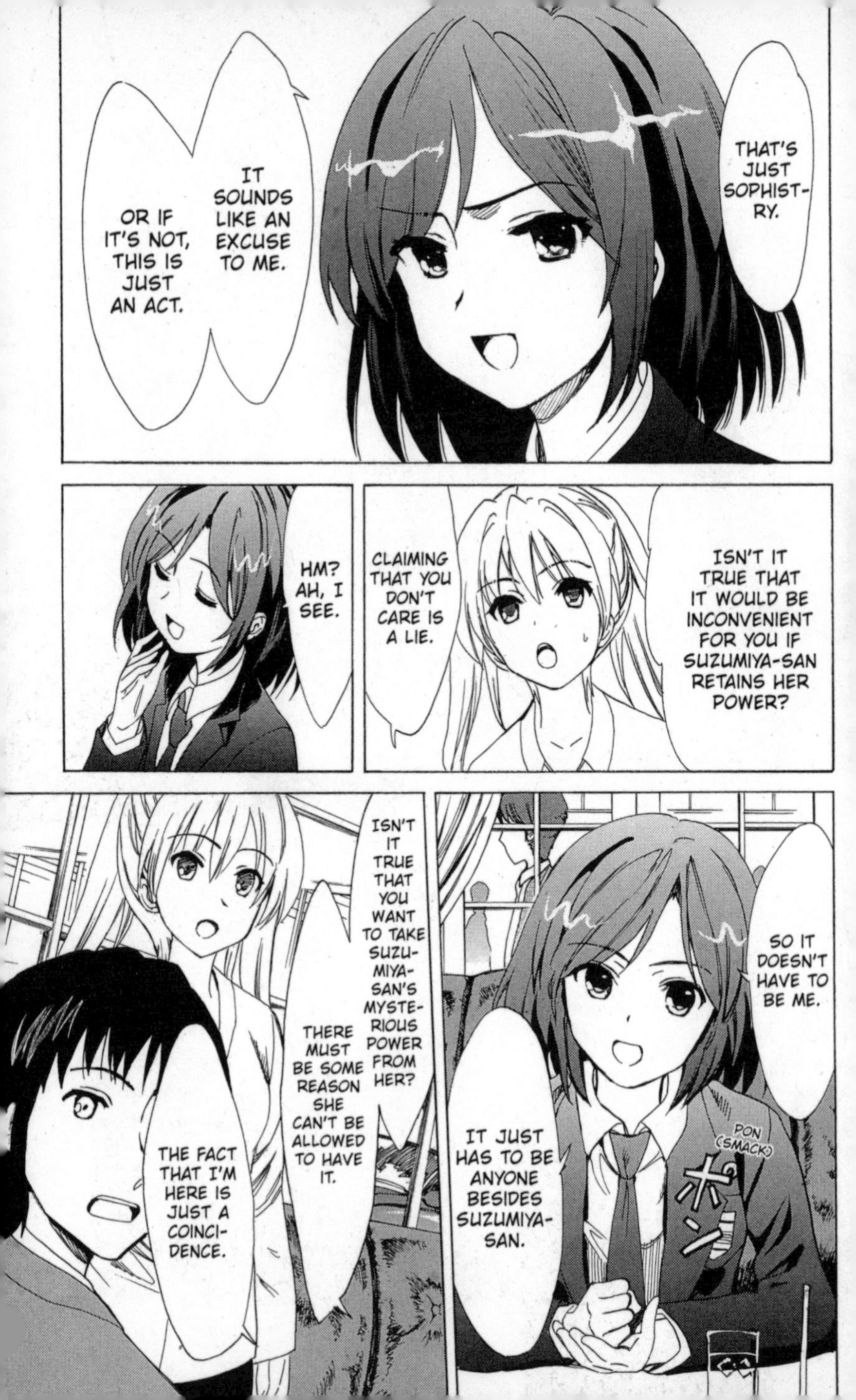
THAT'S JUST SOPHISTRY.
IT SOUNDS LIKE AN EXCUSE TO ME.
OR IF IT'S NOT, THIS IS JUST AN ACT.
ISN'T IT TRUE THAT IT WOULD BE INCONVENIENT FOR YOU IF SUZUMIYA-SAN RETAINS HER POWER?
CLAIMING THAT YOU DON'T CARE IS A LIE.
HM? AH, I SEE.
SO IT DOESN'T HAVE TO BE ME.
PON (SMACK)
IT JUST HAS TO BE ANYONE BESIDES SUZUMIYA-SAN.
ISN'T IT TRUE THAT YOU WANT TO TAKE SUZUMIYA-SAN'S MYSTERIOUS POWER FROM HER?
THERE MUST BE SOME REASON SHE CAN'T BE ALLOWED TO HAVE IT.
THE FACT THAT I'M HERE IS JUST A COINCIDENCE.

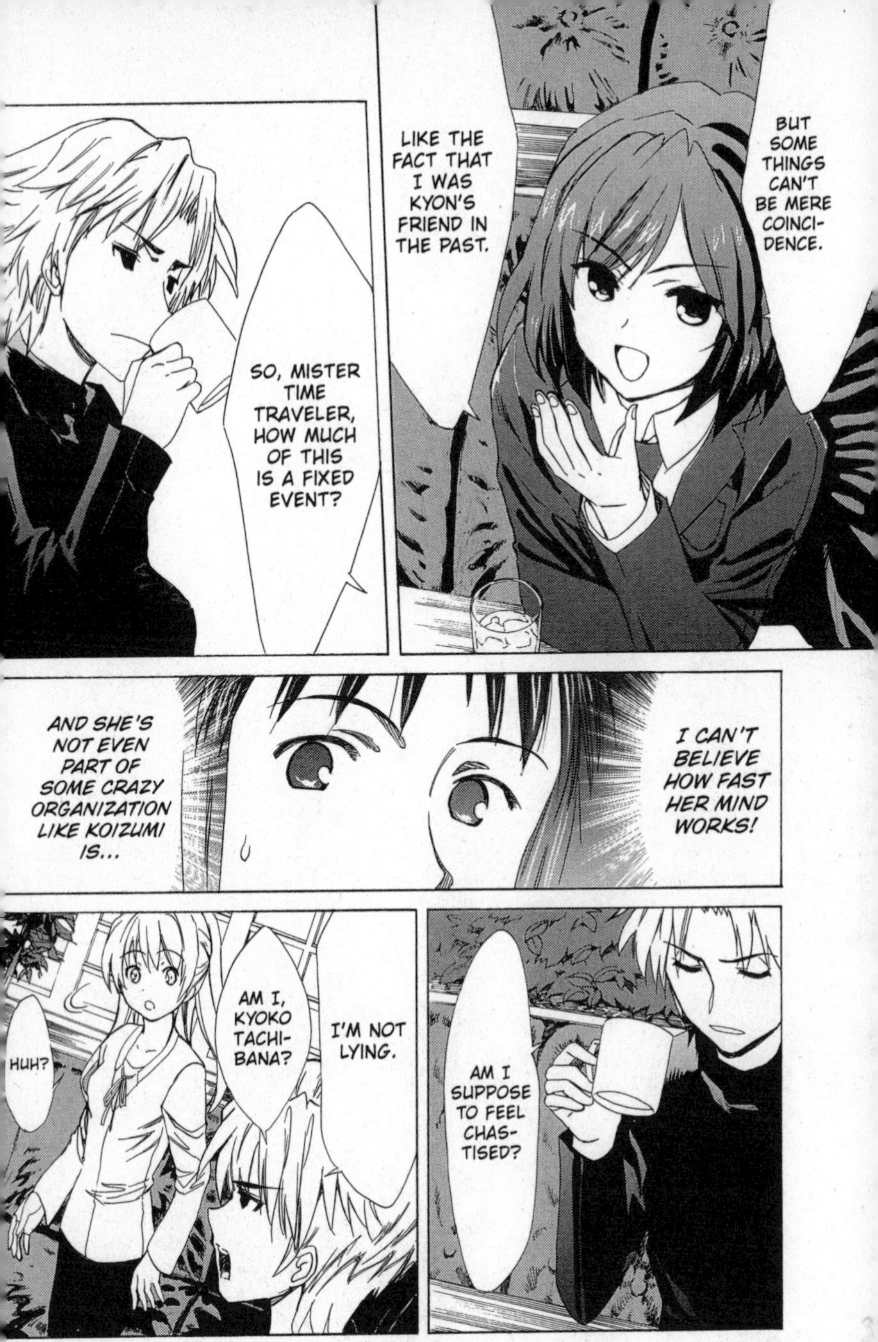
BUT SOME THINGS CAN'T BE MERE COINCIDENCE.
LIKE THE FACT THAT I WAS KYON'S FRIEND IN THE PAST.
SO, MISTER TIME TRAVELER, HOW MUCH OF THIS IS A FIXED EVENT?
I CAN'T BELIEVE HOW FAST HER MIND WORKS!
AND SHE'S NOT EVEN PART OF SOME CRAZY ORGANIZATION LIKE KOIZUMI IS...
AM I SUPPOSE TO FEEL CHASTISED?
I'M NOT LYING.
AM I, KYOKO TACHIBANA?
HUH?

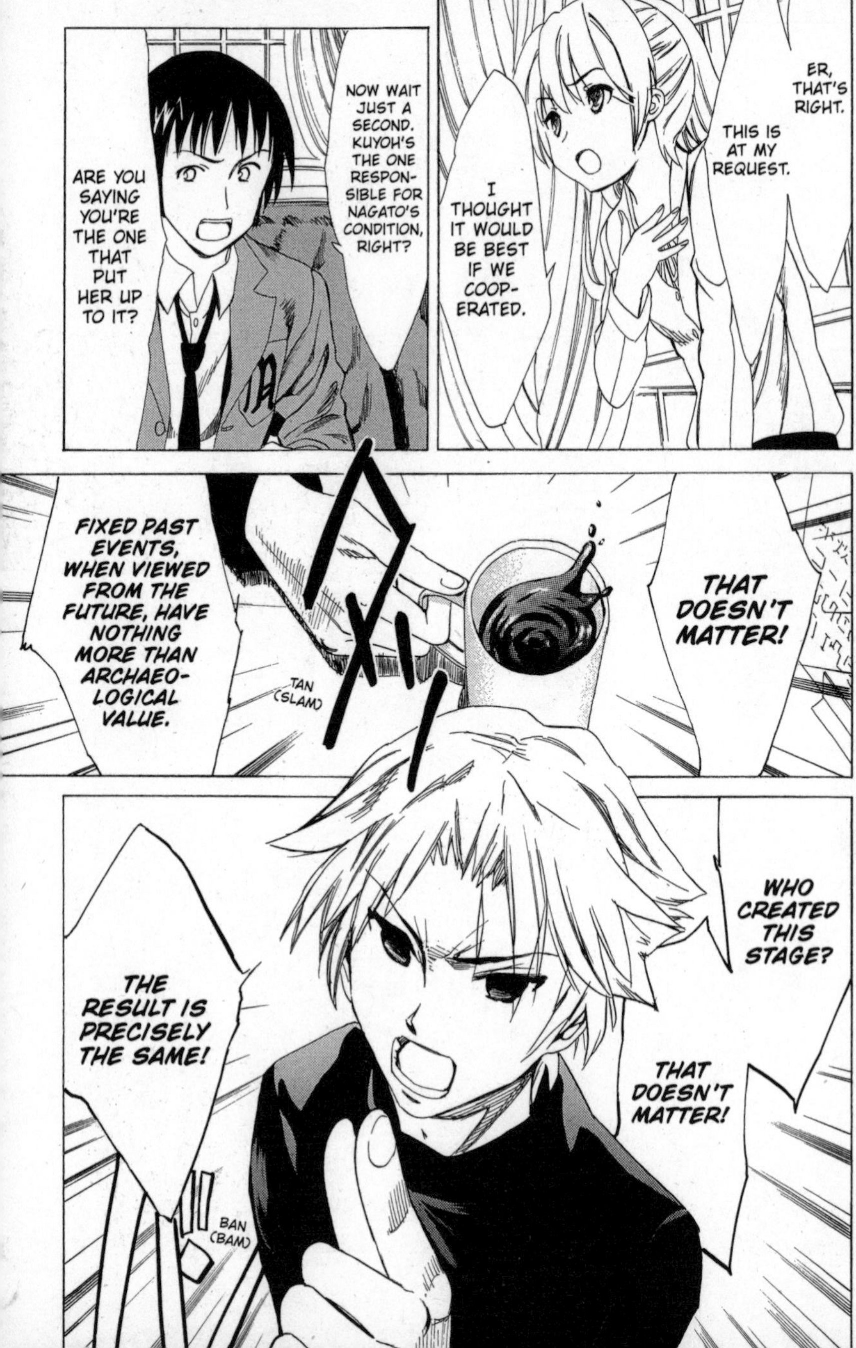
ER, THAT'S RIGHT.
THIS IS AT MY REQUEST.
I THOUGHT IT WOULD BE BEST IF WE COOPERATED.
NOW WAIT JUST A SECOND. KUYOH'S THE ONE RESPONSIBLE FOR NAGATO'S CONDITION, RIGHT?
ARE YOU SAYING YOU'RE THE ONE THAT PUT HER UP TO IT?
THAT DOESN'T MATTER!
TAN (SLAM)
FIXED PAST EVENTS, WHEN VIEWED FROM THE FUTURE, HAVE NOTHING MORE THAN ARCHAEOLOGICAL VALUE.
WHO CREATED THIS STAGE?
THAT DOESN'T MATTER!
THE RESULT IS PRECISELY THE SAME!
BAN (BAM)

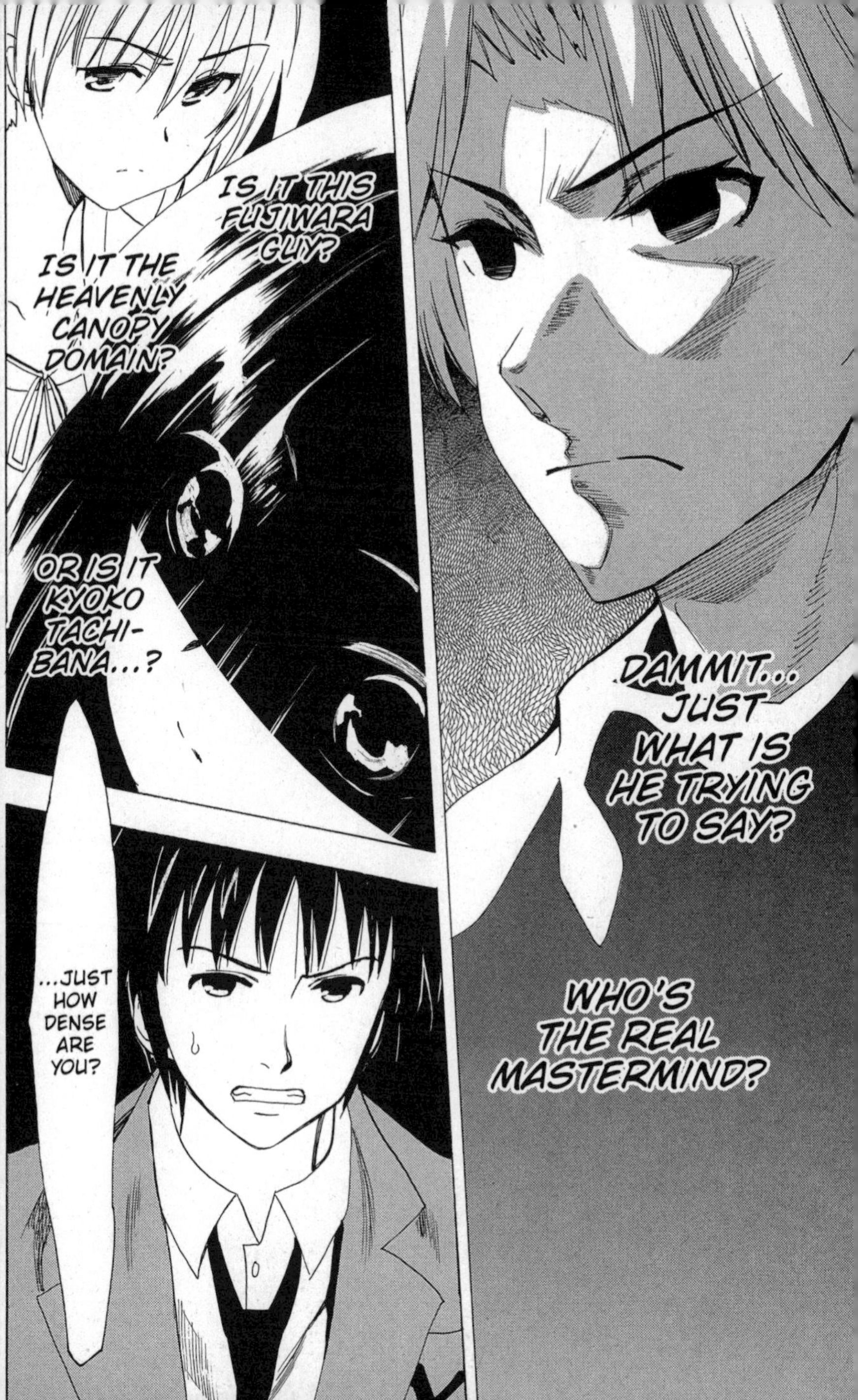
DAMMIT... JUST WHAT IS HE TRYING TO SAY?
WHO'S THE REAL MASTERMIND?
IS IT THIS FUJIWARA GUY?
IS IT THE HEAVENLY CANOPY DOMAIN?
OR IS IT KYOKO TACHIBANA...?
...JUST HOW DENSE ARE YOU?

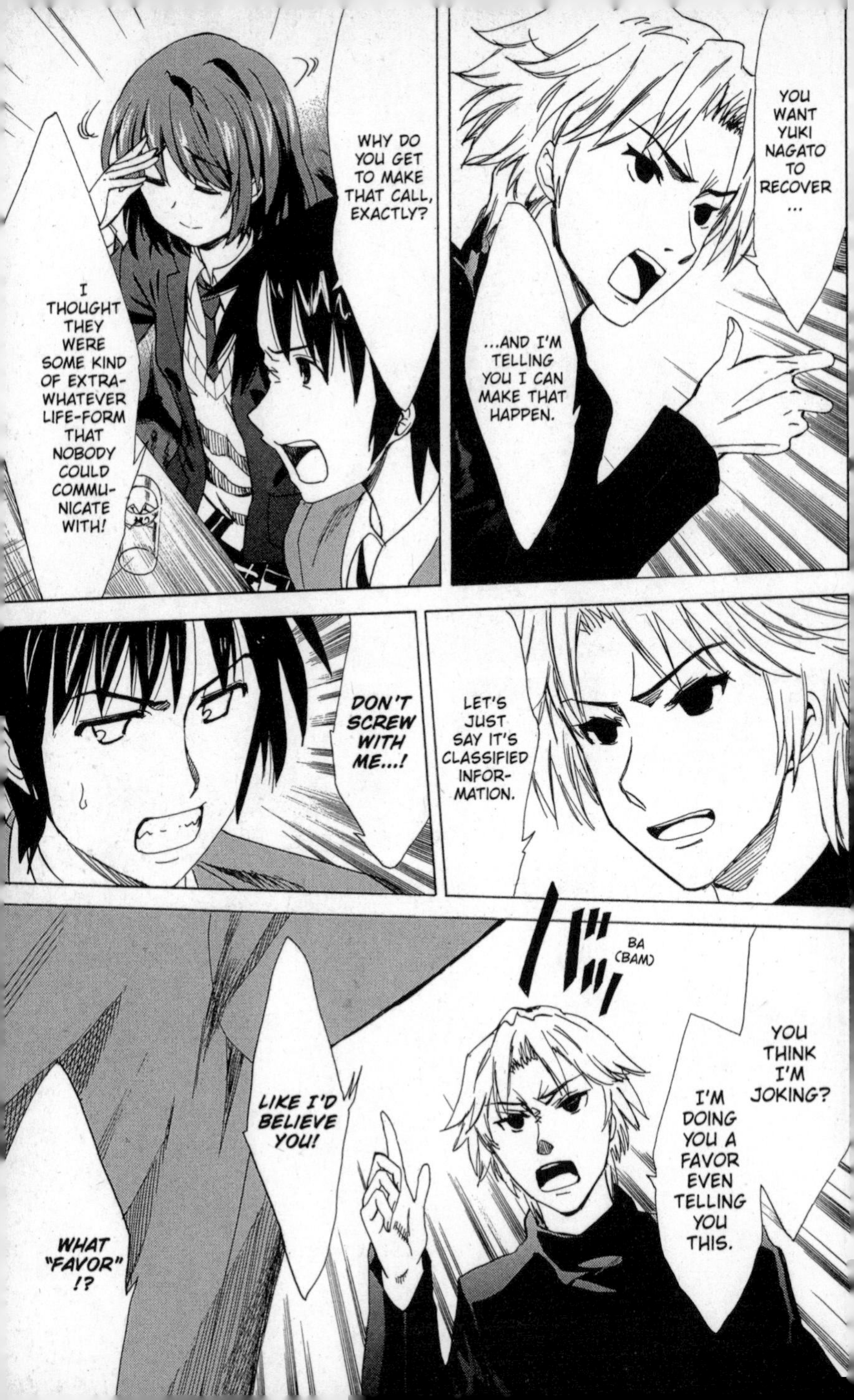
YOU WANT YUKI NAGATO TO RECOVER ...
...AND I'M TELLING YOU I CAN MAKE THAT HAPPEN.
WHY DO YOU GET TO MAKE THAT CALL, EXACTLY?
I THOUGHT THEY WERE SOME KIND OF EXTRA-WHATEVER LIFE-FORM THAT NOBODY COULD COMMUNICATE WITH!
LET'S JUST SAY IT'S CLASSIFIED INFORMATION.
DON'T SCREW WITH ME...!
BA (BAM)
YOU THINK I'M JOKING?
I'M DOING YOU A FAVOR EVEN TELLING YOU THIS.
LIKE I'D BELIEVE YOU!
WHAT "FAVOR"!?

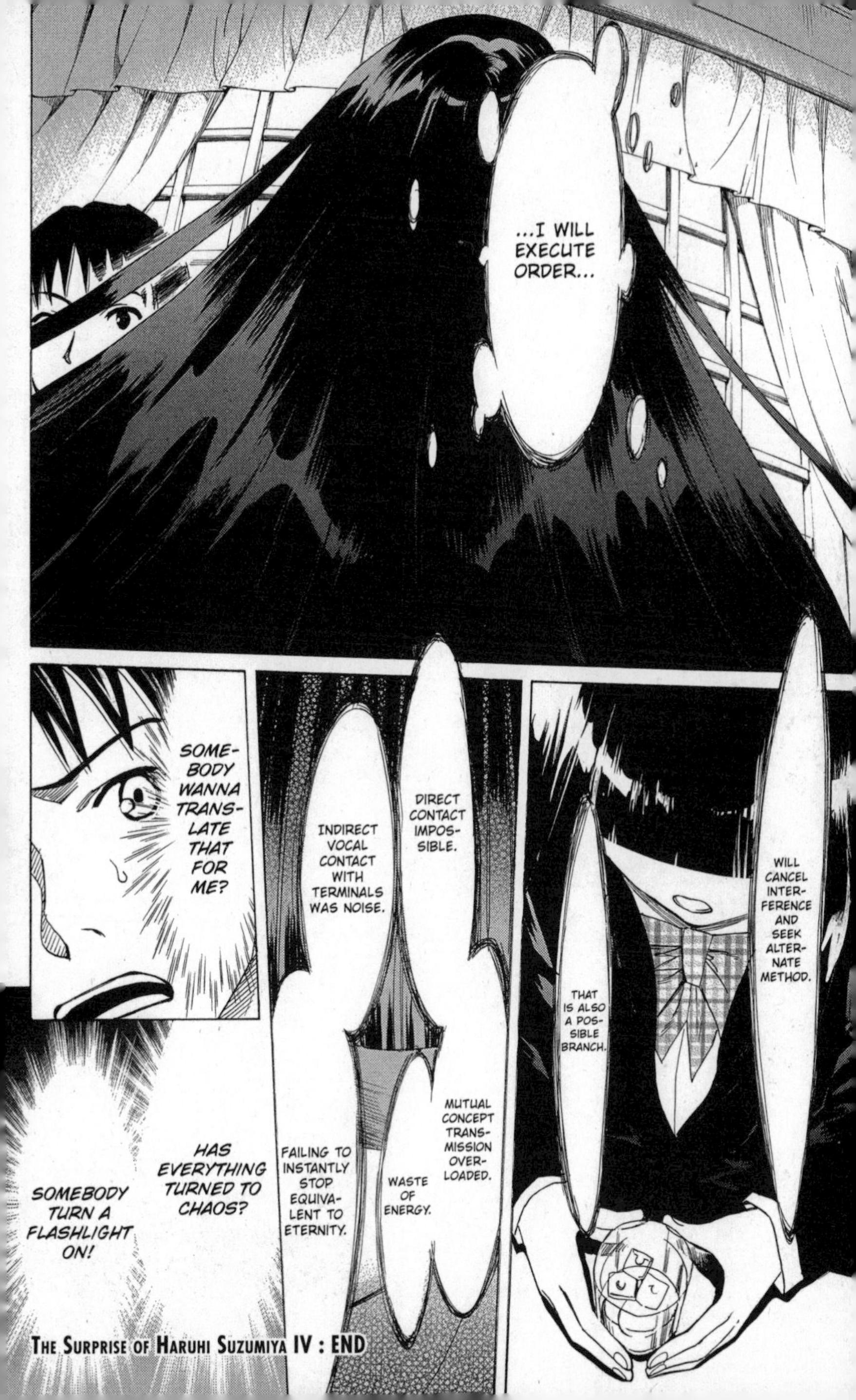
...I WILL EXECUTE ORDER...
WILL CANCEL INTERFERENCE AND SEEK ALTERNATE METHOD.
THAT IS ALSO A POSSIBLE BRANCH.
DIRECT CONTACT IMPOSSIBLE.
INDIRECT VOCAL CONTACT WITH TERMINALS WAS NOISE.
MUTUAL CONCEPT TRANSMISSION OVERLOADED.
WASTE OF ENERGY.
FAILING TO INSTANTLY STOP EQUIVALENT TO ETERNITY.
SOMEBODY WANNA TRANSLATE THAT FOR ME?
HAS EVERYTHING TURNED TO CHAOS?
SOMEBODY TURN A FLASHLIGHT ON!
THE SURPRISE OF HARUHI SUZUMIYA IV : END

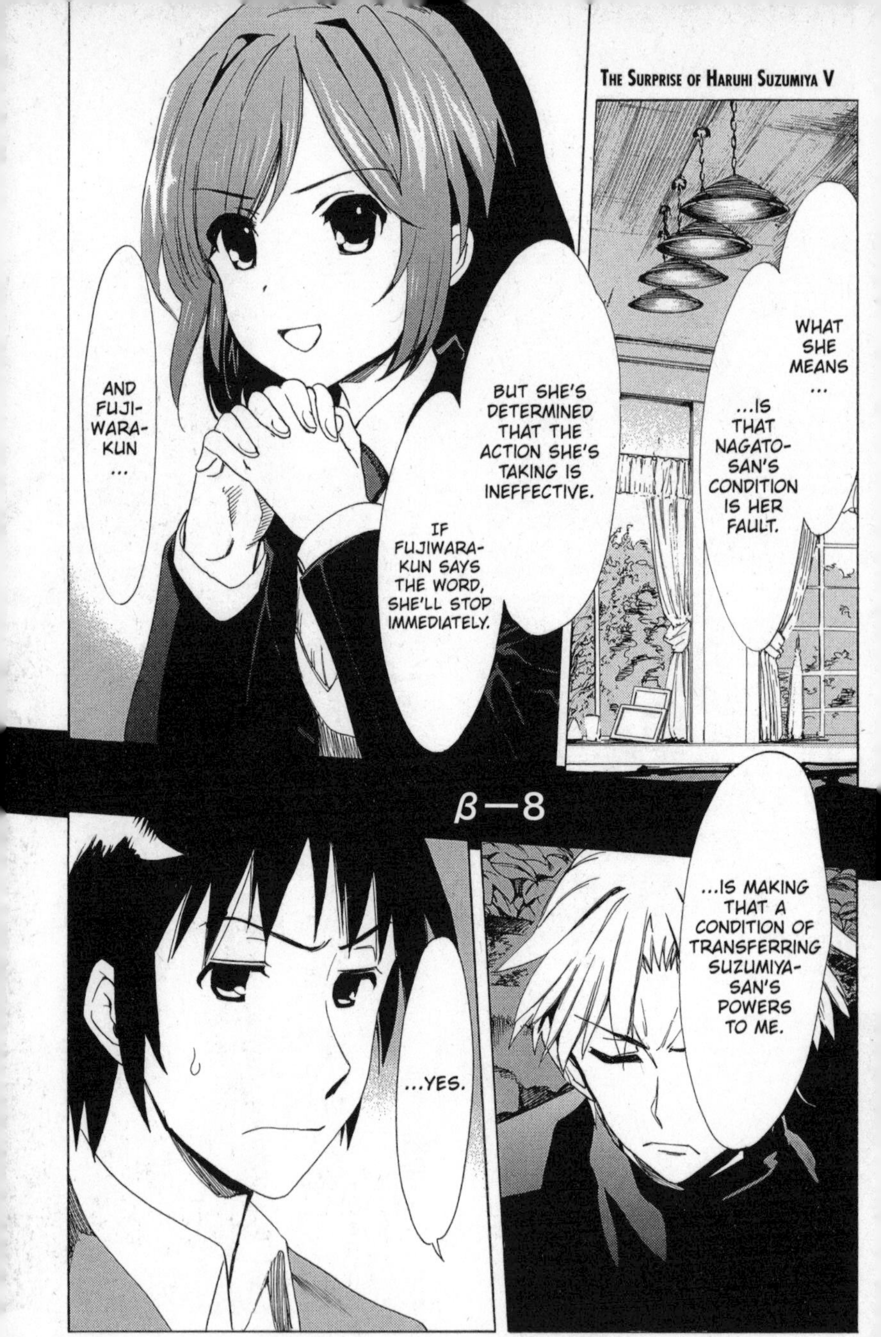
What she means...
...is that Nagato-san's condition is her fault.
But she's determined that the action she's taking is ineffective.
If Fujiwara-kun says the word, she'll stop immediately.
And Fujiwara-kun...
β—8
...is making that a condition of transferring Suzumiya-san's powers to me.
...Yes.

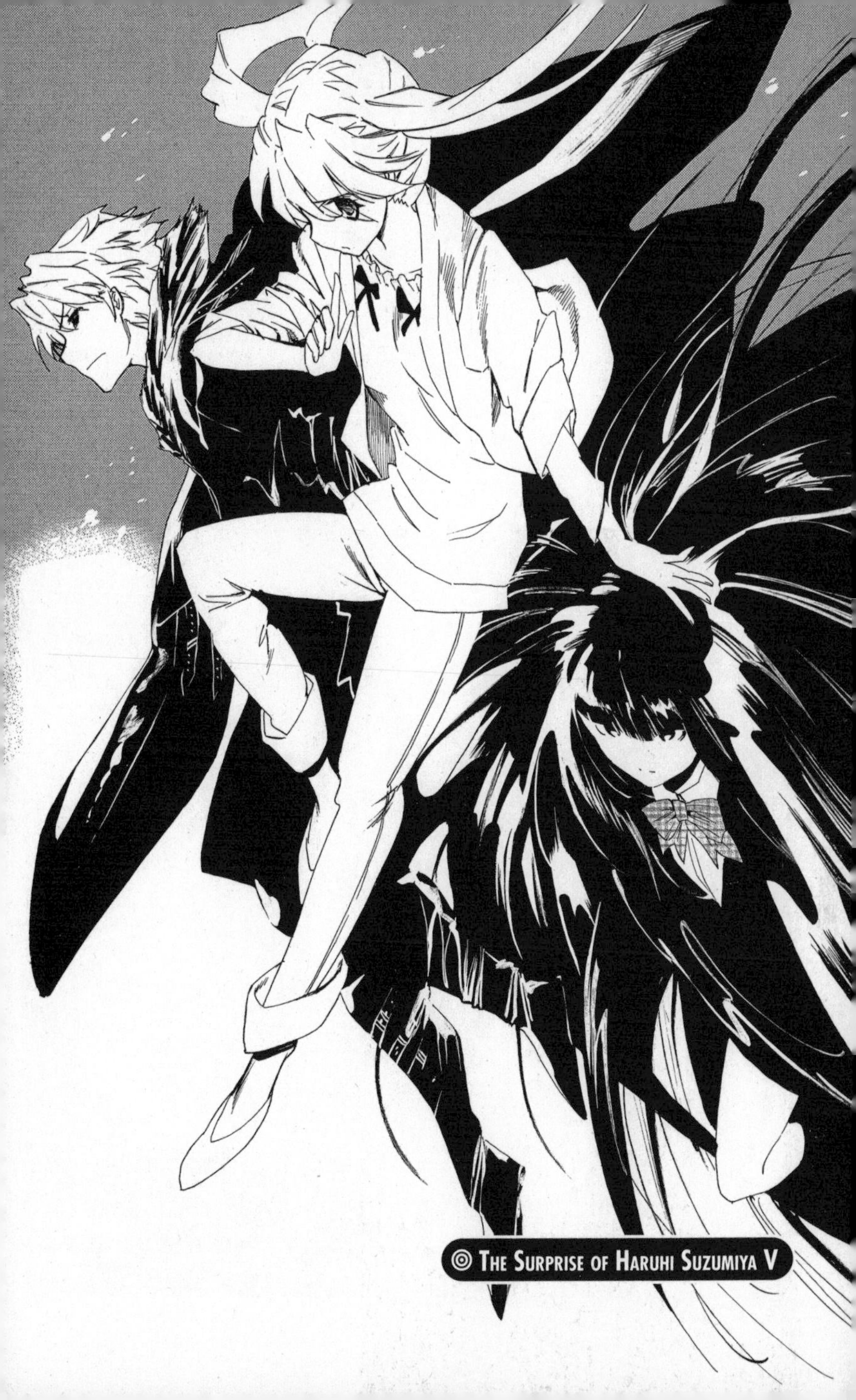
◎ The Surprise of Haruhi Suzumiya V

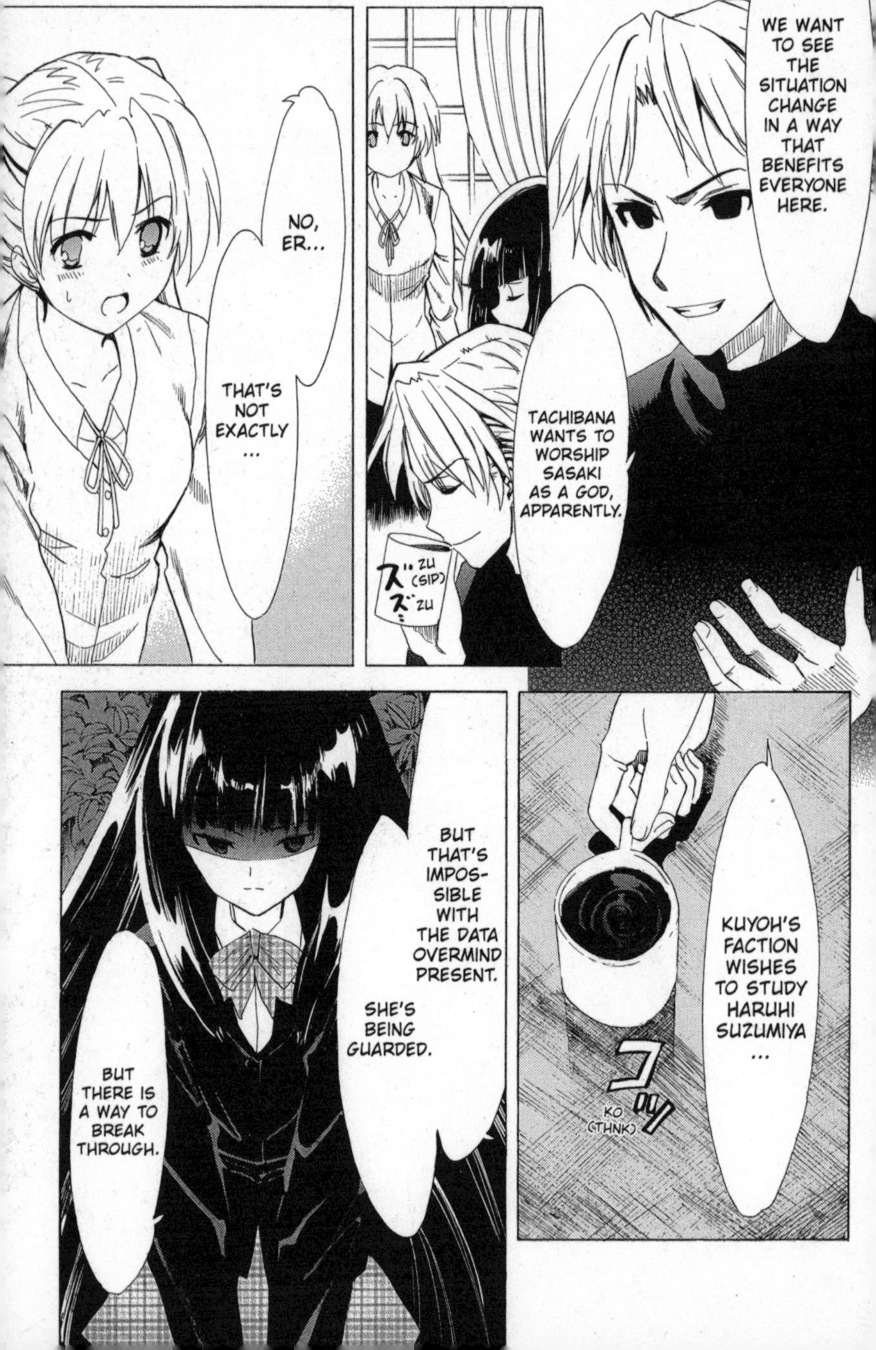
WE WANT TO SEE THE SITUATION CHANGE IN A WAY THAT BENEFITS EVERYONE HERE.
TACHIBANA WANTS TO WORSHIP SASAKI AS A GOD, APPARENTLY.
ZU ZU (SIP)
NO, ER...
THAT'S NOT EXACTLY ...
KUYOH'S FACTION WISHES TO STUDY HARUHI SUZUMIYA ...
KO (THNK)
BUT THAT'S IMPOSSIBLE WITH THE DATA OVERMIND PRESENT.
SHE'S BEING GUARDED.
BUT THERE IS A WAY TO BREAK THROUGH.

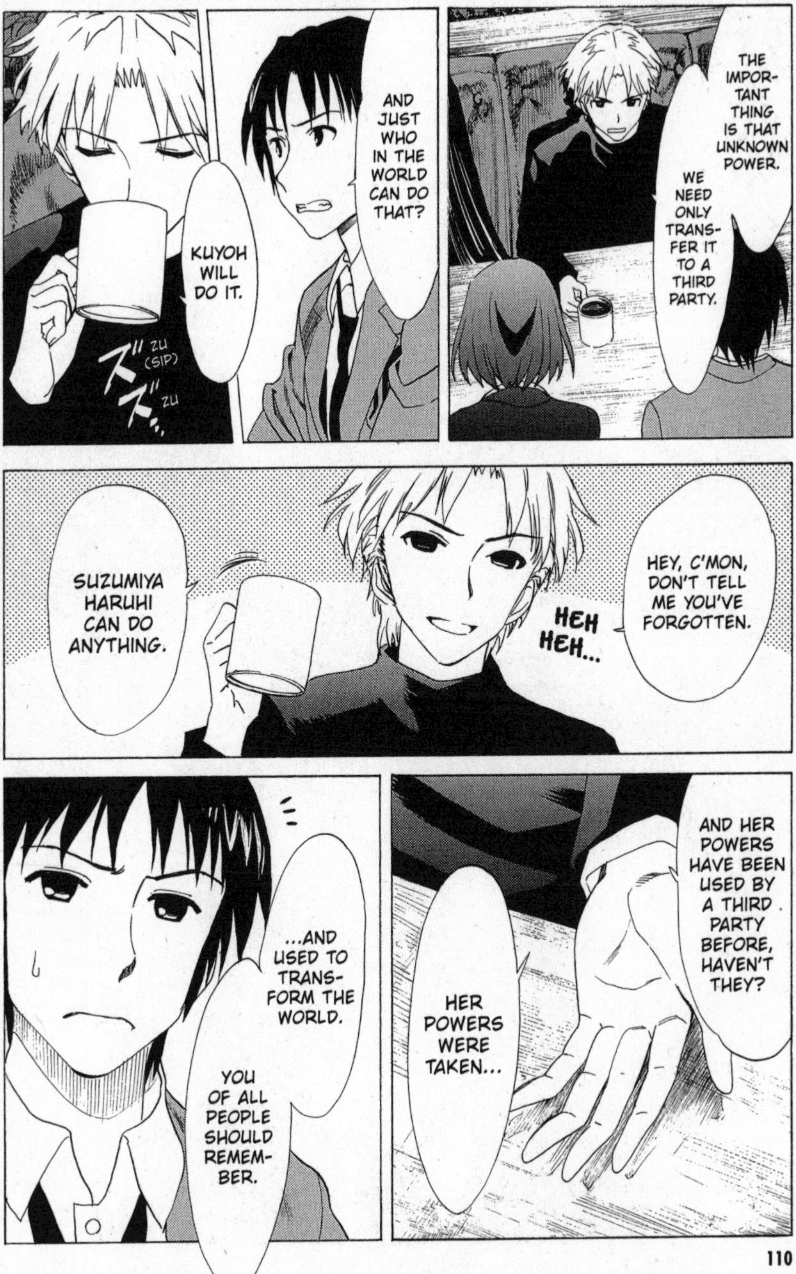
THE IMPORTANT THING IS THAT UNKNOWN POWER.
WE NEED ONLY TRANSFER IT TO A THIRD PARTY.
AND JUST WHO IN THE WORLD CAN DO THAT?
KUYOH WILL DO IT.
ZU (SIP)
ZU
HEY, C'MON, DON'T TELL ME YOU'VE FORGOTTEN.
HEH HEH...
SUZUMIYA HARUHI CAN DO ANYTHING.
AND HER POWERS HAVE BEEN USED BY A THIRD PARTY BEFORE, HAVEN'T THEY?
HER POWERS WERE TAKEN...
...AND USED TO TRANSFORM THE WORLD.
YOU OF ALL PEOPLE SHOULD REMEMBER.

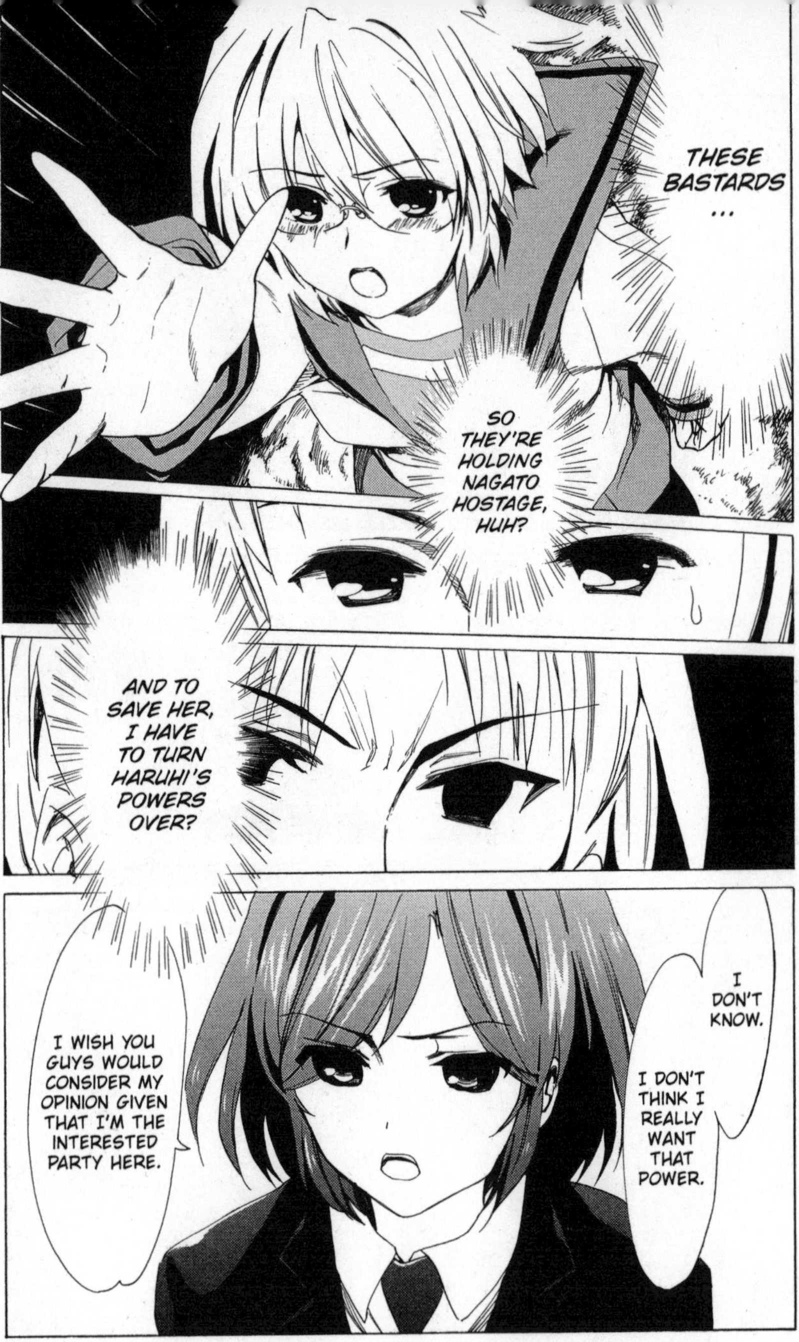
THESE BASTARDS...
SO THEY'RE HOLDING NAGATO HOSTAGE, HUH?
AND TO SAVE HER, I HAVE TO TURN HARUHI'S POWERS OVER?
I DON'T KNOW.
I DON'T THINK I REALLY WANT THAT POWER.
I WISH YOU GUYS WOULD CONSIDER MY OPINION GIVEN THAT I'M THE INTERESTED PARTY HERE.

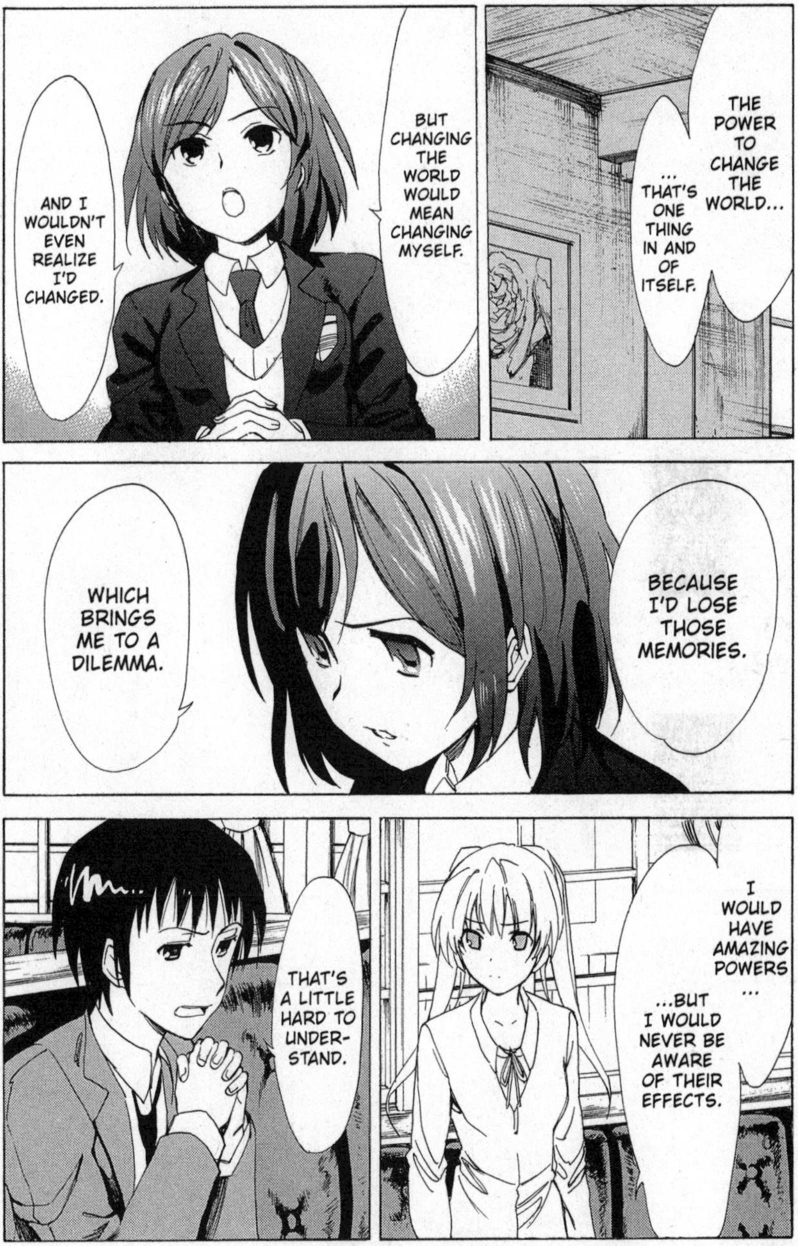
THE POWER TO CHANGE THE WORLD...
...THAT'S ONE THING IN AND OF ITSELF.
BUT CHANGING THE WORLD WOULD MEAN CHANGING MYSELF.
AND I WOULDN'T EVEN REALIZE I'D CHANGED.
BECAUSE I'D LOSE THOSE MEMORIES.
WHICH BRINGS ME TO A DILEMMA.
I WOULD HAVE AMAZING POWERS ...
...BUT I WOULD NEVER BE AWARE OF THEIR EFFECTS.
Mm...
THAT'S A LITTLE HARD TO UNDER-STAND.

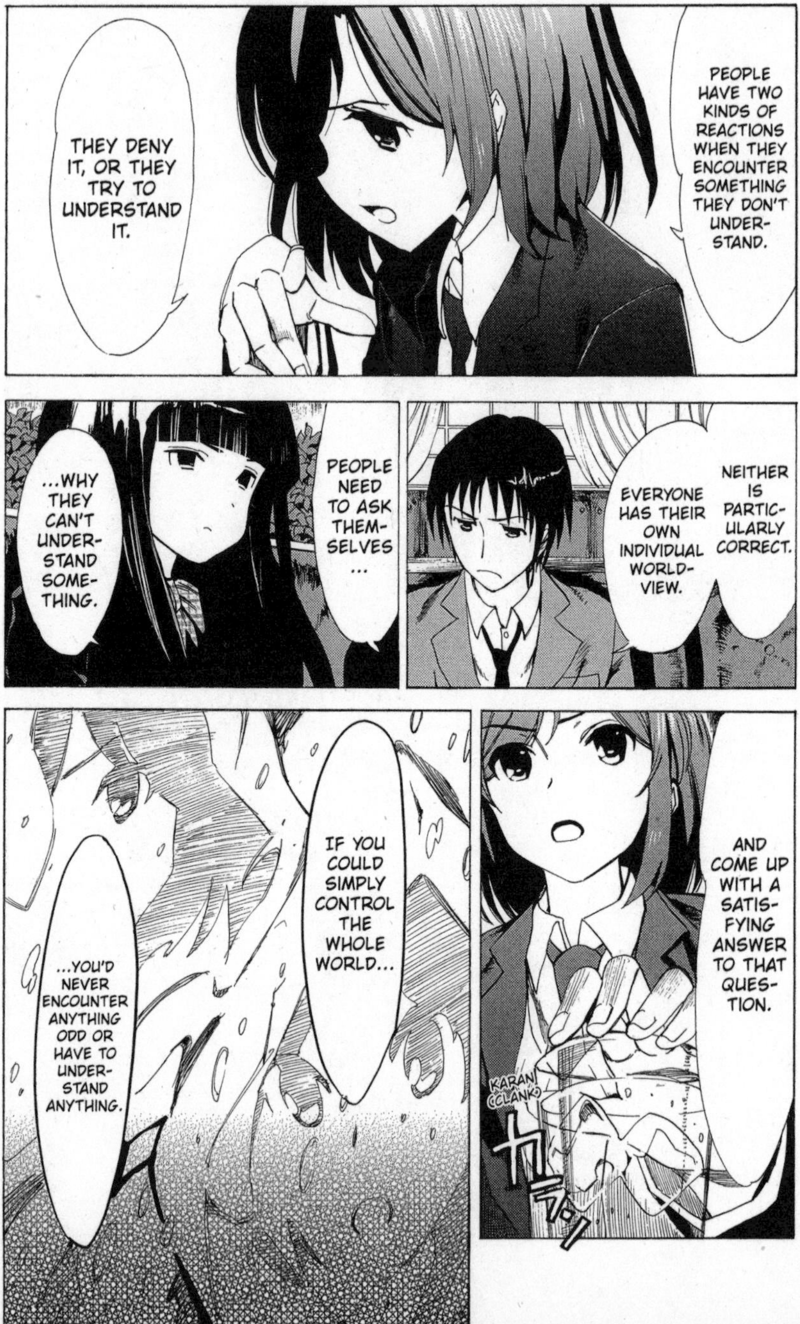
PEOPLE HAVE TWO KINDS OF REACTIONS WHEN THEY ENCOUNTER SOMETHING THEY DON'T UNDERSTAND.
THEY DENY IT, OR THEY TRY TO UNDERSTAND IT.
NEITHER IS PARTICULARLY CORRECT.
EVERYONE HAS THEIR OWN INDIVIDUAL WORLDVIEW.
PEOPLE NEED TO ASK THEMSELVES...
...WHY THEY CAN'T UNDERSTAND SOMETHING.
AND COME UP WITH A SATISFYING ANSWER TO THAT QUESTION.
KARAN (CLANK)
IF YOU COULD SIMPLY CONTROL THE WHOLE WORLD...
...YOU'D NEVER ENCOUNTER ANYTHING ODD OR HAVE TO UNDERSTAND ANYTHING.

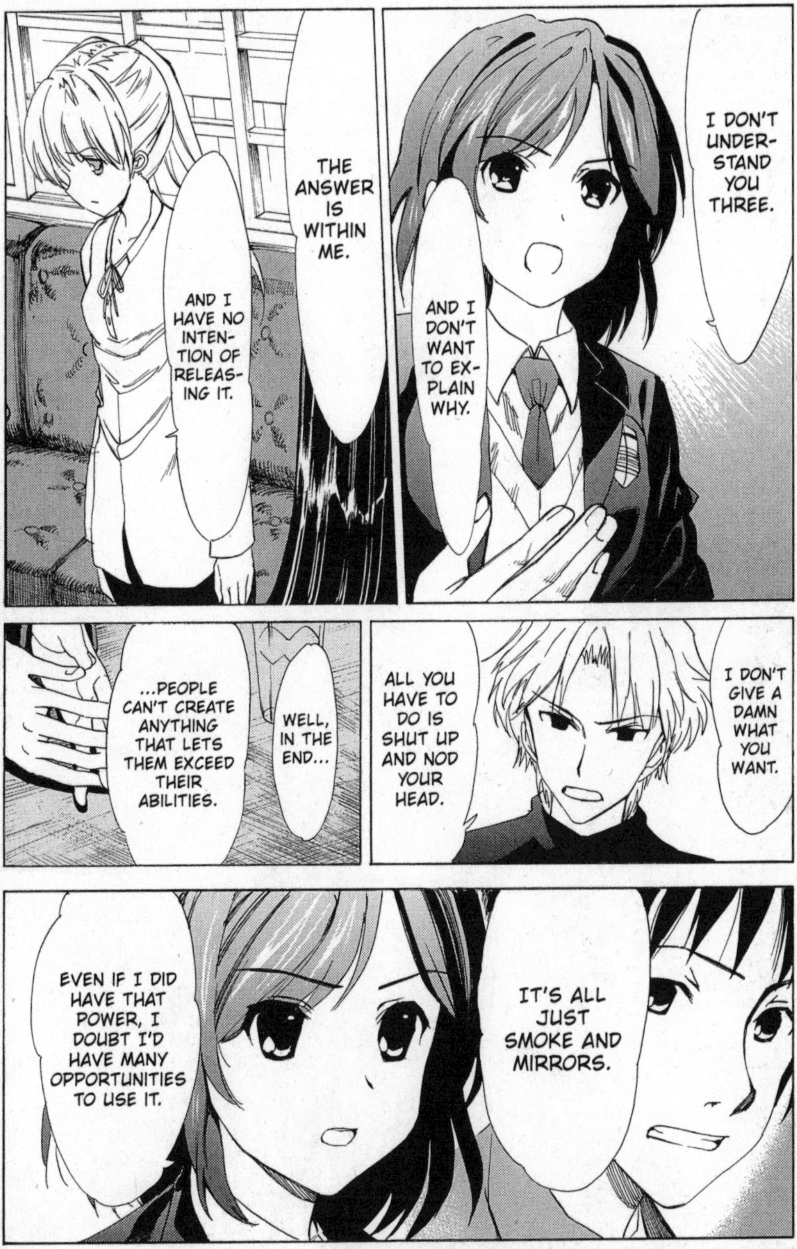
I DON'T UNDERSTAND YOU THREE.
AND I DON'T WANT TO EXPLAIN WHY.
THE ANSWER IS WITHIN ME.
AND I HAVE NO INTENTION OF RELEASING IT.
I DON'T GIVE A DAMN WHAT YOU WANT.
ALL YOU HAVE TO DO IS SHUT UP AND NOD YOUR HEAD.
WELL, IN THE END...
...PEOPLE CAN'T CREATE ANYTHING THAT LETS THEM EXCEED THEIR ABILITIES.
IT'S ALL JUST SMOKE AND MIRRORS.
EVEN IF I DID HAVE THAT POWER, I DOUBT I'D HAVE MANY OPPORTUNITIES TO USE IT.

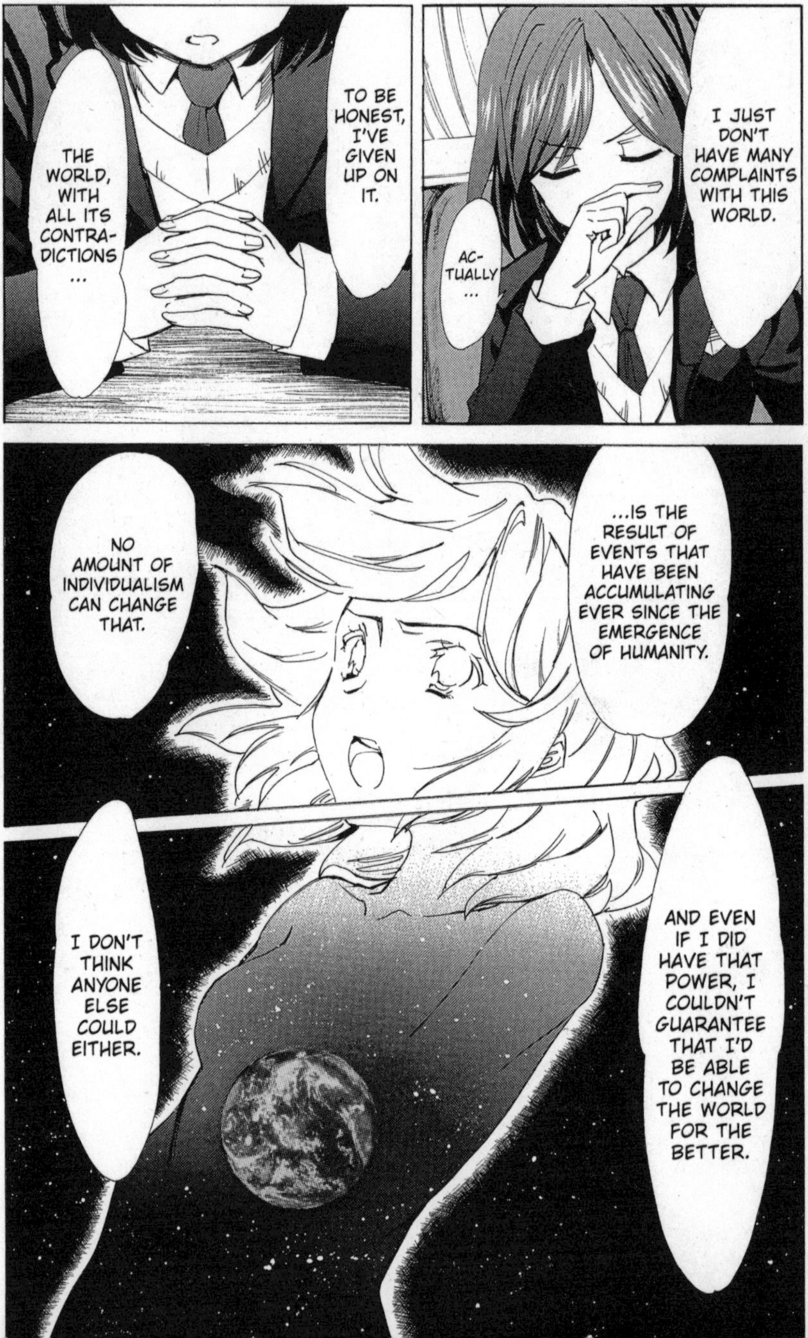
I JUST DON'T HAVE MANY COMPLAINTS WITH THIS WORLD.
AC-TUALLY...
TO BE HONEST, I'VE GIVEN UP ON IT.
THE WORLD, WITH ALL ITS CONTRA-DICTIONS...
...IS THE RESULT OF EVENTS THAT HAVE BEEN ACCUMULATING EVER SINCE THE EMERGENCE OF HUMANITY.
NO AMOUNT OF INDIVIDUALISM CAN CHANGE THAT.
AND EVEN IF I DID HAVE THAT POWER, I COULDN'T GUARANTEE THAT I'D BE ABLE TO CHANGE THE WORLD FOR THE BETTER.
I DON'T THINK ANYONE ELSE COULD EITHER.

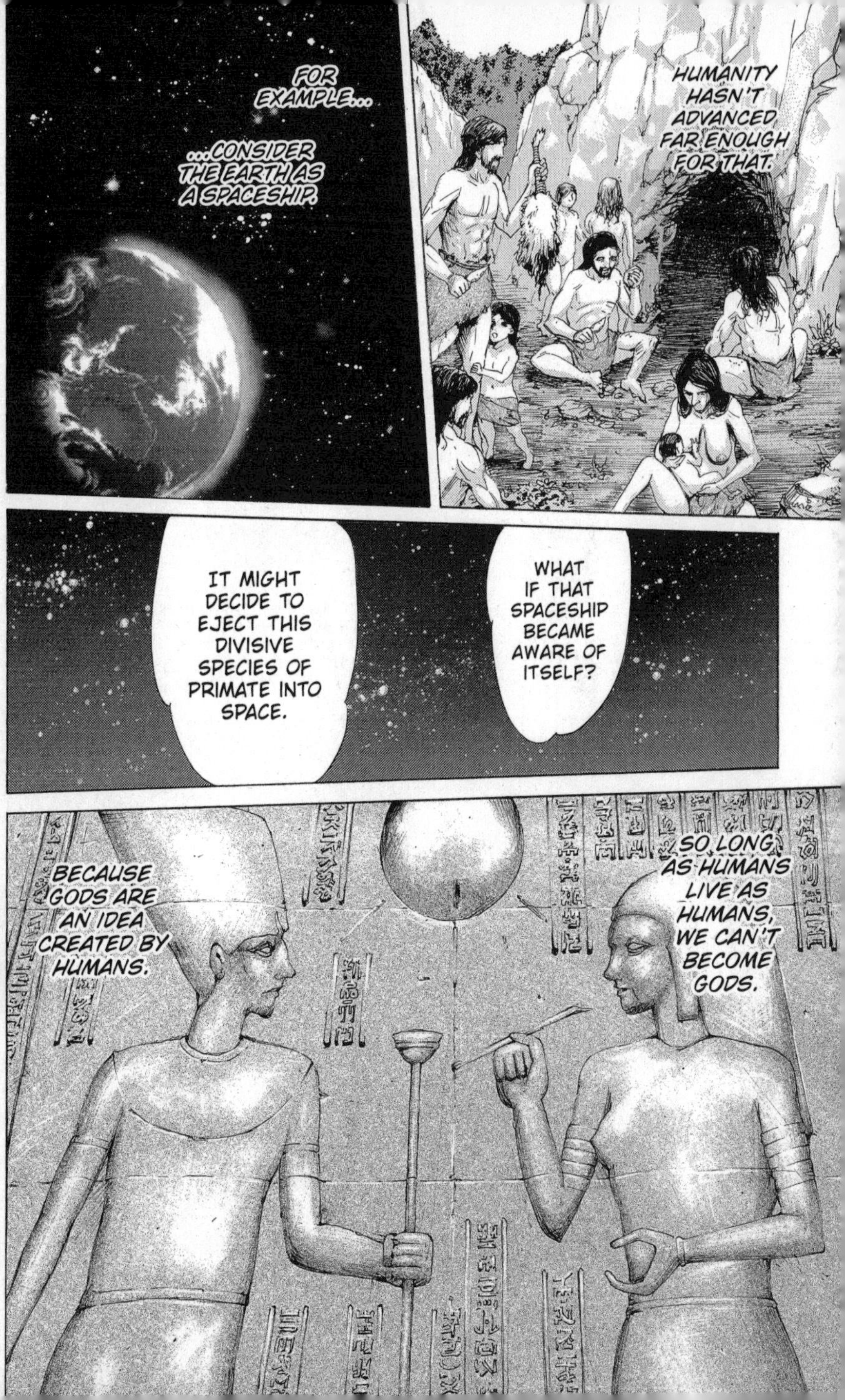
HUMANITY HASN'T ADVANCED FAR ENOUGH FOR THAT.
FOR EXAMPLE...
...CONSIDER THE EARTH AS A SPACESHIP.
WHAT IF THAT SPACESHIP BECAME AWARE OF ITSELF?
IT MIGHT DECIDE TO EJECT THIS DIVISIVE SPECIES OF PRIMATE INTO SPACE.
SO LONG AS HUMANS LIVE AS HUMANS, WE CAN'T BECOME GODS.
BECAUSE GODS ARE AN IDEA CREATED BY HUMANS.

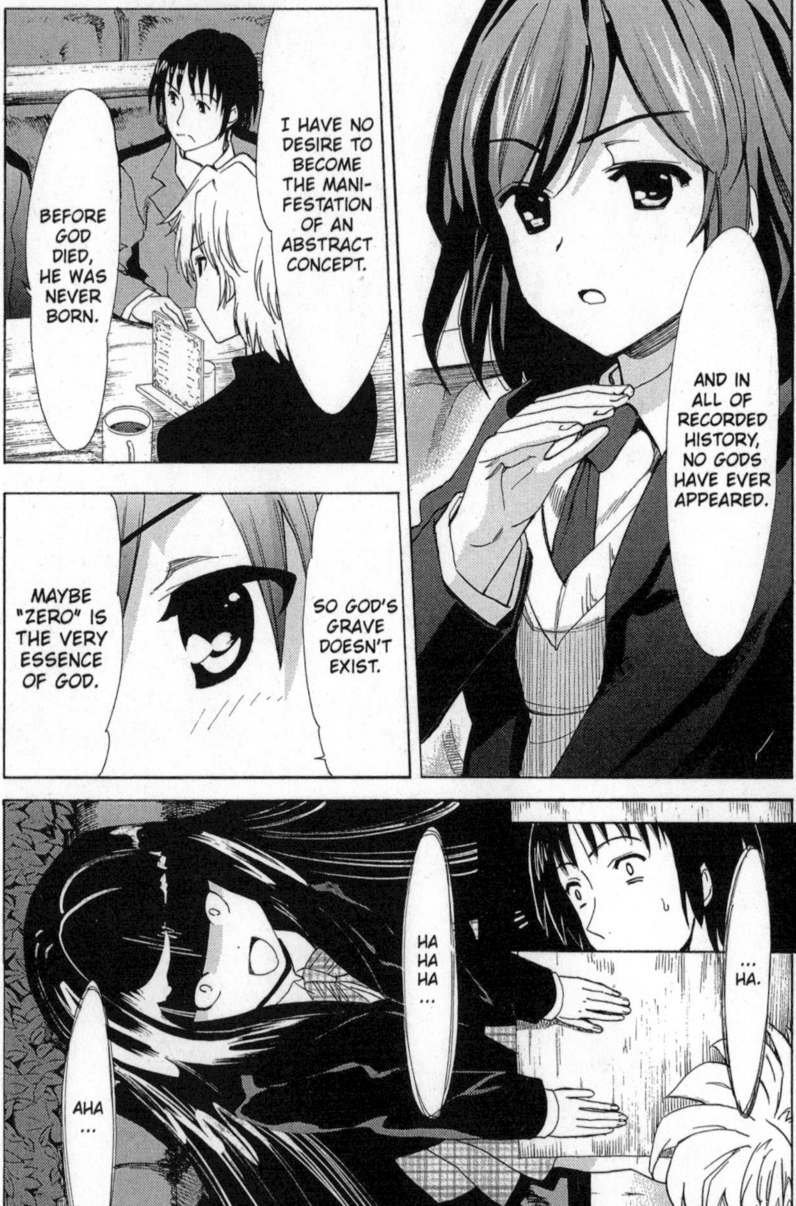
AND IN ALL OF RECORDED HISTORY, NO GODS HAVE EVER APPEARED.
I HAVE NO DESIRE TO BECOME THE MANI-FESTATION OF AN ABSTRACT CONCEPT.
BEFORE GOD DIED, HE WAS NEVER BORN.
SO GOD'S GRAVE DOESN'T EXIST.
MAYBE "ZERO" IS THE VERY ESSENCE OF GOD.
...HA.
HA HA HA ...
AHA ...

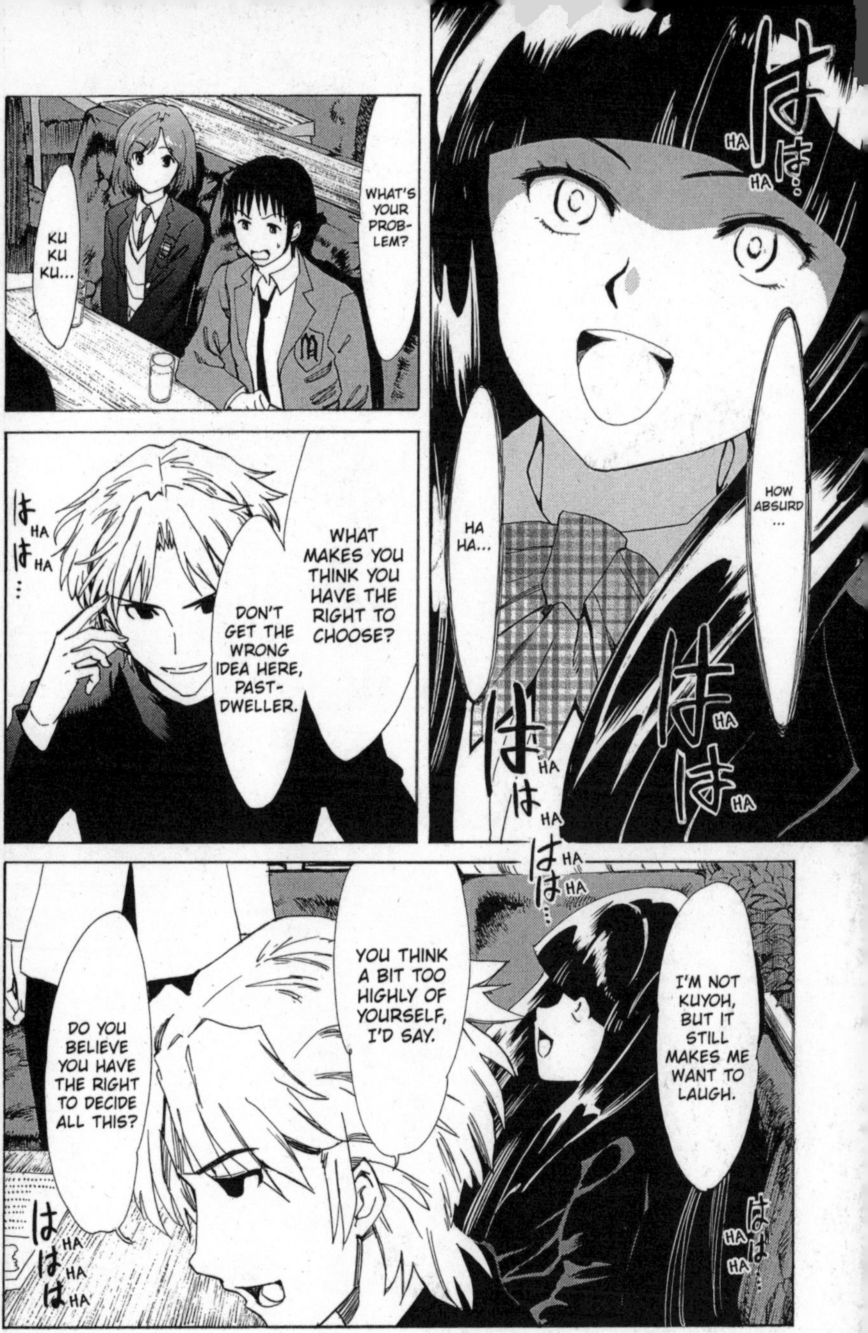
はは。 HA HA
HOW ABSURD...
HA HA...
ははは HA HA HA
はは HA HA
WHAT'S YOUR PROB-LEM?
KU KU KU...
WHAT MAKES YOU THINK YOU HAVE THE RIGHT TO CHOOSE?
DON'T GET THE WRONG IDEA HERE, PAST-DWELLER.
はは… HA HA
はは… HA HA
I'M NOT KUYOH, BUT IT STILL MAKES ME WANT TO LAUGH.
はは… HA HA
YOU THINK A BIT TOO HIGHLY OF YOURSELF, I'D SAY.
DO YOU BELIEVE YOU HAVE THE RIGHT TO DECIDE ALL THIS?
ははは HA HA HA

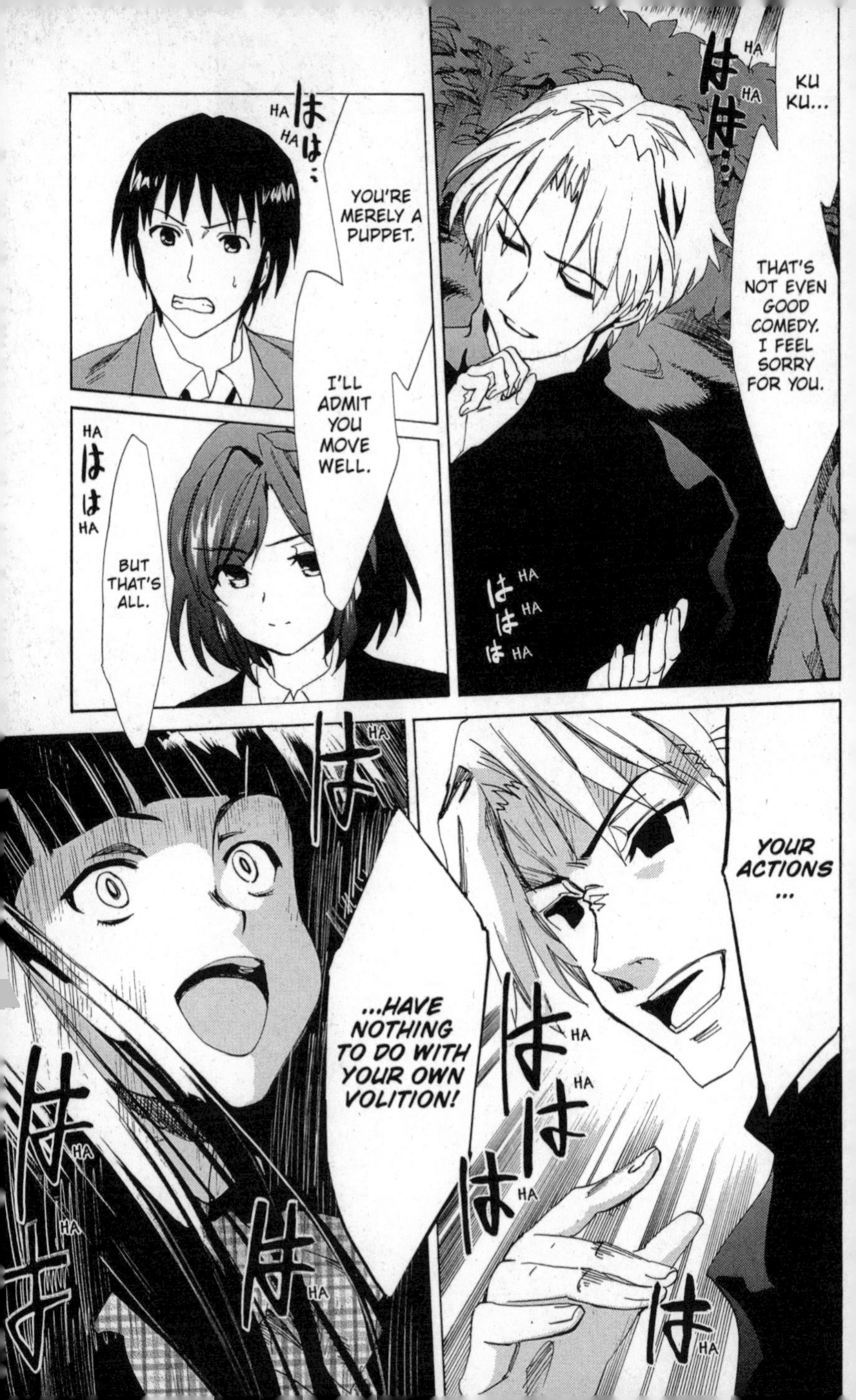

KU KU...
はは… HA HA
THAT'S NOT EVEN GOOD COMEDY. I FEEL SORRY FOR YOU.
ははは HA HA HA
はは… HA HA
YOU'RE MERELY A PUPPET.
I'LL ADMIT YOU MOVE WELL.
はは HA HA
BUT THAT'S ALL.
YOUR ACTIONS ...
ははは HA HA HA
は HA
は HA
...HAVE NOTHING TO DO WITH YOUR OWN VOLITION!
はは HA HA
は HA

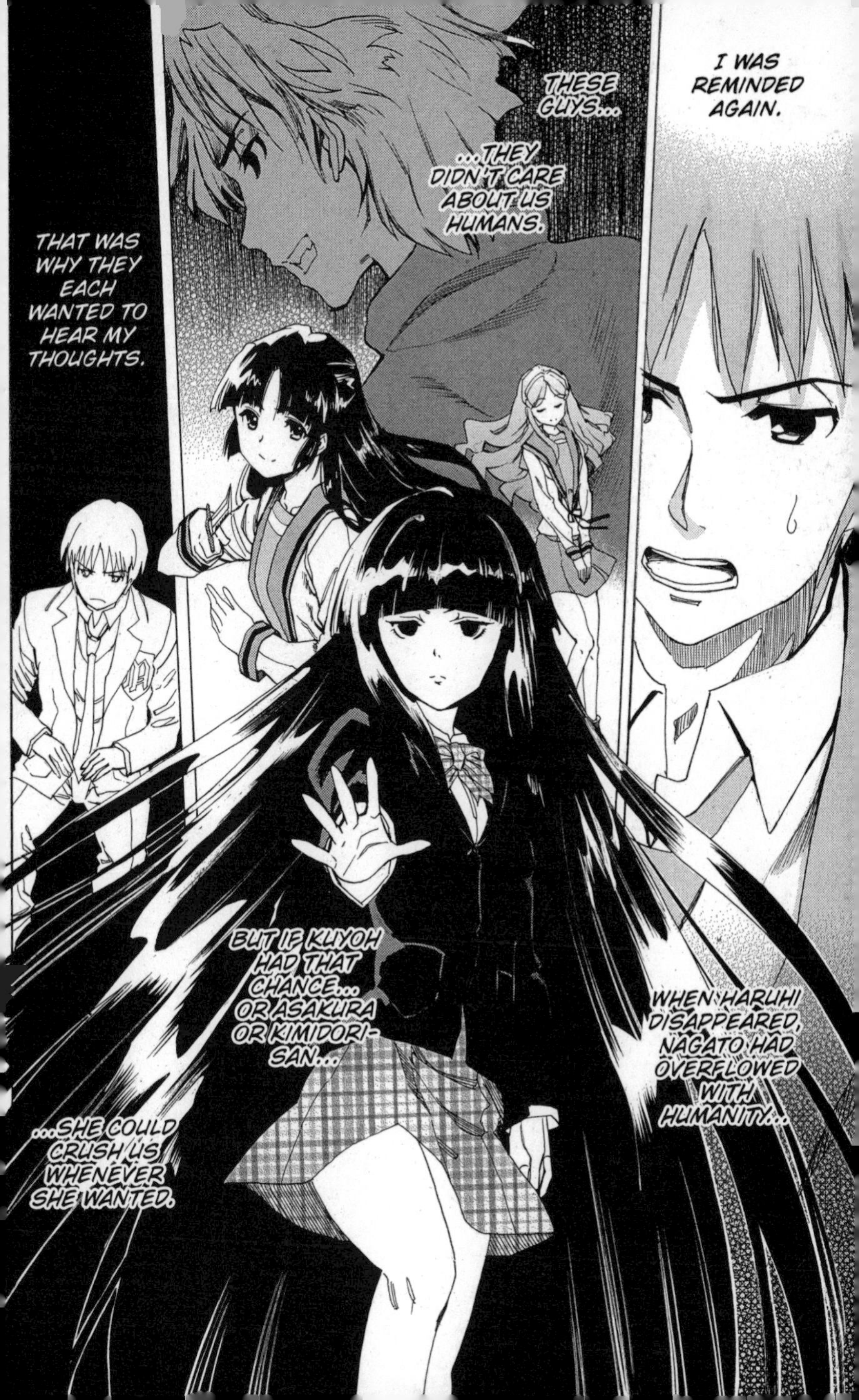
I WAS REMINDED AGAIN.
THESE GUYS...
...THEY DIDN'T CARE ABOUT US HUMANS.
THAT WAS WHY THEY EACH WANTED TO HEAR MY THOUGHTS.
WHEN HARUHI DISAPPEARED, NAGATO HAD OVERFLOWED WITH HUMANITY...
BUT IF KUYOH HAD THAT CHANCE... OR ASAKURA OR KIMIDORI-SAN...
...SHE COULD CRUSH US WHENEVER SHE WANTED.

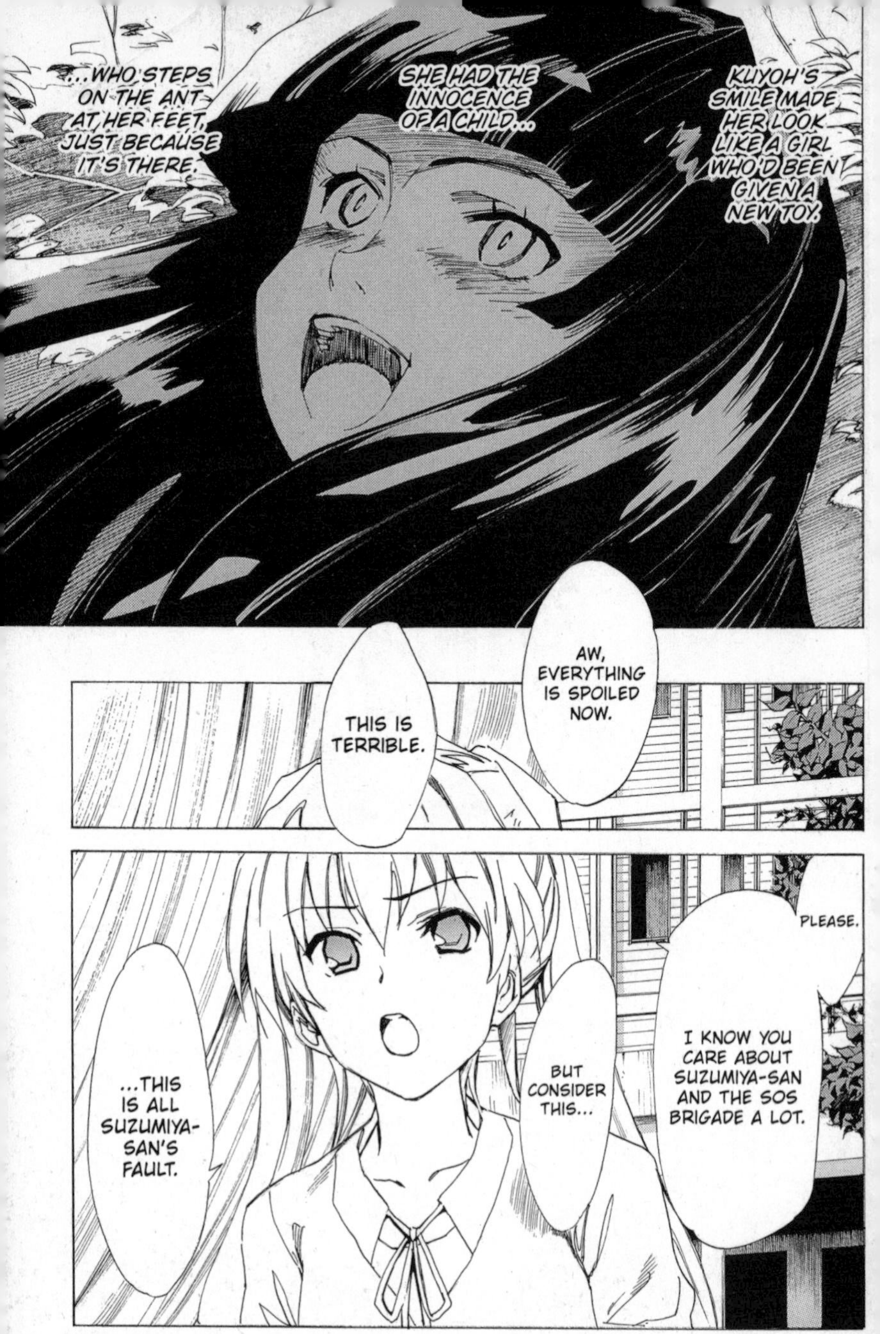
KUYOH'S SMILE MADE HER LOOK LIKE A GIRL WHO'D BEEN GIVEN A NEW TOY.
SHE HAD THE INNOCENCE OF A CHILD...
...WHO STEPS ON THE ANT AT HER FEET, JUST BECAUSE IT'S THERE.
AW, EVERYTHING IS SPOILED NOW.
THIS IS TERRIBLE.
PLEASE.
I KNOW YOU CARE ABOUT SUZUMIYA-SAN AND THE SOS BRIGADE A LOT.
BUT CONSIDER THIS...
...THIS IS ALL SUZUMIYA-SAN'S FAULT.

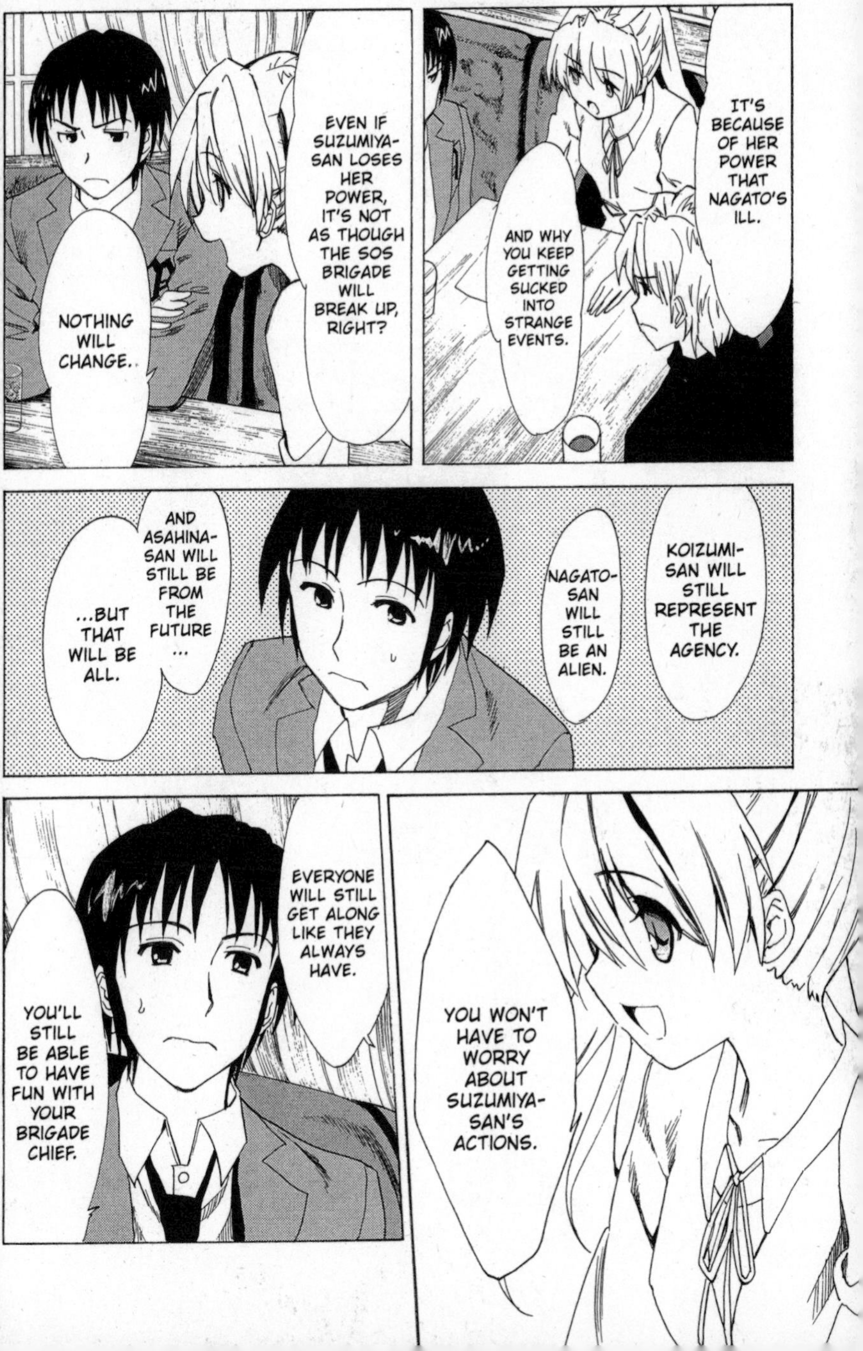
IT'S BECAUSE OF HER POWER THAT NAGATO'S ILL.
AND WHY YOU KEEP GETTING SUCKED INTO STRANGE EVENTS.
EVEN IF SUZUMIYA-SAN LOSES HER POWER, IT'S NOT AS THOUGH THE SOS BRIGADE WILL BREAK UP, RIGHT?
NOTHING WILL CHANGE..
KOIZUMI-SAN WILL STILL REPRESENT THE AGENCY.
NAGATO-SAN WILL STILL BE AN ALIEN.
AND ASAHINA-SAN WILL STILL BE FROM THE FUTURE...
...BUT THAT WILL BE ALL.
YOU WON'T HAVE TO WORRY ABOUT SUZUMIYA-SAN'S ACTIONS.
EVERYONE WILL STILL GET ALONG LIKE THEY ALWAYS HAVE.
YOU'LL STILL BE ABLE TO HAVE FUN WITH YOUR BRIGADE CHIEF.

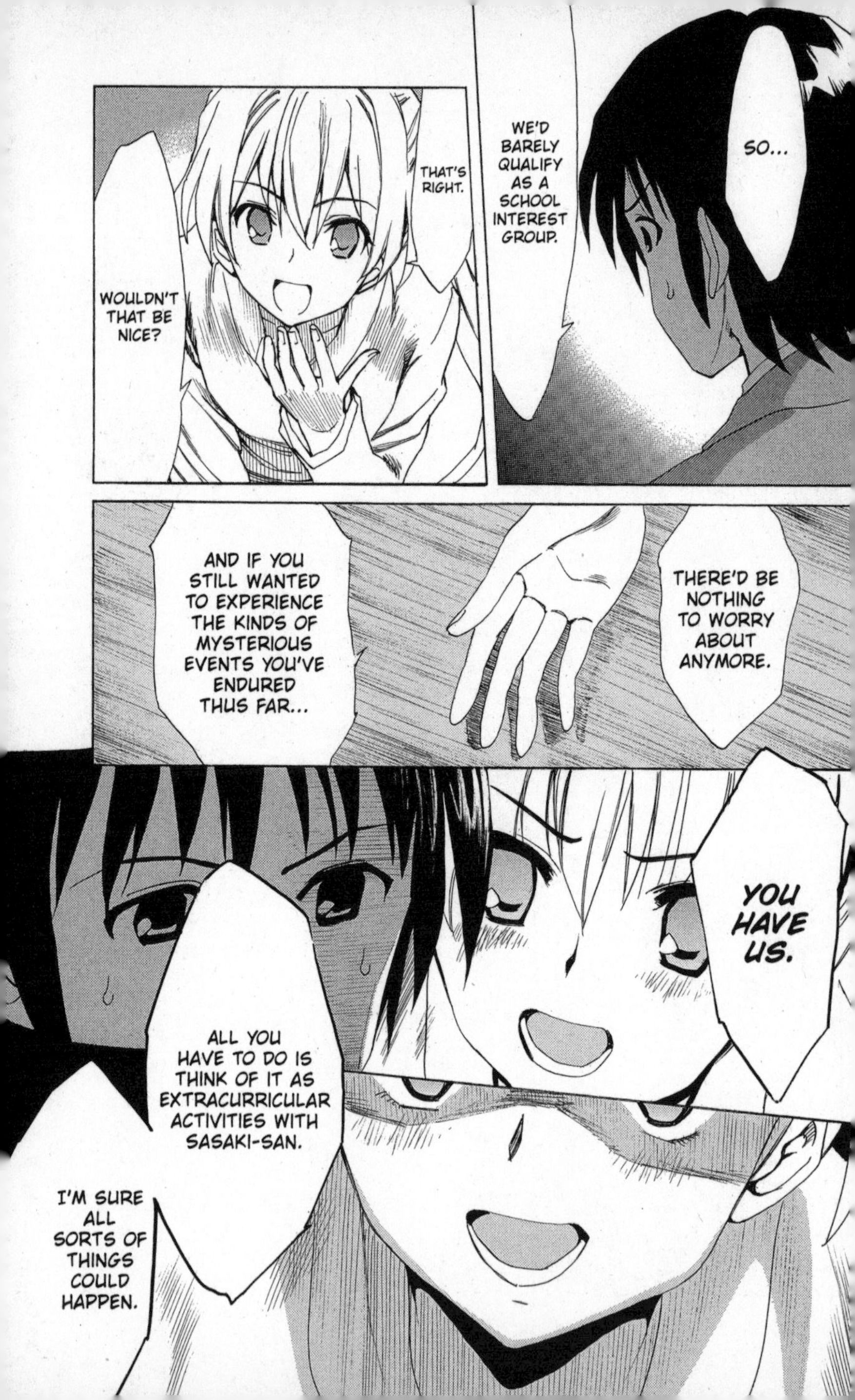
SO...
WE'D BARELY QUALIFY AS A SCHOOL INTEREST GROUP.
THAT'S RIGHT.
WOULDN'T THAT BE NICE?
THERE'D BE NOTHING TO WORRY ABOUT ANYMORE.
AND IF YOU STILL WANTED TO EXPERIENCE THE KINDS OF MYSTERIOUS EVENTS YOU'VE ENDURED THUS FAR...
YOU HAVE US.
ALL YOU HAVE TO DO IS THINK OF IT AS EXTRACURRICULAR ACTIVITIES WITH SASAKI-SAN.
I'M SURE ALL SORTS OF THINGS COULD HAPPEN.

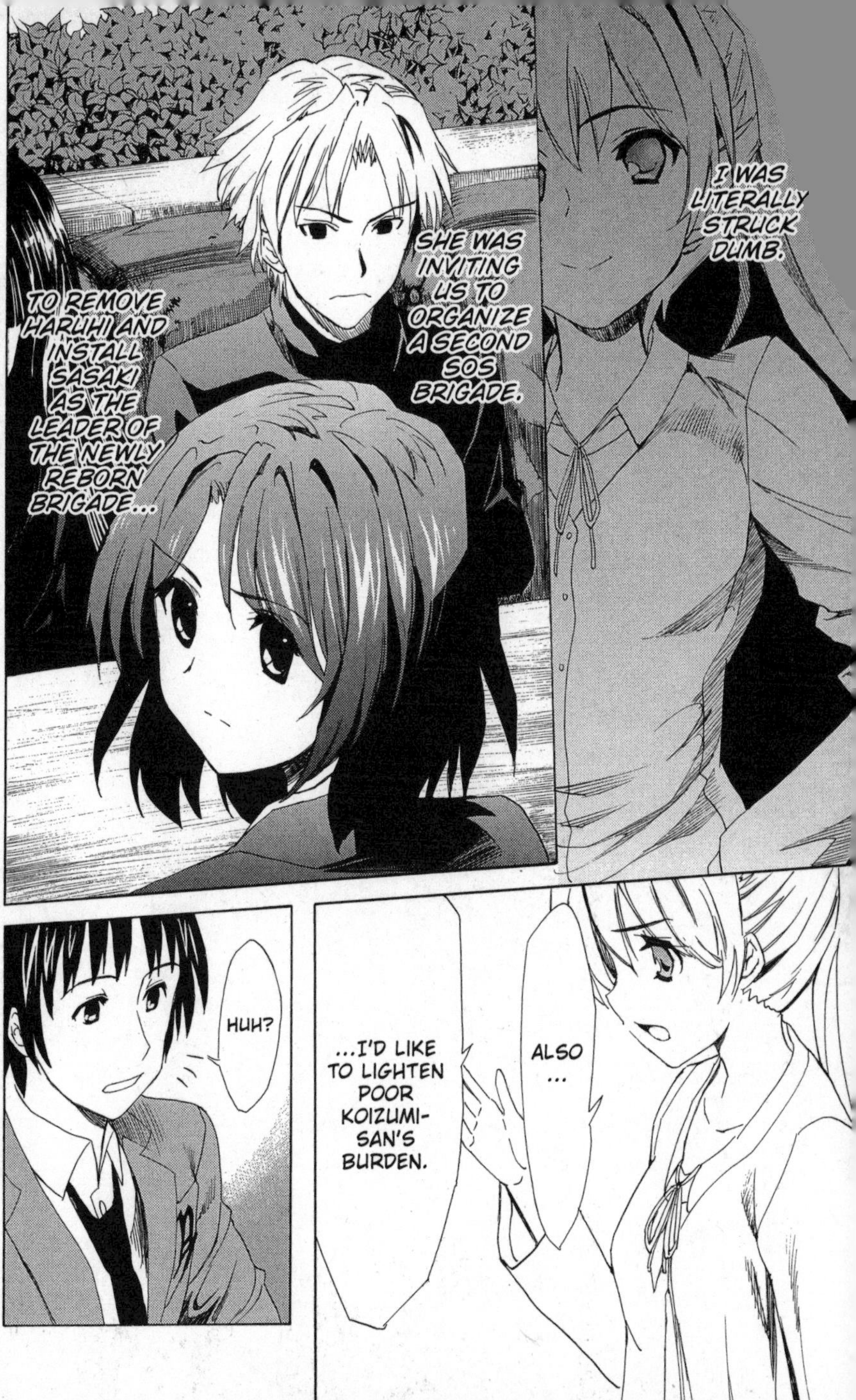
I WAS LITERALLY STRUCK DUMB.
SHE WAS INVITING US TO ORGANIZE A SECOND SOS BRIGADE.
TO REMOVE HARUHI AND INSTALL SASAKI AS THE LEADER OF THE NEWLY REBORN BRIGADE...
ALSO ...
...I'D LIKE TO LIGHTEN POOR KOIZUMI-SAN'S BURDEN.
HUH?

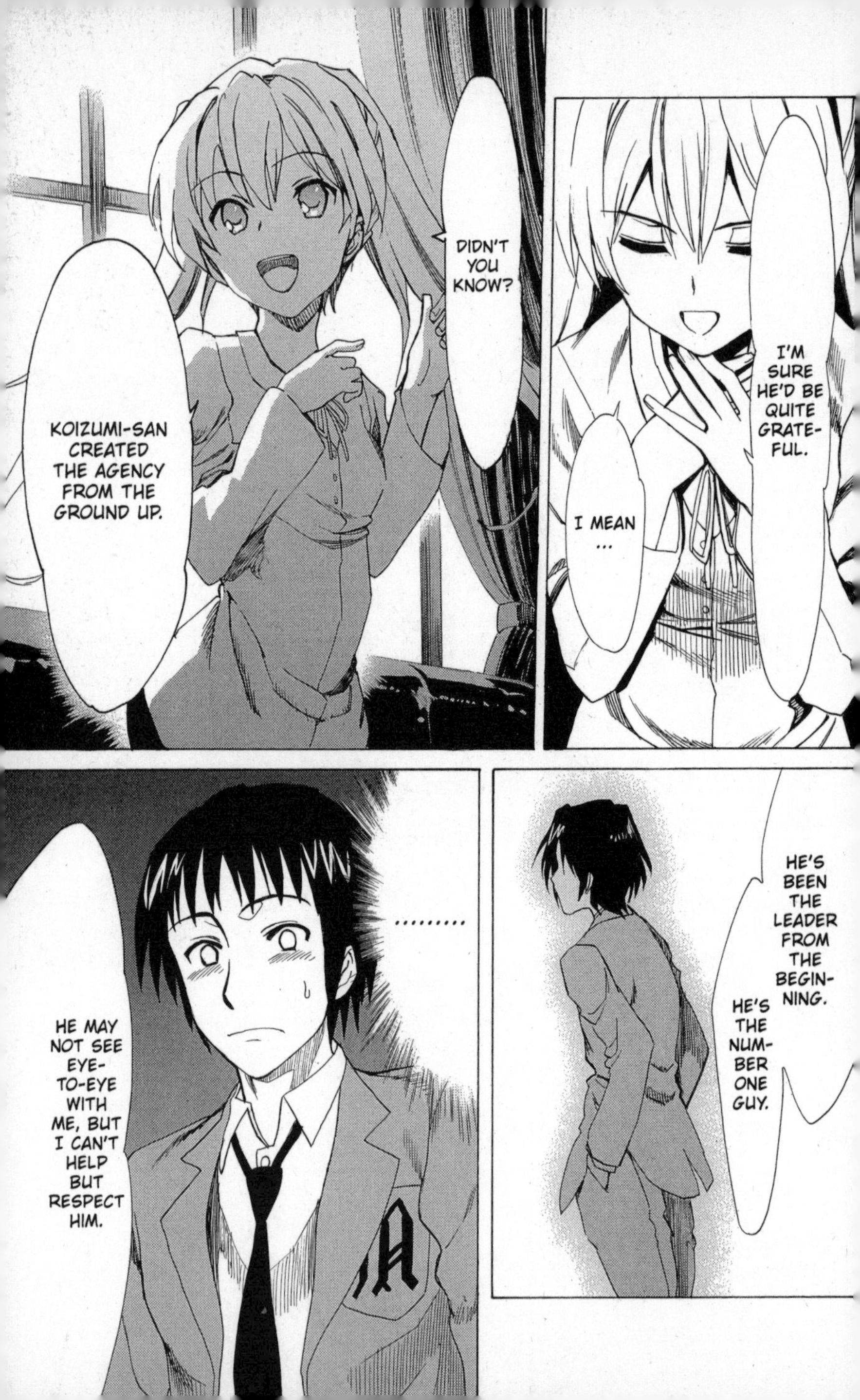
I'M SURE HE'D BE QUITE GRATE-FUL.
I MEAN ...
DIDN'T YOU KNOW?
KOIZUMI-SAN CREATED THE AGENCY FROM THE GROUND UP.
HE'S BEEN THE LEADER FROM THE BEGIN-NING.
HE'S THE NUM-BER ONE GUY.
....
HE MAY NOT SEE EYE-TO-EYE WITH ME, BUT I CAN'T HELP BUT RESPECT HIM.

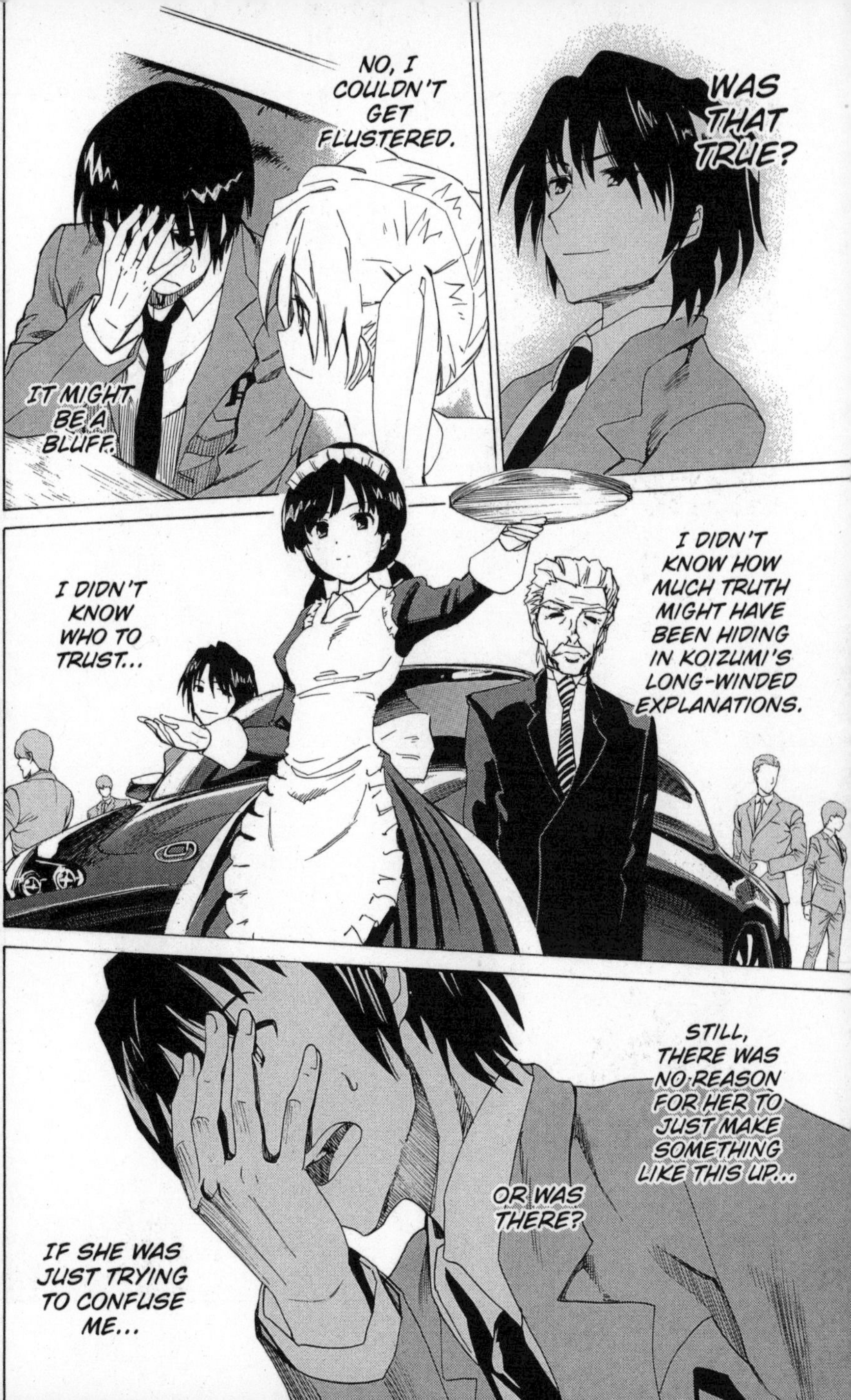
WAS THAT TRUE?
NO, I COULDN'T GET FLUSTERED.
IT MIGHT BE A BLUFF.
I DIDN'T KNOW HOW MUCH TRUTH MIGHT HAVE BEEN HIDING IN KOIZUMI'S LONG-WINDED EXPLANATIONS.
I DIDN'T KNOW WHO TO TRUST...
STILL, THERE WAS NO REASON FOR HER TO JUST MAKE SOMETHING LIKE THIS UP...
OR WAS THERE?
IF SHE WAS JUST TRYING TO CONFUSE ME...

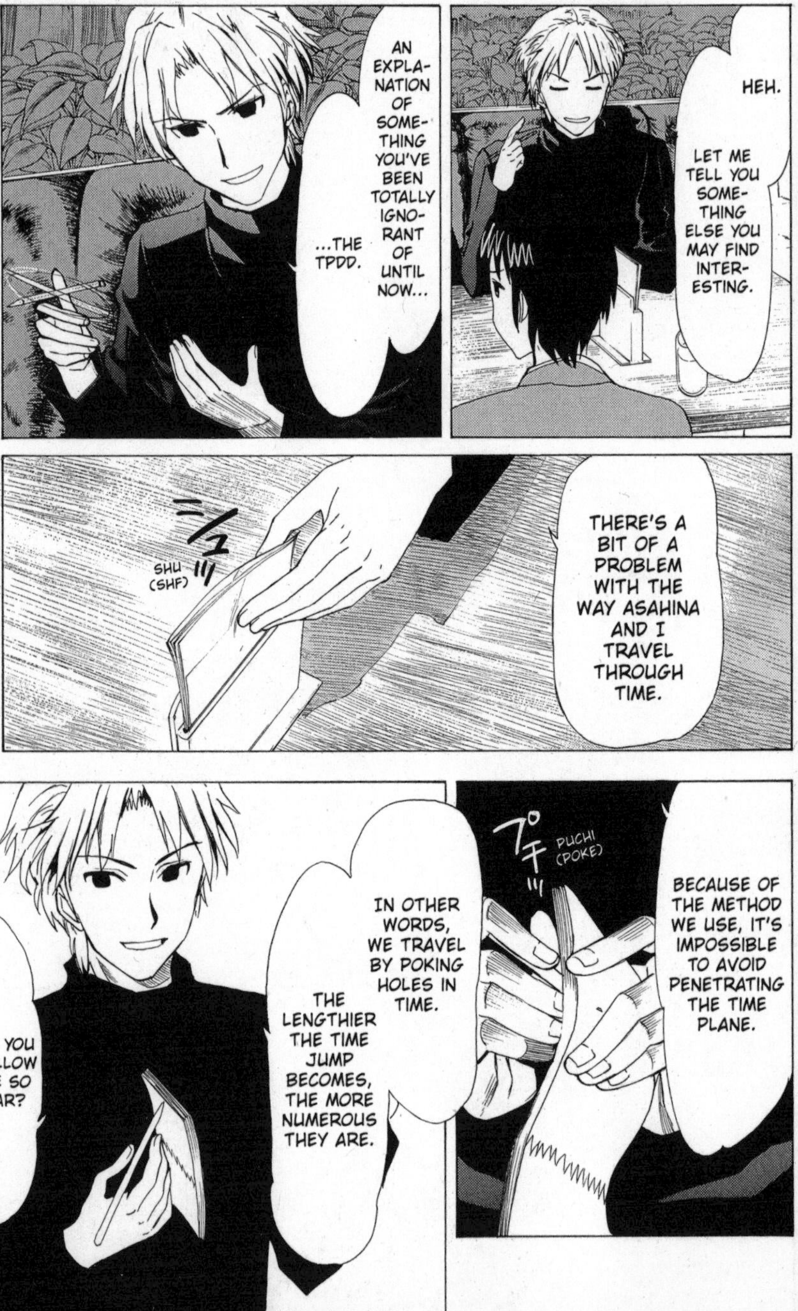
HEH.
LET ME TELL YOU SOMETHING ELSE YOU MAY FIND INTERESTING.
AN EXPLANATION OF SOMETHING YOU'VE BEEN TOTALLY IGNORANT OF UNTIL NOW...
...THE TPDD.
THERE'S A BIT OF A PROBLEM WITH THE WAY ASAHINA AND I TRAVEL THROUGH TIME.
SHU (SHF)
PUCHI (POKE)
BECAUSE OF THE METHOD WE USE, IT'S IMPOSSIBLE TO AVOID PENETRATING THE TIME PLANE.
IN OTHER WORDS, WE TRAVEL BY POKING HOLES IN TIME.
THE LENGTHIER THE TIME JUMP BECOMES, THE MORE NUMEROUS THEY ARE.
DO YOU FOLLOW ME SO FAR?

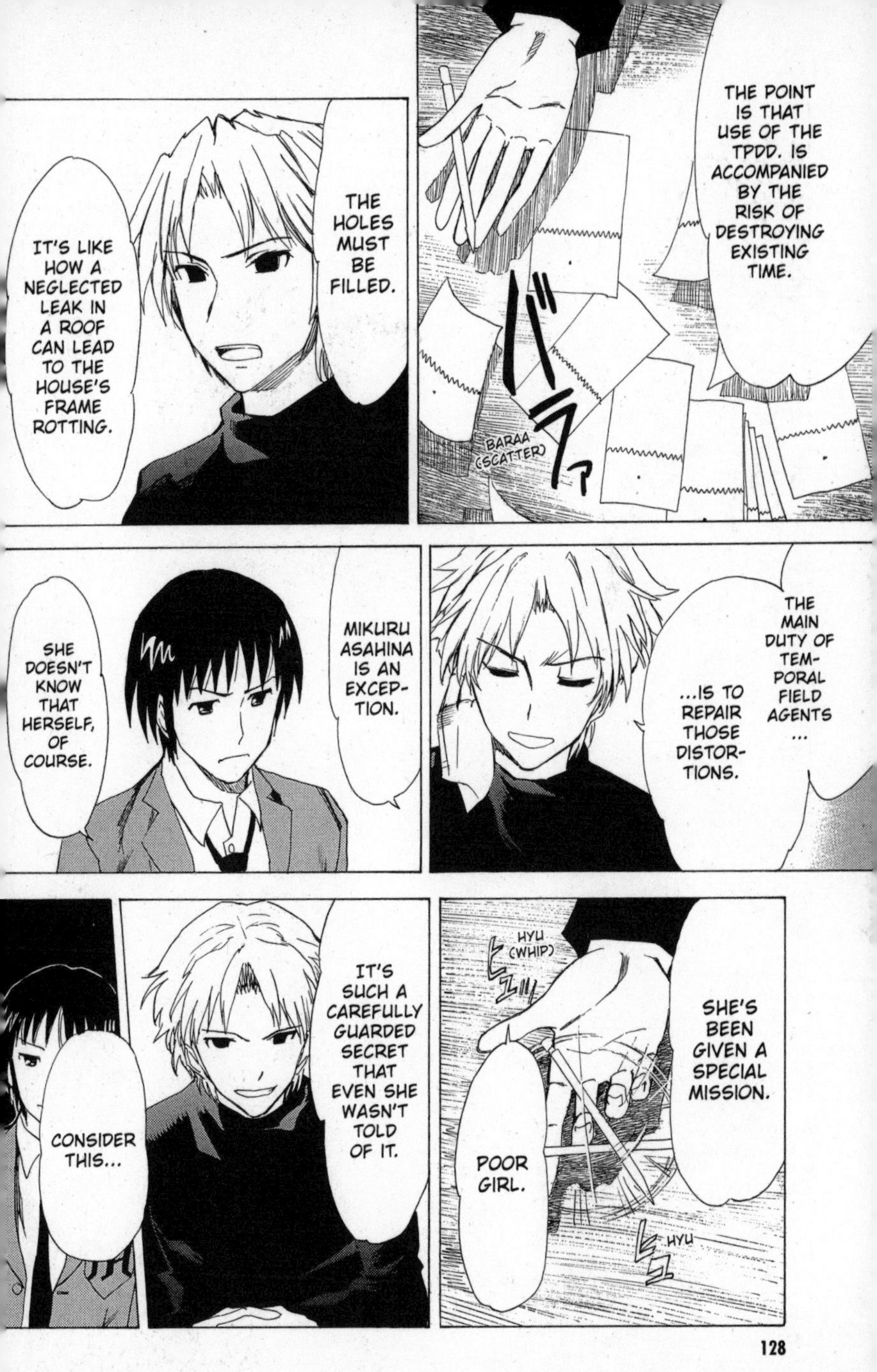
THE POINT IS THAT USE OF THE TPDD. IS ACCOMPANIED BY THE RISK OF DESTROYING EXISTING TIME.
BARAA (SCATTER)
THE HOLES MUST BE FILLED.
IT'S LIKE HOW A NEGLECTED LEAK IN A ROOF CAN LEAD TO THE HOUSE'S FRAME ROTTING.
THE MAIN DUTY OF TEM-PORAL FIELD AGENTS...
...IS TO REPAIR THOSE DISTOR-TIONS.
MIKURU ASAHINA IS AN EXCEP-TION.
SHE DOESN'T KNOW THAT HERSELF, OF COURSE.
HYU (WHIP)
SHE'S BEEN GIVEN A SPECIAL MISSION.
POOR GIRL.
HYU
IT'S SUCH A CAREFULLY GUARDED SECRET THAT EVEN SHE WASN'T TOLD OF IT.
CONSIDER THIS...

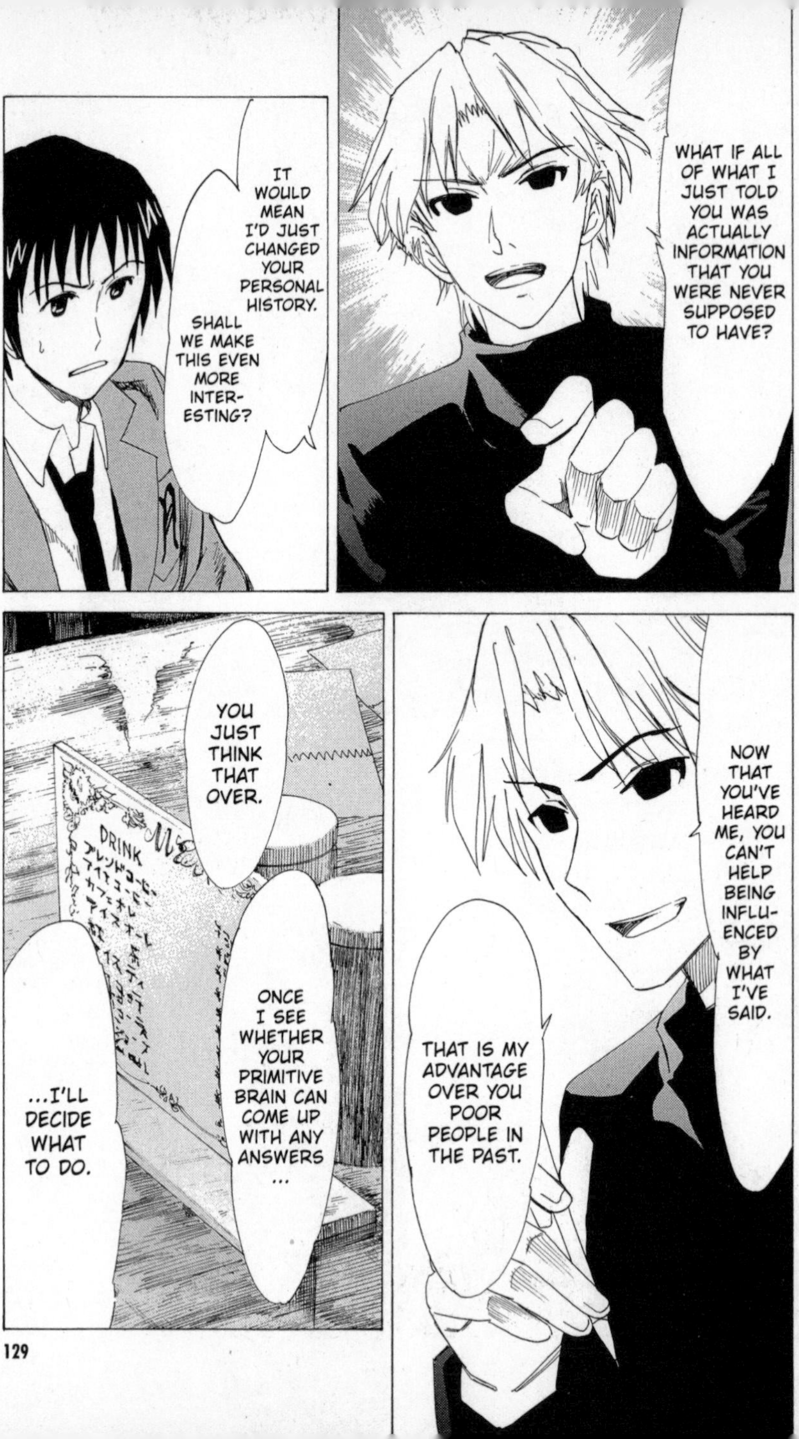
WHAT IF ALL OF WHAT I JUST TOLD YOU WAS ACTUALLY INFORMATION THAT YOU WERE NEVER SUPPOSED TO HAVE?
IT WOULD MEAN I'D JUST CHANGED YOUR PERSONAL HISTORY.
SHALL WE MAKE THIS EVEN MORE INTERESTING?
NOW THAT YOU'VE HEARD ME, YOU CAN'T HELP BEING INFLU-ENCED BY WHAT I'VE SAID.
THAT IS MY ADVANTAGE OVER YOU POOR PEOPLE IN THE PAST.
YOU JUST THINK THAT OVER.
DRINK
ONCE I SEE WHETHER YOUR PRIMITIVE BRAIN CAN COME UP WITH ANY ANSWERS...
...I'LL DECIDE WHAT TO DO.

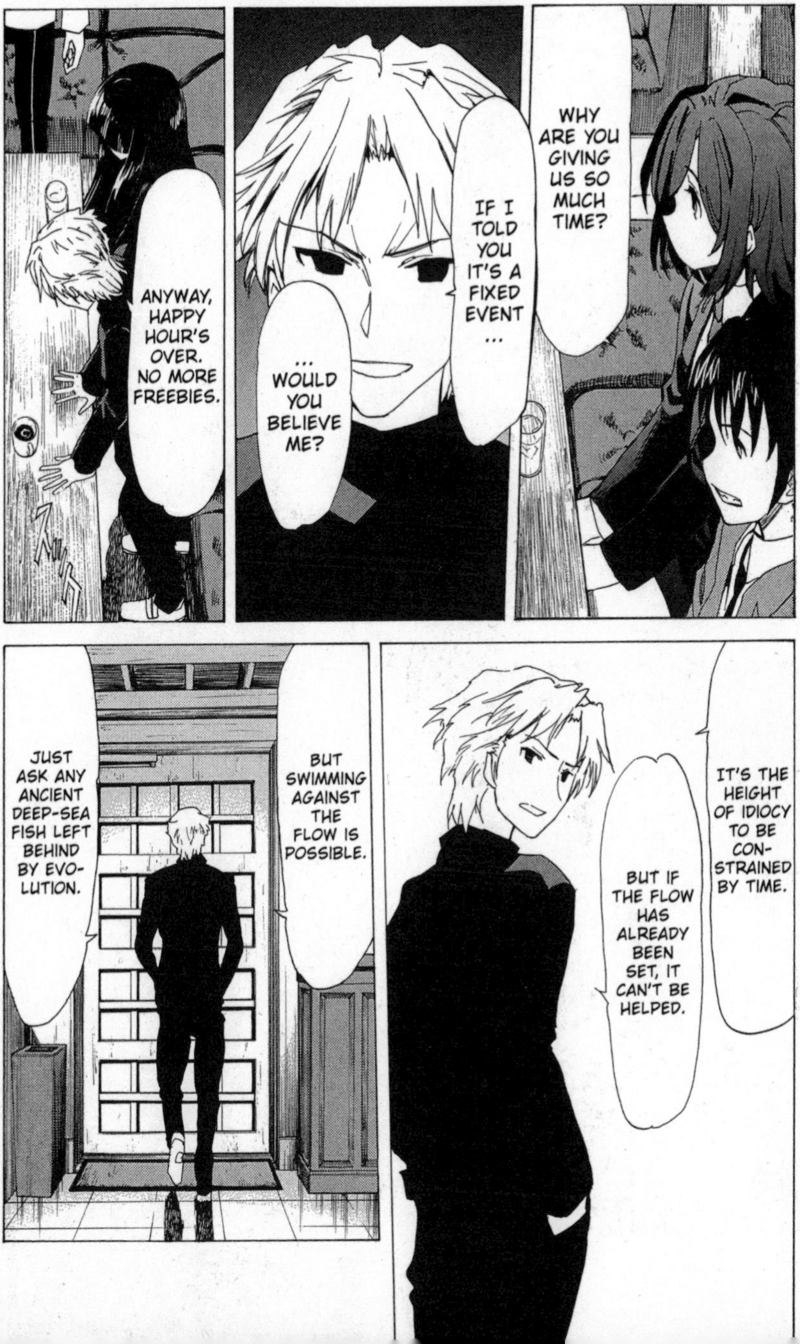
WHY ARE YOU GIVING US SO MUCH TIME?
IF I TOLD YOU IT'S A FIXED EVENT ...
... WOULD YOU BELIEVE ME?
ANYWAY, HAPPY HOUR'S OVER. NO MORE FREEBIES.
IT'S THE HEIGHT OF IDIOCY TO BE CONSTRAINED BY TIME.
BUT IF THE FLOW HAS ALREADY BEEN SET, IT CAN'T BE HELPED.
BUT SWIMMING AGAINST THE FLOW IS POSSIBLE.
JUST ASK ANY ANCIENT DEEP-SEA FISH LEFT BEHIND BY EVOLUTION.

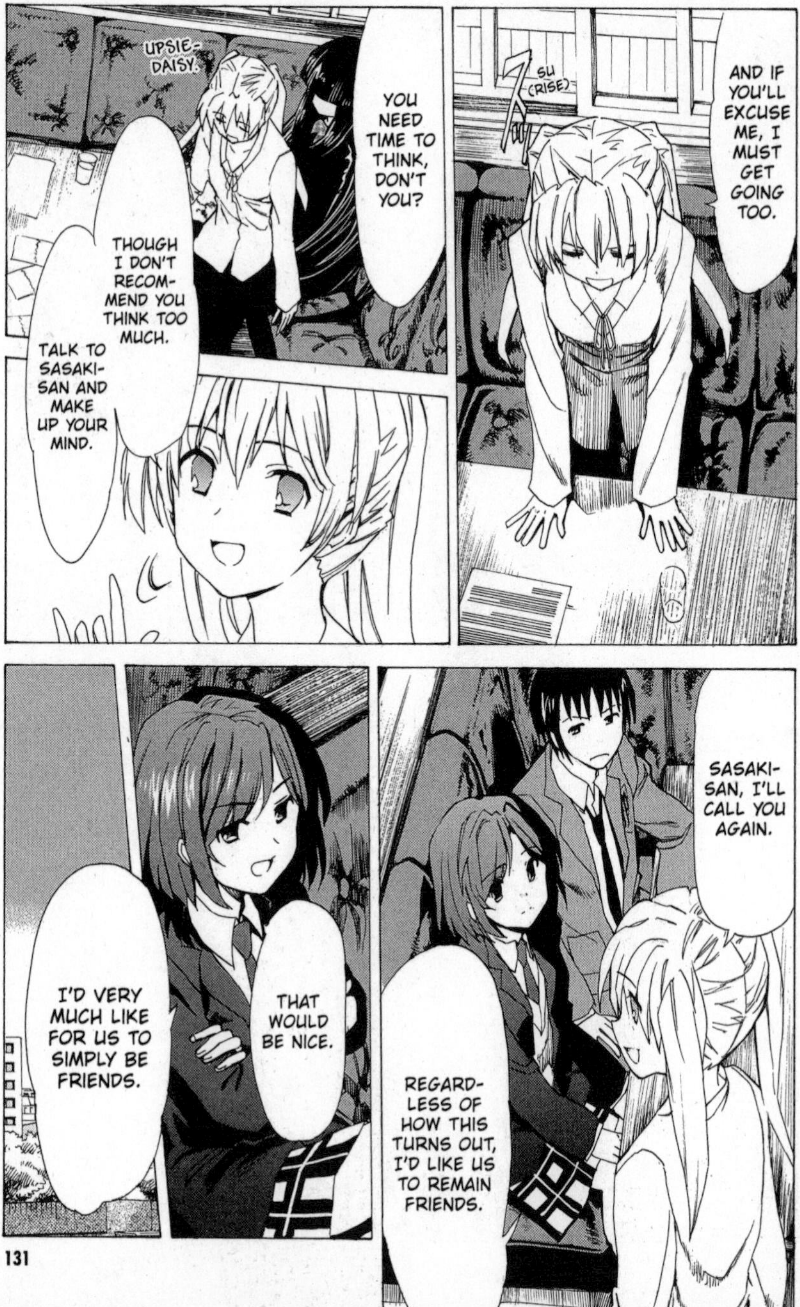
SU (RISE)
AND IF YOU'LL EXCUSE ME, I MUST GET GOING TOO.
YOU NEED TIME TO THINK, DON'T YOU?
UPSIE-DAISY.
THOUGH I DON'T RECOM-MEND YOU THINK TOO MUCH.
TALK TO SASAKI-SAN AND MAKE UP YOUR MIND.
SASAKI-SAN, I'LL CALL YOU AGAIN.
REGARD-LESS OF HOW THIS TURNS OUT, I'D LIKE US TO REMAIN FRIENDS.
THAT WOULD BE NICE.
I'D VERY MUCH LIKE FOR US TO SIMPLY BE FRIENDS.

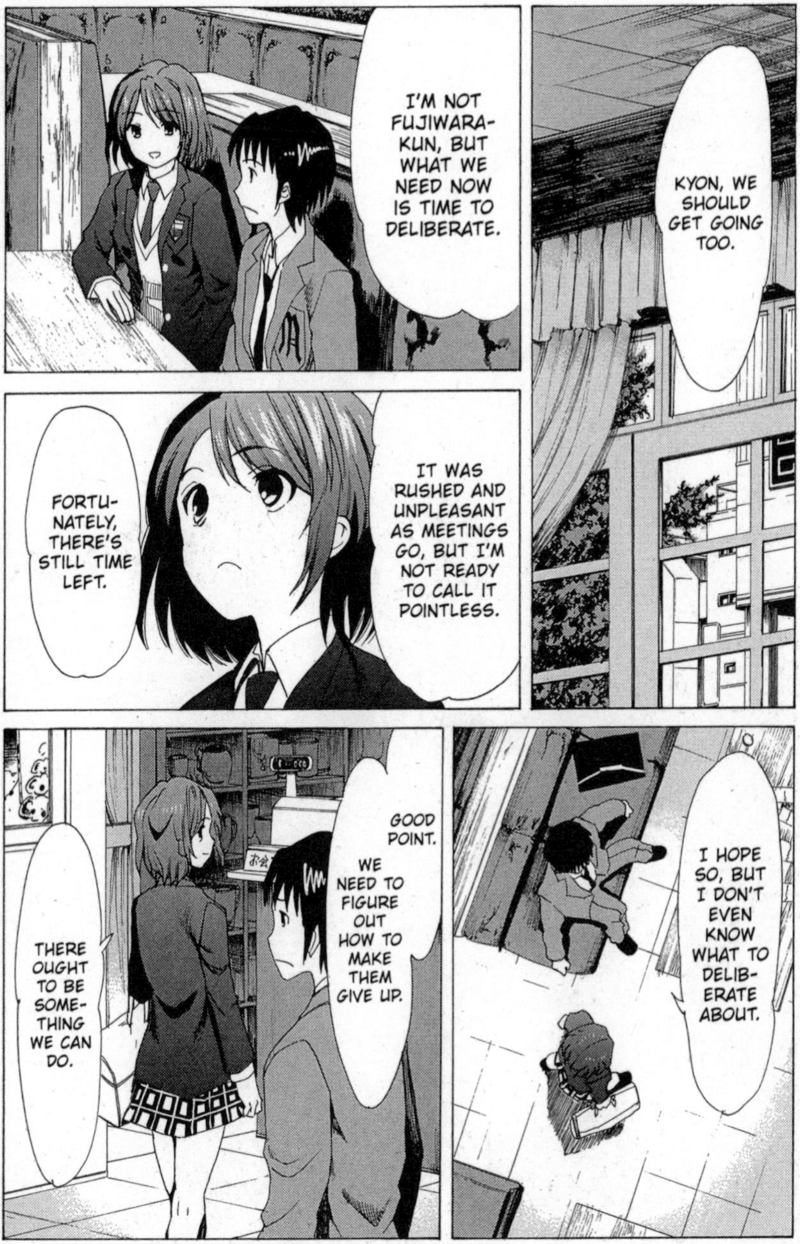
KYON, WE SHOULD GET GOING TOO.
I'M NOT FUJIWARA-KUN, BUT WHAT WE NEED NOW IS TIME TO DELIBERATE.
IT WAS RUSHED AND UNPLEASANT AS MEETINGS GO, BUT I'M NOT READY TO CALL IT POINTLESS.
FORTUNATELY, THERE'S STILL TIME LEFT.
I HOPE SO, BUT I DON'T EVEN KNOW WHAT TO DELIBERATE ABOUT.
GOOD POINT.
WE NEED TO FIGURE OUT HOW TO MAKE THEM GIVE UP.
THERE OUGHT TO BE SOMETHING WE CAN DO.

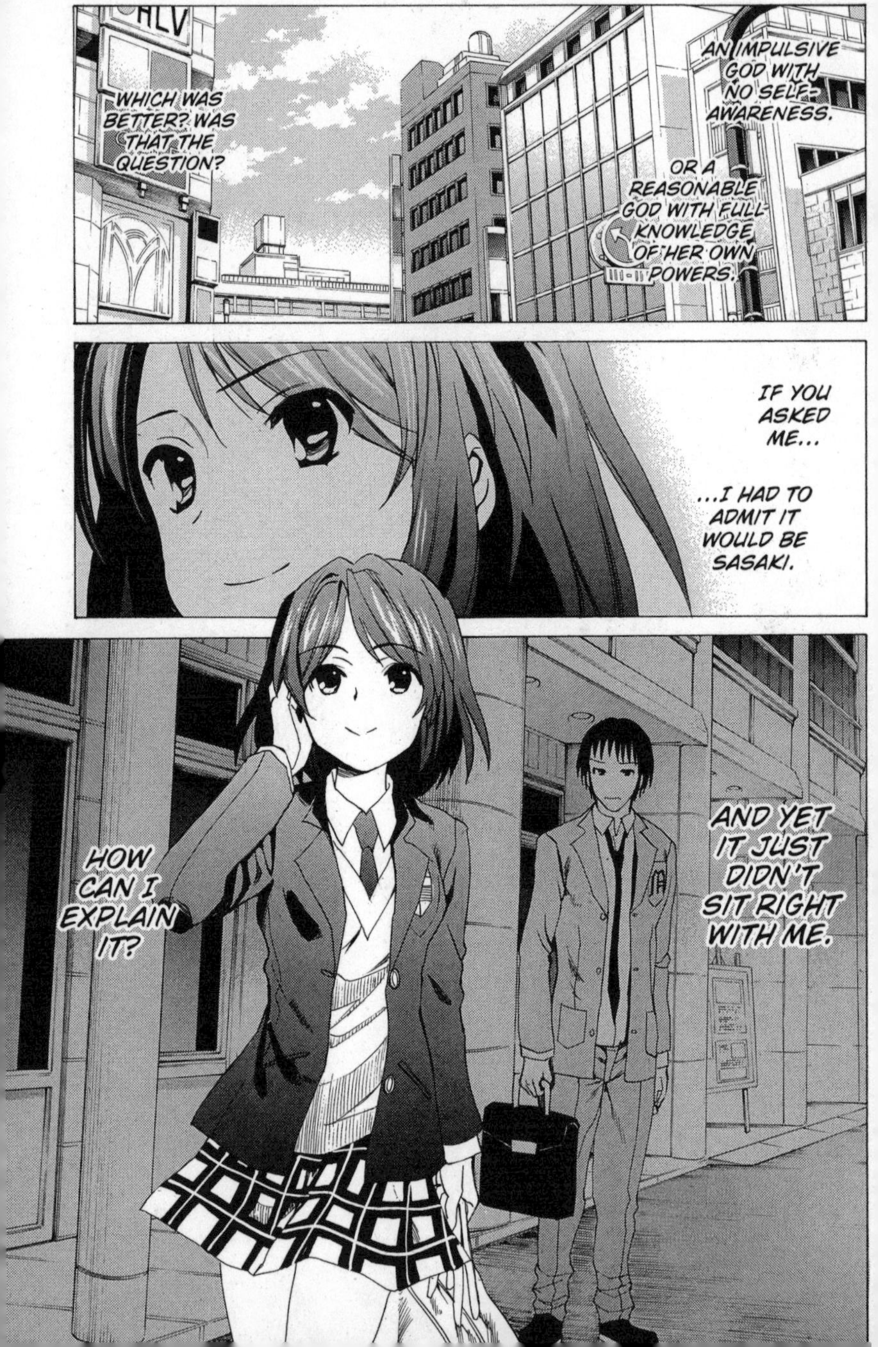
AN IMPULSIVE GOD WITH NO SELF-AWARENESS.
OR A REASONABLE GOD WITH FULL KNOWLEDGE OF HER OWN POWERS.
WHICH WAS BETTER? WAS THAT THE QUESTION?
IF YOU ASKED ME...
...I HAD TO ADMIT IT WOULD BE SASAKI.
AND YET IT JUST DIDN'T SIT RIGHT WITH ME.
HOW CAN I EXPLAIN IT?

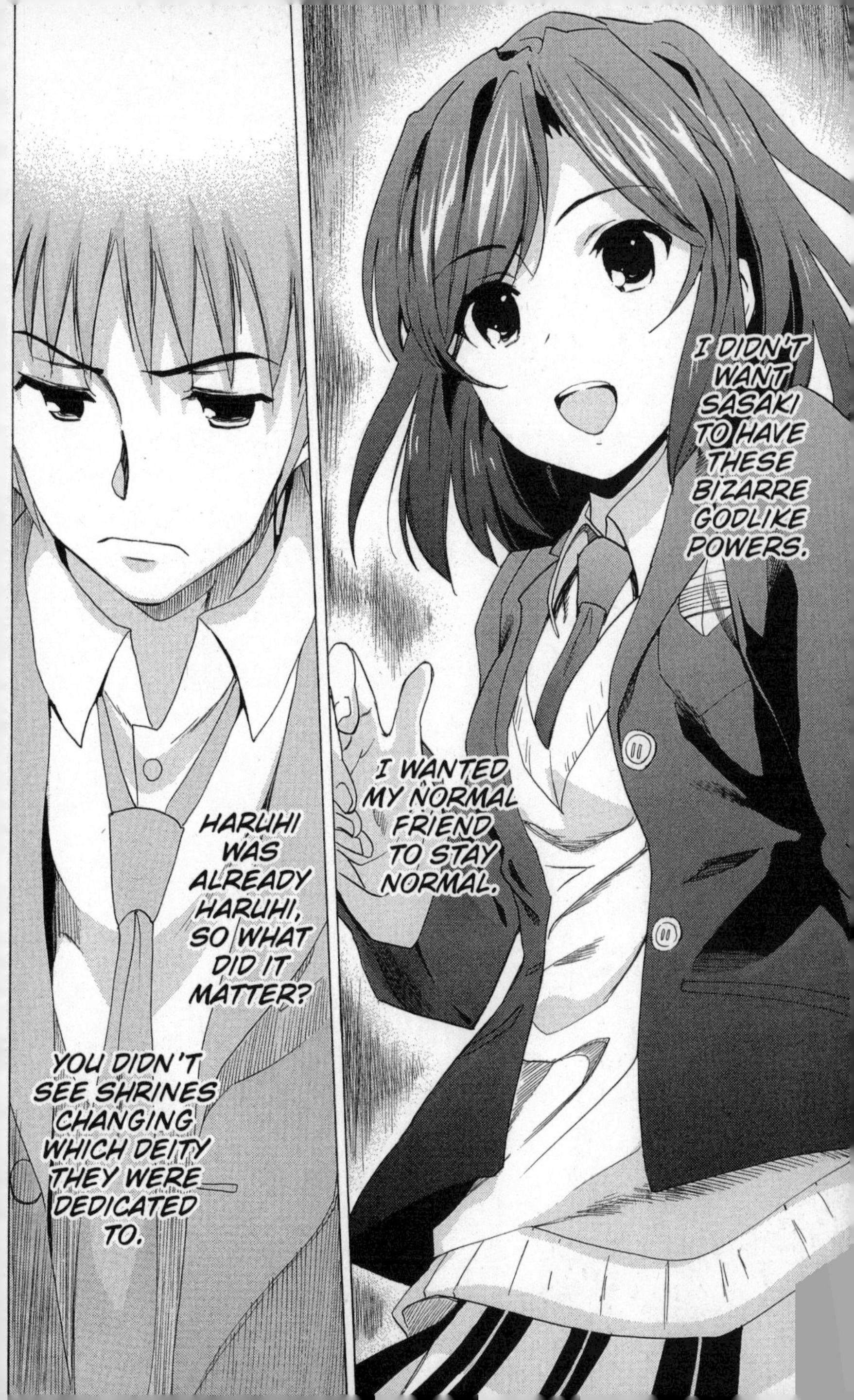
I DIDN'T WANT SASAKI TO HAVE THESE BIZARRE GODLIKE POWERS.
I WANTED MY NORMAL FRIEND TO STAY NORMAL.
HARUHI WAS ALREADY HARUHI, SO WHAT DID IT MATTER?
YOU DIDN'T SEE SHRINES CHANGING WHICH DEITY THEY WERE DEDICATED TO.

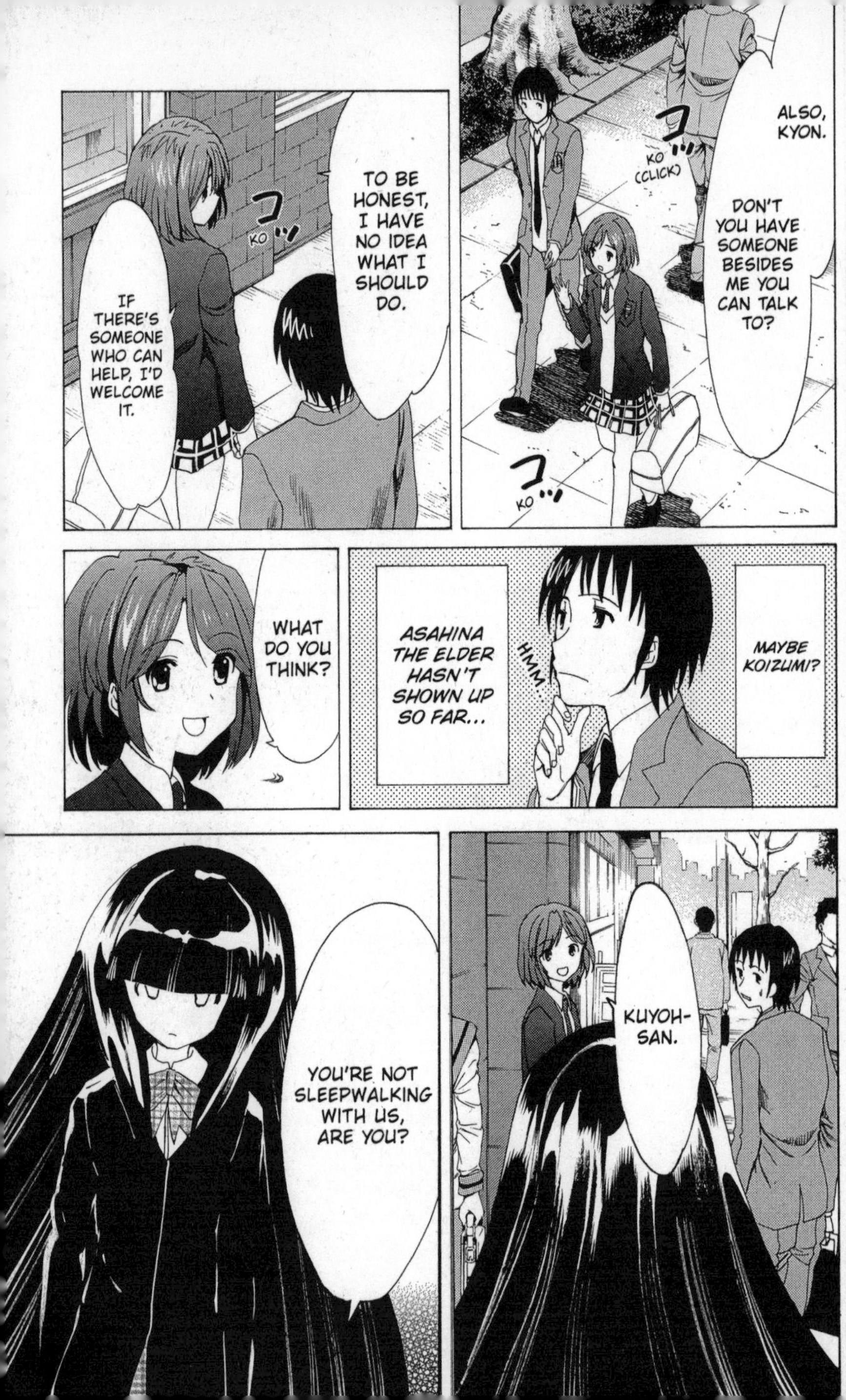
ALSO, KYON.
KO (CLICK)
DON'T YOU HAVE SOMEONE BESIDES ME YOU CAN TALK TO?
KO
TO BE HONEST, I HAVE NO IDEA WHAT I SHOULD DO.
KO
IF THERE'S SOMEONE WHO CAN HELP, I'D WELCOME IT.
MAYBE KOIZUMI?
HMM...
ASAHINA THE ELDER HASN'T SHOWN UP SO FAR...
WHAT DO YOU THINK?
KUYOH-SAN.
YOU'RE NOT SLEEPWALKING WITH US, ARE YOU?

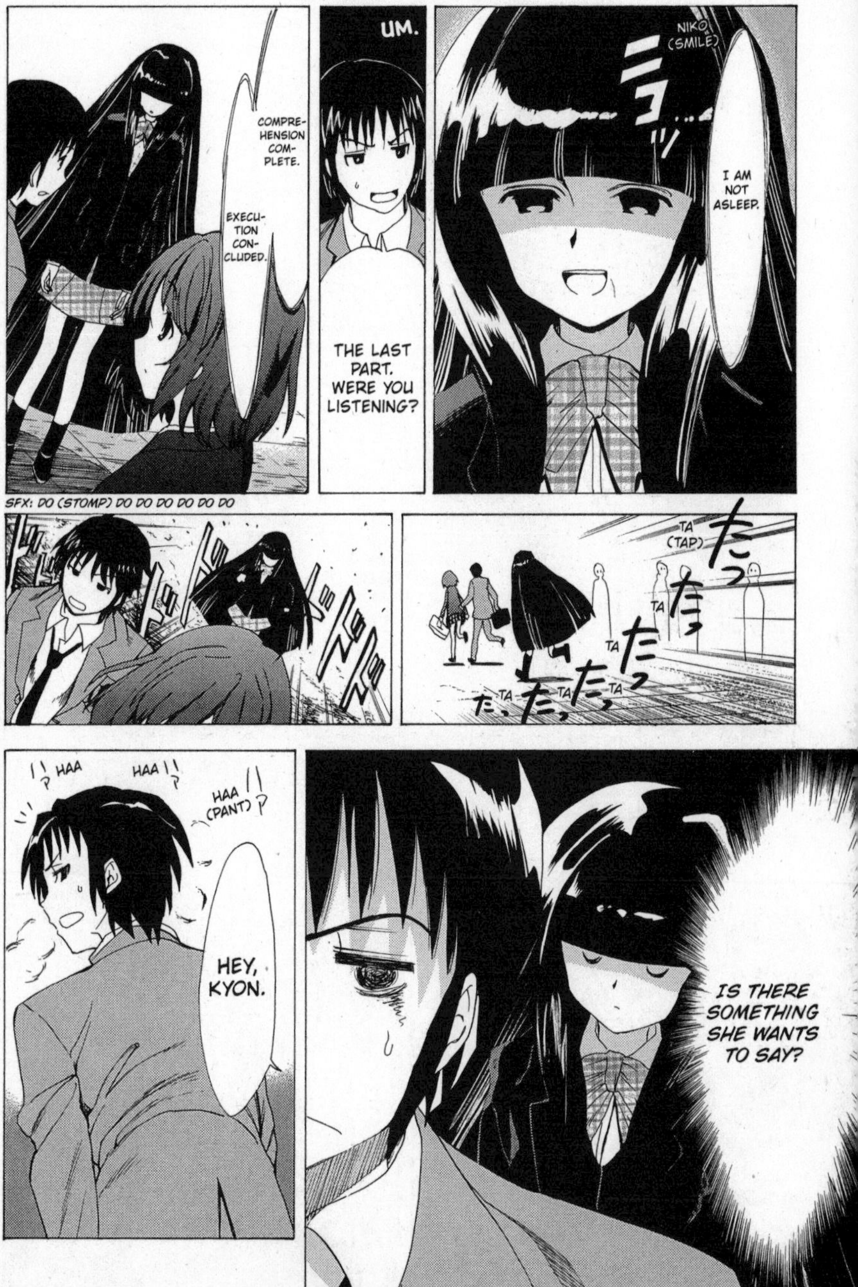
NIKO (SMILE)
I AM NOT ASLEEP.
UM.
THE LAST PART. WERE YOU LISTENING?
COMPRE-HENSION COM-PLETE.
EXECU-TION CON-CLUDED.
SFX: DO (STOMP) DO DO DO DO DO DO
TA (TAP) TA TA TA TA TA TA
IS THERE SOMETHING SHE WANTS TO SAY?
HAA HAA HAA (PANT)
HEY, KYON.

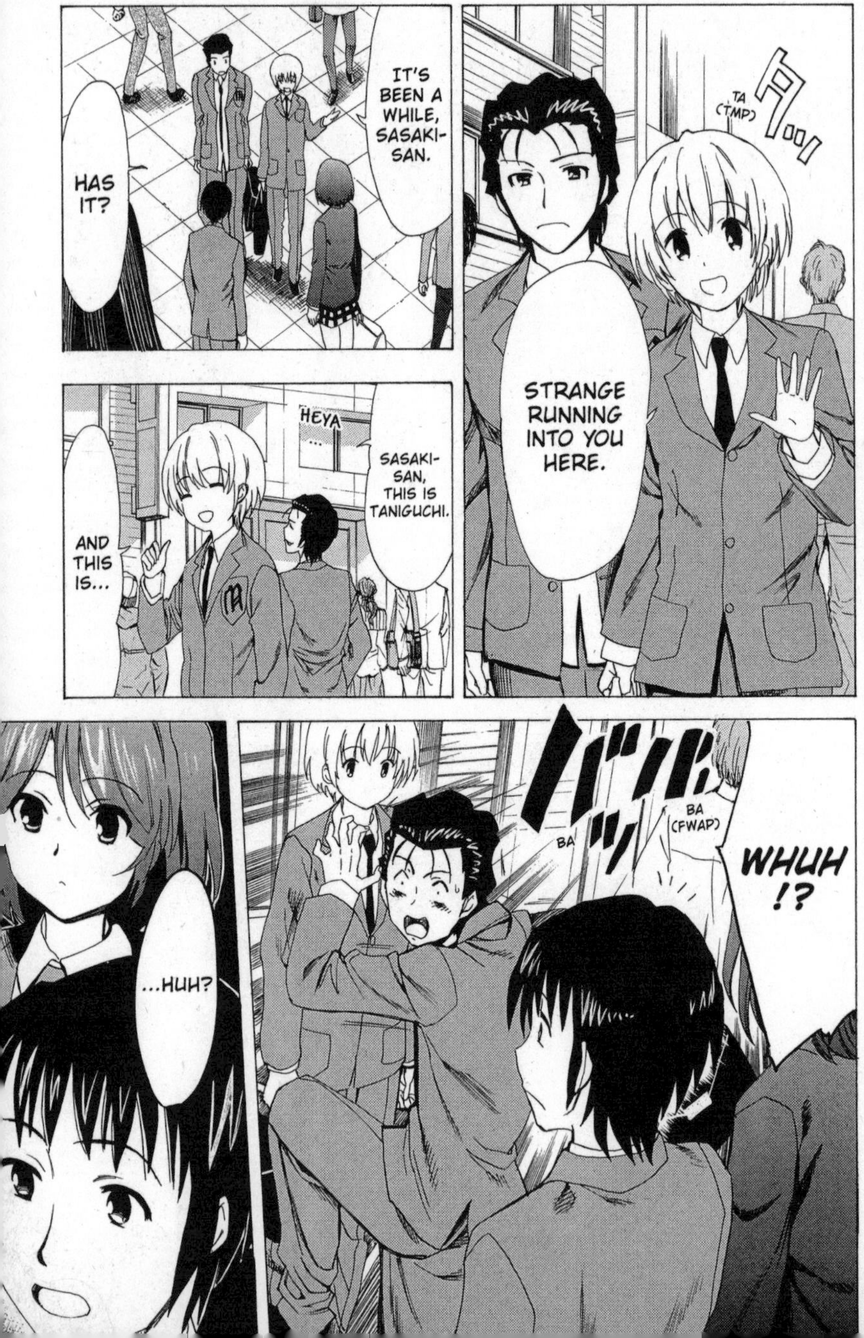
TA (TMP)
STRANGE RUNNING INTO YOU HERE.
IT'S BEEN A WHILE, SASAKI-SAN.
HAS IT?
HEYA ...
SASAKI-SAN, THIS IS TANIGUCHI.
AND THIS IS...
WHUH !?
BA (FWAP)
BA
...HUH?

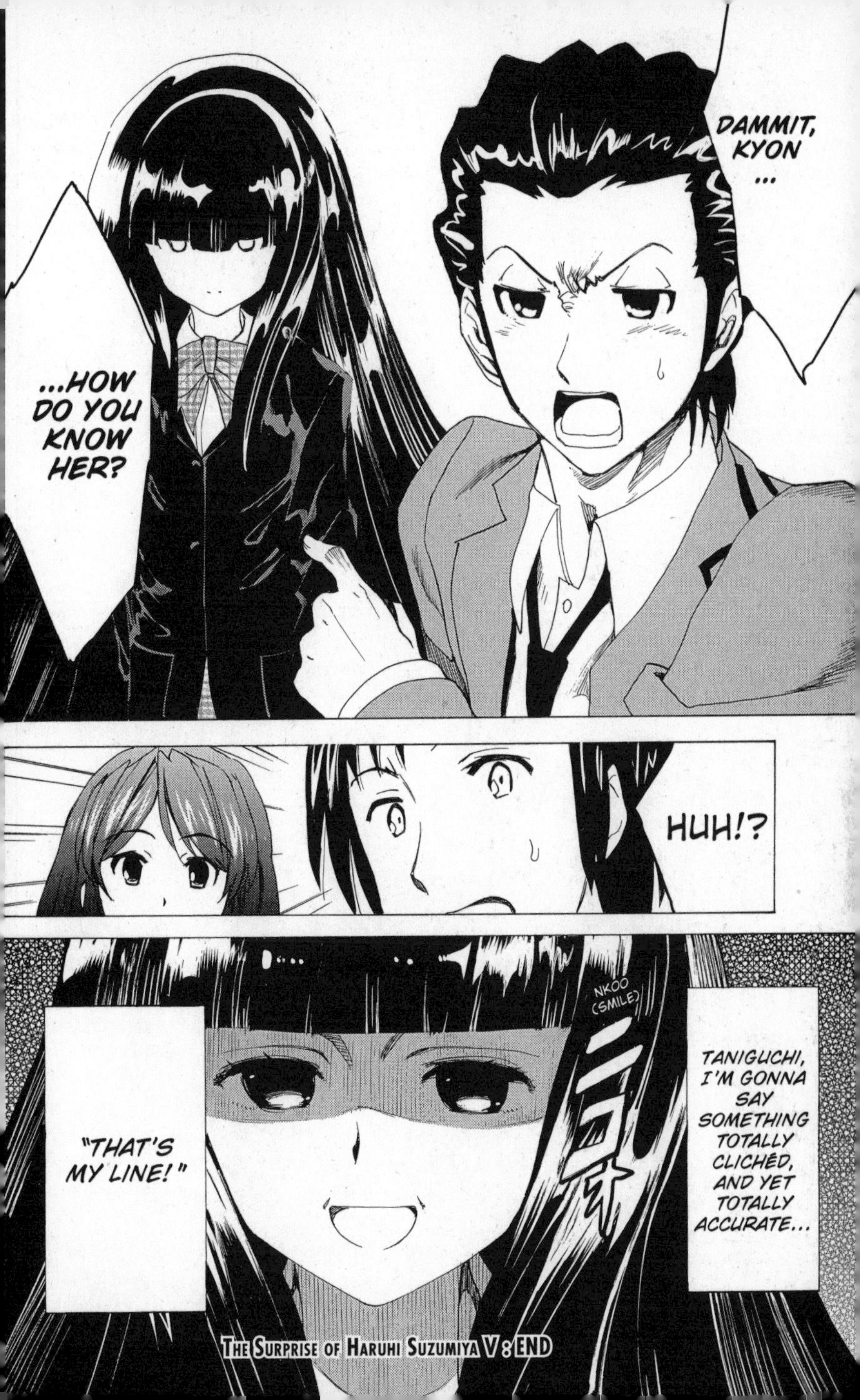
DAMMIT, KYON ...
...HOW DO YOU KNOW HER?
HUH!?
TANIGUCHI, I'M GONNA SAY SOMETHING TOTALLY CLICHÉD, AND YET TOTALLY ACCURATE...
NKOO (SMILE)
"THAT'S MY LINE!"
THE SURPRISE OF HARUHI SUZUMIYA V : END

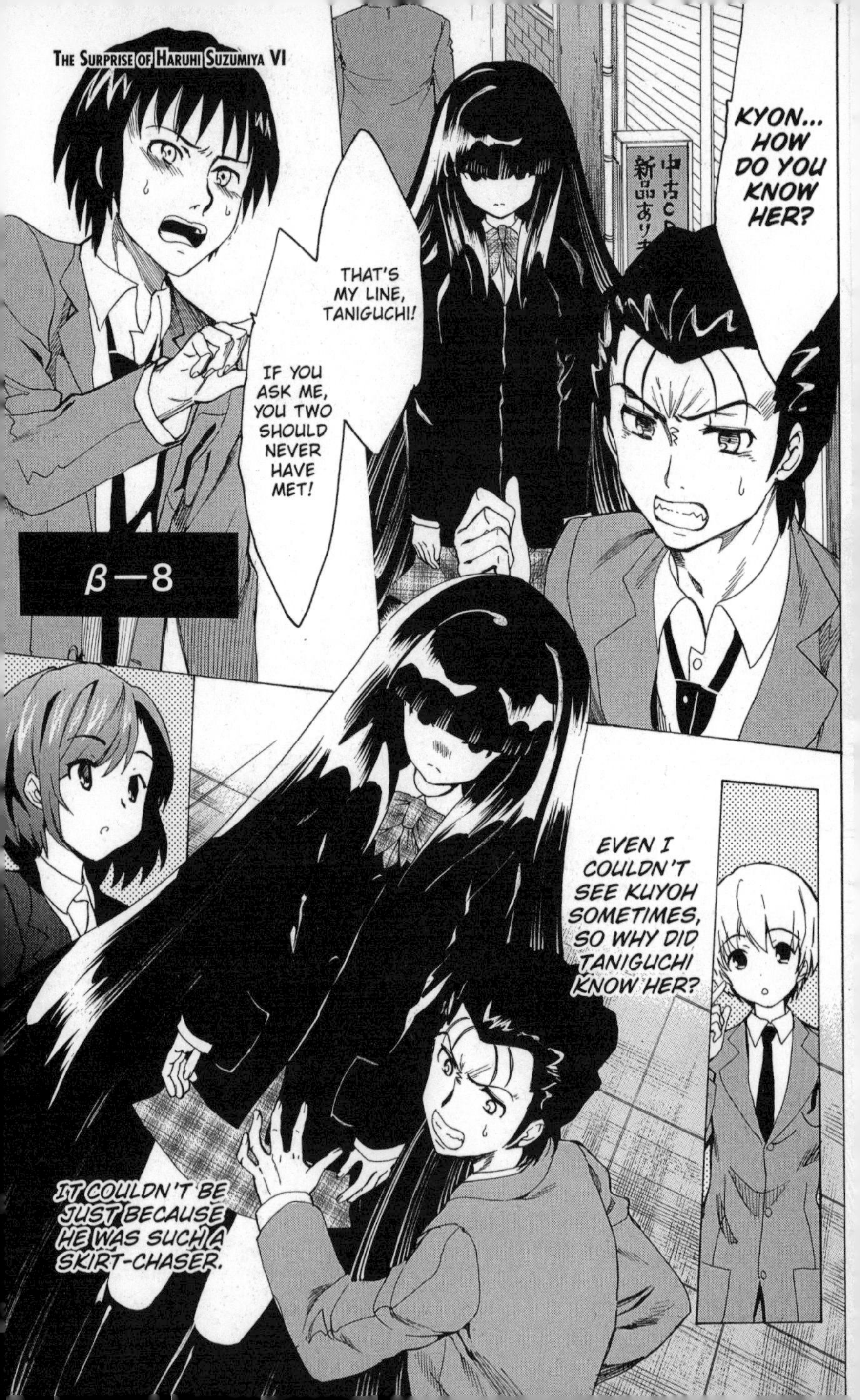
KYON... HOW DO YOU KNOW HER?
THAT'S MY LINE, TANIGUCHI!
IF YOU ASK ME, YOU TWO SHOULD NEVER HAVE MET!
β—8
EVEN I COULDN'T SEE KUYOH SOMETIMES, SO WHY DID TANIGUCHI KNOW HER?
IT COULDN'T BE JUST BECAUSE HE WAS SUCH A SKIRT-CHASER.

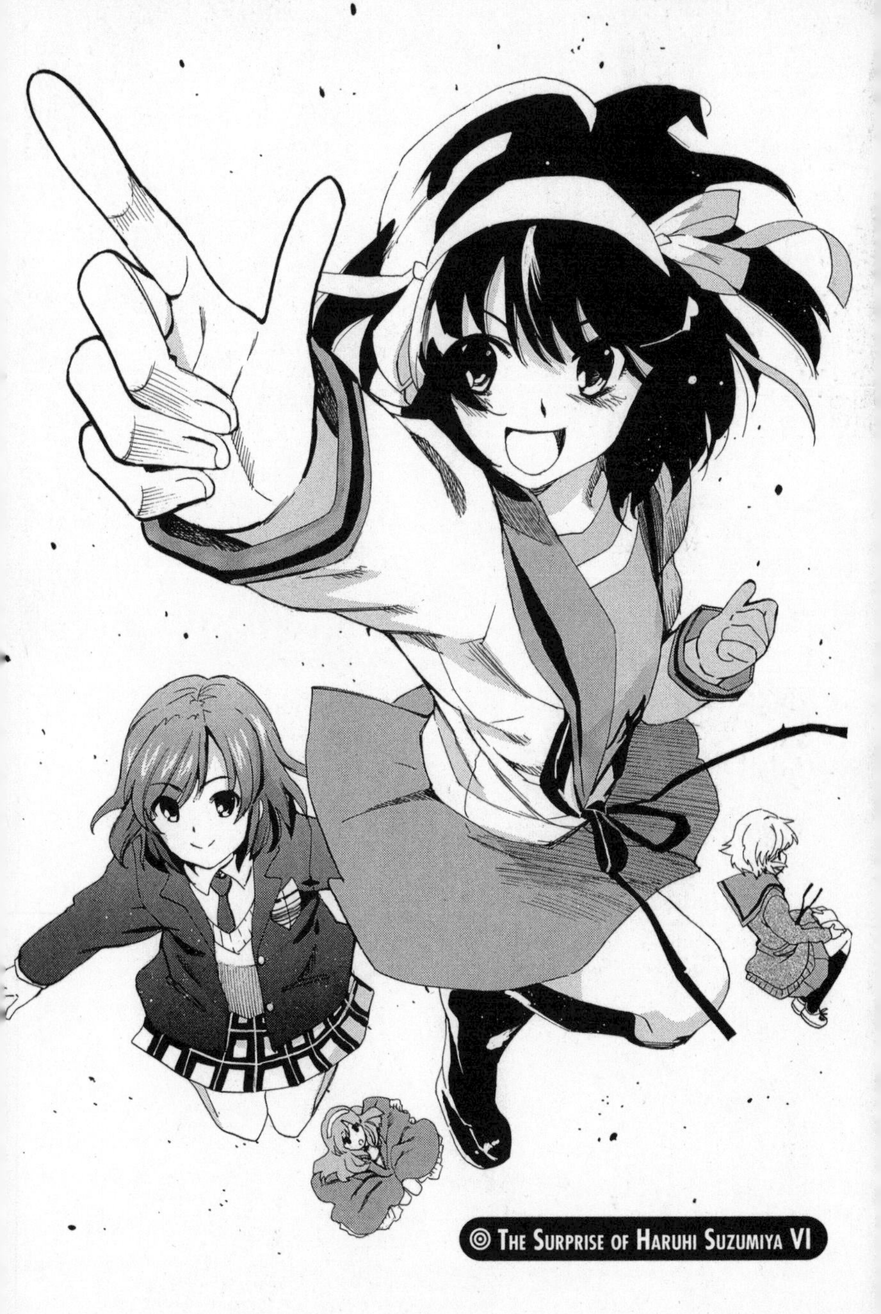

◎ The Surprise of Haruhi Suzumiya VI

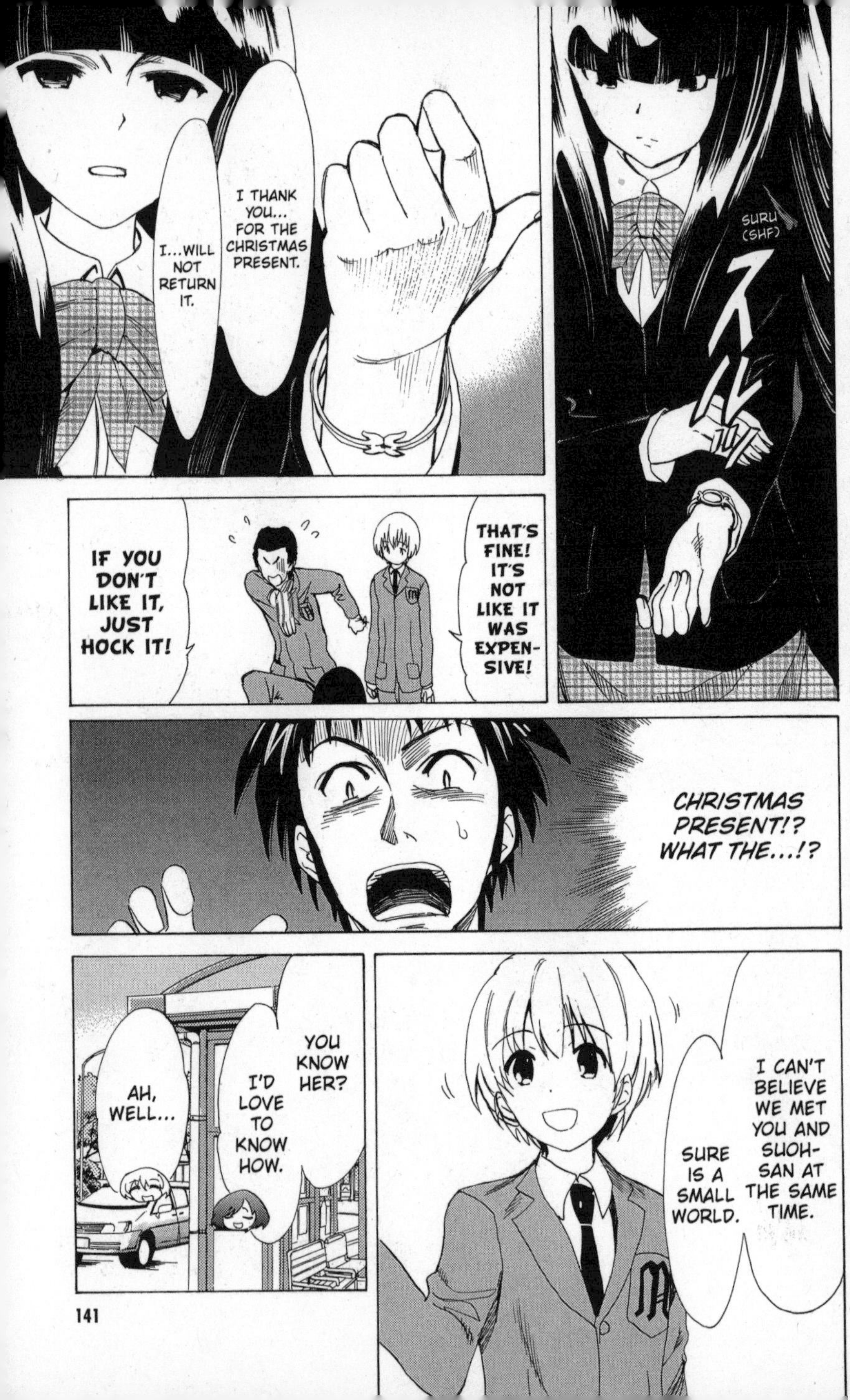
SURU (SHF)
I THANK YOU... FOR THE CHRISTMAS PRESENT.
I...WILL NOT RETURN IT.
THAT'S FINE! IT'S NOT LIKE IT WAS EXPENSIVE!
IF YOU DON'T LIKE IT, JUST HOCK IT!
CHRISTMAS PRESENT!? WHAT THE...!?
I CAN'T BELIEVE WE MET YOU AND SUOH-SAN AT THE SAME TIME.
SURE IS A SMALL WORLD.
YOU KNOW HER?
I'D LOVE TO KNOW HOW.
AH, WELL...

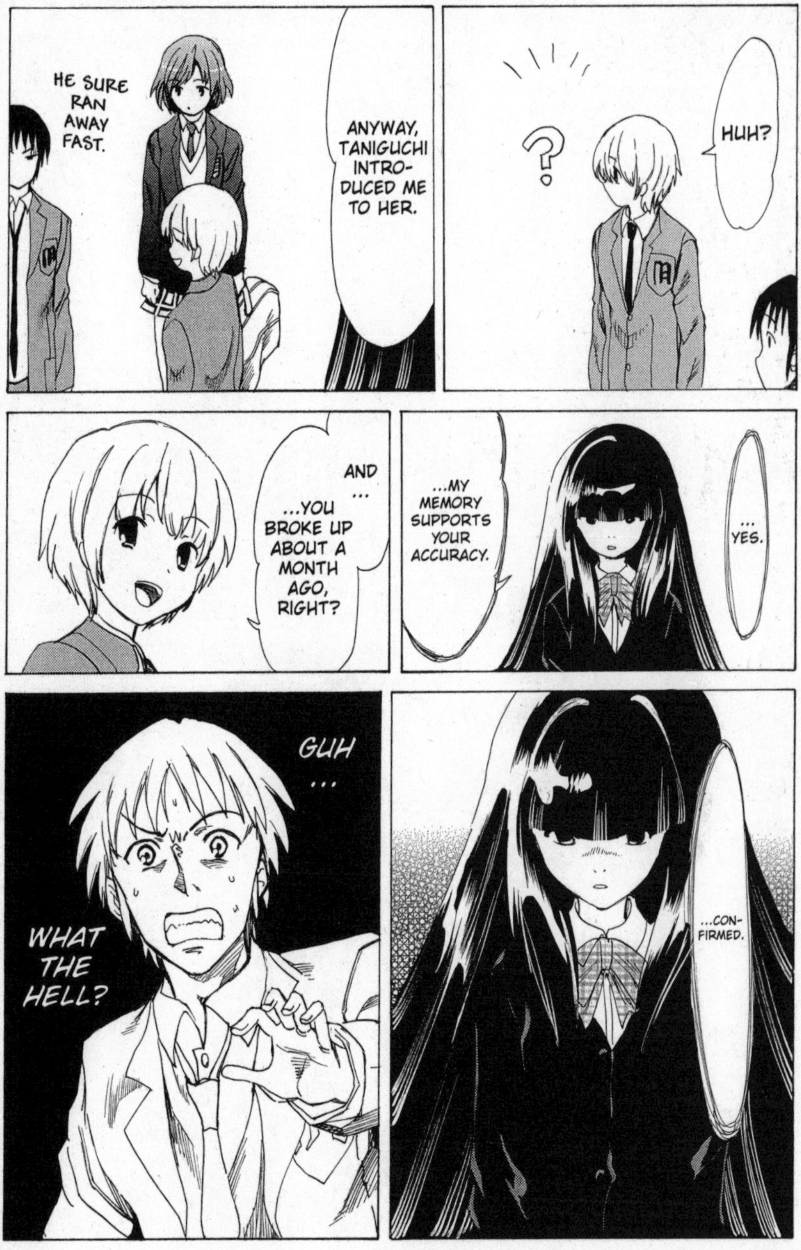
HUH?
ANYWAY, TANIGUCHI INTRO-DUCED ME TO HER.
HE SURE RAN AWAY FAST.
... YES.
...MY MEMORY SUPPORTS YOUR ACCURACY.
AND ...
...YOU BROKE UP ABOUT A MONTH AGO, RIGHT?
...CON-FIRMED.
GUH ...
WHAT THE HELL?

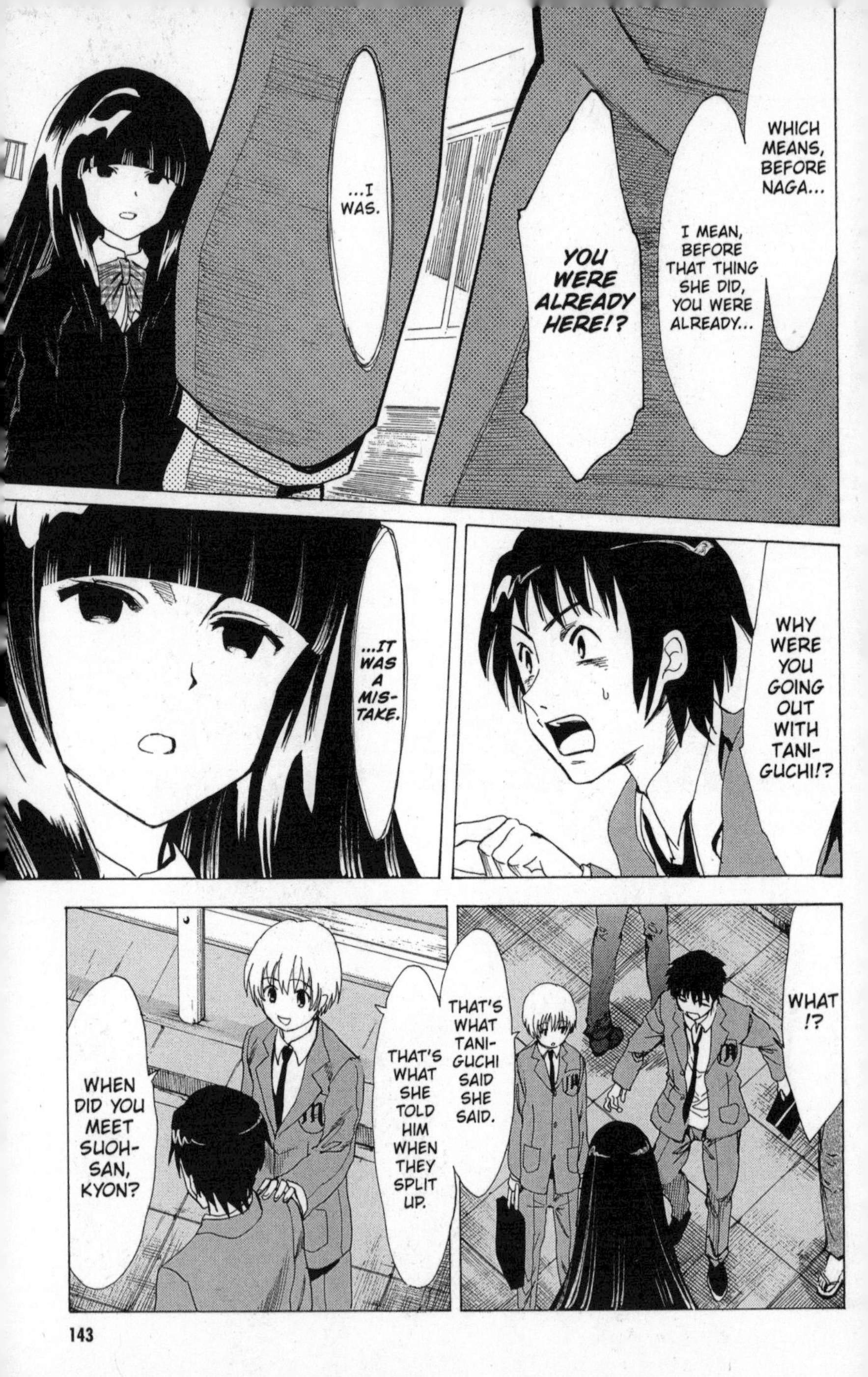
WHICH MEANS, BEFORE NAGA...
I MEAN, BEFORE THAT THING SHE DID, YOU WERE ALREADY...
YOU WERE ALREADY HERE!?
...I WAS.
WHY WERE YOU GOING OUT WITH TANI-GUCHI!?
...IT WAS A MIS-TAKE.
WHAT!?
THAT'S WHAT TANI-GUCHI SAID SHE SAID.
THAT'S WHAT SHE TOLD HIM WHEN THEY SPLIT UP.
WHEN DID YOU MEET SUOH-SAN, KYON?

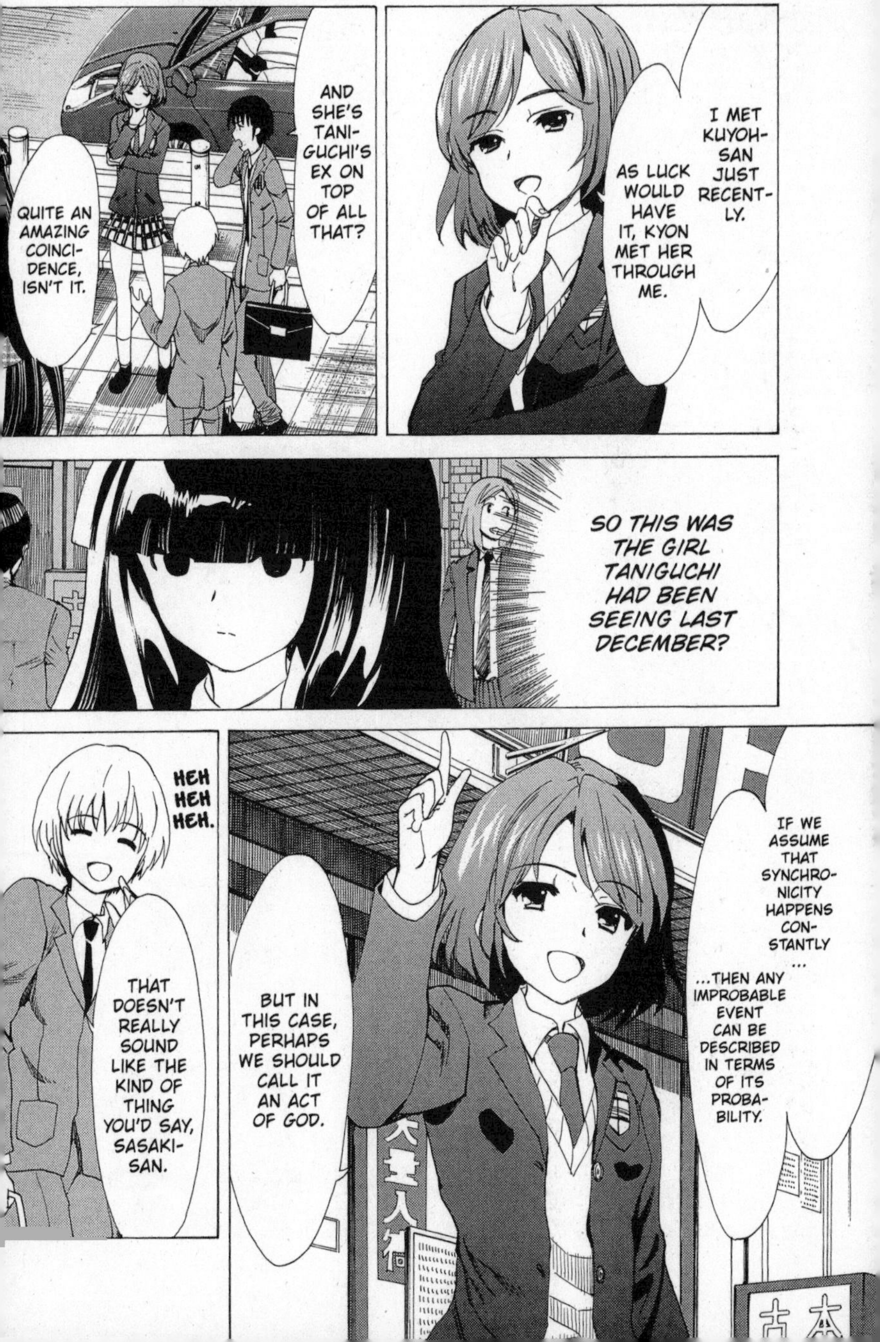
I MET KUYOH-SAN JUST RECENTLY.
AS LUCK WOULD HAVE IT, KYON MET HER THROUGH ME.
AND SHE'S TANIGUCHI'S EX ON TOP OF ALL THAT?
QUITE AN AMAZING COINCIDENCE, ISN'T IT.
SO THIS WAS THE GIRL TANIGUCHI HAD BEEN SEEING LAST DECEMBER?
IF WE ASSUME THAT SYNCHRONICITY HAPPENS CONSTANTLY...
...THEN ANY IMPROBABLE EVENT CAN BE DESCRIBED IN TERMS OF ITS PROBABILITY.
BUT IN THIS CASE, PERHAPS WE SHOULD CALL IT AN ACT OF GOD.
HEH HEH HEH.
THAT DOESN'T REALLY SOUND LIKE THE KIND OF THING YOU'D SAY, SASAKI-SAN.
古本

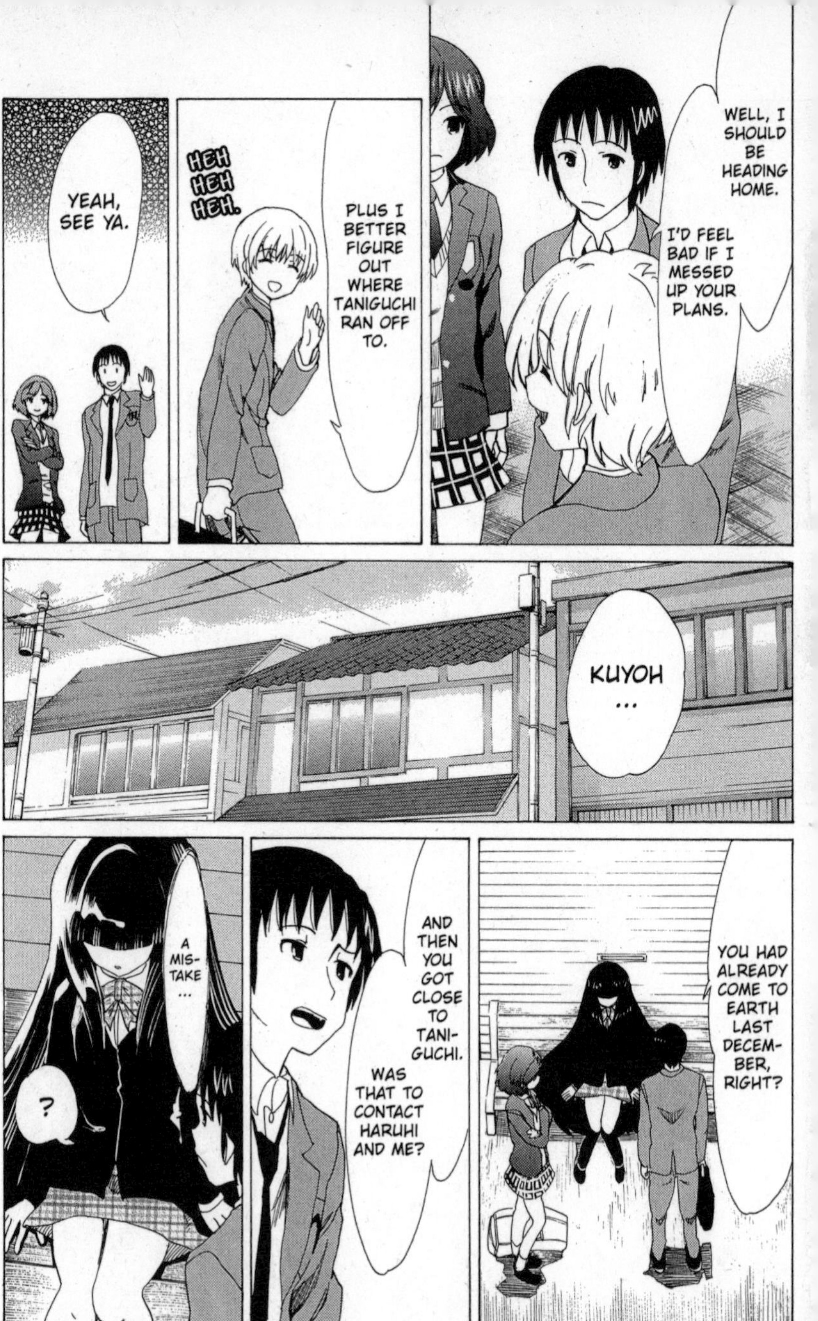
WELL, I SHOULD BE HEADING HOME.
I'D FEEL BAD IF I MESSED UP YOUR PLANS.
HEH HEH HEH.
PLUS I BETTER FIGURE OUT WHERE TANIGUCHI RAN OFF TO.
YEAH, SEE YA.
KUYOH ...
YOU HAD ALREADY COME TO EARTH LAST DECEMBER, RIGHT?
AND THEN YOU GOT CLOSE TO TANIGUCHI.
WAS THAT TO CONTACT HARUHI AND ME?
A MISTAKE ...
?

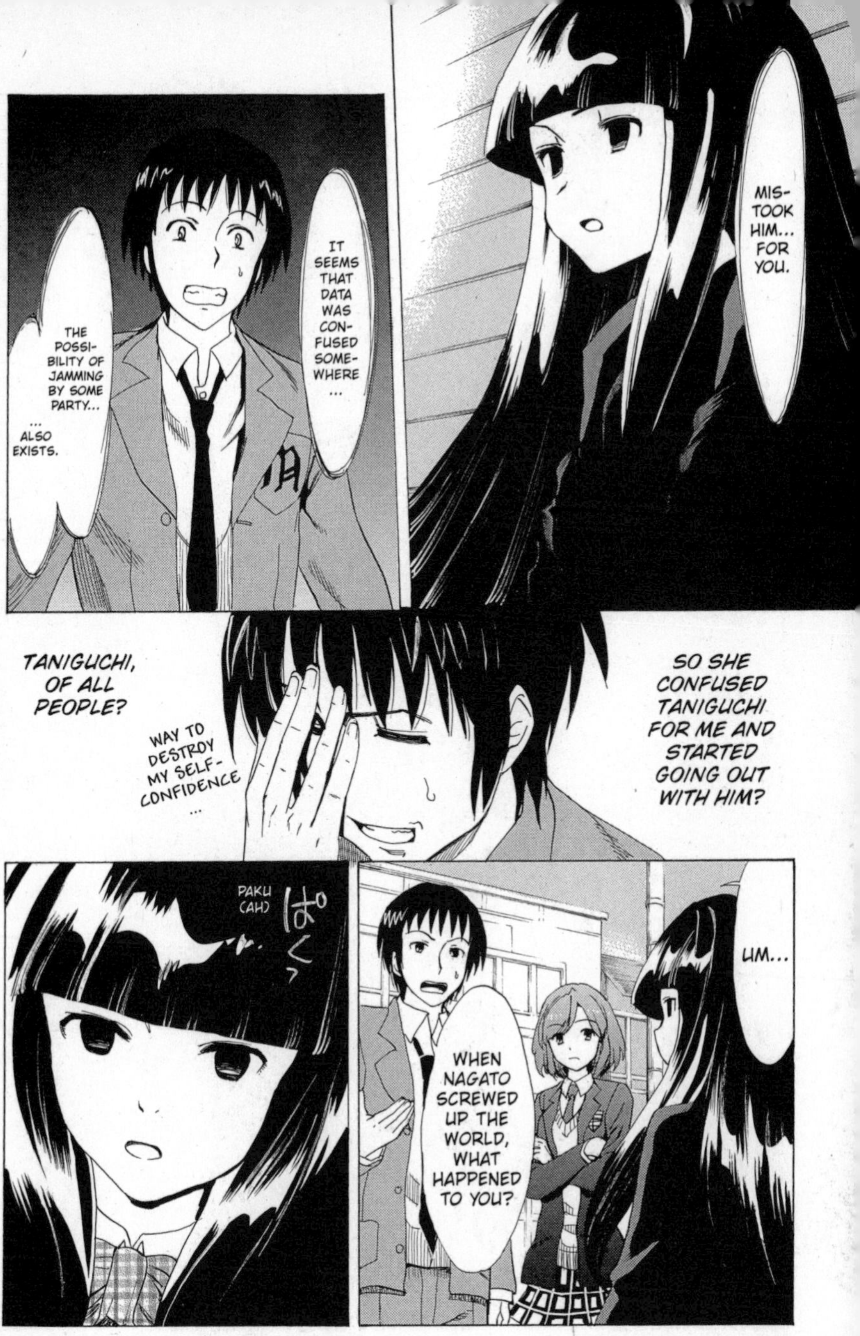
MIS-TOOK HIM... FOR YOU.
IT SEEMS THAT DATA WAS CON-FUSED SOME-WHERE ...
THE POSSI-BILITY OF JAMMING BY SOME PARTY... ... ALSO EXISTS.
SO SHE CONFUSED TANIGUCHI FOR ME AND STARTED GOING OUT WITH HIM?
TANIGUCHI, OF ALL PEOPLE?
WAY TO DESTROY MY SELF-CONFIDENCE ...
UM...
WHEN NAGATO SCREWED UP THE WORLD, WHAT HAPPENED TO YOU?
PAKU (AH)
ぱくっ

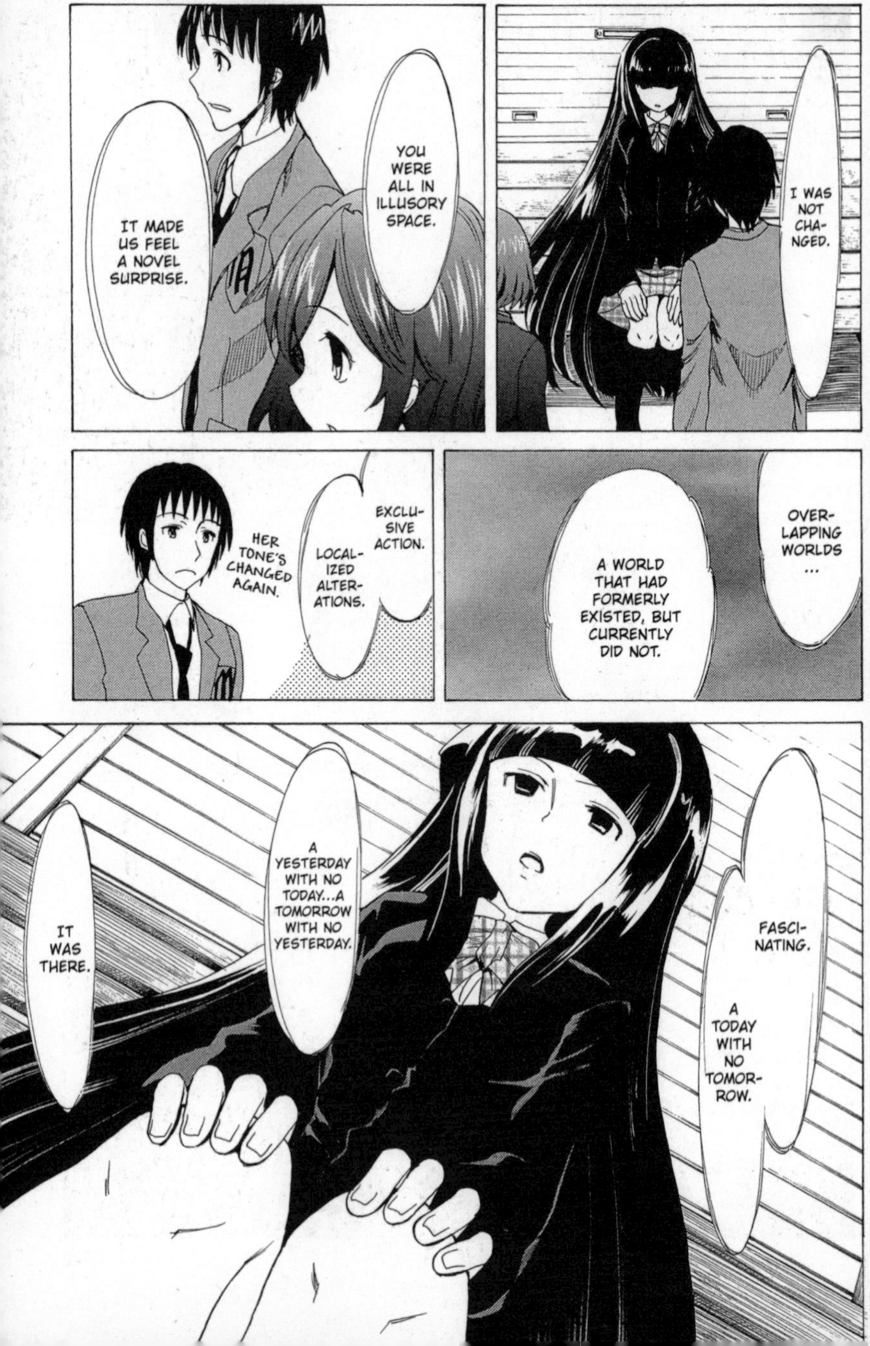
I WAS NOT CHANGED.
YOU WERE ALL IN ILLUSORY SPACE.
IT MADE US FEEL A NOVEL SURPRISE.
OVERLAPPING WORLDS...
A WORLD THAT HAD FORMERLY EXISTED, BUT CURRENTLY DID NOT.
EXCLUSIVE ACTION.
LOCALIZED ALTERATIONS.
HER TONE'S CHANGED AGAIN.
FASCINATING.
A TODAY WITH NO TOMORROW.
A YESTERDAY WITH NO TODAY...A TOMORROW WITH NO YESTERDAY.
IT WAS THERE.

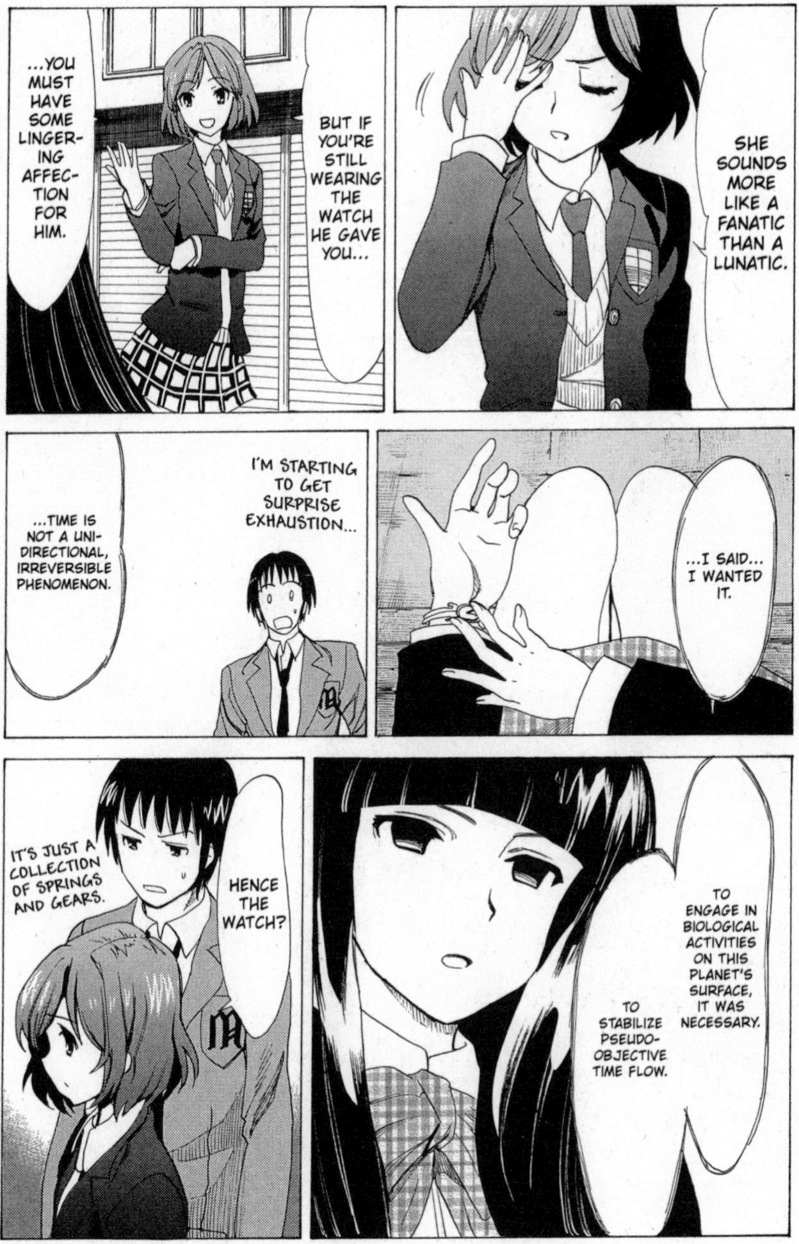
SHE SOUNDS MORE LIKE A FANATIC THAN A LUNATIC.
BUT IF YOU'RE STILL WEARING THE WATCH HE GAVE YOU...
...YOU MUST HAVE SOME LINGERING AFFECTION FOR HIM.
...I SAID... I WANTED IT.
I'M STARTING TO GET SURPRISE EXHAUSTION...
...TIME IS NOT A UNIDIRECTIONAL, IRREVERSIBLE PHENOMENON.
TO ENGAGE IN BIOLOGICAL ACTIVITIES ON THIS PLANET'S SURFACE, IT WAS NECESSARY.
TO STABILIZE PSEUDO-OBJECTIVE TIME FLOW.
HENCE THE WATCH?
IT'S JUST A COLLECTION OF SPRINGS AND GEARS.

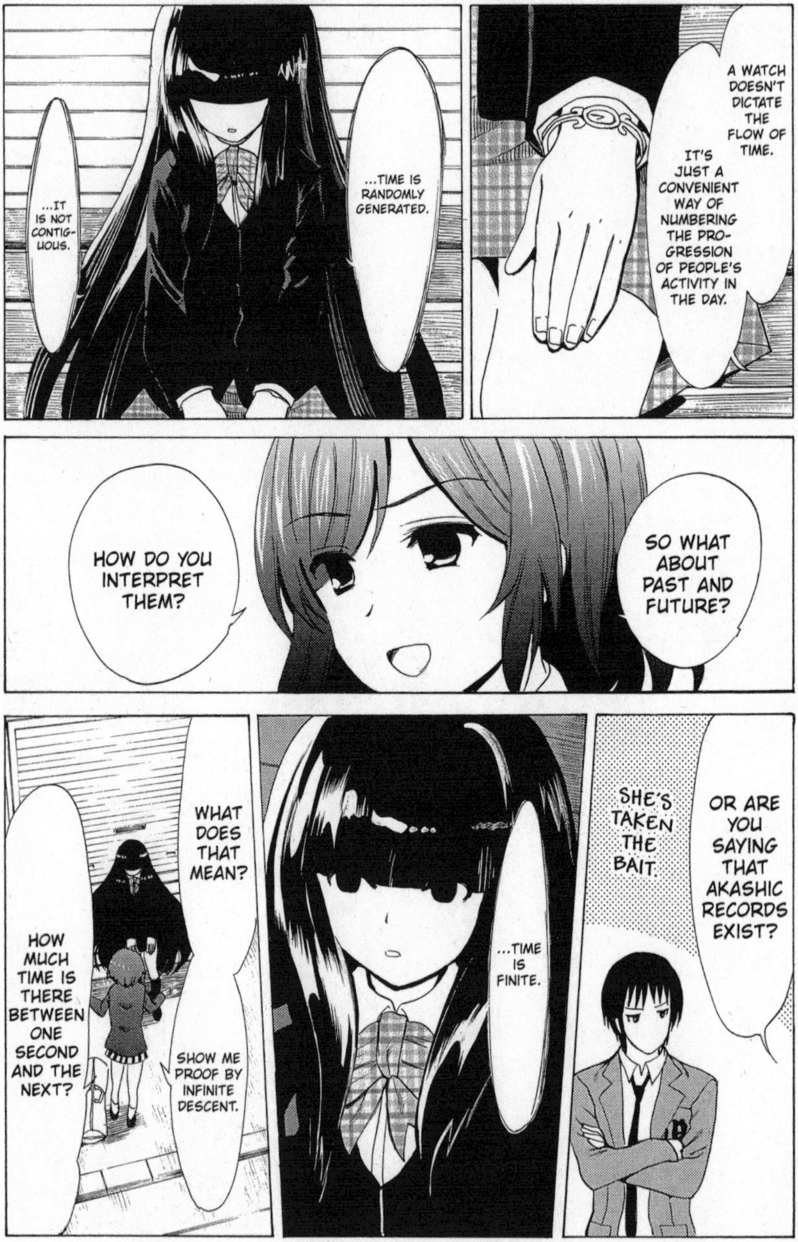
A WATCH DOESN'T DICTATE THE FLOW OF TIME.
IT'S JUST A CONVENIENT WAY OF NUMBERING THE PROGRESSION OF PEOPLE'S ACTIVITY IN THE DAY.
...TIME IS RANDOMLY GENERATED.
...IT IS NOT CONTIGUOUS.
SO WHAT ABOUT PAST AND FUTURE?
HOW DO YOU INTERPRET THEM?
OR ARE YOU SAYING THAT AKASHIC RECORDS EXIST?
SHE'S TAKEN THE BAIT.
...TIME IS FINITE.
WHAT DOES THAT MEAN?
SHOW ME PROOF BY INFINITE DESCENT.
HOW MUCH TIME IS THERE BETWEEN ONE SECOND AND THE NEXT?

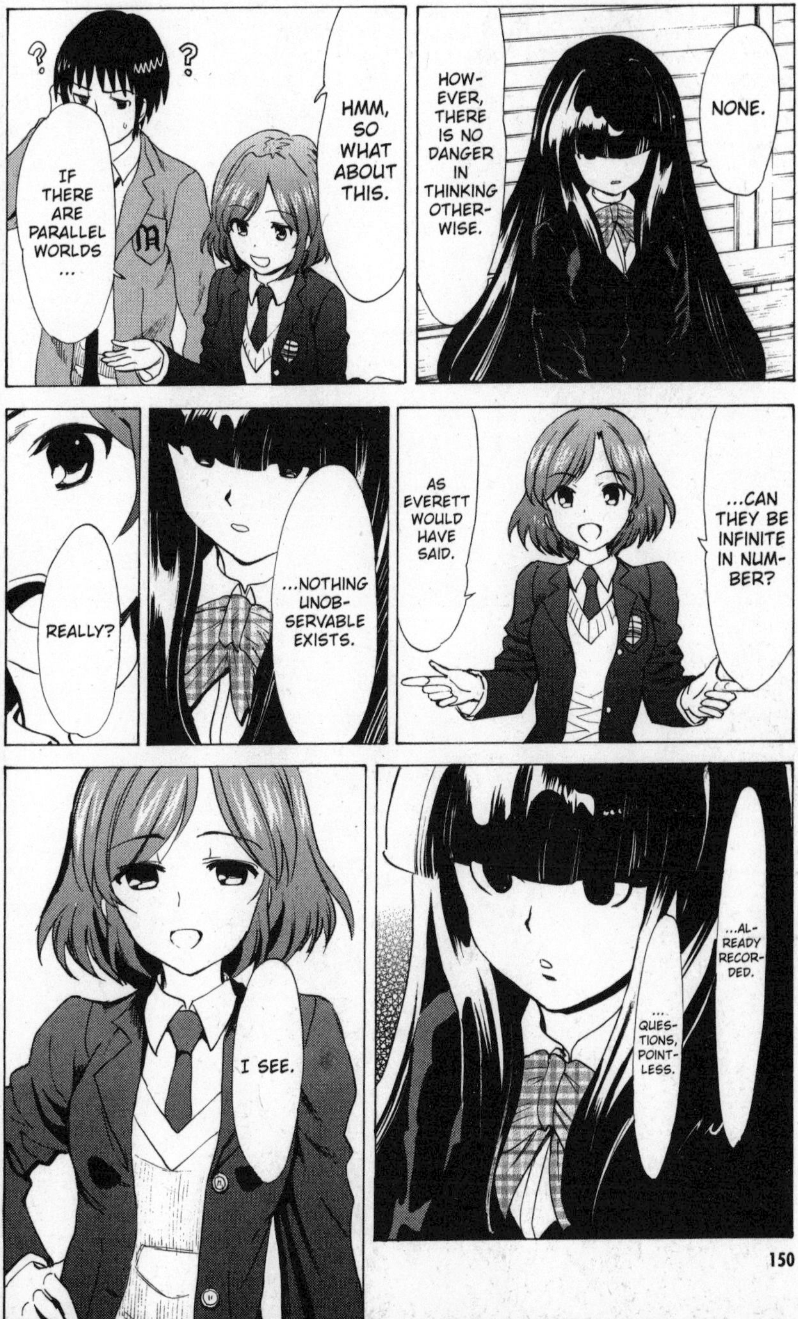
NONE.
HOW-EVER, THERE IS NO DANGER IN THINKING OTHER-WISE.
HMM, SO WHAT ABOUT THIS.
IF THERE ARE PARALLEL WORLDS ...
...CAN THEY BE INFINITE IN NUM-BER?
AS EVERETT WOULD HAVE SAID.
...NOTHING UNOB-SERVABLE EXISTS.
REALLY?
...AL-READY RECOR-DED.
... QUES-TIONS, POINT-LESS.
I SEE.

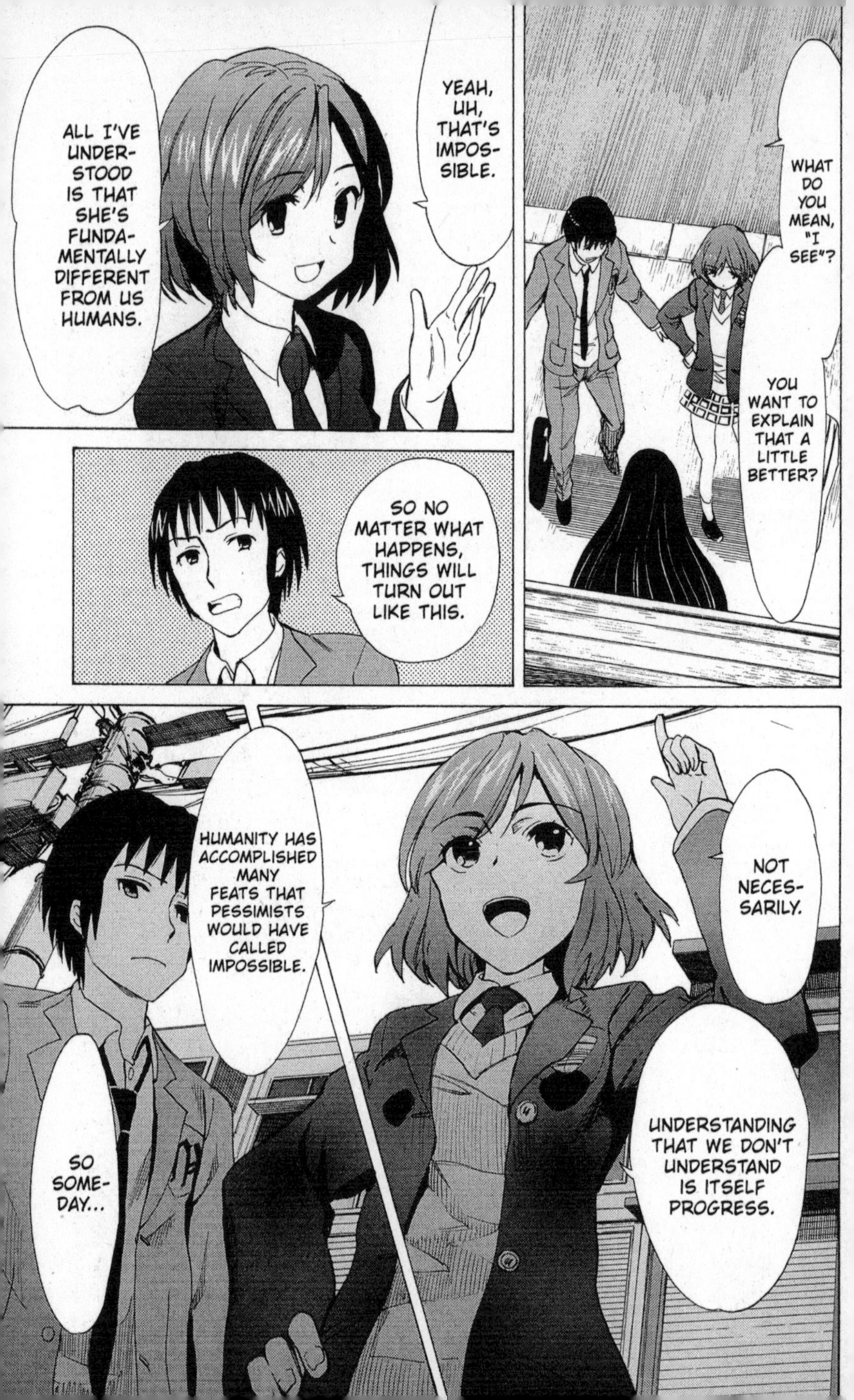
WHAT DO YOU MEAN, "I SEE"?
YOU WANT TO EXPLAIN THAT A LITTLE BETTER?
YEAH, UH, THAT'S IMPOSSIBLE.
ALL I'VE UNDERSTOOD IS THAT SHE'S FUNDAMENTALLY DIFFERENT FROM US HUMANS.
SO NO MATTER WHAT HAPPENS, THINGS WILL TURN OUT LIKE THIS.
NOT NECESSARILY.
HUMANITY HAS ACCOMPLISHED MANY FEATS THAT PESSIMISTS WOULD HAVE CALLED IMPOSSIBLE.
UNDERSTANDING THAT WE DON'T UNDERSTAND IS ITSELF PROGRESS.
SO SOMEDAY...

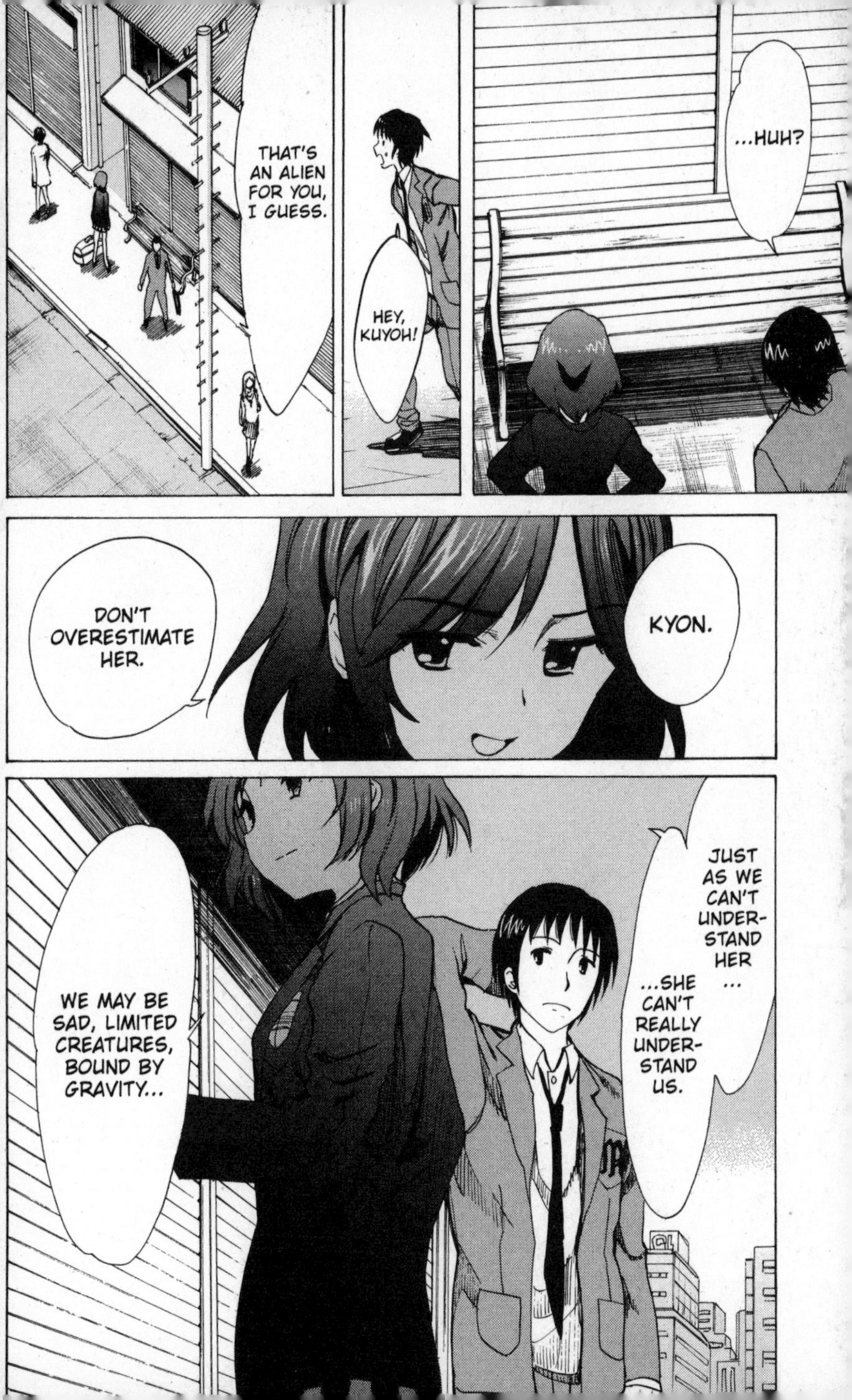
...HUH?
HEY, KUYOH!
THAT'S AN ALIEN FOR YOU, I GUESS.
KYON.
DON'T OVERESTIMATE HER.
JUST AS WE CAN'T UNDER-STAND HER ...
...SHE CAN'T REALLY UNDER-STAND US.
WE MAY BE SAD, LIMITED CREATURES, BOUND BY GRAVITY...

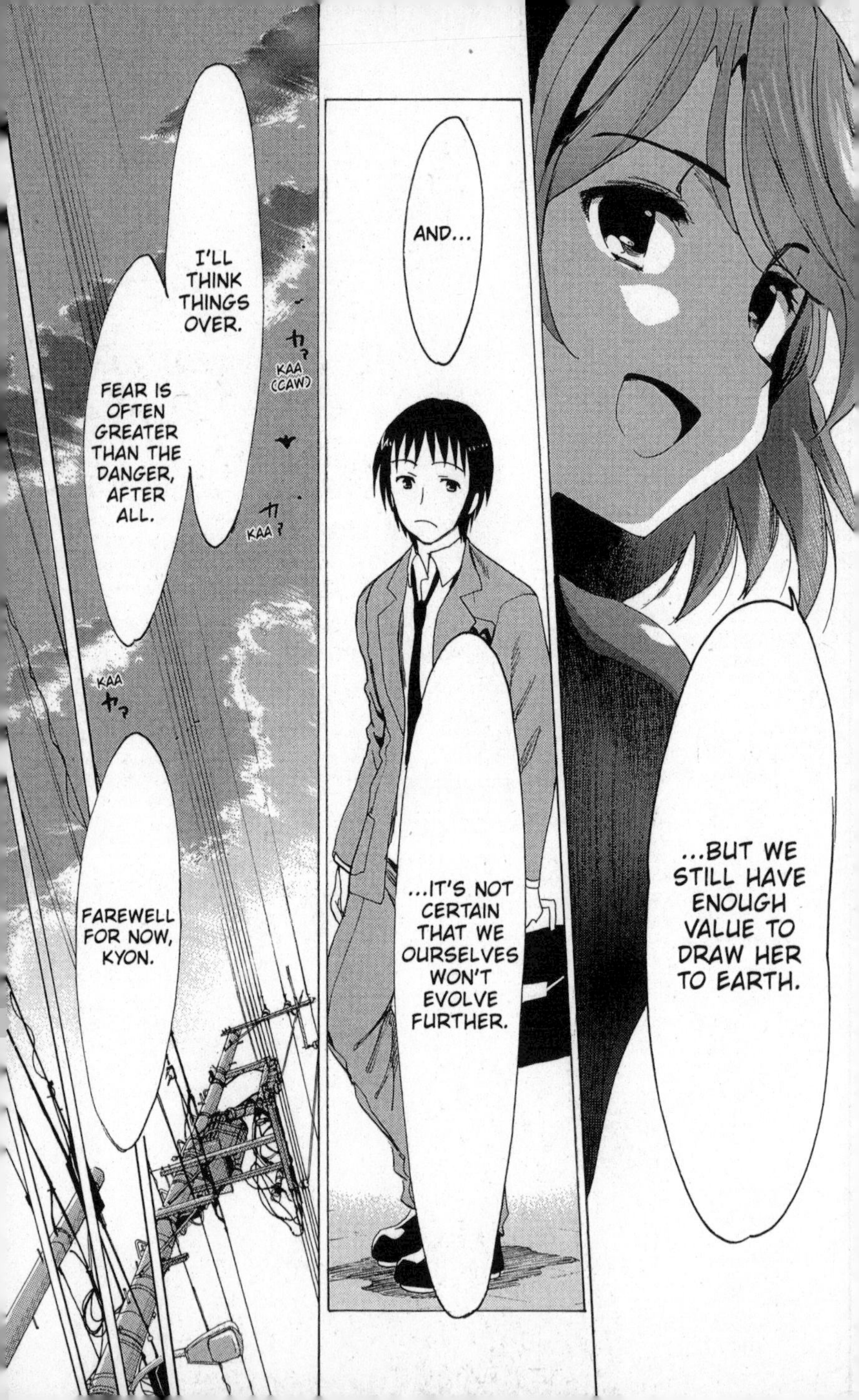
...BUT WE STILL HAVE ENOUGH VALUE TO DRAW HER TO EARTH.
AND...
...IT'S NOT CERTAIN THAT WE OURSELVES WON'T EVOLVE FURTHER.
I'LL THINK THINGS OVER.
KAA (CAW)
FEAR IS OFTEN GREATER THAN THE DANGER, AFTER ALL.
KAA
KAA
FAREWELL FOR NOW, KYON.

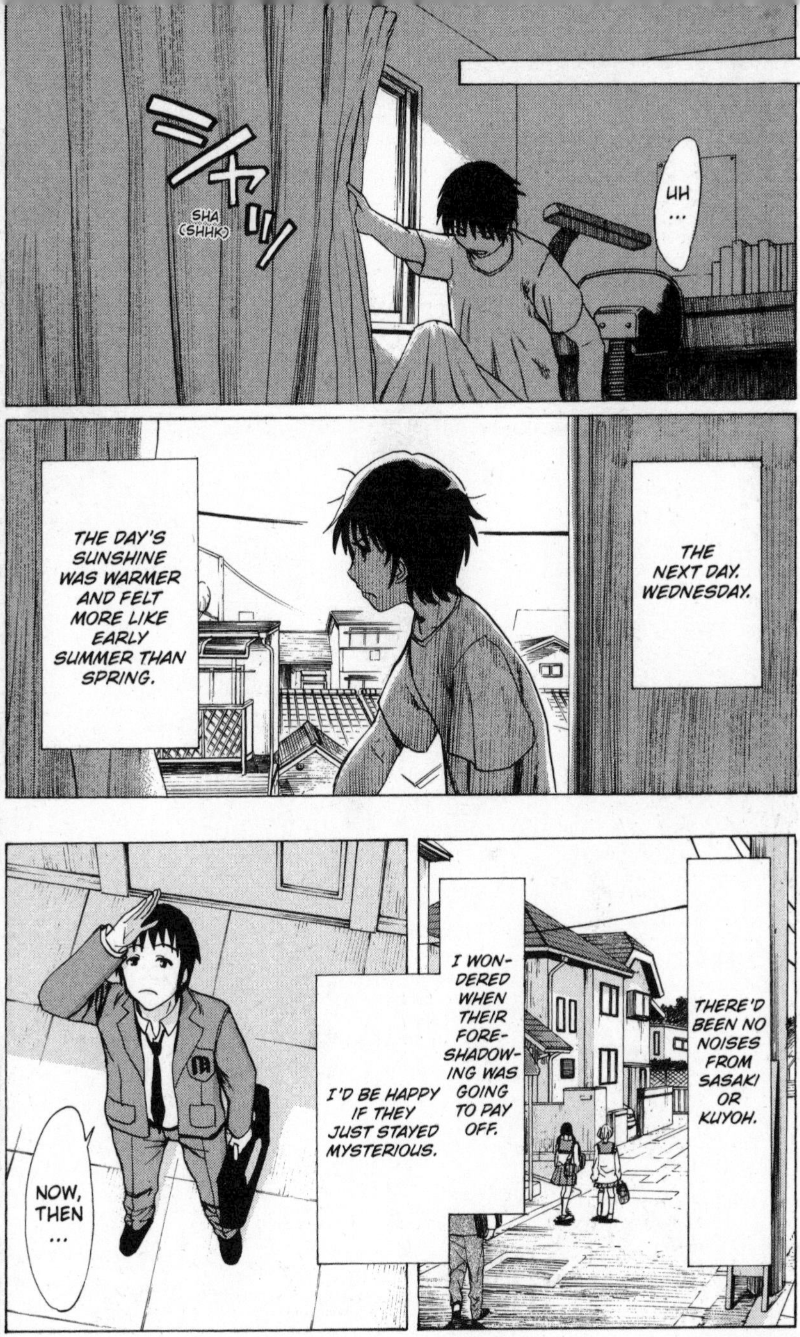
UH ...
シャッ
SHA (SHHK)
THE NEXT DAY. WEDNESDAY.
THE DAY'S SUNSHINE WAS WARMER AND FELT MORE LIKE EARLY SUMMER THAN SPRING.
THERE'D BEEN NO NOISES FROM SASAKI OR KUYOH.
I WONDERED WHEN THEIR FORESHADOWING WAS GOING TO PAY OFF.
I'D BE HAPPY IF THEY JUST STAYED MYSTERIOUS.
NOW, THEN ...

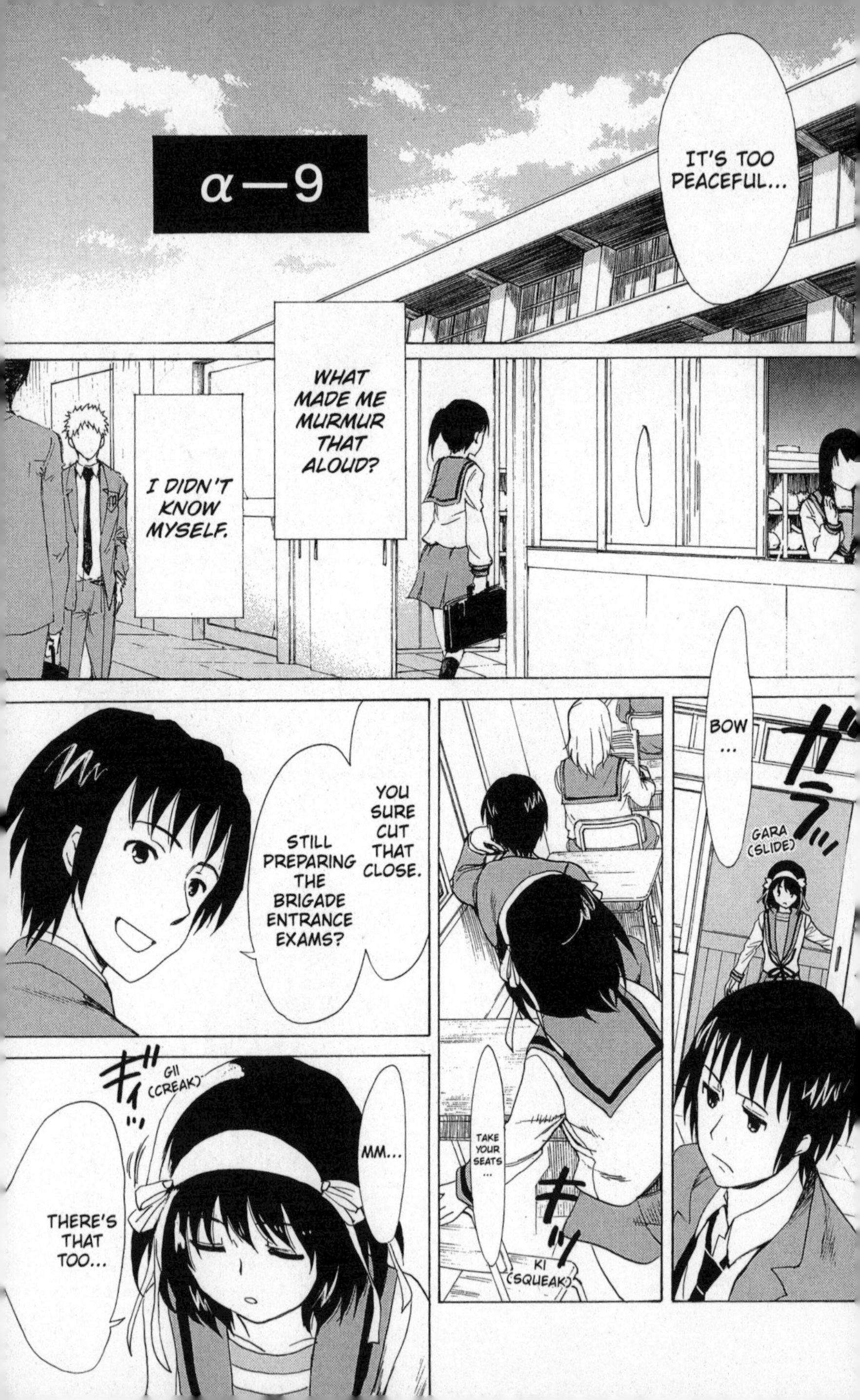

IT'S TOO PEACEFUL...
α—9
WHAT MADE ME MURMUR THAT ALOUD?
I DIDN'T KNOW MYSELF.
BOW ...
GARA (SLIDE)
TAKE YOUR SEATS ...
KI (SQUEAK)
YOU SURE CUT THAT CLOSE.
STILL PREPARING THE BRIGADE ENTRANCE EXAMS?
GII (CREAK)
MM...
THERE'S THAT TOO...

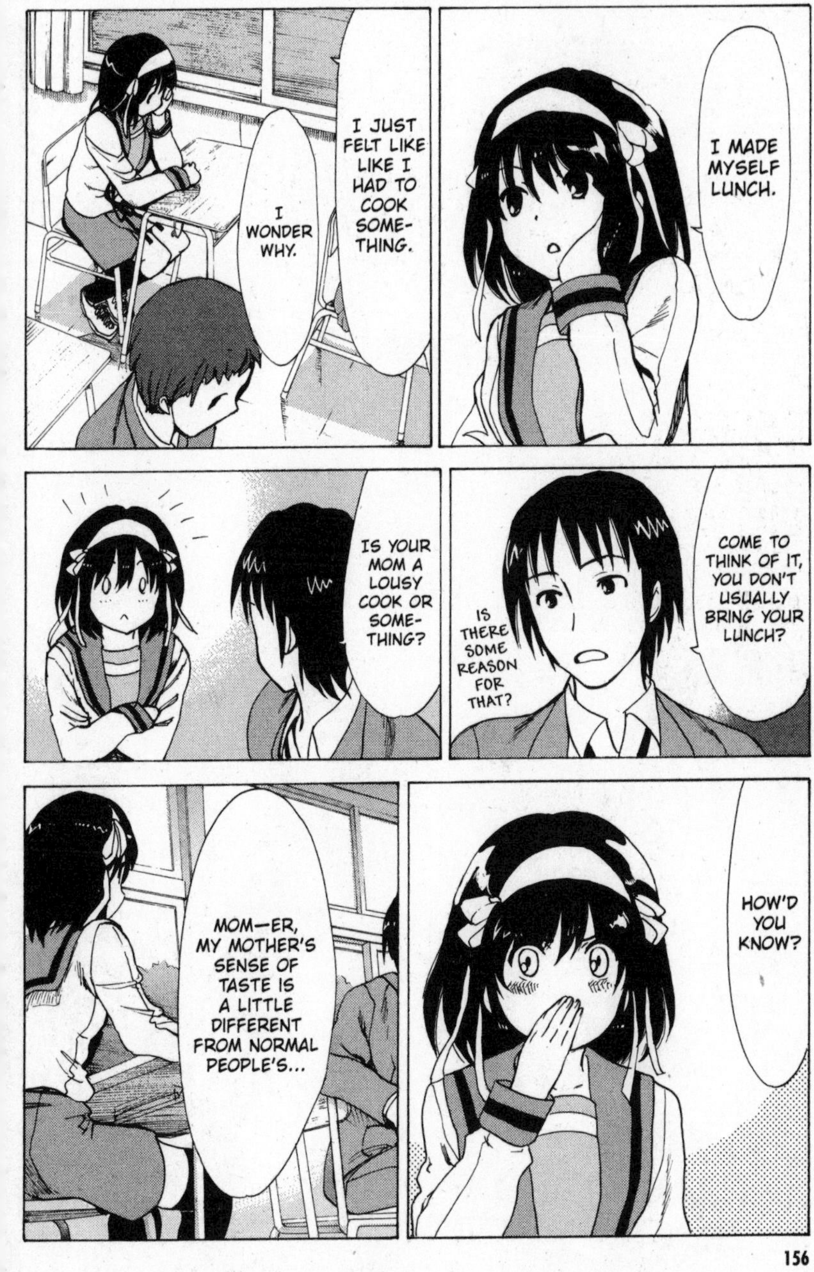
I MADE MYSELF LUNCH.
I JUST FELT LIKE LIKE I HAD TO COOK SOME-THING.
I WONDER WHY.
COME TO THINK OF IT, YOU DON'T USUALLY BRING YOUR LUNCH?
IS THERE SOME REASON FOR THAT?
IS YOUR MOM A LOUSY COOK OR SOME-THING?
HOW'D YOU KNOW?
MOM—ER, MY MOTHER'S SENSE OF TASTE IS A LITTLE DIFFERENT FROM NORMAL PEOPLE'S...

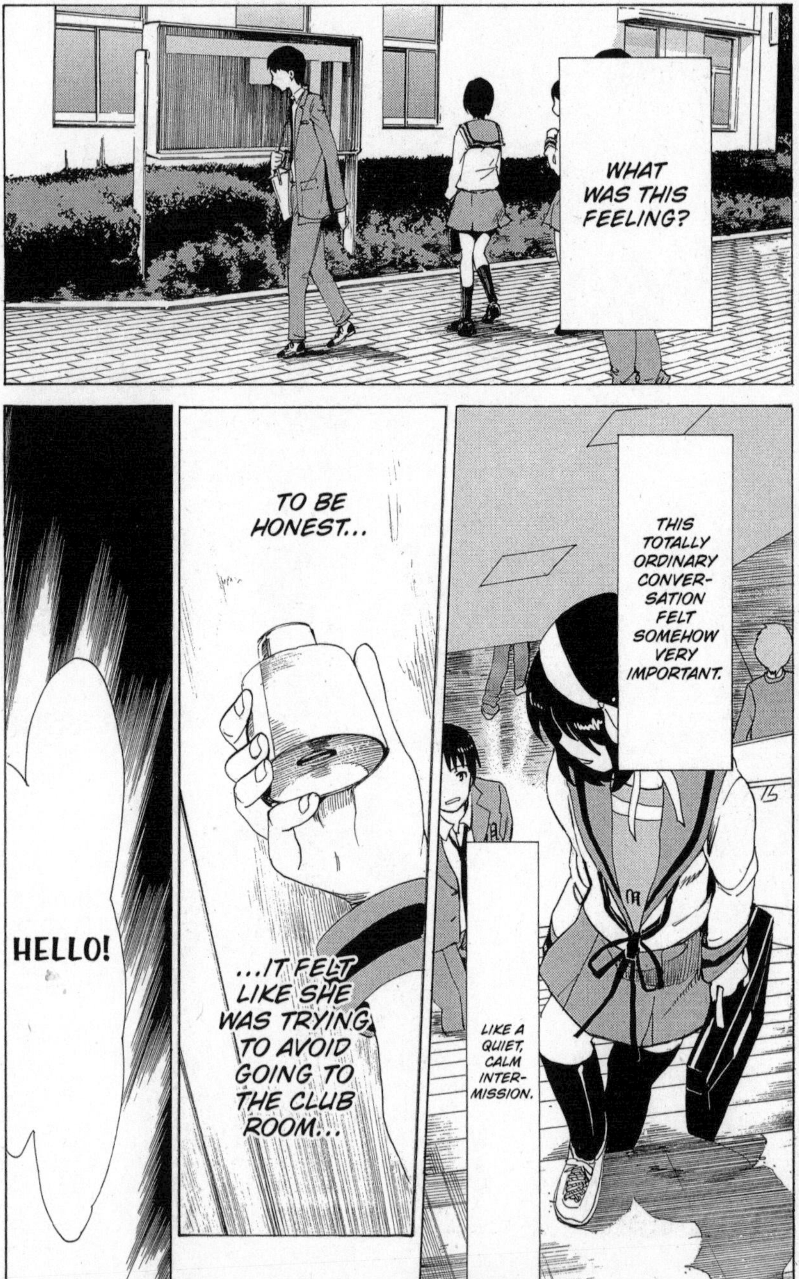
WHAT WAS THIS FEELING?
THIS TOTALLY ORDINARY CONVER-SATION FELT SOMEHOW VERY IMPORTANT.
LIKE A QUIET, CALM INTER-MISSION.
TO BE HONEST...
...IT FELT LIKE SHE WAS TRYING TO AVOID GOING TO THE CLUB ROOM...
HELLO!

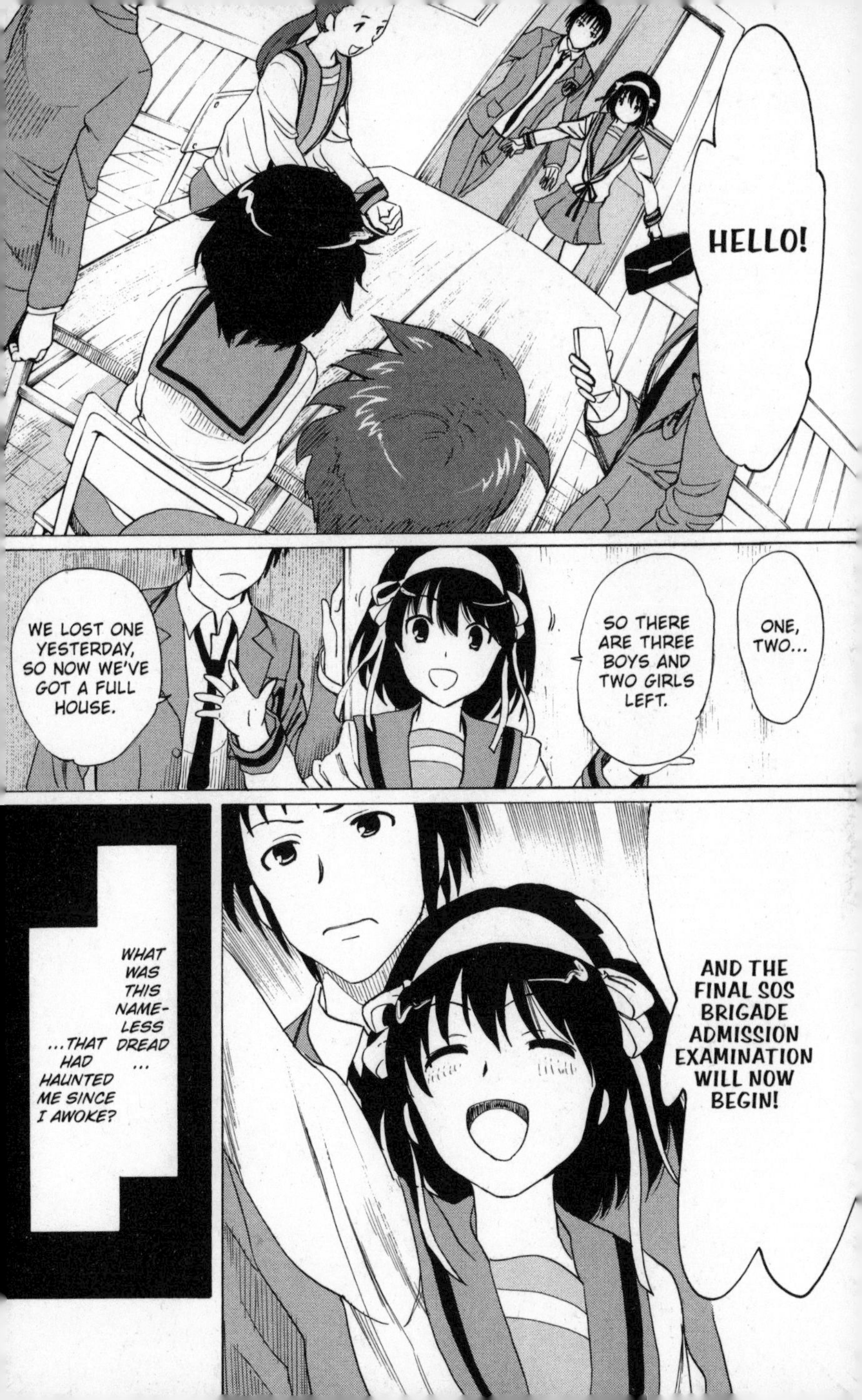
HELLO!
ONE, TWO...
SO THERE ARE THREE BOYS AND TWO GIRLS LEFT.
WE LOST ONE YESTERDAY, SO NOW WE'VE GOT A FULL HOUSE.
AND THE FINAL SOS BRIGADE ADMISSION EXAMINATION WILL NOW BEGIN!
WHAT WAS THIS NAMELESS DREAD...
...THAT HAD HAUNTED ME SINCE I AWOKE?

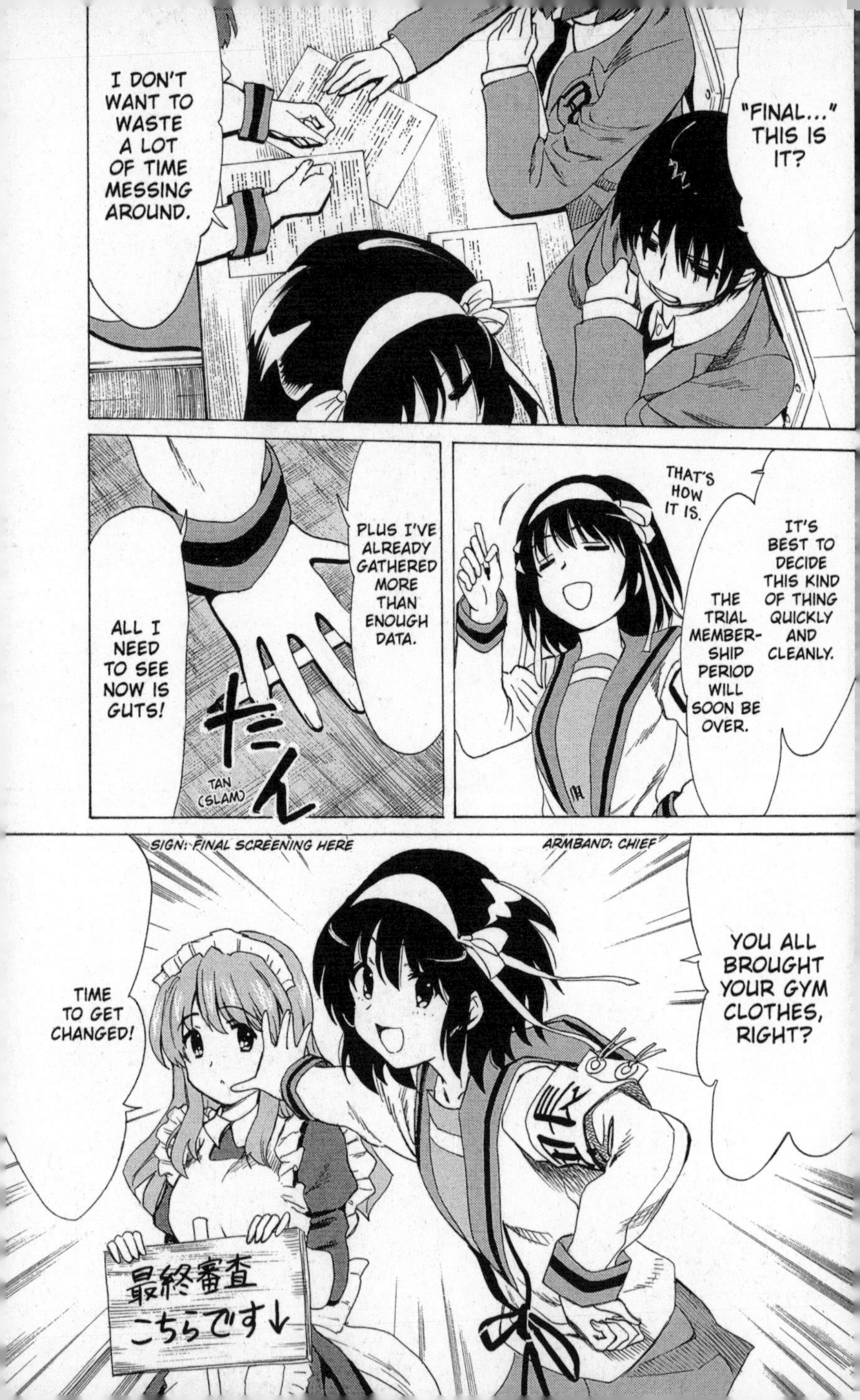
"FINAL..." THIS IS IT?
I DON'T WANT TO WASTE A LOT OF TIME MESSING AROUND.
THAT'S HOW IT IS.
IT'S BEST TO DECIDE THIS KIND OF THING QUICKLY AND CLEANLY.
THE TRIAL MEMBERSHIP PERIOD WILL SOON BE OVER.
PLUS I'VE ALREADY GATHERED MORE THAN ENOUGH DATA.
ALL I NEED TO SEE NOW IS GUTS!
たん
TAN (SLAM)
ARMBAND: CHIEF
SIGN: FINAL SCREENING HERE
YOU ALL BROUGHT YOUR GYM CLOTHES, RIGHT?
TIME TO GET CHANGED!
最終審査
こちらです↓

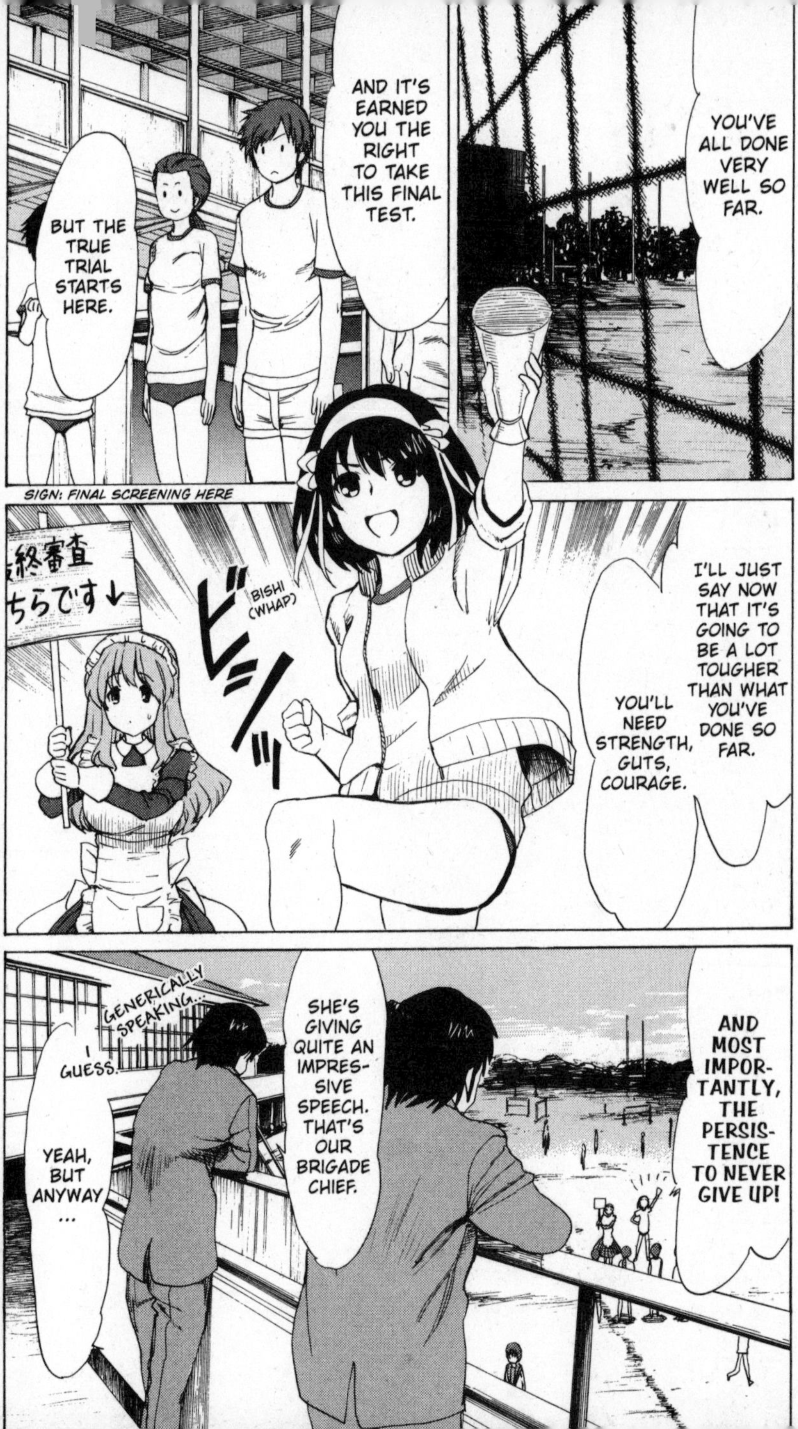
YOU'VE ALL DONE VERY WELL SO FAR.
AND IT'S EARNED YOU THE RIGHT TO TAKE THIS FINAL TEST.
BUT THE TRUE TRIAL STARTS HERE.
SIGN: FINAL SCREENING HERE
I'LL JUST SAY NOW THAT IT'S GOING TO BE A LOT TOUGHER THAN WHAT YOU'VE DONE SO FAR.
YOU'LL NEED STRENGTH, GUTS, COURAGE.
ビシッ
BISHI (WHAP)
終審査
ちらです↓
AND MOST IMPOR-TANTLY, THE PERSIS-TENCE TO NEVER GIVE UP!
SHE'S GIVING QUITE AN IMPRES-SIVE SPEECH. THAT'S OUR BRIGADE CHIEF.
GENERICALLY SPEAKING... I GUESS.
YEAH, BUT ANYWAY...

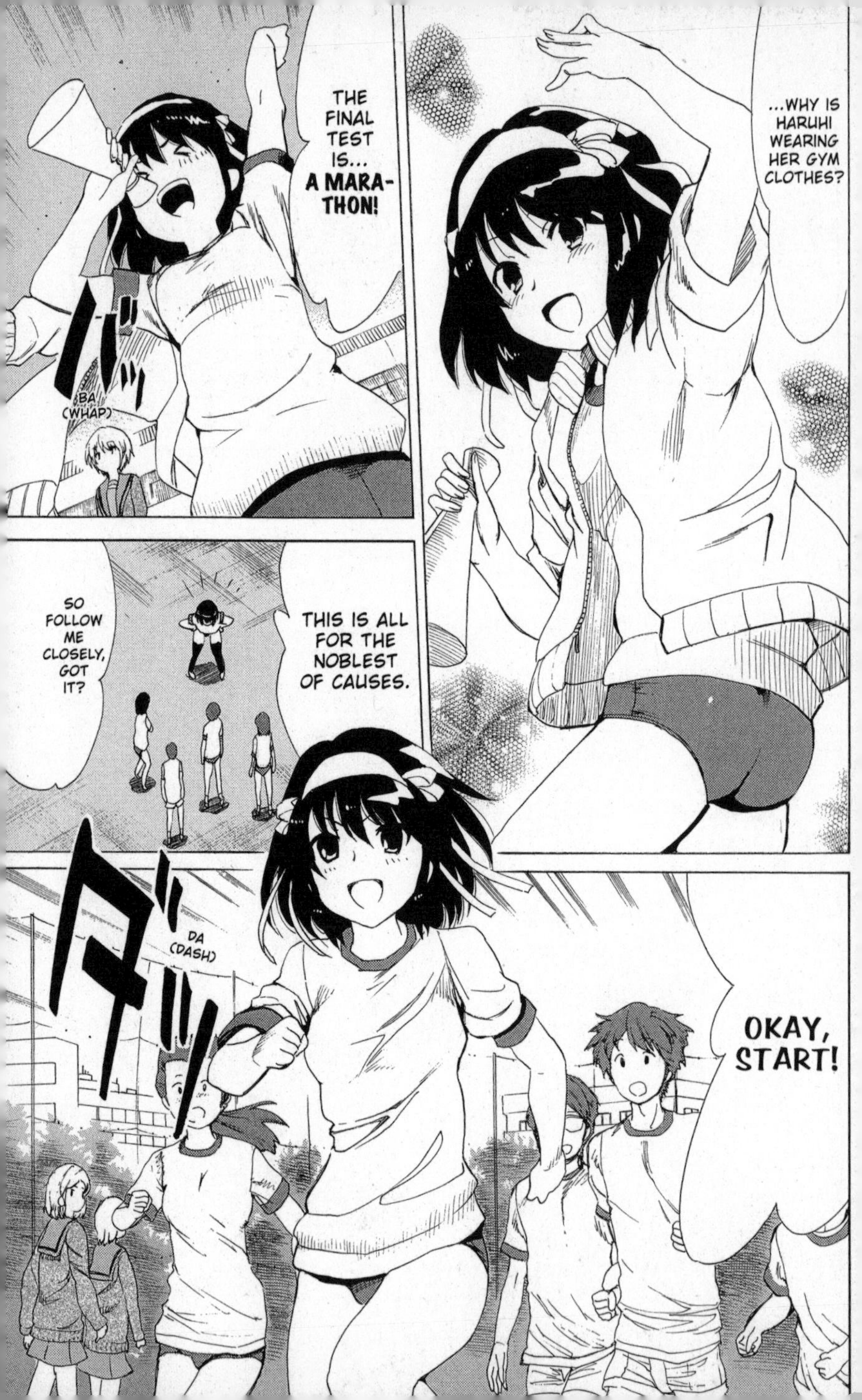
...WHY IS HARUHI WEARING HER GYM CLOTHES?
THE FINAL TEST IS... A MARATHON!
BA (WHAP)
THIS IS ALL FOR THE NOBLEST OF CAUSES.
SO FOLLOW ME CLOSELY, GOT IT?
OKAY, START!
DA (DASH)

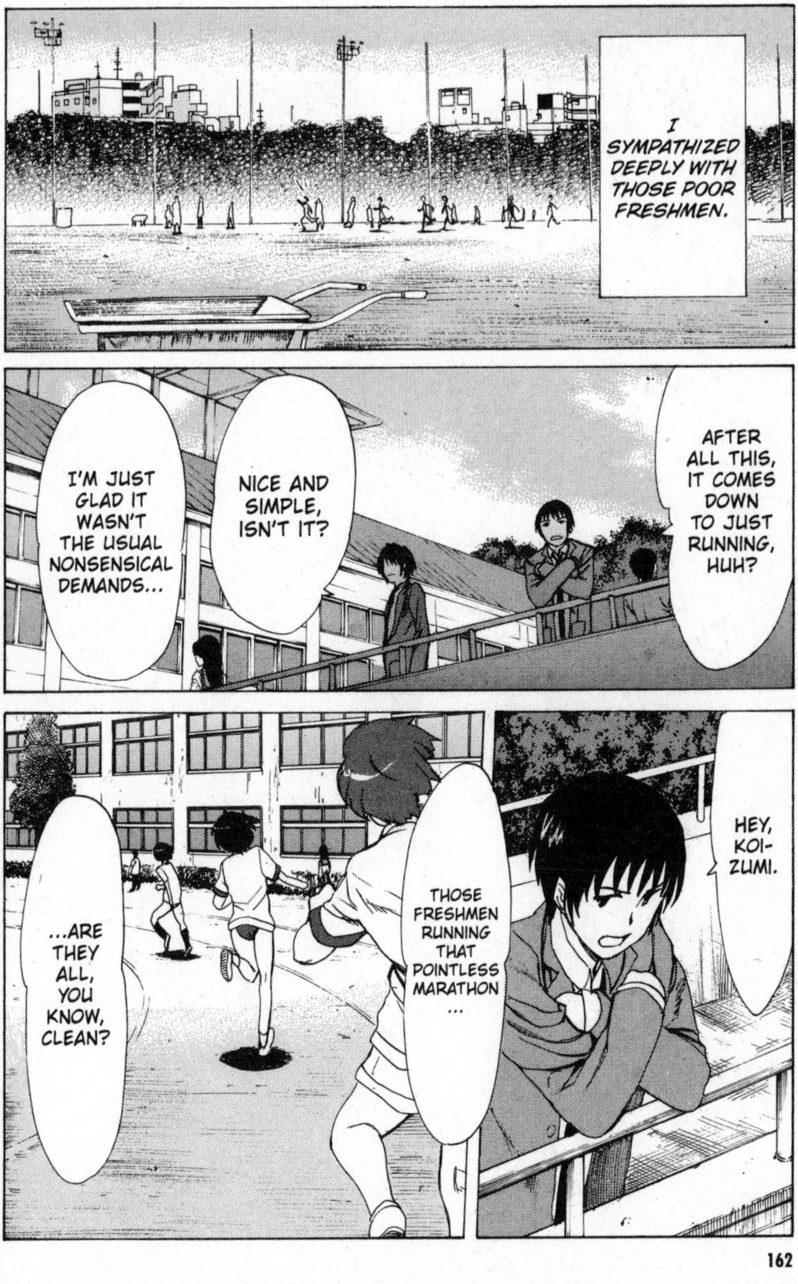
I SYMPATHIZED DEEPLY WITH THOSE POOR FRESHMEN.
AFTER ALL THIS, IT COMES DOWN TO JUST RUNNING, HUH?
NICE AND SIMPLE, ISN'T IT?
I'M JUST GLAD IT WASN'T THE USUAL NONSENSICAL DEMANDS...
HEY, KOI-ZUMI.
THOSE FRESHMEN RUNNING THAT POINTLESS MARATHON ...
...ARE THEY ALL, YOU KNOW, CLEAN?

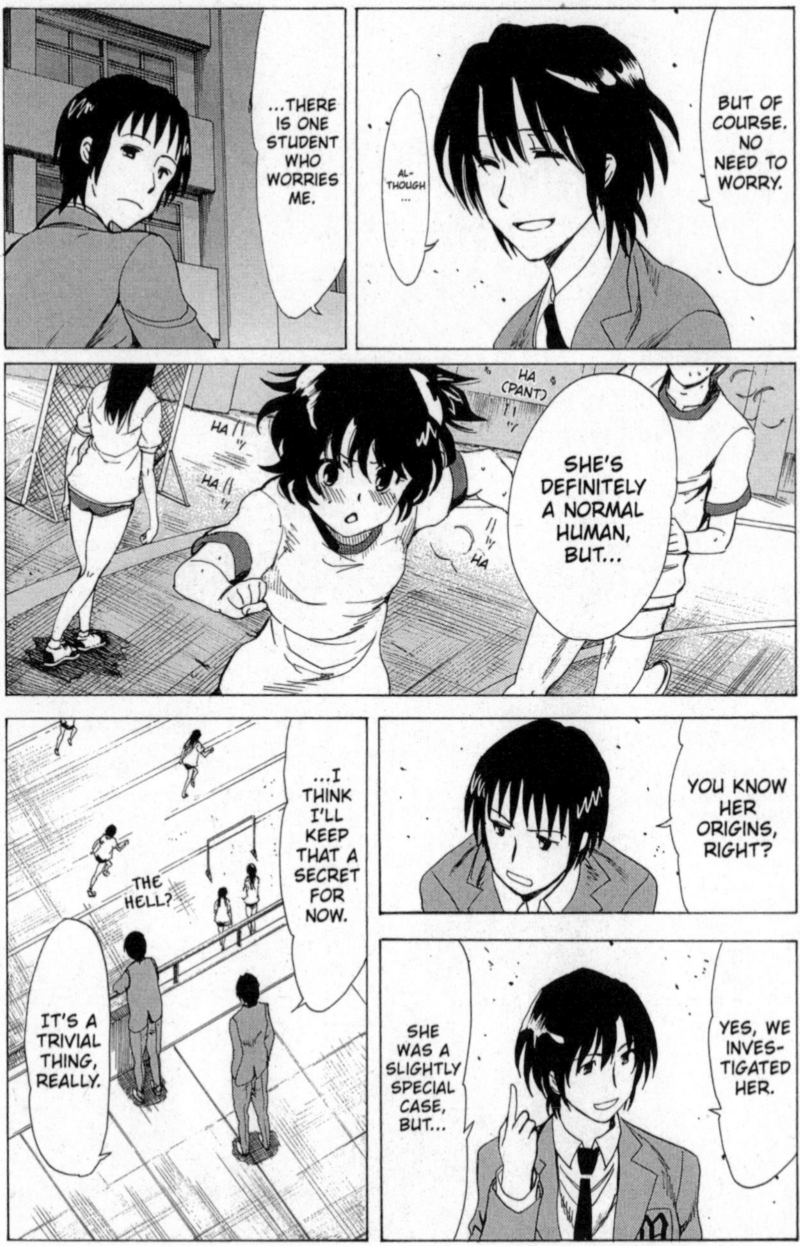
BUT OF COURSE. NO NEED TO WORRY.
AL-THOUGH...
...THERE IS ONE STUDENT WHO WORRIES ME.
HA (PANT)
SHE'S DEFINITELY A NORMAL HUMAN, BUT...
HA
HA
HA
YOU KNOW HER ORIGINS, RIGHT?
YES, WE INVES-TIGATED HER.
SHE WAS A SLIGHTLY SPECIAL CASE, BUT...
...I THINK I'LL KEEP THAT A SECRET FOR NOW.
THE HELL?
IT'S A TRIVIAL THING, REALLY.

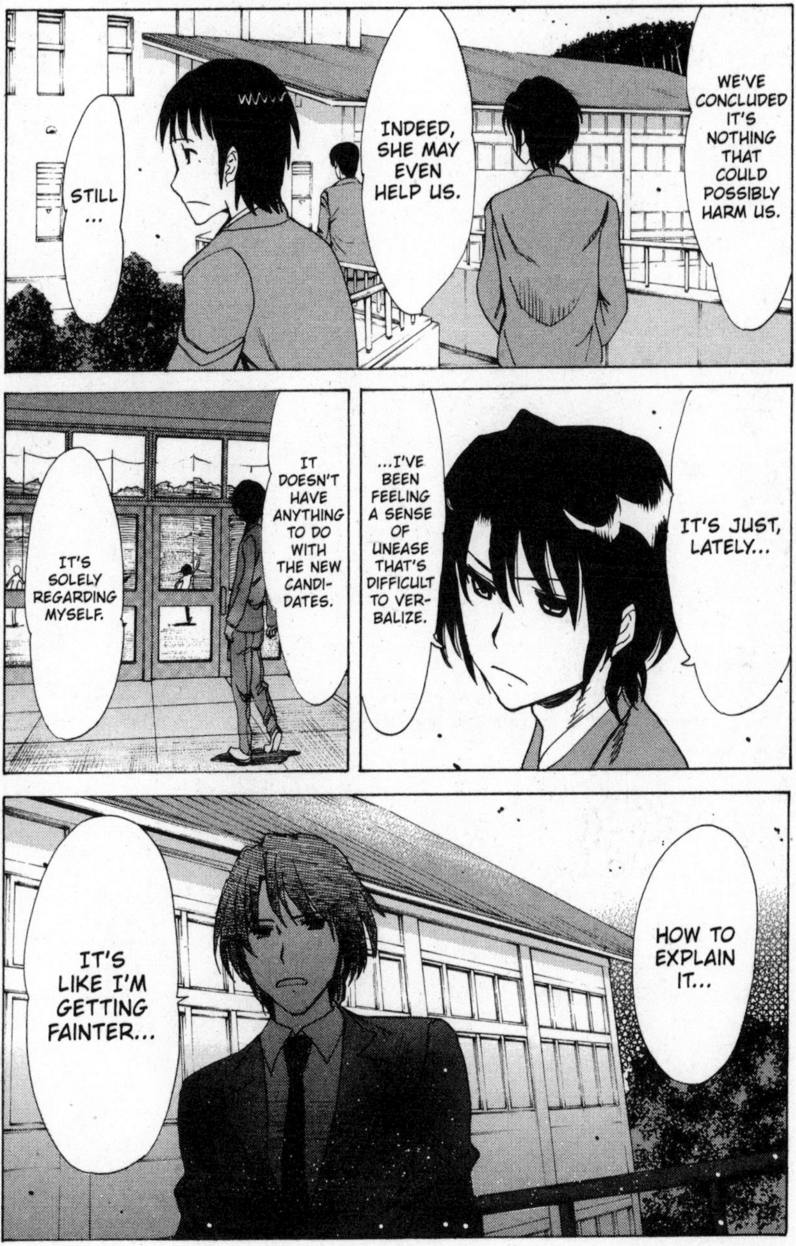
WE'VE CONCLUDED IT'S NOTHING THAT COULD POSSIBLY HARM US.
INDEED, SHE MAY EVEN HELP US.
STILL ...
IT'S JUST, LATELY...
...I'VE BEEN FEELING A SENSE OF UNEASE THAT'S DIFFICULT TO VERBALIZE.
IT DOESN'T HAVE ANYTHING TO DO WITH THE NEW CANDIDATES.
IT'S SOLELY REGARDING MYSELF.
HOW TO EXPLAIN IT...
IT'S LIKE I'M GETTING FAINTER...

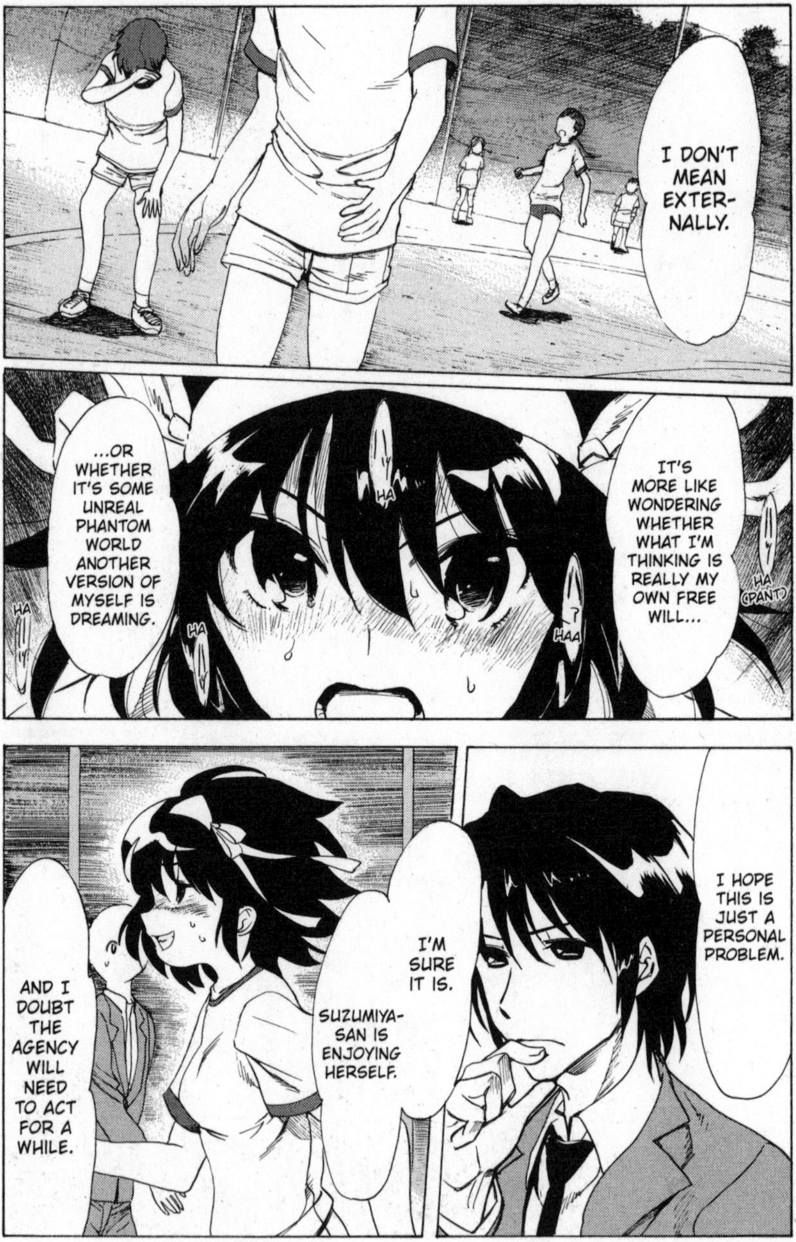
I DON'T MEAN EXTERNALLY.
IT'S MORE LIKE WONDERING WHETHER WHAT I'M THINKING IS REALLY MY OWN FREE WILL...
HA (PANT)
HA
HAA
...OR WHETHER IT'S SOME UNREAL PHANTOM WORLD ANOTHER VERSION OF MYSELF IS DREAMING.
HA
HA
I HOPE THIS IS JUST A PERSONAL PROBLEM.
I'M SURE IT IS.
SUZUMIYA-SAN IS ENJOYING HERSELF.
AND I DOUBT THE AGENCY WILL NEED TO ACT FOR A WHILE.

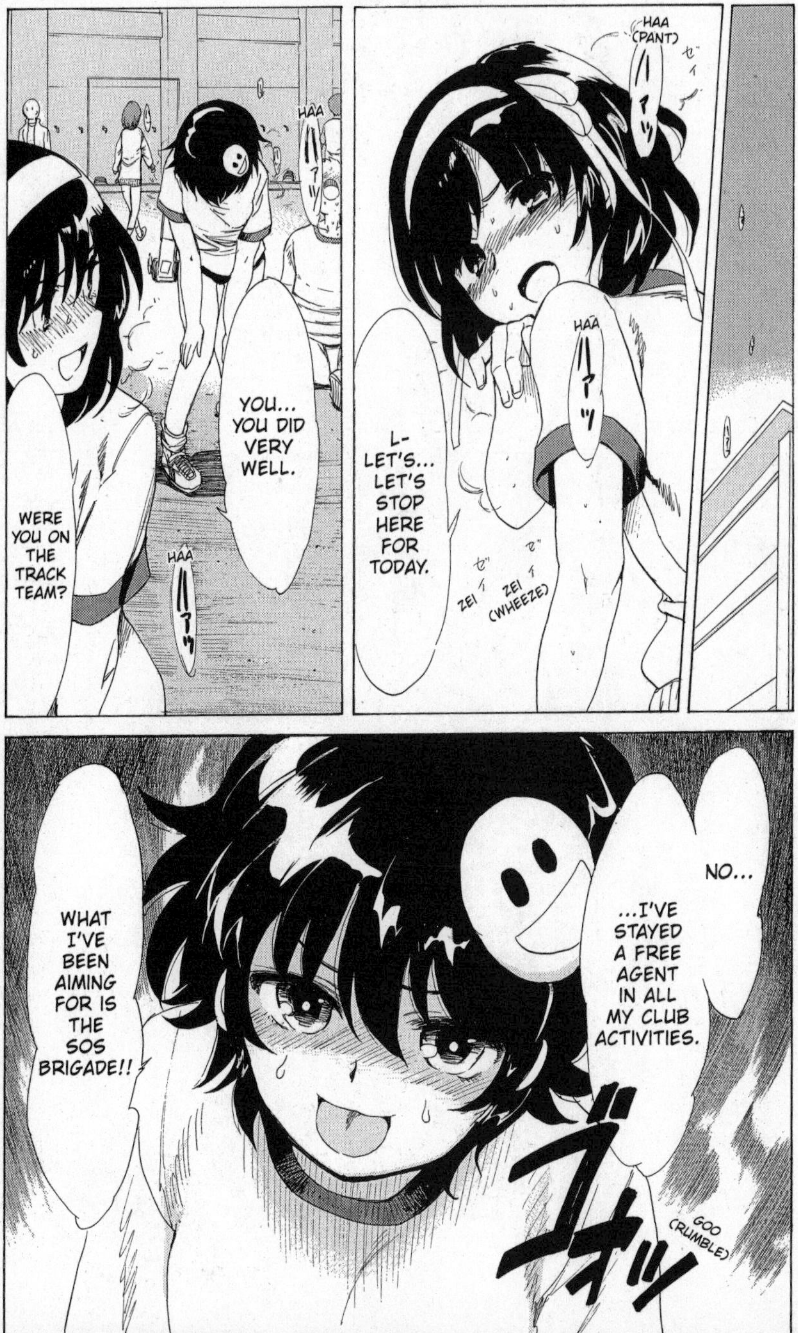
HAA (PANT)
HAA
L- LET'S... LET'S STOP HERE FOR TODAY.
ZEI ZEI (WHEEZE)
HAA
YOU... YOU DID VERY WELL.
WERE YOU ON THE TRACK TEAM?
HAA
NO...
...I'VE STAYED A FREE AGENT IN ALL MY CLUB ACTIVITIES.
WHAT I'VE BEEN AIMING FOR IS THE SOS BRIGADE!!
GOO (RUMBLE)

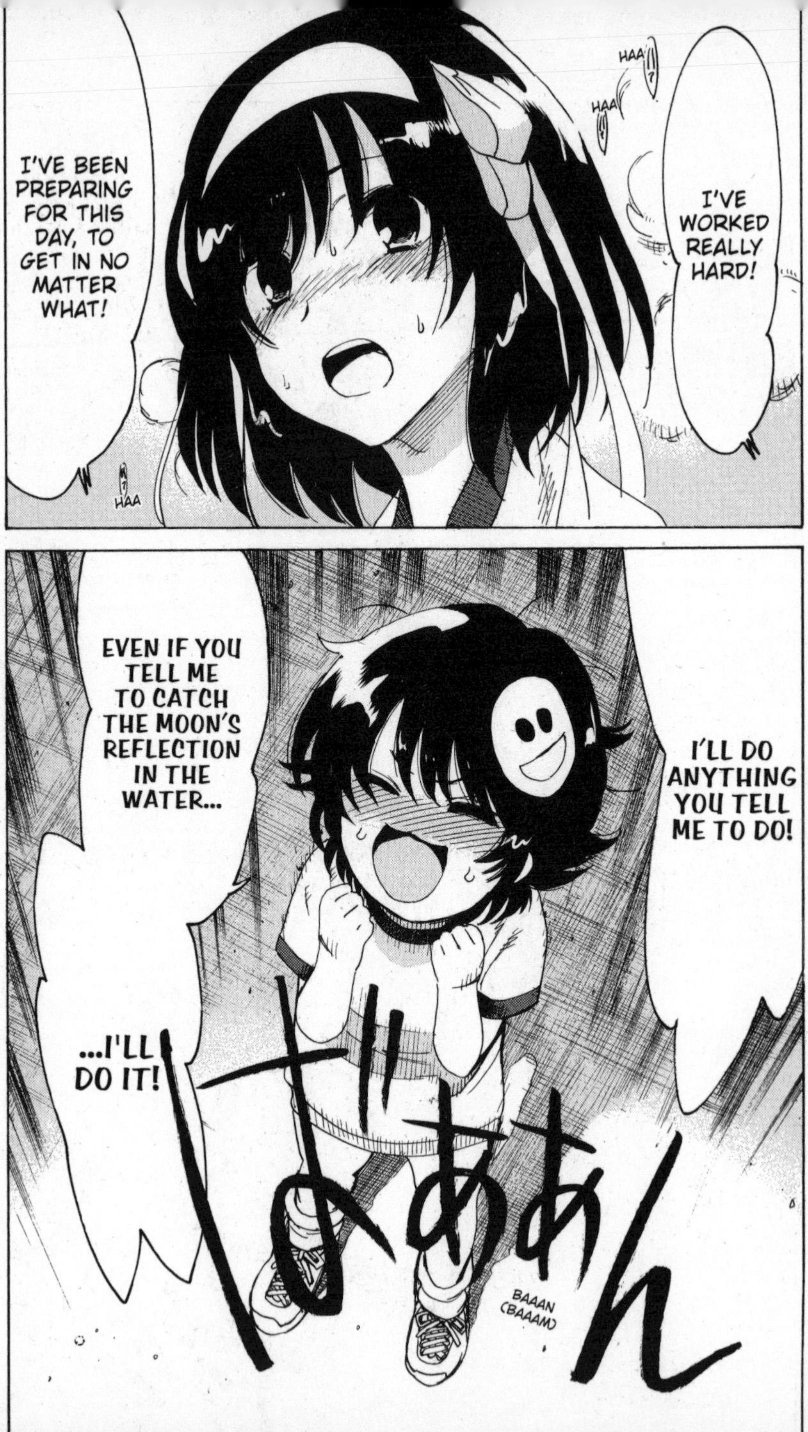

HAA
HAA
I'VE WORKED REALLY HARD!
I'VE BEEN PREPARING FOR THIS DAY, TO GET IN NO MATTER WHAT!
HAA
I'LL DO ANYTHING YOU TELL ME TO DO!
EVEN IF YOU TELL ME TO CATCH THE MOON'S REFLECTION IN THE WATER...
...I'LL DO IT!
BAAAN (BAAAM)

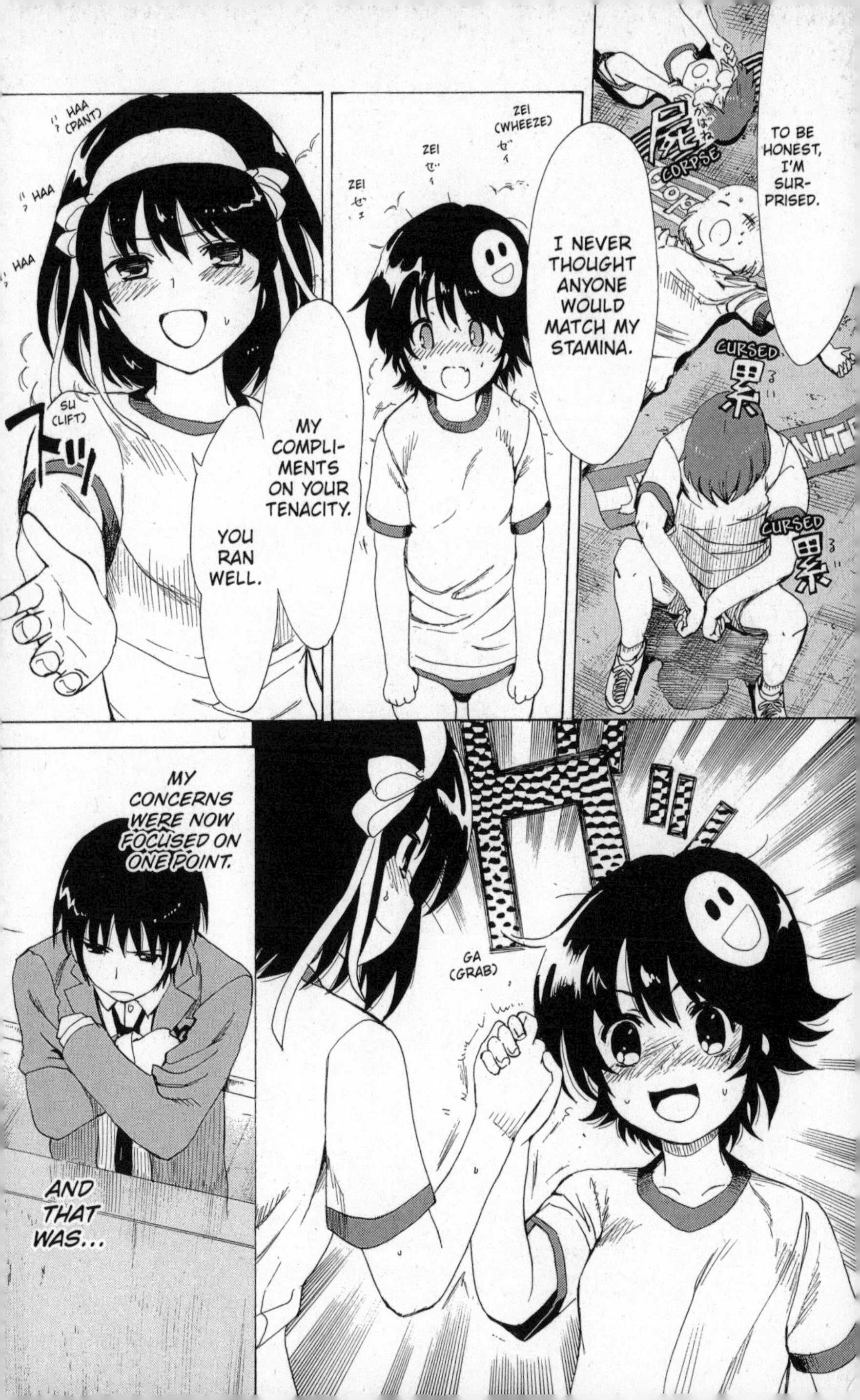
TO BE HONEST, I'M SURPRISED.
CORPSE
CURSED
CURSED
ZEI (WHEEZE)
ZEI
ZEI
I NEVER THOUGHT ANYONE WOULD MATCH MY STAMINA.
HAA (PANT)
HAA
HAA
SU (LIFT)
MY COMPLIMENTS ON YOUR TENACITY.
YOU RAN WELL.
GA (GRAB)
MY CONCERNS WERE NOW FOCUSED ON ONE POINT.
AND THAT WAS...

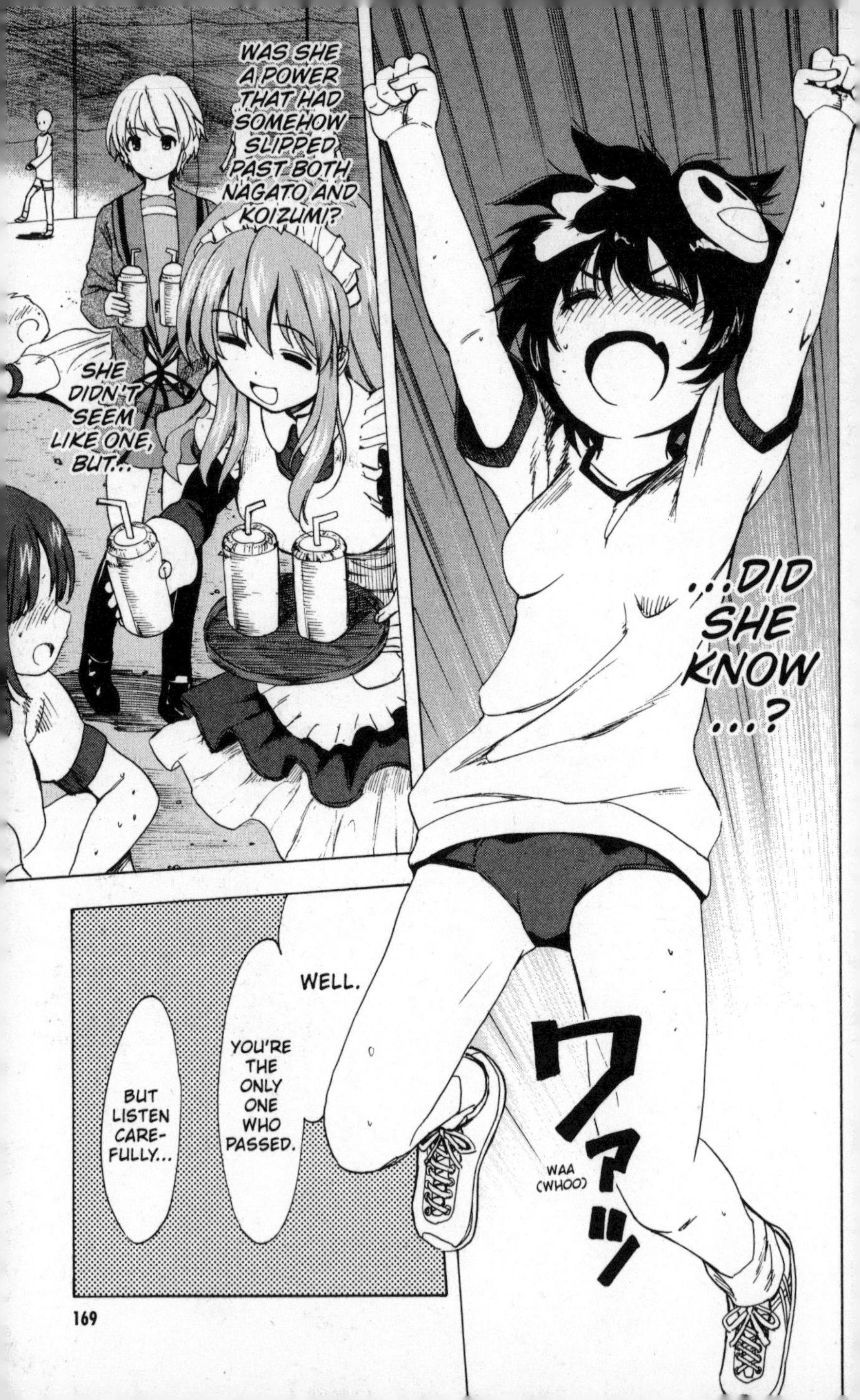
...DID SHE KNOW...?
WAA (WHOO)
WAS SHE A POWER THAT HAD SOMEHOW SLIPPED PAST BOTH NAGATO AND KOIZUMI?
SHE DIDN'T SEEM LIKE ONE, BUT...
WELL.
YOU'RE THE ONLY ONE WHO PASSED.
BUT LISTEN CAREFULLY...

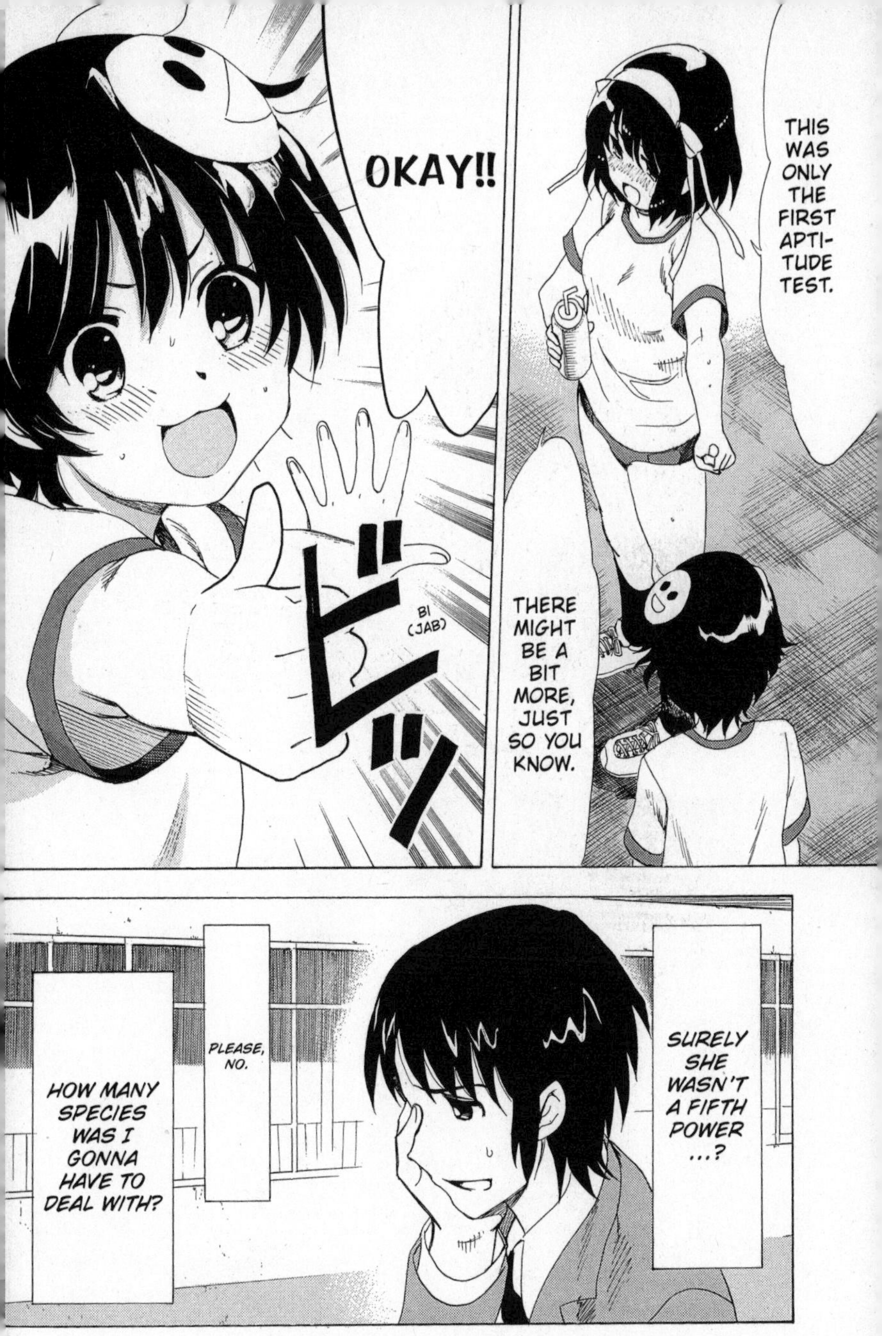
THIS WAS ONLY THE FIRST APTI-TUDE TEST.
THERE MIGHT BE A BIT MORE, JUST SO YOU KNOW.
OKAY!!
BI (JAB)
SURELY SHE WASN'T A FIFTH POWER ...?
PLEASE, NO.
HOW MANY SPECIES WAS I GONNA HAVE TO DEAL WITH?

The Surprise of Haruhi Suzumiya VI : END

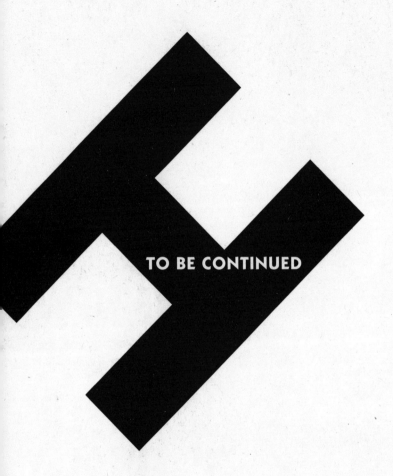

TO BE CONTINUED

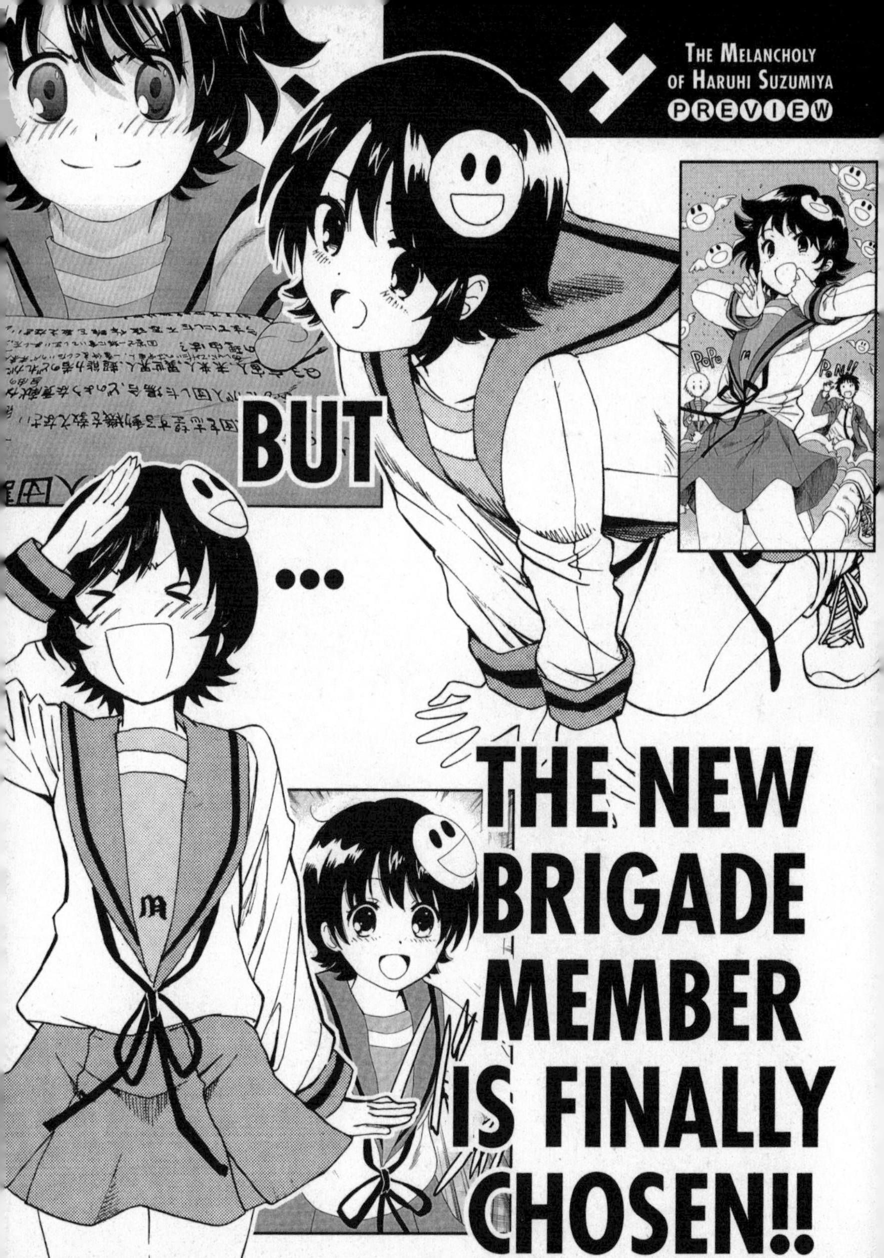
THE MELANCHOLY OF HARUHI SUZUMIYA
PREVIEW
BUT
...
THE NEW BRIGADE MEMBER IS FINALLY CHOSEN!!

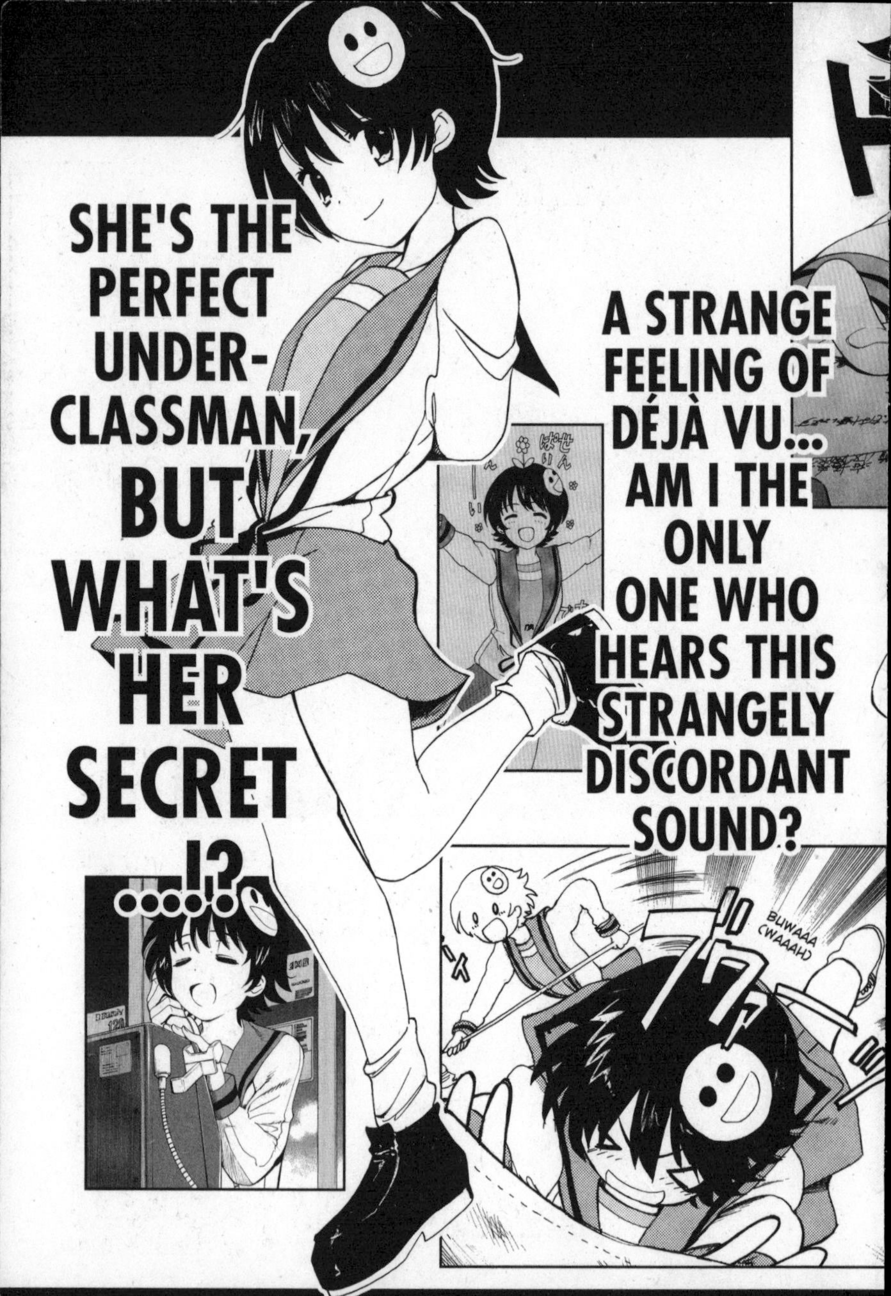
SHE'S THE PERFECT UNDER-CLASSMAN, BUT WHAT'S HER SECRET ...!?
A STRANGE FEELING OF DÉJÀ VU... AM I THE ONLY ONE WHO HEARS THIS STRANGELY DISCORDANT SOUND?
BUWAAA (WAAAH)

CHEMICAL REACTIONS AND HUMAN RELATIONSHIPS ABOUND IN THE CONTINUING SURPRISE ARC!

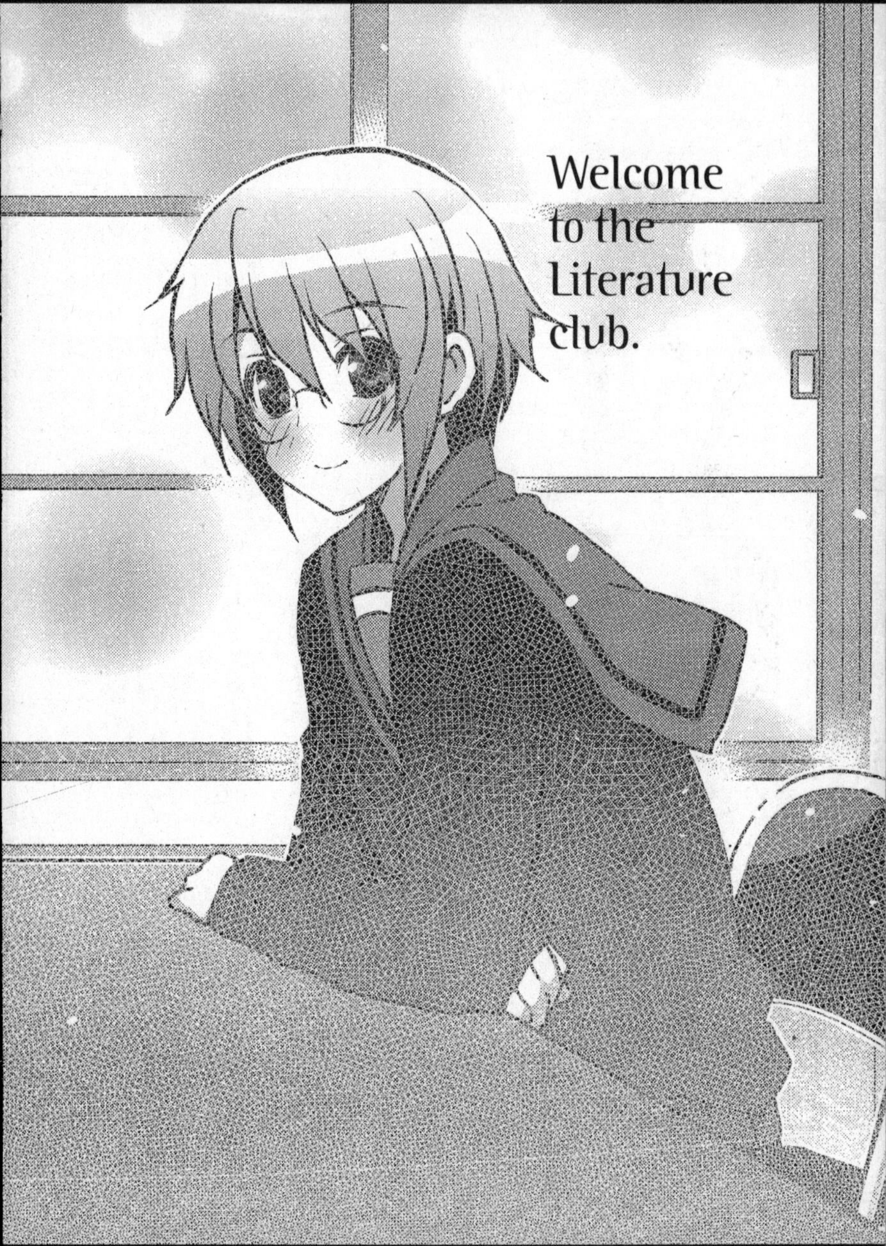
Welcome
to the
Literature
club.

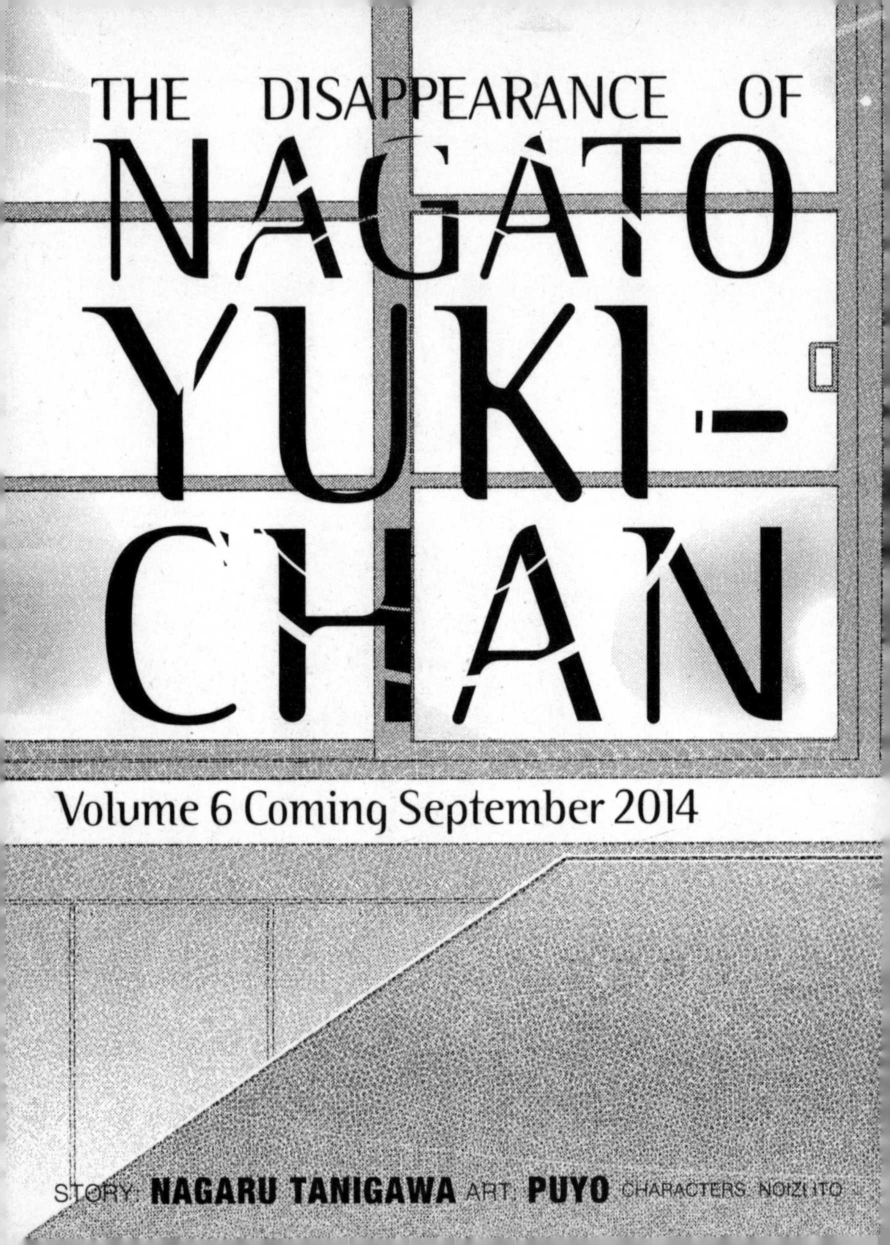
THE DISAPPEARANCE OF
NAGATO
YUKI-
CHAN
Volume 6 Coming September 2014
STORY: NAGARU TANIGAWA ART: PUYO CHARACTERS: NOIZI ITO

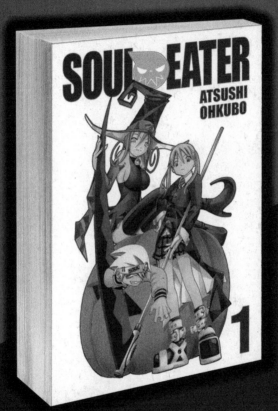

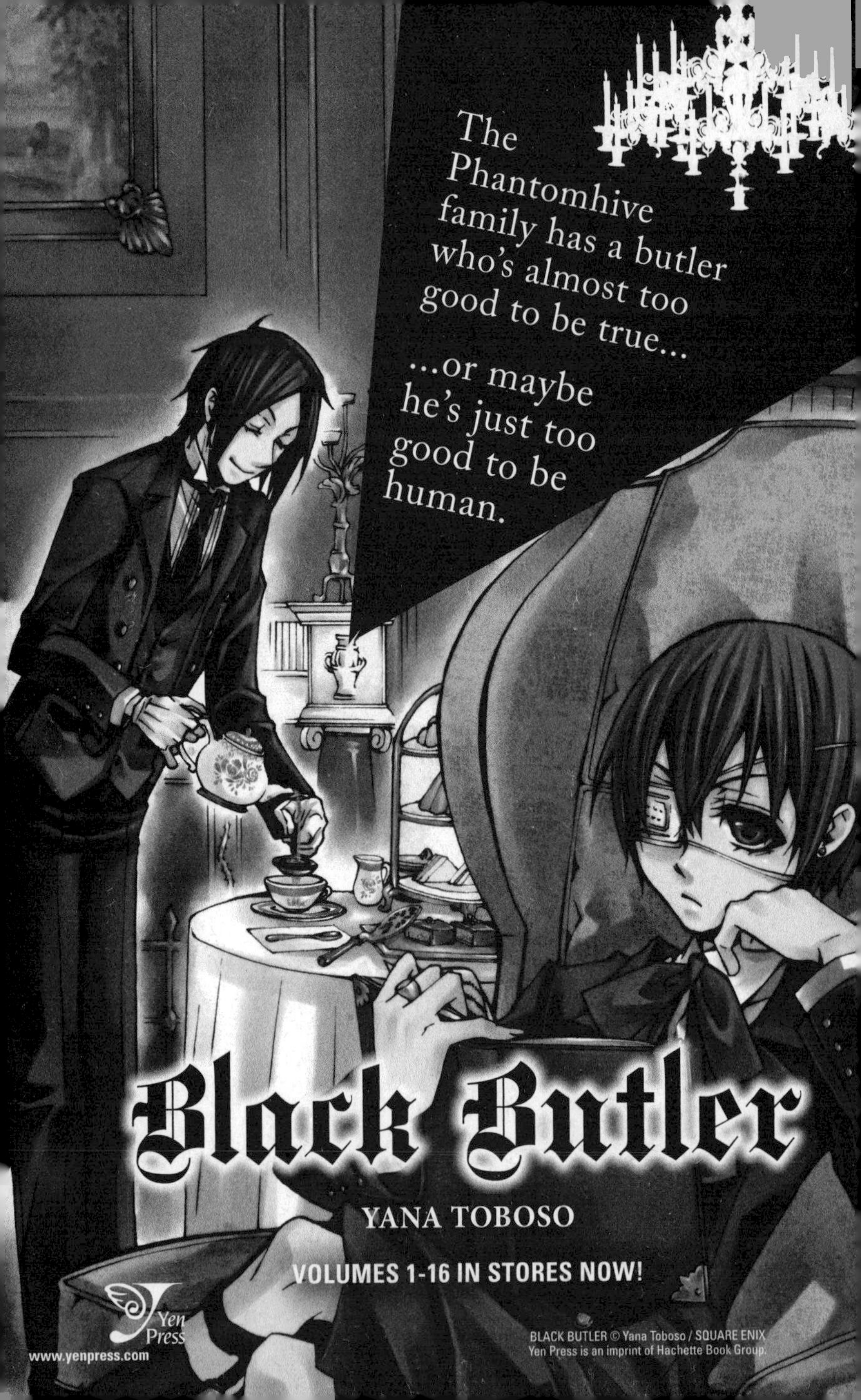
The Phantomhive family has a butler who's almost too good to be true...
...or maybe he's just too good to be human.
Black Butler
YANA TOBOSO
VOLUMES 1-16 IN STORES NOW!
Yen Press
www.yenpress.com
BLACK BUTLER © Yana Toboso / SQUARE ENIX
Yen Press is an imprint of Hachette Book Group.

THE MELANCHOLY OF

⑱

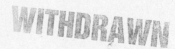

Original Story: Nagaru Tanigawa
Manga: Gaku Tsugano
Character Design: Noizi Ito

Translation: Paul Starr
Lettering: Alexis Eckerman

SUZUMIYA HARUHI NO YUUTSU Volume 18 © Nagaru TANIGAWA • Noizi ITO 2013 © Gaku TSUGANO 2013. Edited by KADOKAWA SHOTEN. First published in Japan in 2013 by KADOKAWA CORPORATION, Tokyo. English translation rights arranged with KADOKAWA CORPORATION, Tokyo, through Tuttle-Mori Agency, Inc., Tokyo.

English translation © 2014 by Hachette Book Group, Inc.

Yen Press
Hachette Book Group
237 Park Avenue, New York, NY 10017

www.HachetteBookGroup.com
www.YenPress.com

Yen Press is an imprint of Hachette Book Group, Inc. The Yen Press name and logo are trademarks of Hachette Book Group, Inc.

First Yen Press Edition: May 2014

ISBN: 978-0-316-28678-7

10 9 8 7 6 5 4 3 2 1

BVG

Printed in the United States of America